INDEX

History of the Ancient & Medieval World

Volume 12

Index

Marshall Cavendish
New York Toronto Sydney

Published in 1996 by
Marshall Cavendish Corporation
99 White Plains Road
Tarrytown, NY 10591-9001
U.S.A.

Editor: Henk Dijkstra
Executive Editor: Stasja Cornelissen
Art Director: Henk Oostenrijk, Studio 87, Utrecht, The Netherlands
Index Editors: Schuurmans & Jonkers, Leiden, The Netherlands

The History of the Ancient and Medieval World is a completely revised and
updated edition of *The Adventure of Mankind*.
©1996 HD Communication Consultants BV, Hilversum, The Netherlands
This edition ©1996 by Marshall Cavendish Corporation, Tarrytown, New York and HD Communication Consultants BV,
Hilversum, The Netherlands

Library of Congress Cataloging-in-Publication Data

History of the ancient and medieval world / edited by Henk Dijkstra.
p. cm.
Completely rev. and updated ed. of : The Adventure of mankind (second edition 1996).
Contents:—v.12. Index
ISBN 0-7614-0363-9 (v.12).—ISBN 0-7614-0315-5 (lib.bdg.:set)
1. History, Ancient—Juvenile literature. 2. Middle Ages—History—Juvenile literature. I. Dijkstra, Henk. II. Title: Adventure of mankind
D117.H57 1996
930—dc20/95-35715

CONTENTS

Chronicles

1 Anglo-Saxon Kingdoms

Kingdom of Kent
Hengest (455-488)
Ooisc (488-512)
Octa (512-522)
Aethelbert I (560-616)
Eadbald (616-640)
Earconbert (640-664)
Egbert I (664-673)
Hlothere (673-685)
Eadric (685-686)
Oswine (686-690)
Swaefhard (689-694)
Wihtred (690-725)
Aethelbert II (725-748)
Eadberht I (748-762)
Sigered (762-764)
Heaberht (764-770)
Egbert II (765-784)
Ealhmund (784-785)
Eadberht II (796-798)
Cuthred (798-807)
Baldred (823-825)

Kingdom of Bernicia
Ida (547-559)
Glappa (559-560)
Adda (560-568)
Aethelric (568-572)
Theoderic (572-579)
Frithuwald (579-585)
Hussa (585-592)

Kingdom of Deira
Aelle (569-599)
Aethelric (599-604)

Kingdom of Northumbria
(unified kingdoms of
Deira and Bernicia)
Aethelfrid (592-616)
Edwin (616-633)
Osric (633-634)
Eanfrith (633-634)
St Oswald (634-642)
Oswiu (642-670)
St Oswine (644-651)
Aethelwald (651-655)
Ecgfrith (670-685)
Aldfrith (686-705)
Eadwulf I (705-706)
Osred I (706-716)
Cenred (716-718)
Osric (718-729)
Ceolwulf (729-737)
Eadberht (737-758)
Oswulf (758-759)
Aethelwald (759-765)
Alhred (765-774)
Aethelred I (774-779)
Aelfwald I (779-788)
Osred II (788-790)
Aethelred I (790-796)
Osbald (796)
Eardwulf (796-808)
Aelfwald II (808)
Eardwulf (808-809)
Eanred (809-841)
Aethelred II (841-844)
Redwulf (844)
Aethelred II (844-848)
Osbert (848-866)
Aelle (866-867)
Egbert I (867-873)
Ricsige (873-876)
Egbert II (876-878)

Eadwulf II (878-913)
Aldred (913-927)

Kingdom of Mercia
Penda (633-655)
Wulfhere (658-675)
Aethelred I (675-704)
Cenred (704-709)
Ceolred (709-716)
Aethelbald (716-757)
Beornred (757)
Offa (757-796)
Ecgfrith (796)
Cenwulf (796-821)
Ceolwulf I (821-823)
Beornwulf (823-825)
Ludeca (825-827)
Wiglaf (827-840)
Berhtwulf (840-852)
Burgred (852-874)
Ceolwulf II (874-879)
Aethelred II (879-911)
Aethelflaed (911-918)
Aelfwyn (918-919)

Kingdom of Wessex
Cerdic (519-534)
Cynric (534-560)
Ceawlin (560-591)
Ceol (591-597)
Ceolwulf (597-611)
Cynegils (611-642)
Cenwalh (642-672)
Seaxburh (672-674)
Aescwine (674-676)
Centwine (676-685)
Caedwalla (685-688)
Ine (688-726)
Aethelheard (726-740)
Cuthred (740-756)
Sigeberht (756-757)
Cynewulf (757-786)
Berhtric (786-802)
Egbert of Wessex (802-839)

Kingdom of England
Egbert of Wessex (802-839)
Ethelwulf (839-858)
Ethelbald (860-860)
Ethelbert (856-865)
Ethelred I (865-871)
Alfred the Great (871-899)
Edward the Elder (899-924)
Aelfweard (924)
Athelstan (924-939)
Edmund I (939-946)
Edred (946-955)
Edwy (955-959)
Edgar the Peaceful (957-975)
St Edward the Martyr (975-978)
Ethelred II the Unready (978-1016)
Edmund II Ironside (1016)
Canute the Great (1016-1035)
Harold I Harefoot (1037-1040)
Harthacanute (1040-1042)
St Edward the Confessor (1042-1066)
Harold II (1066)
William I the Conqueror (1066-1087)
William II Rufus (1087-1100)
Henry I (1100-1135)
Stephen (1135-1154)
Henry II (1154-1189)
Richard I (1189-1199)
JohnLackland (1199-1216)
Henry III (1216-1272)
Edward I (1272-1307)
Edward II (1307-1327)

Edward III (1327-1377)
Richard II (1377-1399)
Henry IV (1399-1413)
Henry V (1413-1422)
Henry VI (1422-1461)
Edward IV (1461-1483)
Edward V (1483)
Richard III (1483-1485)
Henry VII (1485-1509)
Henry VIII (1509-1547)
Edward VI (1547-1553)

2 Assyrian Rulers

Adasi
Belu-bani (1698-1689)
Libaya (1688-1672)
Sharma-Adad I (1671-1660)
Iptar-Sin (1659-1648)
Bazaya (1647-1620)
Lullaya (1619-1604)
Shu-Ninua (1613-1600)
Sharma-Adad II (1599-1597)
Erishum III (1596-1584)
Ishme-Dagan II (1577-1562)
Ashur-nirari I (1545-1520)
Puzur-Ashur III (1519-1496)
Enlil-nasir I (1495-1483)
Nur-ili (1482-1471)
Ashur-shanudi (1471)
Ashur-rabi I (1470-1451)
Ashur-nadin-ahhe I (1450-1431)
Enlil-nasir II (1430-1425)
Ashur-nirari II (1424-1418)
Ashur-bel-nisheshu (1417-1409)
Ashur-ra'im-nisheshu (1408-1401)
Ashur-nadin-ahhe II (1400-1391)
Eriba-Adad I (1390-1364)
Ashur-uballit I (1363-1328)
Enlil-nirari (1327-1318)
Arik-den-ili (1317-1306)
Adad-nirari I (1305-1274)
Shalmaneser I (1273-1244)
Tukulti-Ninurta I (1243-1207)
Ashur-nadin-apli (1206-1203)
Ashur-nirari III (1202-1197)
Enlil-kudurri-usur (1196-1192)
Ninurta-apil-Ekur (1191-1179)
Ashur-dan I (1178-1133)
Ninurta-tukulti-Ashur
Mutakkil-Nusku
Ashur-resh-ishi I (1132-1115)
Tiglath-Pileser I (1114-1076)
Ashared-apil-Ekur (1075-1074)
Ashur-bel-kala (1073-1056)
Eriba-Adad II (1055-1054)
Ashurnasirpal I (1049-1031)
Shalmaneser II (1030-1019)
Ashur-nirari IV (1018-1013)
Ashur-rabi II (1012-972)
Ashur-resh-ishi II (971-967)
Tiglath-Pileser II (966-935)
Ashur-dan II (934-912)
Adad-nirari II (911-891)
Tukulti-Ninurta II (890-884)
Ashurnasirpal II (883-859)
Shalmaneser III (858-824)
Shamshi-Adad V (823-811)
Adad-nirari III (810-783)
Shalmaneser IV (782-773)
Ashur-dan III (772-755)
Ashur-nirari V (754-745)
Tiglath-Pileser III (744-727)
Shalmaneser V (726-722)
Sargon II (721-705)
Sennacherib (704-681)
Esarhaddon (684-669)

Ashurbanipal (669-631)
Ashur-etil-ilani (631-?)
Sin-shumu-lishir
Sin-shar-ishkun (?-612)
Ashur-uballit II (611-609)

3 The Aztec Empire

Acamapichtli (1372-1391)
Huitzilihuitl (1391-1416)
Chimalpopoca (1416-1427)
Itzcoatl (1427-1440)
Motecuhzoma I Ilhuicamina (1440-1468)
Axayacatl (1468-1481)
Tizoc (1481-1486)
Ahuitzotl (1486-1502)
Motecuhzoma II Xocoyotzin (1502-1520)
Cuitlahuac (1520)
Cuauhtemoc (1520-1521)
Spanish conquest of the Aztec empire (1519-1521)

4 Babylonian Rulers

Sumuabum (1894-1881)
Sumulael (1880-1845)
Sabium (1844-1831)
Apil-Sin (1830-1813)
Sinmuballit (1812-1793)
Hammurabi (1792-1750)
Samsuiluna (1749-1712)
Abi-eshuh (1711-1684)
Ammi-ditana (1683-1647)
Ammisaduqa (1646-1626)
Samsuditana (1625-1595)
Gandash (1729-1704)
Agum I (1703-1682)
Kashtiliash I (1681-1660)
Urzigurumash
Harba
Burna-Buriash I
Kara-indash
Kadashman-Harbe I
Kurigalzu I
Kadashman-Enlil I (1374-1360)
Burna-Buriash II (1359-1333)
Kara-hardash (1333)
Nazi-Mugash (1333)
Kurigalzu II (1332-1308)
Nazi-Maruttash (1307-1282)
Kadashaman-Turgu (1281-1264)
Kadashaman-Enlil II (1263-1255)
Kudur-Enlil (1254-1246)
Shagarakti-Shuriash (1245-1233)
Kashtiliash IV (1232-1225)
Tukulti-Ninurta I of Assyria (1225)
Enlil-nadin-shumi (1224)
Kadashaman-Harbe II (1223)
Adad-shuma-iddina (1222-1217)
Adad-shuma-usur (1216-1187)
Meli-Shipak (1186-1172)
Merodachbaladan I (1171-1159)
Zababa-shuma-iddina (1158)
Enlil-nadin-ahi (1157-1155)
Marduk-kabit-ahheshu (1157-1140)
Itti-Marduk-balatu (1139-1132)
Ninurta-nadin-shumi (1131-1126)
Nebuchadrezzar I (1125-1104)
Enlil-nadin-apli (1103-1100)
Marduk-nadin-ahhe (1099-1082)
Marduk-shapik-zeri (1081-1069)
Adad-apla-iddina (1068-1047)
Marduk-ahhe-eriba (1046)
Marduk-zer (1045-1034)
Nabu-shumu-libur (1033-1026)
Simbar-Shipak (1025-1008)
Ea-mukin-zeri (1008)
Kashshu-nadin-ahhe (1007-1005)
Eulmash-shakin-shumi (1004-988)
Ninurta-kudurri-usur I (987-985)
Shirikti-Shuqamuna (985)
Mar-biti-apla-usur (984-979)
Nabu-mukin-aph (978-943)
Ninurta-kudurri-usur II (943)
Mar-biti-ahhe-iddina (942-?)
Shamash-mudammiq
Nabu-shuma-ukin I
Nabu-apal-iddina

Marduk-zakir-shumi I
Marduk-balassu-iqbi (?-813)
Baba-aha-iddina (812-?)
Ninurta-apl
Marduk-bel-zeri
Marduk-apla-usur
Eriba-Marduk
Nabu-shuma-ishkun
Nabonassar (?-748)
Nabu-nadin-zeri (747-734)
Nabu-shuma-ukin II (733-732)
Nabu-mukin-zeri (732)
Tiglath-Pileser III of Assyria 731-729
Shalmaneser V of Assyria (726-722)
Merodach-Baladan II (721-710)
Sargon II of Assyria (709-705)
Sennacherib of Assyria (704-703)
Marduk-zakir-shumi II (703)
Merodach-Baladan II (703)
Bel-ibni (702-700)
Ashur-nadin-shumi (699-694)
Nergal-ushezib (693)
Mushezib-Marduk (692-689)
Sennacherib of Assyria (688-681)
Esarhaddon of Assyria (689-669)
Ashurbanipal of Assyria (668)
Shamash-shum-ukin (667-648)
Kandalanu (647-627)
Nabopolassar (626)
Nebuchadezzar II (605-562)
Awil-Marduk (561-560)
Labashi-Marduk (559-556)
Nabonidus and Belshazzar (556-539)
Persian conquest

5 Byzantine or Eastern Emperors

Arcadius (395-408)
Theodosius II (408-450)
Marcianus (450-457)
Leo I (457-474)
Leo II (474)
Zeno (474-491)
Anastasius I (491-518)
Justin I (518-527)
Justinian I (527-565)
Justin II (565-578)
Tiberius II, Constantinus (578-582)
Mauritius (582-602)
Phocas I (602-610)
HeracliusI (610-641)
Constantine III (641)
Heracleon (641)
Constans II (641-668)
Constantine IV (668-685)
Justinian II (685-695)
Leontius (695-698)
Tiberius III (698-705)
Justinian II (restored) (705-711)
Philippicus (711-713)
Anastasius II (713-715)
Theodosius III (715-717)
Leo III, the Isaurian (717-740)
Constantine V (740-775)
Leo IV (775-779)
Constantine VI (779-797)
Irene (797-802)
Nicephorus I (802-811)
Stauracius (811)
Michael I (811-813)
Leo V, the Armenian (813-820)
Michael II, the Armorian (820-829)
Theophilus III (829-842)
Michael III, the Drunkard (842-867)
Basil I, the Macedonian (867-886)
Leo VI, the Wise (886-912)
Alexander III (912-913)
Constantine VII Porphyrogenitus (913-959)
Romanus I Lecapenus (920-944)
Christopher (921-931)
Romanus II (959-963)
Nicephorus II Phocas (963-969)
John I Tzimisces (969-976)
Basil II Bulgaroktonus (976-1025)
Constantine VIII (1025-1028)
Romanus III Argyropolus (1028-1034)
Michael IV, the Daphlagonian (1034-1041)

Michael V Calaphates (1041-1042)
Constantine IX Monomachus (1042-1055)
Theodora (1055-1056)
Michael VI Stratioticus (1056-1057)
Isaac I Comnenus (1057-1059)
Constantine X Ducas (1059-1067)
Andronicus (1067)
Constantine XI (1067)
Romanus IV Diogenes (1068-1071)
Michael VII Parapinakes (1071-1078)
Nicephorus III Botaniates (1078-1081)
Alexius I Comnenus (1081-1118)
John IV Calus (1118-1143)
Manuel I (1143-1180)
Alexius II (1180-1183)
Andronicus I (1183-1185)
Isaac II Angelus (1185-1195)
Alexius III (1195-1203)
Alexius IV (1203-1204)
Alexius V (1204)
Theodore I Lascaris (1204-1222)
John III Vatatzes (1222-1254)
Theodore II Lascaris (1254-1258)
John IV Lascaris (1258-1261)
Michael VIII Palaeologus (1261-1282)
Andronicus II (1282-1328)
Michael IX (1294-1320)
Andronicus III (1382-1341)
John V (restored) (1341-1376)
John VI Cantacuzene (1347-1354)
John V (restored) (1355-1376)
Andronicus IV (1376-1379)
John V (restored) (1379-1390)
John VII (1390)
Manuel II (1391-1425)
John VIII (1425-1448)
Constantine XI (1448-1453)

6 Chinese Dynasties

Chin in Dynasty
Zheng of Qin (221-201)
Erh Shih Huang Ti (210-207)
Ch'in Wang (207)

Western Han Dynasty
Liu Pang (Kao Tsu) (207-195)
Hiu Ti (195-188)
Lü Hou (188-180)
Wên Ti (180-157)
Ching Ti (157-141)
Wu Ti (141-87)
Chao Ti (87-74)
Hsüan Ti (74-48)
Yüan Ti (48-33)
Ch'êng Ti (33-7)
Ai Ti (7-1)
P'ing Ti (1-6)
Ju-tzu Ying (6-9)

Hsin Dynasty
Chia Huang Ti (Wang Mang) (9-23)
Huai-yang Wang (Liu Hsüan) (23-25)

Eastern Han Dynasty
Kuang Wu Ti (Liu Hsiu) (25-57)
Ming Ti (57-75)
Chang Ti (75-88)
Ho Ti (88-106)
Shang Ti (106)
An Ti (106-125)
Shun Ti (125-144)
Ch'ung Ti (144-145)
Chih Ti (145-146)
Huan Ti (146-168)
Ling Ti (168-189)
Shao Ti (189)
Hsien Ti (189-220)

The Three Kingdoms

Wei Dynasty
Wên Ti (220-226)
Ming Ti (226-239)
Fei Ti (239-264)
Shao Ti
Yüan Ti

Shu Dynasty
Chao Lieh Ti (221-260)
Hou Chu (260-263)

Wu Dynasty
Ta Ti (221-252)
Fei Ti (252-258)
Ching Ti (258-264)
Mo Ti (264-280)

Western Chin Dynasty
Wu Ti (Ssu-ma Yen) (266-290)
Hiu Ti (290-307)
Huai Ti (307-311)
Min Ti (313-316)

Southern Dynasties

Eastern Chin Dynasty
Yüan Ti (Ssu-ma Jui) (317-323)
Ming Ti (323-325)
Ch'eng Ti (325-342)
K'ang Ti (342-344)
Mu Ti (344-361)
Ai Ti (361-365)
Hai-hsi Kung (365-372)
Chien Wen Ti (372)
Hsiao Wu Ti (372-396)
An Ti (396-419)
Kung Ti (419-420)

Liu Sing Dynasty
Wu Ti (Liu Wu) (420-422)
Shao Ti (422-424)
Wen Ti (424-453)
Hsiao Wu Ti (453-464)
Ch'ien Fei Ti (464-466)
Ming Ti (466-472)
Hou Fei Ti (472-477)
Shun Ti (477-479)

Southern Ch'i Dynasty
Kao Ti (479-482)
Wu Ti (482-493)
Yü-lin Wang (493-494)
Hai-ling Wang (494)
Ming Ti (494-498)
Tung-hun Hou (498-501)
Ho Ti (501-502)

Liang Dynasty
Wu Ti (Hsiao Yen) (502-549)
Chien Wen Ti (549-551)
Yü-chang Wang (551)
Yüan Ti (552-555)
Ching Ti (555-557)

Ch'ên Dynasty
Wu Ti (557-559)
Wên Ti (559-566)
Lin-hai Wang (566-568)
Hsüan Ti (569-582)
Hou Chu (582-589)

Northern Dynasties

Northern Wei Dynasty (Hsien-pei)
Tao Wu Ti (386-409)
Ming Yüan Ti (409-423)
T'ai Wu Ti (423-452)
Nan-an Wang (452)
Wên Ch'êng Ti (452-465)
Hsien Wên Ti (465-471)
Hsiao Wên Ti (471-499)
Hsüan Wu Ti (499-515)
Hsiao Ming Ti (515-528)
Lin-t'ao Wang (528)
Hsiao Chuang Ti (528-530)
Tung-hai Wang (530-531)
Chieh Min Ti (531-532)
An-ting Wang (532)
Hsiao Wu Ti (532-535)

Eastern Wei Dynasty (Hsien-pei)
Hsiao Ching Ti (535-550)

Northern Ch'i Dynasty
Wên Hsüan Ti (550-559)
Fei Ti (559-560)
Hsiao Chao Ti (560-561)
Wu Ch'êng Ti (561-565)
Hou Chu (565-577)
Yu Chu (577)

Western Wei Dynasty
Wên Ti (535-551)
Fei Ti (551-554)
Kung Ti (554-557)

Northern Chou Dynasty
Hsiao Min Ti (557)
Ming Ti (557-560)
Wu Ti (560-578)
Hsüan Ti (578-579)
Ching Ti (579-581)

Sui Dynasty
Wên Ti (581-604)
Yang Ti (604-617)
Kung Ti (617-618)

T'ang Dynasty
Kao Tsu (618-626)
T'ai Tsung (626-649)
Kao Tsung (649-683)
Chung Tsung (684)
Jui Tsung (684-690)
Wu Hou (690-705)
Chung Tsung (705-710)
Jui Tsung (710-712)
Hsüan Tsung (712-756)
Su Tsung (756-762)
Tai Tsung (762-779)
Tê Tsung (779-805)
Shun Tsung (805)
Hsien Tsung (805-820)
Mu Tsung (820-824)
Ching Tsung (824-827)
Wên Tsung (827-840)
Wu Tsung (840-846)
Hsiuan Tsung (846-859)
I Tsung (859-873)
Hsi Tsung (873-888)
Chao Tsung (888-904)
Ai Ti (904-907)

The Five Dynasties

Later Liang Dynasty
T'ai Tsu (907-912)
Ying Wang (912-913)
Mo Ti (913-923)

Later T'ang Dynasty
Chuang Tsung (923-926)
Ming Tsung (926-933)
Min Ti (933-934)
Fei Ti (934-937)

Later Chin Dynasty
Kao Tsu (937-942)
Ch'u Ti (942-947)

Later Han Dynasty
Kao Tsu (947-948)
Yin Ti (948-951)

Later Chou Dynasty
T'ai Tsu (951-954)
Shih Tsung (954-959)
Kung Ti (959-960)

The Border Empires

Liao Dynasty
T'ai Tsu (907-926)
T'ai Tsung (927-947)
Shih Tsung (947-951)
Mu Tsung (951-969)
Ching Tsung (969-982)
Shêng Tsung (982-1031)
Hsing Tsung (1031-1055)
Tao Tsung (1055-1101)

T'ien-tso Ti (1101-1125)

Chin Dynasty
T'ai Tsu (1115-1123)
T'ai Tsung (1123-1135)
Hsi Tsung (1135-1150)
Hai-ling Wang (1150-1161)
Shih Tsung (1161-1189)
Chang Tsung (1189-1208)
Wei-shao Wang (1208-1213)
Hsüan Tsung (1213-1224)
Ai Tsung (1224-1234)
Mo Ti (1234)

Northern Sung Dynasty
T'ai Tsu (960-976)
T'ai Tsung (976-997)
Chên Tsung (997-1022)
Jên Tsung (1022-1063)
Ying Tsung (1063-1067)
Shên Tsung (1067-1085)
Chê Tsung (1085-1100)
Hui Tsung (1100-1126)
Ch'in Tsung (1126-1127)

Southern Sung Dynasty
Kao Tsung (1127-1162)
Hsiao Tsung (1162-1189)
Kuang Tsung (1189-1194)
Ning Tsung (1194-1224)
Li Tsung (1224-1264)
Tu Tsung (1264-1274)
Kung Ti (1274-1276)
Tuan Tsung (1276-1278)
Ti Ping (1278-1279)

Yüan Dynasty
T'ai Tsu (1206-1227)
T'ai Tsung (1229-1241)
Ting Tsung (1246-1248)
Hsien Tsung (1251-1259)
Shih Tsu (1260-1294)
Ch'eng Tsung (1294-1307)
Wu Tsung (1307-1311)
Jen Tsung (1311-1320)
Ying Tsung (1320-1323)
T'ai-ting Ti (1323-1328)
Wen Tsung (1328-1329)
Ming Tsung (1329)
Wen Tsung (1329-1332)
Ning Tsung (1332)
Shun Ti (1333-1368)

Ming Dynasty
Hung Wu (1368-1398)
Chien Wen (1398-1402)
Yung Lo (1402-1424)
Hunh Hsi (1424-1425)
Hsüan Te (1425-1435)
Cheng T'ung (1435-1449)
Ching T'ai (1449-1457)
T'ien Shun (1457-1464)
Cheng Hua (1464-1487)
Hung Chih (1487-1505)
Cheng Te (1505-1521)
Chia Ching (1521-1567)
Lung ch'ing (1567-1572)
Wan Li (1572-1620)
T'ai Ch'ang (1620)
T'ien Ch'i (1620-1627)
Ch'ung Chen (1627-1644)

7 Egyptian pharaos

New Kingdom (74-1085)

Dynasty XVIII (1574-1320) at Thebes
Ahmose I(1574-1550)
Amenhotep I (1550-1530)
Thutmose I (1530-)
Thutmose II (?-1503)
Hatshepsut (1503-1482)
Thutmose III (1503-1450)
Amenhotep II (1450-1425)
Thutmose IV (1425-1417)
Amenhotep III (1417-1379)
Akhenaton (1379-1362)

Tutankhamen (1361-1352)
Ay (1352-1348)
Horenhab (1348-1320)

Dynasty XIX (1320-1200) at Thebes
Rameses I (1320-1318)
Seti I (1318-1304)
Rameses II (1304-1237)
Merneptah (1236-1218)
Amenmesses (1217-1213)
Seti II (1212-1207)
Merneptah Siptah (1206-1200)
Tewosret (1206-1200)

Dynasty XX (1200-1085) at Thebes
Setnakht (1194-1162)
Rameses III (1194-1162)
Rameses IV (1162-1156)
Rameses V (1156-1152)
Rameses VI (1152-1146)
Rameses VII
Rameses VIII
Rameses IX
Rameses X
Rameses XI (1115-1085)

Period of the Decline (1085-332)

Dynasty XXI (1085-950) at Tanis
Smendes
Psusennes I
Nefercheres
Amenophthis
Siamon
Psusennes II

Dynasty XXII (950-720), Lybians, and Dynasty XXIII
(810-720) at Tanis
Sheshonk I (c. 950)
Takelot I (c. 900)
Osorkon I
Osorkon II
Sheshonk II
Takelot II
Sheshonk IV (767-730)

Dynasty XXIV (720-701) at Sais
Tefnakht (720-715)
Bocchoris (715-701)

Dynasty XXV (c.701-663), Ethiopians or Nubians
Shabaka (701-689)
Shabataka (701-689)
Taharka (689-664)
Tanutaman (663-661)

Dynasty XXVI (663-525) at Sais
Necho I (663)
Psamtik I (663-610)
Necho II (609-594)
Psamtik II (594-588)
Apries (588-568)
Ahmose II (568-526)
Psamtik III (526-525)

Dynasty XXVII (525-405), Persians

Dynasty XXVIII (404-398) at Sais
Amyrteos (404-398)
Dynasty XXIX (398-378) at Mendes
Nepherites I (398-392)
Psammouthis (392-390)
Achoris (390-378)
Nepherites II (378)

Dynasty XXX (378-341) at Sebennytos
Nectanebo (378-360)
Teos (361-357)
Nectanebo II (359-341)

Dynasty XXXI (341-332), Persian

Conquest by Alexander the Great of Macedon (332)

8 The Frankish Empire

The Carolingian House
Charles Martel (719-741)
Pépin the Short (751-768)
Charlemagne (768-814)
Louis I the Pious (814-840)
Charles I the Bald (843-877)
Louis II the Stammerer (877-879)
Louis III (879-882)
Carloman (879-884)
Charles II the Fat (885-888)

The Robertian House
Odo of Anjou (888-898)

The Carolingian House
Charles III the Simple (893-923)

The Robertian House
Robert I (922-923)
Rudolph (923-936)

The Carolingian House
Louis IV of Outremer (936-954)
Lothair (954-986)
Louis V, the Sluggard (986-987)

The Capetian House
Hugh Capet (987-996)
Robert II the Pious (996-1031)
Henry I (1031-1060)
Philip I (1060-1108)
Louis VI the Fat (1108-1137)
Louis VII the Younger (1137-1180)
Philip II Augustus (1180-1223)
Louis VIII the Lion (1223-1226)
St Louis IX (1226-1270)
Philip III the Bold (1270-1285)
Philip IV the Fair (1285-1314)
Louis X the Stubborn (1314-1316)
Philip V the Tall (1316-1322)
Charles IV the Fair (1322-1328)

The House of Valois
Philip VI (1328-1350)
John II the Good (1350-1364)
Charles V the Wise (1364-1380)
Charles VI the Mad (1380-1422)
Charles VII the Victorious (1422-1461)
Louis XI (1461-1483)
Charles VIII (1483-1498)

9 The Frankish Kingdom

The Merovingian house
Merovech (c. 450)
Childeric I (457-482)
Clovis (482-511)
Chlodomer (511-524)
Theuderic I (511-533)
Childebert I (511-558)
Chlotar I (558-561)
Theudebert I (533-547)
Theudebald (547-555)
Charibert I (561-567)
Sigebert I (561-575)
Chilperic I (561-584)
Guntram (561-593)
Childebert II (575-596)
Chlotar II (613-629)
Theudebert II (596-612)
Theuderic II (596-613)
Sigebert II (613)
Dagobert I (629-639)
Charibert II (630-634)
St Sigebert III (634-656)
ClovisII (639-657)
Chlotar III (657-673)
Childeric II (662-675)
St Dagobert II (676-679)
Theuderic III (679-690)
Clovis III (690-694)
Childebert III (694-711)
Dagobert III (711-715)
Chilperic II (715-721)
Chlotar IV (717-719)

Theuderic IV (721-737)
Childeric III (743-751)

10 The Hebrew Kingdoms

Saul (1025-1000)
David (1000-965)
Solomon (965-925)

Kingdom of Judah
Rehoboam (934-917)
Abijah (915-913)
Asa (913-873)
Jehoshaphat (873-849)
Jehoram (849-842)
Ahaziah (841)
Athaliah (841-836)
Jehoash (835-796)
Amaziah (795-767)
Uzziah (766-740)
Jotham (739-732)
Ahaz (730-715)
Hezekiah (714-686)
Manasseh (685-641)
Amon (640-639)
Josiah (639-609)
Jehoahaz (609)
Jehoiakim (608-598)
Jehoiachin (598-597)
Zedekiah (596-586)

Kingdom of Israel
Jeroboam I (922-901)
Nadab (901-900)
Baasha (900-877)
Elah (877-876)
Zimri (876)
Tibni (876-875)
Omri (rival king) (876-869)
Ahab (874-853)
Ahaziah (853-852)
Jehoram (852-841)
Jehu (841-814)
Jehoahaz (813-797)
Jehoash (796-781)
Jeroboam II (781-754)
Zechariah (754-753)
Shallum (753)
Menahem (753-742)
Pekahiah (742-741)
Pekah (740-731)
Hoshea (731-723)

Assyrian Conquest

11 The Hellenistic World

The Kingdom of Macedonia
Perdiccas I (c. 700)
Argaeus I
Philip I (c.100)
Aëropus I
Alcetas
Amyntas I (?-498)
Alexander I (495-452)
Perdiccas II (452-413)
Archelaus (413-399)
Orestes (399-397)
Aëropus II (397-394)
Amyntas II (394-393)
Pausanias(rival king) (394-393)
Amyntas III (393-385)
Argaeus II (385-383)
Amyntas III (383-370)
Alexander II (370-368)
Ptolemy of Alorus (368-365)
Perdiccas III (365-359)
Philip II (359-336)
Alexander III the Great (336-323)
Philip III (323-317)
Alexander IV (317-309)
Antigonus the One-eyed (306-301)
Cassander (305-297)
Philip IV (297)
Alexander V (297-294)
Antipater I (297-294)
Demetrius I the Besieger (294-287)

Pytthus of Epirus (287-285)
Lysimachus (285-281)
Ptolemy Ceraunus (281-279)
Meleager (279)
Antipater II Etesias (279)
Sosthenes (279-277)
Antigonus II Gonatas (277-239)
Demetrius II (239-229)
Antigonus III Doson (227-221)
Philip V (221-179)
Perseus (179-168)

Roman Conquest of Macedonia

The Kingdom of Syracuse
Cleander (505-498)
Hippocrates (498-491)
Gelon I (491-478)
Hiero I (478-466)
Thrasybulus (466-465)
Dionysius I (405-367)
Dionysius II (367-357)
Dion (357-354)
Calippus (354-353)
Hipparinus (353-351)
Nysaeus (351-347)
Dionysius II (347-344)
Timoleon (344-337)
Agathocles (317-289)
Hiero II (270-215)
Gelon II (coregent) (?-216)
Hieronymus (215-214)

Roman Conquest of Syracuse

The Ptolemaic Dynasty
Ptolemy I Soter (323-285)
Ptolemy II Philadelphus (285-246)
Ptolemy III Euergetes (246-221)
Ptolemy IV Philopator (221-205)
Ptolemy V Epiphanes (204-180)
Ptolemy VI Philometor (180-145)
Ptolemy VII Noes Philopator (145-144)
Ptolemy VIII Euergetes II (144-116)
Ptolemy IX Soter II (116-107)
Ptolemy X Alexander I (107-88)
Ptolemy IX Soter II (88-80)
Ptolemy XI Alexander II (80)
Ptolemy XII Neos Dionysus (80-51)
Ptolemy XIII Philopator (51-47)
Cleopatra Philopator (51-30)
Ptolemy XIV Philopator (47-44)
Ptolemy XV Caesar Philopator Philometor (44-30)

Roman rule starts

The Seleucid Dynasty
Seleucus I Nicator (312-281)
Antiochus I Soter (281-261)
Seleucus I (280-267)
Antiochus II Theos (261-246)
Seleucus II Callinicus (246-226)
Seleucus III Soter (226-223)
Antiochus III the Great (223-187)
Seleucus IV Philopator (187-175)
Antiochus IV Epiphanes (175-164)
Antiochus V Eupator (164-162)
Demetrius I (162-150)
Alexander I Balas (Epiphenes) (150-145)
Antiochus VI Epiphanes Dionysus (145-142)
Demetrius II Nicator (145-139)
Tryphon (142-138)
Antiochus VII Euergetes (139-129)
Demetrius II Nicator (129-125)
Alexander II (128-122)
Cleopatra Thea (125-120)
Seleucus V (125)
Antiochus VIII (125-121)
Antiochus IX (113-95)
Seleucus VI Epiphanes Nicator (96-95)
Demetrius III (95-88)
Antiochus X Eusebes (95-93)
Antiochus XI Epiphanes Philadelphus (95)
Philip I Epiphanes Philadelphus (95-83)
Antiochus XII Dionysus (87-84)
Tigranes the Great (95-69)
Philip II (69-64)

Antiochus XIII Philadelphus (69-64)

Roman rule of Syria

12 The Holy Roman Empire

Charles I the Great (Charlemagne) (800-814)
Louis I the Pious (814-840)
Lothar I (840-855)
Louis II (855-875)
Charles II the Bald (875-877)
Charles III the Fat (881-887)
Arnulf of Carinthia (887-899)
Louis III the Child (900-911)
Conrad I (911-918)
Henry I the Fowler (919-936)
Otto I the Great (936-973)
Otto II (973-983)
Otto III (983-1002)
St Henry II (1002-1024)
Conrad II (1024-1039)
Henry III (1039-1056)
Henry IV (1056-1105)
Rudolf of Swabia (1077-1080)
Herman of Salm (1081-1088)
Conrad (1087-1098)
Henry V (1105-1125)
Lothair II of Saxony (1125-1137)
Conrad III (1138-1152)
Henry (1147-1150)
Frederick I Barbarossa (1152-1190)
Henry VI (1190-1197)
Philip of Swabia (1198-1208)
Otto IV of Brunswick (1198-1214)
Frederick II (1214-1250)
Henry (1220-1235)
Henry Raspe of Thuringia (1246-1247)
William of Holland (1247-1256)
Conrad IV (1250-1254)
Richard of Cornwall (1257-1272)
Rudolph of Hapsburg I (1273-1291)
Adolf of Nassau (1292-1298)
Albert I of Austria (1298-1308)
Henry VII (1308-1313)
Louis IV of Bavaria (1314-1347)
Frederick of Austria (1314-1330)
Charles IV (1346-1378)
Wenceslas (1378-1400)
Rupert of the Palatinate (1400-1410)
Sigismund (1410-1437)
Albert II of Austria (1438-1439)
Frederick III (1440-1493)
Maximilian I (1493-1519)

13 The Inca Empire

The Kingdom of Cuzco
Manco Capac (c.1200-?)
Sinchi Roca
Lloque Yupanqui
Mayta Capac
Tupac Yupanqui
Inca Roca
Yahuar Huacac
Inca Viracocha

The Empire
Pachacuti Inca (1438-1471)
Topa Inca (1471-1493)
Huanyna Capac (1493-1524)
Huáscar (1524-1532)
Atahualpa (1532)

Spanish conquest of the Inca Empire

14 The Islamic Caliphs

Orthodox Caliphate
Abū Bakr (632-634)
Umar I (634-644)
Uthman (644-656)
Ali Ibn Abi Talib (656-661)
Umayyad Dynasty
Mu'āwiyah I (661-680)
Yazid I (680-683)
Mu'āwiya II (683-684)
Marwan I (684-685)

Abd al-Malik (685-705)
Al-Walid I (705-715)
Süleyman (715-717)
Umar II (717-720)
Yazid II (720-724)
Hisham (724-743)
Al-Walid II (743-744)
Yazid III (744)
Ibrahim (744)
Marwan II (744-750)

Abbasid Dynasty
Abū al-Abbās al-Saffah (750-754)
Al-Mansūr (754-775)
Al-Mahdi (775-785)
Al-Hadi (785-786)
Harun al-Rashid (786-809)
Al-Amin (809-813)
Al-Mamun (813-833)
Al-Mutasim (833-842)
Al-Wathiq (842-847)
Al-Mutawakkil (847-861)
Al-Muntasir (861-862)
Al-Mustain (862-866)
Al-Mutazz (866-869)
Al-Muhtadi (869-870)
Al-Mutamid (870-892)
Al-Mutadid (892-902)
Al-Muktafi (902-908)
Al-Muqtadir (908-932)
Al-Qahir (932-934)
Al-Radi (934-940)
Al-Muttaqi (940-944)
Al-Mustakfi (944-946)
Al-Muti (946-974)
Al-Ta'i' (974-991)
Al-Qadir (991-1031)
Al-Qa'im (1031-1075)
Al-Muqtadi (1075-1094)
Al-Mustazhir (1094-1118)
Al-Mustarshid (1118-1135)
Al-Rashid (1135-1136)
Al-Mustafi (1136-1160)
Al-Mustanjid (1160-1170)
Al-Mustadi (1170-1180)
Al-Nasir (1180-1225)
Al-Zahir (1225-1126)
Al-Mustansir (1126-1242)
Al-Mustasim (1242-1258)

Mongol conquest of Iraq

15 The Medieval Kingdom of Italy

Berengar I of Friuli (888-924)
Guy of Spoleto(rival king) (889-894)
Lambert of Spoleto (894-898)
Louis of Provence (900-905)
Rudolf II of Burgundy (922-926)
Hugh of Arles (926-948)
Lothair (948-950)
Berengar II of Ivrea (950-963)
Adalbert (950-963)

16 The Persian Empire

The Achaemenid Dynasty
Cyrus the Great (559-530)
Cambyses (529-522)
Smerdis (Bardiya) (522)
Darius I (521-486)
Xerxes I (485-465)
Artaxerxes I (464-424)
Xerxes II (424)
Sogdianus (424)
Darius II (423-405)
Artaxerxes II (404-359)
Artaxerxes III (358-338)
Arses (Xerxes III) (337-336)
Darius III (335-330)

Macedonian conquest of the Persian Empire

The Sasanids
Ardashir I (224-241)
Shapur I (241-272)
Ormuz I (272-273)

Bahram I (273-276)
Bahram II (276-293)
Bahram III (293)
Narses (293-302)
Ormuz II (302-309)
Shapur II (309-379)
Ardashir II (379-383)
Shapur III (383-388)
Bahram IV (388-399)
Yazdgerd I (399-420)
Bahram V the Wild Ass (420-438)
Yazdgerd II (438-457)
Hormizd III (457-459)
Peroz (459-484)
Balash (484-488)
Kavadh I (488-497)
Zamasp (497-499)
Kavadh I (499-531)
Khusrau I (531-579)
Ormuz IV (579-590)
Bahram VI Chubin (590-591)
Khusrau II the Victorious 590-628
Kavad II (628)
Ardashir III (628-630)
Shahrbaraz (630)
Boran (630-631)
Azarmedukhr (631-632)
Yazdgerd III (632-651)

Arab conquest of Sasanid Empire

17 The Il-Khans of Persia

Chingizid Dynasty
Hülegü (conquered Persia in 1256-1258)1256-1265
Abaqa (1265-1282)
Tegüder (1282-1284)
Arghün (1284-1291)
Gaikhatu (1291-1295)
Baidu (1295)
Gházán (1295-1304)
Öljeitü (1304-1316)
Abu Sa'id (1316-1335)
Arpa (1335-1336)
Musa (1336-1337)
Muhammad (1336-1338)
Sati Beg (1338-1339)
Jahan Temür (1339-1340)
Süleyman (1339-1343)

18 Roman or Western Emperors

Augustus (27-14)
Tiberius (14-37)
Gaius Caesar (Caligula) (37-41)
Claudius (41-54)
Nero (54-68)
Galba (68-69)
Otho (69)

Vitellius (69)
Vespasian (69-79)
Titus (79-81)
Domitian (81-96)
Nerva (96-98)
Trajan (98-117)
Hadrian (117-138)
Antoninus Pius (138-161)
Marcus Aurelius and Lucius Verus (161-169)
Marcus Aurelius (169-177)
Marcus Aurelius and Commodus (177-180)
Commodus (180-192)
Pertinax (193)
Didius Julianus (193)
Septimius Severus (193-198)
Septimius Severus and Antoninus (Caracalla) (198-209)
Septimius Severus, Antoninus (Caracalla) and Geta (209-211)
Antoninus (Caracalla) and Geta (211-212)
Antoninus (Caracalla) (212-217)
Macrinus (217-218)
Macrinus and Diadumenianus (218)
Antoninus (Elagabalus) (218-222)
Severus Alexander (222-235)
Maximinus Thrax (235-238)
Gordianus I and II (238)
Pupienus and Balbinus (238)
Gordianus III (238-244)
Philip the Arabian (244-247)
Philip the Arabian and Philip (247-249)
Decius (249-251)
Trebonianus Gallus and Volusianus (251-253)
Aemilianus (253)
Valerian and Gallienus (253-260)
Gallienus (260-268)
Claudius II (Gothicus) (268-270)
Quintillus (270)
Aurelianus (270-275)
Tacitus (275-276)
Florian (276)
Probus (276-282)
Carus (282-283)
Carinus and Numerianus (283-284)
Diocletian (284-286)
Diocletian and Maximian (286-305)
Constantius I and Galerius (305-306)
Galerius, Severus and Constantine I (306-307)
Galerius, Licinius and Constantine I (307-310)
Galerius, Licinius, Constantine I and Maximinus Daia (310-311)
Licinius and Constantine I (311-324)
Constantine I (324-337)
Constantine II, Constantius II and Constans (337-340)
Constantius II and Constans (340-350)
Constantius II (350-361)
Julian (the Apostate) (361-363)
Juvian (363-364)
Valentinian I and Valens (364-367)
Valentinian I, Valens and Gratian (367-375)

Valens, Gratian and Valentinian II (375-378)
Gratian, Valentinian II and Theodosius I (379-383)
Valentinian II, Theodosius I and Arcadius (383-392)
Theodosius I and Arcadius (392-393)
Theodosius I, Arcadius and Honorius (393-395)
Honorius, Flavius (395-423)
Constantius III (421)
John (423-425)
Valentinian III (425-455)
Petronius Maximus (455)
Avitus, Marcus Maecilius (455-456)
Majorian (457-461)
Severus Libius (461-465)
Anthemius (467-472)
Olybrius Anicius (472)
Glycerius (473)
Nepos Julius (473-475)
Romulus Augustulus (475-476)

19 The Visigothic Kingdom (Spain)

Alaric I (395-410)
Ataulf (410-415)
Sigeric (415)
Wallia (415-418)
Theodoric I (418-451)
Thorismund (451-453)
Theodoric II (453-466)
Euric (466-484)
Alaric II (484-507)
Gesalic (507-511)
Amalaric (511-531)
Theudis (531-548)
Theudegisil (548-549)
Agila I (549-555)
Athanagild (555-567)
Liuva I (567-572)
Leovigild (568-586)
Reccared I (586-601)
Liuva II (601-603)
Witteric (603-610)
Gundemar (610-612)
Sisebut (612-621)
Reccared II (621)
Suinthila (621-631)
Sisenand (631-636)
Chintila (636-639)
Tulga (639-642)
Chindasuinth (642-653)
Reccesuinth (653-672)
Wamba (672-680)
Erwig (680-687)
Egica (687-702)
Wittiza (702-710)
Roderic (710-711)
Agila II (711-714)

Muslim conquest of Visigothic Spain

Time line

Years Ago

3.5 billion Formation of the earth (vol. 1)

248-65 million Mesozoic era (vol. 1)

144-65 million Because of continental drift, dinosaurs are not found on every continent (vol. 1)

70-65 million Dinosaurs dominate the earth; mammals begin to diversify by evolution (vol. 1)

66 million-present Cenozoic era (vol. 1)

40-30 million Oligopithecids and Parapithecids; first mammal with characteristics of anthropoid primates (vol. 1)

35.5-23.3 million Oligocene epoch; first signs of glacial cooling (vol. 1)

23.3-5.2 million Miocene epoch; earth's surface evolves into what is essentially its present form (vol. 1)

23-14 million Proconsul, likely ancestor of both apes and monkeys of the Old World (vol. 1)

5.2-1.6 million Pliocene epoch; large ice sheets form on northern continents (vol. 1)

3.5-2.6 million *Australopithecus afarensis*; the oldest species of Australopithecus (vol. 1)

3-2 million *Australopithecus africanus* (vol. 1)

2.5 million-200,000 Lower Paleolithic Age (vol. 1)

2.4-1.8 million "Early Homo" (*Homo habilis* and *Homo rudolphensis*); first tool-producing human ancestors (vol. 1)

1.8 -1.6 million *Homo erectus*; possibly the first human ancestor to migrate out of Africa (vol. 1)

1.6 million-15,000 Pleistocene epoch; constant fluctuations between warm and intensely cold global climates (vol. 1)

700,000 *Homo sapiens*, also known as Neandertaler; Ubeidiya, Israel; earliest recorded human settlement in the Near East (vol. 1)

400,000 Earliest evidence for controlled use of fire (vol. 1)

200,000 *Homo sapiens sapiens*, Anatomically Modern Human, gradually expands from Africa to parts of Asia and the Near East (vol. 1); First people in Japan (vol. 11)

100,000-30,000 The Mousterian culture (generally associated with Neandertals) flourishes in Europe and the Near East (vol. 1)

40,000-32,000 *Homo sapiens sapiens* spread into Europe with more sophisticated technologies and cognitive abilities than the Neandertals (vol. 1)

35,000-28,000 Earliest art in human and animal figurines (vol. 1)

30,000-25,000 Settlement of Melanesians on the islands of the Pacific (vol. 3)

30,000-20,000 First groups of hunters migrate from North to South America (vol. 11)

18,000-11,000 Global climate gradually gets warmer; glaciers retreat to northern latitudes (vol. 1)

c. 10,000 Neolithic revolution in the Near East; domestication of plants and animals, increased sedentary lifestyle, and social complexity (vol. 1)

BC

c. 7000 Farming takes hold in Greece and Southeast Europe; European Mesolithic culture (vol. 1); Earliest agricultural settlement near Knossos, Greece (vol. 2)

5000 Settlement of earliest population between Euphrates and Tigris in Mesopotamia (vol. 2)

4500-4000 First habitation of the Nile Delta, Egypt (vol. 2)

c. 4000-3000 Urban revolution in the Near East (vol. 1)

4000 Addition of two new population groups, the Semites and the Sumerians in Mesopotamia (vol. 2)

3300-2000 Early Minoan culture on Crete, Greece; period when palaces were built (vol. 2)

3150-2650 Archaic period, the first two dynasties rule in Egypt, pharaohs were buried in clay stone tombs dried by the sun (vol. 2)

c. 3000 Invention of writing in Mesopotamia (vol. 1); introduction of the cylinder seal from Mesopotamia evolves into hieroglyphics in Egypt; the cities of Lower Mesopotamia slowly expand their powers and become city-states (vol. 2)

2650-2150 Egypt, the Ancient Kingdom. From the Third through the Sixth Dynasties the empire is centralized (vol. 2)

2650 Pharaoh Djoser builds the first pyramid (Egypt) (vol. 2)

2613-2498 During the Fourth Dynasty pyramid building in Egypt reaches its zenith (vol. 2)

c. 2500-2000 Palestine inhabited by Semitic peoples (vol. 3)

2500-1750 Harappa or Indus Valley culture (vol. 3)

2500-1500 Micronesians invade the Pacific Ocean as far as Polynesia (vol. 3)

2340-2200 Foundation of the Empire of Sumer and Akkad, Mesopotamia by Sargon I, Golden Age of Mesopotamian civilization (vol. 2)

c. 2200 Guthians destroy Akkad, rule Mesopotamia as barbarians (vol. 2); legendary dynasty of Xia reigns in China (vol. 3)

2125 End of the rule by the kings of Memphis, Egypt; start of the First Interregnum (vol. 2)

2125-2060 Beginning of the Eleventh Dynasty in Thebes, division between Upper and Lower Egypt (vol. 2)

2112 Ur dynasty rules major part of Mesopotamia (vol. 2)

2040-1640 Middle Kingdom, Upper and Lower Egypt are united under Mentuhotpe; Thebes becomes seat of government of the Middle Kingdom, building of temples throughout the empire (vol .2)

c. 2000 Entry of two new population groups in Mesopotamia, the Hurrians and Indo-Europeans (vol. 2); introduction of the horse-drawn chariot in Hittite Empire; Bronze Age of the Shang, first Chinese dynasty (vol. 3); beginning of the Preclassical Maya civilization (vol. 11)

c. 2000-1750 Hebrews migrate into Palestine, Abraham travels to Palestine (vol. 3)

2000-1700 Indo-Aryans interact with and conquer the people of the Indus Valley (vol. 3)

2000-1600 Middle Minoan period on Crete (vol. 2)

2000-1300 Metallurgy becomes widespread in Europe (vol. 1)

1880 Amorite dynasty of Babylon, Mesopotamia (vol. 2)

1800 *Mari Letters* provide fascinating look on society on the Euphrates (vol. 2)

c. 1800-1200 In the Punjab, a series of hymns, the *Rig-Veda*, is composed; the Indian religion is dominated by the priests or Brahmans (vol. 7)

1792-1750 Hammurabi is sixth king of Babylon, *Hammurabi's Code* (vol. 2)

1780-1720 Influx of foreigners into Egyptian society (vol. 2)

c. 1750 Abraham forms convenant with God (vol. 3)

1750-1555 In the Nile Delta non-Egyptian states led by desert rulers/Hyksos arise (vol. 2)

1750-1700 Mycenae rises to great power and wealth in Greece (vol. 2)

1700 Internal strife on Crete and domination of Knossos marks a period of decline; Linear A script on Crete developed (vol. 2)

1700-1450 The palaces on Crete are decorated with mural paintings, "House of the Frescoes" in Knossos (vol. 2)

c. 1650 Cities rise around the palaces on Crete, the oldest cities in Europe (vol. 2); Hattusili I fights to hold the Hittite Empire together (vol. 3)

c. 1650-1250 Stay of the Israelites in Egypt (vol. 3)

1640-1550 Seventeenth Dynasty in Thebes (Egypt) subjucated to the Hyksos kings (vol. 2)

1600 Rise of Mycenaen culture on the mainland of Greece (vol. 2)

1594 Old Babylon destroyed by the Hittites (vol. 2)

c. 1550 Earliest settlement on the site of subsequent Rome (vol. 5)

1550-1300 The New Egyptian Kingdom starts with Ahmose, founder of the Eighteenth Dynasty; pharaohs were buried in closed rock tombs with a separate mortuary temple (vol. 2)

1500-1360 Golden Age of the Phoenician city of Ugarit (vol. 3)

c. 1500 Writing of civil code in Hittite Empire; Earliest sections of Vedas written in India (vol. 3)

1480-1430 Tuthmosis III, the Egyptian Kingdom reaches its greatest size (vol. 2)

1450 Linear B related to Greek is especially spoken in the Mycenaean royal fortresses (vol .2)

1450-1200 International trade by Crete extends to Europe; Golden Age and widest expansion of Mycenaean civilization (vol. 2)

1400-1350 Building of the Citadel and the Lion's Gate in Mycenae (vol. 2)

1400-1300 Middle Assyrian period, renewal of Assyria, strong imperialism (vol. 2)

1391-1353 The Egyptian refined art and colossal temples are funded by agricultural production and Nubian gold (vol. 2)

1380 Suppiluliuma, founder of the New Empire of the Hitttites (vol. 3)

1306 Beginning in Egypt of the Nineteenth Dynasty with Ramses I (vol. 2)

c. 1300 Destruction of the palace of Knossos on Crete (vol. 2); beginning of the Olmec civilization on the Caribbean coast (vol. 11)

1300-1000 Urnfield culture dominates Europe (vol. 1)

1290-1224 Under Ramses II great construction activity in Egypt, including his own grave, the "Ramesseum" (vol. 2)

1286 Battle at Kadesh, the Egyptian Pharaoh Ramses II defeated by Hittite army (vol. 2)

c. 1250 Development of the Phoenician alphabet (vol. 3)

c. 1224-1214 Exodus of the Hebrews from Egypt to Palestine led by Moses, prophet and lawgiver (vol. 3)

c. 1200 The Nineteenth Dynasty in Egypt destroyed by domestic unrest and short-reigning kings; Mycenaean civilization is repeatedly ravaged by destruction; destruction of Babylon by Tukulti-Ninurta I, Assyrian king. (vol. 2); Ten Commandments (vol. 3)

1200-900 Fall of the Hittite Empire (vol. 2)

1098 Pharaoh's power declines considerably under Ramses XI (vol. 2)

1050 Beginning of the Dark Ages in Greece (vol. 2)

c. 1050-750 Emergence of city-states and aristocracy in the Greek world (vol. 4)

1027 China, the Zhou dynasty conquers the Shang dynasty (vol. 7)

c. 1000 Use and production of iron spreads quickly across Europe (vol. 1); David chosen as king of the Israelites; consolidation of power and growth of the states in China (vol. 3)

c. 950 Plain of Eurotas conquered by Dorian Greeks (vol. 4)

926-722 Kingdom of Israel; rise of the prophets (vol. 3)

925-587 Kingdom of Judah (vol. 3)

c. 900 Restoration of the Assyrian Empire (vol. 2); Phoenicians trade from Asia Minor to Egypt, from Arabia to southern Spain (vol. 3); rise of the Chimú civilization in South America (vol. 11)

c. 900-700 Creation of Spartan form of government with kings, warriors, helots and free residence (vol. 4)

900-600 Several settlements on the hills surrounding Rome (vol. 5)

c. 880-660 *Brahmanas*, books explaining the hymns and their ritual application in the Indian religion (vol. 7)

814 Foundation of the colony of Carthage by the Phoenicians (vol. 3)

800 Babylon becomes part of the Assyrian Empire (vol. 2)

c. 800-500 The *Aranyakas* and *Upanishads* teach the inner meaning of offerings in the Indian religious culture (vol. 7)

753 Legendary foundation of Rome by Romulus (vol. 5)

750-700 Homer composes the *Iliad* and *Odyssey* (vol. 4)

c. 750-550 Archaic period in Greece, power in the hands of the aristocracy, foundation of Greek coastal settlements on the Mediterranean and the Black Seas (vol. 4)

743 Attack on the Syrian city-states and their allies (vol. 2)

722-705 Sargon II defeats coalition of Syrian and Phoenician cities (vol. 2)

c. 700 Conquest of Messenia by Sparta; Athens is governed by nine archons of aristocratic descent (vol. 4)

c. 700-500 Under Greek influence a Mediterranean urban culture develops in central Italy (vol. 4)

689 Babylon completely destroyed by Assyrian king, Nineveh becomes new residence of the Assyrian Empire (vol. 2)

660 Legendary foundation of Japan by Emperor Jimmu Tenno (vol. 11)

650-500 Tyranny, the most prevalent type of government in the Greek world, undermines the position of the aristocracy and clears the way for democracy (vol. 4)

c. 625 Valley between Palatine and Capitoline Hills is built up, origin of the settlement of Rome, controlled by king and Senate (vol. 5)

616-509 Three Etruscan kings rule Rome (vol. 5)

612 Nineveh, capital of the Assyrian Empire falls, beginning of the New Babylon Empire (vol. 2)

610-547 Anaximander of Miletus produces a world map and a sun dial (vol. 4)

c. 600-400 Legalism and Daoism, the two main philosophies in China (vol. 3)

594-593 Through his reforms, Solon ends the worst abuses under Athenian law, such as the enslavement of debtors (vol. 4)

586 Fall of Jerusalem, Jewish people in Babylonian exile (vol. 2, 3, 7)

c. 580-480 Xenophanes, Greek poet and philosopher (vol. 4)

563-483 The Buddha, Siddharta Gautama, announces his new "teaching of the eightfold path" (vol. 3, 7)

561 Tyranny of Peisistratus in Athens (vol. 4)

561-510 Athens becomes the center of the Ionian Greeks (vol. 4)

559-529 The Persian king Cyrus II conquers the Median Empire (vol. 3)

551-479 Confucius (Kong Fuzi) Chinese political thinker (vol. 3, 7)

539 New Babylonian Empire and Babylon conquered by the Persians (vol. 2, 3)

536 The Jews are allowed to return to Palestine (vol. 2, 3, 7)

525 Egypt integrated in the Persian Empire (vol. 2)

521-486 Darius I rules the Persian Empire (vol. 3)

c. 520 Carthage sends an expedition to found colonies beyond Gibraltar (vol. 3)

510 End of tyranny in Athens, restoration of democracy (vol. 4)

510-508/7 Political reforms under Cleisthenes; the populace (demos) gains in importance, introduction of the boulè (Council of 500) in Athens (vol. 4)

509 End of Etruscan power, start of the Roman republic, power in the hands of two consuls, the Senate, and the popular assembly (vol. 5)

c. 500 Scythians emerge as powerful warriors from Eastern Europe (vol. 1); Forum Romanum being used as cultural and political center of the Roman Republic (vol. 5); legendary Chinese figure of Laozi (vol. 7)

c. 500-400 Increase in number of Roman citizens (vol. 5)

500-250 Expansion of the Celts (vol. 1)

c. 500-221 Period of the battling states in China (vol. 3)

497-406/5 Sophocles, Greek writer of tragedies (vol. 4)

495 Greeks lose a major battle at sea against the Persians (vol. 4)

493 Rome included in the Latin League (vol. 5)

491 Persian king demands submission of the Greek city-states, Athens and Sparta refuse (vol. 4)

490 Greek victory over the Persians at Marathon (vol. 4)

490-480 Under Themistocles, Athens becomes a naval power (vol. 4)

486 Rome defeats the Latin army (vol. 5)

480 Sparta claims military hegemony over Athens, battle of Salamis (vol. 4)

480-420 Herodotus, Greek historian, the "Father of History" (vol. 4)

480-221 Period of the Warring States in China (vol. 7)

478/477 Foundation of the Delian League against

Persia, led by Athens (vol. 4)

470 Persian army of Darius I defeated by the Greeks (vol. 3)

470-399 Socrates, Greek philosopher died by drinking poison (vol. 4)

460-429 The Athenian Pericles active as general and orator (vol. 4)

460-400 The Greek historian Thucydides (vol. 4)

457 Ezra, Jewish scholar of law institutes religious reforms (vol. 7)

455 Euripides's *Peliades* (vol. 5)

c. 450 Hippocrates searches for natural explanations of diseases (vol. 4); recording of the current common law in Rome (vol. 5)

450-385 Aristophanes, Greek writer of comedies (vol. 4)

447-406 Beginning of the reconstruction of the Acropolis in Athens (vol. 4)

445 Thirty Years Peace between Sparta and Athens (vol. 5)

443 Athens founds the colony of Thurii in Southern Italy (vol. 4)

431-404 Peloponnesian War between Sparta and Athens and their allies (vol. 5)

429-347 Greek philosopher Plato (vol. 4)

425 Completion of the temple of Athena Nike and the Erechtheum on the Acropolis in Athens (vol. 5)

421-418 Peace of Nicias between Athens and Sparta (vol. 5)

404 Capture of Athens and destruction of their fleet by Lysander, end of the Athenian democracy and start of the oligarchy under the "Thirty Tyrants," Spartan hegemony over all of Greece (vol. 5)

403 Civil war ends the rule of the Thirty Tyrants, restoration of democracy in Athens (vol. 5)

c. 400-200 Carthage evolves into a powerful state (vol. 5)

387 Peace dictated by Persia between Sparta and some Greek cities such as Athens; Plato founds his Academia in Athens (vol. 5)

384-322 Aristotle, Greek philosopher (vol. 4)

375 Rome has hegemony in the Latin League (vol. 5)

372-289 According to the Chinese thinker Mencius restoration of the Chinese empire is possible only through the virtue of the ruler (vol. 3, 7)

366-347 Plato's *Theory of Ideas* (vol. 5)

365-275 Pyrrho of Elis founds the School of Skeptics (vol. 5)

359 Philip II king of Macedonia (vol. 5)

358 Rome forces all Latins into a closer alliance (vol. 5)

356 Appointment of the first plebeian dictator in Rome (vol. 5)

c. 350 Xenophon, Athenian historian (vol. 4)

348 Treaty between Rome and Carthage (vol. 5)

340-338 Latin League rises up against Roman domination, resulting in the dissolution of the League (vol. 5)

336 Alexander the Great succeeds Philip II as king of Macedonia (vol. 5)

335-263 Zeno of Cition; teachings of the Stoa in Athens (vol. 5)

332 Alexander the Great conquers Egypt and Palestine (vol. 2, 5, 7)

331 Foundation of Alexandria in Egypt by Alexander the Great, who emphasizes his descendance from the gods (vol. 5)

330 Alexander the Great crushes the Persian world empire (vol. 3, 5)

327 Invasion of India as far as the Indus Valley by Alexander the Great (vol. 3, 5)

324 Chandra Gupta Maurya creates a power base in Punjab, establishes the Maurya dynasty in India (vol. 3, 7)

323 Death of Alexander the Great; succeded by Alexander IV and Philip III; actual power in the hands of the diadochs (vol. 5)

323-306/304 Battle of the diadochs brings about the formation of new kingdoms in Greece and Asia Minor (vol. 5)

c. 320-305 Foundation of the Mouseion in Alexandria (vol. 5)

306 Antigones and Demetrius kings of Asia Minor, dynasty of the Antigonids (vol. 5)

305 Ptolemy king of Egypt, Palestine, Cyprus, and Cyrenaica, founder of the dynasty of the Ptolemies (vol. 5, 7)

305-304 Seleucus II, founder of the dynasty of the Seleucids, king from Sardis to Kabul (vol. 5)

c. 300 Plebeian majority in the Roman Senate (vol. 5); rise of Tiwanaku civilization in South America (vol. 11)

287 *Lex Hortensia* renews the Roman government (vol. 5)

287-212 Law of Archimedes (vol. 5)

c. 270-232 Golden Age of India under Asoka, king of the entire Indian subcontinent (vol. 3, 7)

270 Italy south of the Po in Roman hands (vol. 5)

264-241 First Punic War between Carthago and Rome (vol. 5)

c. 225 Confucius's (Kong Fuzi's) teachings become state ideology (vol. 3)

221 Zheng of Qin, first emperor of united China, beginning of the Han dynasty, building of the first Great Wall (vol. 3, 7)

218-201 Second Punic War; Rome declares war on Carthage, Hannibal marches over the Alps (vol. 5)

209 Roman consul Scipio captures Carthago Nova (vol. 5)

202 Beginning of the Han dynasty in China (vol. 7)

c. 200 Composition in India of the *Bhagavad-Gita*, one of the holiest poems of Hinduism; *The Septuagint*, translation of the Bible into Greek (vol. 7)

198 The Syrian Antiochus conquers the Ptolemies' possessions in Palestine (vol. 7)

190 Rome eclipses all Hellenistic empires (vol. 5)

171 War between Rome and Macedonia (vol. 5)

167 Violent revolt in Jerusalem, the Maccabees start a guerilla warfare against Syrian rule (vol. 7)

167-160 Judas Maccabaeus frees the majority of Palestine (vol. 7)

c. 150 Compilation of definitive text of the *Iliad* and *Odyssey* (vol. 4)

149-146 Third Punic War (vol. 5)

138 Simon coins the first Jewish money (vol. 7)

133-123 The brothers Gracchi want to weaken the power of the Optimates in the Roman Senate (vol. 5)

c. 121 China conquers the Tarim Basin (vol. 11)

107 Marius reforms the Roman army (vol. 5)

106-43 Roman orator Cicero (vol. 5)

88-82 Civil war in the Roman Empire (vol. 5)

82-78 Sulla occupies Rome as a dictator, Senate obtains all powers (vol. 5)

70 Pompey and Crassus consuls of the Roman Republic; Cicero begins his oratorial fame (vol. 6)

63 The Roman general Pompey brings Palestine within the Roman sphere of influence (vol. 7)

60 First Triumvirate, Crassus, Pompey and Caesar, rule Rome (vol. 6)

52 Pompey is sole consul (vol. 6)

49-48 Caesar defeats Pompey in a civil war (vol. 6)

46-44 Caesar rules as a dictator over the Roman world, brings about calendar reforms (vol. 6)

43-36 Second Triumvirate, Antony, Octavian and Lepidus, rule in Rome (vol. 6)

29 The Roman writer Virgil begins his *Aeneid* (vol. 6)

28 Livy begins his *History of Rome from the Foundation of the City* (vol. 6)

27 Start of the Principate in the Roman Empire, Octavian goes now by the name Augustus (vol. 6)

25-4 Herod the Great rules as king of Palestine under Roman protection, John the Baptist announces that the kingdom of God is approaching (vol. 7)

14 Textbook by the Roman Vitruvius on architecture (vol. 6)

9 Rhine and Danube become borders of the Roman Empire (vol. 6)

6 Birth of Jesus in Bethlehem (vol. 7)

AD

14 Mausoleum of Augustus is built in Rome (vol. 6)

14-37 Tiberius rules as Roman emperor (vol. 6)

27-30 Jesus preaches among the people; he is called the Messiah (vol. 7)

30 Jesus is crucified at Jerusalem (vol. 7)

37-41 Caligula rules the Roman Empire (vol. 6)

40-50 Essays by Stoic philosopher Seneca (vol. 6)

c. 40 Jesus' followers call themselves Christians and increasingly diverge from traditional Judaism (vol. 7)

41-54 The Roman Emperor Claudius (vol. 6)

54 First epistle of Paul to the Corinthians (vol. 7)

54-68 Nero rules the Roman Empire; building of Nero's Golden House (vol. 6)

64 Great fire in Rome, persecution of the Christians (vol. 6); death of the apostle Peter (vol. 7)

66-70 Jewish uprising against Rome (vol. 7)

67 Death of the apostle Paul (vol. 7)

68-69 Year of the four Roman Emperors and civil war (vol. 6)

70 The Temple in Jerusalem is destroyed, beginning of the Diaspora (vol. 7)

c. 70-100 Compilation of the gospels (vol. 7)

71 Start on the building of the Colosseum (vol. 6)

79 Eruption of Mount Vesuvius, Pompeii is destroyed (vol. 6)

98-117 Trajan is Roman emperor, prohibits active searches for Christians (vol. 6, 7)

c. 100 Buddhism in China (vol. 7); construction of the Pyramid of the Sun in Teotihuacán (vol. 11)

c.100-200 Christianity spreads in the eastern parts of the Roman Empire (vol. 7)

114-117 Trajan's war against the Parthians, the Roman army conquers Mesopotamia (vol. 6)

115 Historical works by the Roman Tacitus (vol. 6)

117-138 Roman emperor Hadrian (vol. 6)

132-135 Last major Jewish revolt in Judaea by the Roman suppressed (vol. 6)

c. 150 Teotihuacán becomes a state in Central America (vol. 11)

161-180 Marcus Aurelius rules the Roman Empire (vol. 6)

190 Works by the Christian writers Tertulian and Irenaeus (vol. 6)

c. 210 Roman history by the Greek Cassius Dio (vol. 6)

212 Caracalla absolute ruler over the Roman Empire (vol. 6)

220-280 Chinese Empire breaks into three states, invasions by Mongols and Hsiung-nu (vol. 11)

c. 225 The Christians constitute one of the largest religious communities in the Roman Empire (vol. 7); Confucianism becomes state religion in China (vol. 11)

235-285 Period of anarchy in the Roman Empire, the soldier-emperors (vol. 6); Christianity attracts a great number of followers, construction of the catacombs in Rome (vol. 7)

242-272 Sapor is king of the Persians (vol. 8)

248-251 Decius as Roman emperor, general order to worship Roman gods results in Christian persecution (vol. 6, 7)

257 Start of new Christian persecution in the Roman Empire (vol. 6)

c. 260 Influence of Christianity in the New Persian Empire (vol. 8)

270-275 Roman emperor Aurelian restores the empire unity (vol. 6)

284 Diocletian is proclaimed Roman emperor, start of large-scale reorganization and consolidation in the empire (vol. 6)

285 Maximian is made co-emperor in the west of the Roman Empire, start of multiple emperorship (vol. 6)

285-305 The Emperor Diocletian creates a tetrarchy (vol. 8)

c. 300-400 Cultural flowering in India, golden age of Buddhism and Brahmanism (vol. 7)

c. 300-900 Beginning of classical Maya culture in the Yucatán (vol. 11)

306 Rise of the Chin dynasty in the east of China (vol. 11)

309-379 The Persian king Sapor II conquers large parts of Eastern Syria (vol. 8)

311 Edict of tolerance, making it legal to be a Christian (vol. 7)

312 Constantine the Great conquers Rome, becomes the new emperor; he testifies to his belief in Christianity (vol. 7)

313 Edict of Milan: Christians are entitled to practice their religion freely (vol. 7)

320-499 Nearly all of northern India is ruled by the Gupta dynasty (vol. 7)

324 Constantine, the sole ruler of the Roman Empire, donates vast possessions to the Christian church (vol. 7)

325 Emperor Constantine the Great calls the first Council of Nicaea where Arians are branded as heretics (vol. 7)

330 Constantine founds the capital of Constantinople (vol. 8)

337 Emperor Constantine is baptized on his deathbed (vol. 7)

337-361 The Roman emperor Constans publicly speaks against paganism (vol. 7)

342-420 The church father Jerome translates the Old Testament into Latin (vol. 7)

c. 350 Buddhism penetrates to the emperor's court of China (vol. 7)

354-430 St. Augustine of Hippo, a church father (vol. 7)

361-363 Julian the Apostate rules the Roman Empire; he tries to restore paganism (vol. 7, 8)

375 Huns destroy the empire of the Ostrogoths (vol. 8)

c. 375-500 The great migration causes the native people to be dominated by a handful of barbarians (vol. 8)

378 Battle of Adrianople, the Goths conquer and reign supreme in the Balkans (vol. 8)

379 Theodosius I becomes Roman emperor; during his reign the altars and sanctuaries of pagan gods are destroyed (vol. 7, 8); the Persian Empire at the zenith of its power (vol. 8)

395 Theodosius divides definitively the Roman Empire into two parts (vol. 7, 8)

409 The Vandals and Suevi reach Spain (vol. 8)

410 Sack of Rome by the leader of the Visigoths Alaric (vol. 8)

413 Church father Augustine writes *De Civitate Dei* (vol. 7)

418 The Visigoths as foederati of the Roman Empire are granted residence in Aquitaine and found the kingdom of Toulouse (vol. 8)

c. 420 Chin dynasty succeeded by Liu Sung dynasty; Wei Empire of the Tartars develops in the north of China (vol. 11)

440-461 Pope Leo I the Great (vol. 8)

441-453 Attila is ruler of the Huns (vol. 8)

c. 450 Increasing importance of Christianity in the Persian Empire, most Christians are followers of the Nestorian church (vol. 8)

455 Vandals invade Italy and plunder Rome (vol. 8)

c. 470 Huns attack the Indian Empire (vol. 11)

476 The last Roman emperor is dethroned by the Teutons, their leader Odoacer sends the imperial insignia to Constantinople (vol. 7, 8)

481 Death of Childeric, who is succeeded by Clovis as king of the Franks (vol. 8)

493 Italy in the hands of the Ostrogoths (vol. 7)

493-526 Under the emperor Theodoric a revival of Latin culture in Italy (vol. 8)

496 Clovis defeats the army of the Alemanni and is baptized as a Christian in Reims (vol. 8)

c. 500-700 Buddhism is slowly forced out of southern and western India (vol. 7)

511 Death of Clovis, the first major unifier of the Frankish Empire (vol. 8, 9)

518-527 Justin rules the Eastern Roman Empire (vol. 8)

527-565 Justinian is emperor of the Eastern Roman Empire, tries to restore the Roman Empire (vol. 7, 8)

531 Chosroes, "Splendid fame," ascends the Persian throne (vol. 8)

532 Nica riot in Constantinople, a revolt against Emperor Justinian; Chosroes expands the Persian Empire to the Caucasus (vol. 8)

534 Completion of the *Corpus Iuris Civilis* (vol. 8)

537 Completion of the Hagia Sophia in Constantinople (vol. 8)

538 Japanese emperor accepts Buddhism (vol. 11)

c. 540 Benedict establishes a monastic rule at Monte Cassino (vol. 7)

c. 550 Tantrism develops in India on the basis of texts and books, the *Kama Sutra* is written (vol. 7); both Visigoths and Burgundians convert to the Christian faith (vol. 8)

568 Italy is conquered by the Lombards (vol. 7, 8)

570 Birth of the Prophet Muhammad in Mecca (vol. 8)

590-604 Pope Gregory I the Great, the papacy regains international prestige (vol. 7)

593-622 Expansion of Buddhism in Japan (vol. 11)

597 The king of England is baptized by St. Augustine of Canterbury (vol. 7)

c. 600 Recording of the prophecies of Muhammad (vol. 8)

600-1000 Rajput dynasty rules in northwestern India (vol. 7)

613 Victory of the Persians over the Byzantines at Antioch, Syria becomes a Persian province (vol. 8)

614 The Persians occupy Jerusalem (vol. 8)

618-907 Tang dynasty rules China, Confucianism again becomes the philosophy of a majority (vol. 7)

618 Under Kao-tsu, China becomes the world's greatest empire (vol. 11)

629 First pilgrimage of Muhammad and his followers to Mecca (vol. 8)

630 The Kaaba in Mecca becomes the center of the teachings of Muhammad (vol. 8)

632 Death of Muhammad, Ab'Bakr becomes the first caliph, almost all Arabs become Muhammadans (vol. 8)

632-634 Beginning of the Jihad, the "Holy War" of the Arabs (vol. 8)

637-641 Arabs conquer Egypt, Persia and Alexandria (vol. 8)

c. 650 Polynesians visit Hawaii for the first time (vol. 3); definitive end of the Sassanid Empire (vol. 8); the Byzantine Empire threatened by Arab armies and Slavic tribes (vol. 9)

661 Beginning of the Umayyad dynasty in the Arab world (vol. 8)

674-679 The Arabs besiege Constantinople (vol. 8)

687 Majordomo Pépin becomes ruler of core Frankish territories (vol. 9)

698 The Arabs conquer Carthage and reach the Atlantic Ocean (vol. 8)

c. 700 Christanization of the conquered territories by Anglo-Saxon monks by request of the Frankish rulers (vol. 9)

711 The Arabs cross the Strait of Gibraltar and conquer the empire of the Visigoths (vol. 8)

712 Beginning of Islamic influence in India (vol. 7, 11)

720 First written history of Japan by Nikon Shoki (vol. 11)

726 Iconoclasm divides the Byzantine Empire (vol. 9)

731 Bede's *Historia Ecclesiastica Gentis Anglorum* (vol. 7)

732 Battle of Poitiers, the king of the Franks Charles Martel halts the advance of the Muslim army which withdraws behind the Pyrenees (vol. 8, 9)

741 Constantine V becomes Byzantine emperor (vol. 9)

c. 750 Writing of the *Donatio Constantini* (vol. 9); invention of the printing press in China (vol. 11)

c. 750-900 No dominant culture in Central America (vol. 11)

754-775 In Iraq, the new capital, Baghdad, of the Muslim world is built (vol. 8)

756 Abd-al-Rahman founds the emirate of Córdoba in Spain (vol. 8)

771 Charlemagne becomes ruler of the Frankish Empire (vol. 9)

792 Empress Irene rules the Byzantine Empire (vol. 9)

794-1185 Heian period in Japanese history (vol. 11)

795 Alcuin of York encourages the study of the *artes liberales* (vol. 9)

800 The pope crowns Charlemagne emperor in Rome (vol. 9); introduction of paper money in China (vol. 11)

820 Michael II rules the Byzantine Empire, beginning of the Armenian dynasty (vol. 9)

822 Rebellion of Thomas the Slav in the Byzantine Empire (vol. 9)

835 Einhard writes *Vita Karoli Magni* (vol. 9)

843 The Treaty of Verdun results in the division of the Frankish Empire in three parts; end of iconoclasm in the Byzantine world (vol. 9)

c. 850 Decline and persecution of Buddhism in China, followed by the rise of Daoism (vol. 7)

858-1160 Fujiwara family controls Japanese government (vol. 11)

867 The Macedonian dynasty in the Byzantine Empire begins with Basil I (vol. 9)

870 Codification of Byzantine law by Basil I (vol. 9)

870-880 By two treaties the central kingdom is divided between the East and the West Frankish Empires (vol. 9)

875 Formalization of the feudal system in Western Europe (vol. 9)

c. 900-1000 Beginning of the Reconquista, the recovery of Muslim territory throughout Spain (vol. 8)

c. 900 Chola founds empire encompassing Sri Lanka and southern India (vol. 11)

910 Founding of the monastic community at Cluny (vol. 9)

911 Death of the last Carolingian king in the East Frankish Empire (vol. 9)

929-1025 The Caliphate of Córdoba in Spain (vol. 8)

936 Otto I the Great becomes king of Germany (vol. 9)

c. 950 The Ottonian state church system undermines the authority of the secular rulers (vol. 9)

955 Otto I defeats the Magyars at Lechfield (vol. 9)

960-1279 Sung dynasty rules in China (vol. 11)

962 Otto I is crowned emperor of the Holy Roman Empire (vol. 9)

969 Cairo founded by the Fatimids (vol. 8)

969-1171 The caliphate of the Fatimids (vol. 8)

978-1005 Vladimir I rules Kyyiv Empire (vol. 11)

1599

987 Hugh Capet becomes king of the West Frankish Empire (vol. 9)

c. 1000 The Byzantine Empire reaches its greatest size and is at the height of its power (vol. 9)

1002 Otto III dies, Duke Henry of Bavaria ascends the throne of the East Frankish Empire (vol. 9)

1019 Great Russian Empire emerges (vol. 11)

1024 Duke Conrad of Swabia is crowned Holy Roman Emperor (vol. 9)

1039 Henry III ascends the German throne (vol. 9)

1042 Edward the Confessor takes the English throne (vol. 10)

c. 1050 Development of Romanesque architecture in Europe (vol. 9)

1054 The Great Schism divides the Christian church (vol. 9)

1066 Battle of Hastings, William the Conquerer seizes England (vol. 10)

1071 Battle of Manzikert, the Byzantine army is defeated by the Seldjuks (vol. 9)

1075 Beginning of the Investiture Controversy between the Pope and the Holy Roman Emperor; *Dictatus Papae* written by Pope Gregory VII (vol. 9)

1076 The Ghanese Empire is plundered by the Almoravids (vol. 11)

1086 *Domesday Book* (vol. 10)

1192 Muhammad of Ghur conquers Hindu Empire (vol. 11)

1096 The First Crusade departs for Jerusalem (vol. 9)

1099 Godfrey of Bouillon is crowned king of Jerusalem (vol. 9)

c. 1100 Boyars become important influence on Russian leader (vol. 11)

c. 1100-1200 Golden Age of Polynesian navigators (vol. 3); Seljuks rule Baghdad (vol. 8)

1120 The new monastic orders of the Cistercians and the Premonstratians receive papal approval (vol. 9)

1122 The Concordat of Worms settles the Investiture Controversy (vol. 9, 10)

1125 Beginning of the dynastic disputes between the Guelphs and Hohenstaufen in Germany (vol. 10)

1125-1279 Beginning of the Sung dynasty in the south of China (vol. 11)

1137 Louis VII takes the French throne and marries Eleanor of Aquitaine (vol. 10)

c. 1150 Development of Gothic architecture in the Île de France (vol. 9); ideology of *Dominium Mundi*, the pope is the ruler of the world (vol. 10); end of the Toltec Empire in Central America (vol. 11)

1152 Frederick I Barbarossa becomes German emperor (vol. 10)

1154 Henry Plantagenet becomes king of English crown (vol. 10)

1160-1185 Tiara clan controls Japanese government (vol. 11)

1161 Foundation of the Hanseatic League in Germany (vol. 10)

1167 Chingiz Khan imposes rule on Mongol tribes (vol. 11)

1170 Creation of the Lombardian League against the German emperor (vol.10)

1176 Battle of Legnano, the army of the German emperor Frederick I Barbarossa is defeated (vol. 10)

1181 Birth of St. Francis of Assisi (vol. 9)

1185-1333 Kamakura period in Japan (vol. 11)

1189 Richard the Lionheart succeeds in England (vol. 10)

1192 Muhammad of Ghur conquers the Hindu kingdom of Delhi (vol. 7)

1200 The Christians reconquer most of Spain (vol. 8, 9)

1202-1204 Fourth Crusade, capture and plunder of Constantinople (vol. 10)

1206 Chingiz Khan declares the Mongols to be one people (vol. 11)

1212-1250 Frederick II becomes German emperor (vol. 10)

1215 The Magna Carta exacted by vassals in England (vol. 10)

1223 Mongol victory over the Russians at Kalka (vol. 11)

1226 The Teutonic Order colonizes the areas east of the Oder (vol. 10)

1227 Death of Mongol leader Chingiz Khan, succeeded by his son Ogodai (vol. 11)

1229-1241 Further conquest by Mongols of Korea, China, and Europe (vol. 11)

1235 Kublai Khan, Mongol leader, becomes sole ruler of the Chin Empire; Sundiata founds the Mali Empire (vol. 11)

1240 Moscow becomes center of Orthodox Christian culture in Russia; Sundiata destroys the old city of Ghana (vol. 11)

1241 Battle at Leignitz ends Mongol offensive (vol. 10, 11)

1243 Mangu becomes khan of the Mongols (vol. 11)

1245 Empire of the Golden Horde, Mongols hold sway in Russia (vol. 11)

1246 Mongols found Beijing in the north of China (vol. 11)

1250 Death of Frederick II, Interregnum in the German Empire (vol. 10)

c. 1250-1275 Venetian Marco Polo travels through China (vol. 11)

c. 1250 Mongols grant Moscow ruler the title "Grand Duke" (vol. 11)

1258 Henry III on the English throne, forced to introduce government reform (vol. 10)

1260 Baghdad is destroyed by the Mongols (vol. 8)

1260-1294 Kublai Khan new leader of the Mongols (vol. 11)

1263-1265 Pope crowns Charles of Anjou as king of Normandy (vol. 10)

1271 Mongol dynasty becomes the Yüan dynasty in China (vol. 11)

1272 Rudolf of Hapsburg becomes emperor of Germany (vol. 10)

1274 First Mongol attack on Japan (vol. 11)

1279 Mongols rule all of China (vol. 11)

1282 Sicilian Vespers, Peter of Aragon receives the crown of Sicily (vol. 10)

1285-1314 Philip the Fair of France strengthens the government (vol. 10)

1291 Acre, the last Christian stronghold in the Middle East, falls (vol. 9)

1294-1303 Reign of Pope BonifaceVIII (vol. 10)

1294 Death of Mongol leader Kublai Khan (vol. 11)

1301 Osman I, founder of the Ottoman Empire (vol. 11)

1302 The papal bull *Unam Sanctum* (vol. 10)

1307 Start of the residence of the Holy See in Avignon, *Babylonian exile*, term first used by Petrarch (vol. 10)

1307-1332 Golden Age of the Mali Empire under Congo Mansu (vol. 11)

c. 1325 Muslim state in India reaches its greatest size under Tughlug dynasty (vol. 11)

1328 Philip VI of Valois takes the French crown (vol. 10)

1331 Japanese Emperor tries to abolish shogunate (vol. 11)

1337 Begining of the Hunderd Years' War (vol. 10)

1345 Tenochtitlán is founded in Central America (vol. 11)

1346 Battle of Crécy, the French are defeated (vol. 10)

c. 1350 New Zealand discovered and populated by Polynesians (vol. 3); the grand dukes of Moscow increase their autonomy (vol. 11)

1356 The Black Prince defeats the French at Poitiers (vol. 10); Süleyman I makes the Ottoman Empire a sea power (vol. 11)

1358 Etiene Marcel takes over the government of Paris, revolt of the *Jacquerie* (vol. 10)

1360 Timur is elected khan of the Mongols and becomes a Muslim (vol. 11)

1366 Peace of Bretigny, between France and England (vol. 10)

1368 Beginning of the Ming dynasty in China (vol. 11)

1377 Pope Gregory IX moves back to Rome, end of the Babylonian exile (vol. 10)

1378 Beginning of the Great Western Schism that divides the Christain church, period of the antipopes; Schism causes cry for Church reform (vol. 10)

1381 Unrest among the English people led by Wat Tyler (vol. 10)

c. 1390 The Russian Church secedes from Eastern Church (vol. 11)

1398 Mongol raids under Timur in India (vol. 11)

1402 Mongols defeat the Ottoman army near Ankara (vol. 11)

1404 Death of Philip the Bold of Burgundy (vol. 10)

1405 Death of Timur, end of the Mongol Empire (vol. 11)

1407 The French internally divided, battle between the Armagnacs and Bourguignons (vol. 10)

1412 Birth of Joan of Arc (vol. 10)

1417 End of the Great Western Schism, Pope Martin V moves back to Rome (vol. 10)

1429 Joan of Arc, symbol of French resistance against English rule, ends the English siege of Orléans, Charles VII is crowned king at Reims (vol. 10)

c. 1430 Beginning of the expansion of the Inca Empire in South America under Viracocha (vol. 11)

1433 Timbuktu conquered by the Tuareg (vol. 11)

1438-1471 Panchacuti Inca Yupanqui rules the Incas (vol. 11)

1440 Frederick III elected Hapsburg emperor (vol. 10)

1445 Tenochtitlán becomes the capital of the Aztec Empire (vol. 11)

1453 End of the Hunderd Years' War (vol. 10); fall of Byzantium by Mehmed II, leader of the Ottoman Empire (vol. 11)

1462-1470 Incas conquer the Chimú Empire (vol. 11)

1462-1505 Ivan III the Great, ruler of Moscow, takes the title of *csar* and keeps Lithuanians and Mongols under control and conquers Novgorod (vol 11)

1465-1492 Sonni Ali rules the Songhai Empire (vol. 11)

1467 Charles the Bold inherits a divided empire of Burgundy and the Netherlands (vol. 11)

1467-1568 Period of the Warring States in Japan (vol. 11)

1477 Maximilian of Austria marries Mary of Burgundy (vol. 10)

1481 Ottoman Turks besiege Rhodos (vol. 11)

1487 Four thousand people sacrificed by Aztec ruler Ahuitzotl (vol. 11)

c. 1490 Guru Nanak founds the Sikh religion in India (vol. 11)

1492 The Catholic kings of Spain conquer Granada (vol. 8); Columbus discovers America (vol. 10)

1496 Marriage between Philip of Austria and Joanna, heiress to the Spanish throne (vol. 10)

c. 1500 Leo Africanus, *The History and Description of Africa*

1510 Portuguese conquer Goa (India), beginning trade monopoly (vol. 11)

1513 Conquest of the Hausa states (Africa) by Askia (vol. 11)

1519-1532 Spaniards land in Central and South America (vol. 11)

1519-1521 Under Hernán Cortés, Spaniards destroy the Aztec Empire (vol. 11)

1520-1566 Süleyman II the Great, sultan of the Ottoman Empire (vol. 11)

1521/1522 Conquest of Belgrade and Rhodos by the Ottoman Turks (vol. 11)

1526 Battle of Mohács between the Ottoman Empire and a Western European army (vol. 11)

1529 First siege of Vienna by a Ottoman army (vol. 11)

1532 Francisco Pizarro disrupts the Inca Empire with Spanish troops (vol. 11)

1543 First Europeans in Japan (vol. 11)

Glossary

Abbasids dynasty of caliphs formed by descendants of Muhammad's uncle Abbas; ruled from Baghdad (750-1258) until it was sacked by Mongols. Accorded purely religious function in Egypt, Abbasids held power there from 1261 to 1517.

Abbevillian culture offshoot of Acheulean Paleolithic culture from 400,000 years ago, named for the northern African town, Abbeville, near which remnants were discovered.

Abraham one of the patriarchs of the Israelites in the Old Testament of the Bible. He moved with his family from the Sumerian city of Ur to Canaan and was said to have been given property rights there by Yahweh in exchange for the promise to worship only Yahweh.

Abū al-`Abbas first *caliph* (successor) of the Abbasid dynasty (750-754); gained power through the influence of Shiite Ab Muslim but actually opposed and persecuted Shiites.

Abū Bakr first leader of Islam after the death of Muhammad (632-634); took the Arabic title *khalifat Rasul Allah* (successor to the Messenger of God); father-in-law and first convert made by Muhammad outside his own family; began *Jihad* (Holy War), seizing Syrian territory from the Persians.

Abū Muslim (died 754) Persian Shiite Muslim who undermined Muslim popular support for the Umayyad dynasty in favor of the first Abbasid caliph Abu al-'Abbas; supported Abbasid Al Mansur's claim to the throne but was later murdered by him.

Achaea old name for Greece; the region inhabited by the descendants of Achaeus. According to Greek mythology, Achaeus was the grandson of Hellen, the legendary ancestor of the Hellenes, or Greeks.

Achaean League alliance of city-states in province of ancient Greece called Achae; had limited autonomy; federal government determined its foreign policies; dissolved in 146 BC and made a dependency of Rome.

Achaeans collective name used by Homer in his epics, the *Iliad* and the *Odyssey*, for the people of ancient Greece.

Achaemenids Persian dynasty in the ancient Persian kingdom and empire (559-330 BC). whose rulers showed tolerance of the defeated peoples. Cyrus established the empire and Darius expanded it, leaving the subjugated territories autonomous. Alexander the Great conquered this dynasty.

Acheulean a stone tool-making tradition that developed around 1.5 million years ago in East Africa. The Acheulean tradition replaced the preceding Oldowan tradition, with its use of stone tools. This cultural change closely corresponds to the biological transition from "early *Homo*" to *Homo erectus.*

Achilles Greek hero of the Trojan War.

aclla daughters of the Inca nobility chosen to spend their lives between the ages of eight and sixteen in a convent serving the king; some were sacrificed, while others became Inti priestesses or were married to yaconas.

acropolis fortified elevated part of an ancient Greek city. The most famous fortress is the Acropolis in Athens, where various large temples were built, including the Parthenon.

Actium place on the Greek northwest coast near where Octavian defeated the fleet of Antony and Cleopatra in 31 BC. This victory gave Octavian definitive power as Roman emperor.

Adelaide widowed queen of Lombardy who, in 951, asked Otto the Great for aid against the usurper Berengar II, making possible Otto's rise to power.

Adeodatus (Latin: gift from God) natural son of Augustine.

administered trade heavily taxed trade strictly regulated by traditional African monarchs; to increase the power of the ruling classes.

Adonis (earlier Tammuz) Phoenician god of vegetation identified with nature's dying in autumn and rebirth in spring. As Adonis he was worshiped by the Greeks and Romans.

adopted emperors emperors of the second century AD, adopted by their predecessors; chosen as successors because of their own organizational and military capacities. Trajan was the first.

aedilis government official in the Roman Republic; oversaw public order, the market, water and grain supplies, and games. Initially, aediles were officers at the temple of Diana in the Latin League.

Aeneas legendary forefather of the Julian line and of the Roman people; fled with his son Julus out of the destroyed city of Troy; established a new empire in Latium; the main character in Virgil's epic *Aeneid*.

Aeolic Greek dialect spoken in northeastern and central Greece, on the island of Lésvos and in the north and west coast of Asia Minor.

Aeschylus (ca. 525-456 BC) Greek tragedian. Seven of his tragedies remain, including the trilogy *Oresteia* and the *Persians*. He introduced the second actor.

Aethelred the Unready (c. 968-1016) Anglo-Saxon king of England (978-1016) called "The Unready" from the Old English *unraed* (bad counsel). His marriage to Emma, daughter of Richard II, duke of Normandy, laid the basis for the Norman claim to the English throne.

Aetolian League alliance of autonomous Greek city-states around Aetolia.

Africa continent inhabited by a great variety of peoples and cultures, including Semites and Hamites. Hunting tribes such as the Bushmen and Pygmies lived in the interior.

Africa the territory on the northern shore of Africa once belonging to and surrounding the city of Carthage; made a province by Rome after the conquest of Carthage in 146 BC.

African states states developed between 800 BC and AD 1000 that were often characterized by social inequality and political friction; trade was controlled by the ruling class.

African Stone Age Africa was inhabited by civilizations that manufactured increasingly more refined stone tools, e.g., the Olduvai culture (32 million years ago) and the Acheulean culture (1.5 million-100,000 years ago). Language evolved slowly. In about 8000 BC, Africa consisted of communities of hunters and gatherers. Around 3000 BC the Sango culture inhabited the jungle, while the Stillbay culture lived in arid areas.

Agesilaus king of Sparta (c. 400 BC); described by the historian Xenophon.

Agni ancient Indian god of fire. He took many forms, including the god of hearth and home and that of the messenger between gods and men who consumed offerings from sacrificial fires and brought them to other gods. He evolved from the prehistoric Indo-Iranian tradition.

agora public square; political, cultural, and commercial center of the Greek city.

agriculture (Africa) around 2000 BC most African peoples had moved on to agriculture and cattle breeding. Permanent settlements arose and the population grew, causing a shortage of land.

ahimsa (Sanskrit: nonviolence) Buddhist doctrine of nonviolence and adopted by Gandhi.

Ahmose pharaoh ca. 1550 BC; drove the Hyksos from Egypt, conquered their territory in western Asia, and subjugated the Kushites. In Thebes, he renovated the temples of Amon and raised Amon's cult to the most important religion in the empire.

Ahura Mazda supreme god of the Persians. He was the creator and god of truth, justice, and purifying fire. The battle and victory of Ahura Mazda over the evil spirit Angra Mainyu was the foundation of the Persian faith as preached by Zarathushtra.

Airyana Vaeja mythological land where both Persians and Indians lived before they separated. It was identified as the first land Ahura Mazda created.

Aisha or Ayeshah (c.614-678) devoted second wife of the Prophet Muhammad, following the death of his first wife, Khadija; daughter of Muhammad's adviser and eventual successor, Abu Bakr; called the Mother of the Believers.

Akhenaton (or Akhenaten) pharaoh from 1364 to 1347 BC. He introduced the monotheistic cult of Aton and built his new residence at Akhetaton.

Akkadian Empire Semitic rule from ca. 2340 to 2200 BC in northern Mesopotamia (Akkad) and southern Mesopotamia (Sumer). A unified state was formed where, instead of the temples, the kings were the major landowners.

Akkadian language of the Semitic population during the third millennium BC, named after Akkad, capital of the Akkadian Empire.

Al Mansūr caliph of the Abbasid dynasty (754); founder of Baghdad; attempted to unify the realm through religion; accorded equal rights to all Muslim men.

Alamanni southern German people who repeatedly threatened Gallic borders; invaded Gaul in the third century AD; conquered eastern Gaul at the end of the fourth century AD.

Alaric (I) (c.370-c.410) king of the Visigoths (395-410); led Visigoths employed by Roman Emperor Theodosius (394); declared king by them after Theodosius s death (395); invaded Corinth, Argos, and Sparta, accepted ransom from Athens in lieu of sacking it; defeated by Roman General Flavius Stilicho; made prefect of Illyricum; invaded Italy and was defeated by Stilicho (402); besieged Rome, was paid ransom, but sacked the city anyway (410).

Alba Longa city in southern Latium, considered the mother city of Rome; according to legend, freed by Romulus and Remus from a usurper; destroyed around 650 BC by King Tullus Hostilius.

Alcaeus (ca. 600 BC) lyric poet from Lésvos.

alphabet set of written symbols representing separate spoken sounds.

Alcibiades (c. 450-404 BC) wealthy ambitious Athenian; general (420 BC); ended the Peace of Nicias, undertaking the Sicilian expedition. Charged with sacrilege, he defected to Sparta; killed by the Persians.

Alcuin (or Albinus) (735-804) Anglo-Saxon scholar and abbot of St. Martin of Tours; at the request of Charlemagne, initiated the Carolingian Renaissance between 781 and 790.

Alemanni southern Germanic people; threatened Roman borders and invaded Gaul in the third century AD; conquered eastern Gaul at the end of the fourth century; defeated by Frankish King Clovis I.

Aleppo city in northern Syria on the Euphrates River that was the capital of the kingdom of Yamhad during the eighteenth and seventeenth centuries BC. Its golden age took place at the end of the seventeenth century. It battled the Hittites and was conquered by Mursilis I.

Alexander III pope (1159-1181); opponent of Frederick Barbarossa who recognized him in 1177.

Alexander the Great (356-323 BC) king of Macedonia (336-323 BC); son of Philip II; conquered the Persian Empire (334-330 BC); conquered Syria and Egypt (333 BC); invaded the Indus Valley (327 BC).

Alexandria city founded in Egypt by Alexander the Great in 333 BC; the name was also given by Alexander to other cities he founded.

Alexius I Comnenus (1048-1118) Byzantine emperor (1081-1118). His request to Urban II for troops to fight the Muslims sparked the First Crusade in 1095.

Alfred the Great (849-899) king of the West Saxons (871-899); king of England (886-899). He provided the basis for English unification.

Ali of Arabia or Ali ibn Abi Talib (died 661) son-in-law of Muhammad, made fourth caliph of Islam (656). His rule was disputed by Mu`awiyah I, kinsman of Uthman, who succeeded him. Ali was assassinated by his own deserting followers, the Kharijites, in 661.

alignments megaliths or prehistoric stone monuments placed in long rows.

Allah Arabic word for God.

Almohads Islamic reformers from North Africa who drove the Almoravids out of southern Spain between 1146 and 1269, establishing a strong caliphate.

Almoravids a fundamentalist Muslim tribe from the southern Sahara who conquered North Africa and aided the Muslims in Córdoba against the Christians between 1086 and 1146.

alphabet phonetic script with characters for each sound, which the Phoenicians modified and spread to the Greeks, among others. The earliest alphabetic evidence is from the Canaanites in the second millennium BC.

Amarna Letters archive of clay tablets written in Babylonian cuneiform script, found in Akhetaton.

Ambrose, Saint (c.340-397) bishop of Milan; doctor of the Church; opposed Arianism; brought Roman emperor Theodosius I to repentance for the massacre of Thessalonians.

Amidism Buddhist religious sect, also called Pure Land, originating in China.

Ammenemes I pharaoh from 1991 to 1962 BC and founder of the twelfth dynasty (1991-1783 BC) during which the Middle Kingdom had its golden age.

Amon (or Amen) originally a local Theban god, he was associated with Re and became the major god of the Egyptian Empire during the New Kingdom.

Amorites Semitic peoples who invaded Mesopotamia from the north and northwest, beginning in ca. 2000 BC, and threatened the cities. They were slowly absorbed into the Mesopotamian population.

Amos Israelite prophet (eighth century BC) who spoke out against social injustice and predicted the fall of the people of Israel, saying that Yahweh would punish them if they did not renounce idol worship.

amphora vase with handles.

Anastasius I (c.430-518) Byzantine emperor (491-518); supporter of Monophysite doctrine; in 512, built the Anastasius Wall west of Constantinople.

anatman (Sanskrit: no soul) Buddhist concept that individual soul does not exist.

Anatomically Modern Humans (AMH) *Homo sapiens sapiens;* present-day humans, once known as Cro-Magnon.

Anaxagoras (ca. 500-428 BC) Greek philosopher whose doctrines on *nous* (eternal intelligence) and the atom had great impact on later Greek philosophy.

Anaximander (sixth century BC) Ionian natural philosopher from Miletus.

Anaximenes (585-525 BC) Ionian natural philosopher from Miletus.

angels spirits venerated by Christians.

Angles Germanic people; settled in eastern England in the fifth century AD.

Anglo-Saxon Church integration of Irish and Christian practices and rites in Britannia.

Anglo-Saxons Germanic tribes made up of Angles, Saxons, and Jutes living in England before the Norman conquest. They gradually conquered Britain over the fifth century.

Angra Mainyu evil spirit and symbol of dishonesty, wickedness, and darkness in the religion of Zarathushtra.

Anthony, Saint (c.251-c.350) early Egyptian Christian hermit and first Christian monk; subject of the first hagiography (saint's life).

Antigonus Gonatas (320-339 BC) son of Demetrius Poliorcetes, king of Macedonia. After a long battle he eventually became king of Macedonia (277-339) and ruler of Greece. The dynasty of the Antigonids ruled Macedonia until the arrival of the Romans in 148 BC.

Antigonus I (382-301 BC) called Monophthalmus (one-eyed) or Cyclops; king of Macedonia (306-301 BC); a general of Alexander the Great and one of the diadochs; obtained control of much of Asia Minor with the division of Alexander's empire in 323 BC. With his son Demetrius I (Poliorcetes), he invaded Egypt; defeated by an alliance of other diodachs.

Antioch (Antaka) founded in 301 BC by Seleucus I, it was the capital city of Syria until Rome's conquest of Syria in 64 BC. In the eleventh century, it was a Muslim center of government. The Christians conquered it in 1098 during the First Crusade, establishing it as a Christian principality under Bohemund of Taranto.

Antioch III the Great. *See* Anitiochus III, the Great

Antiochus I Soter (the Preserver) king of Syria (c.280-262 BC) son of Seleucus I, general, successor of Alexander the Great.

Antiochus III, the Great (242-187 BC) king of Syria (223-187 BC); son of Seleucus II; brother of and successor to Seleucus III; the most important Seleucid; defeated Ptolemy V; seized Palestine and Lebanon; defeated by the Romans at Thermopylae and at Magnesia (Turkey).

Antiochus IV Epiphanes (the Illustrious) king of Syria (175-164 BC); son of Antiochus III; defeated Egyptian kings Ptolemy VI and Ptolemy VII; seized Jerusalem, prohibited Judaism in favor of the worship of Greek gods; ousted by the Maccabees at the end of the Jewish Revolt.

Antipater (c. 398-319 BC) Macedonian general left in charge of Macedonia in 334 BC when Alexander the Great went to conquer the Persian Empire; put down rebellion in Athens after Alexander's death. His descendants ceded power to the Antigonids.

Antony, Mark (Marcus Antonius) (82-30 BC) a member of the Second Triumvirate; defeated Caesar's murderers in 42 BC, afterward holding power in the East. Through the intrigues of the ambitious Egyptian Queen Cleopatra, he fell into conflict with Octavian, who defeated him at Actium in 31 BC.

Anyang capital city of the late Shang period (c.1250) where excavations revealed palaces, temples, living quarters, royal graves, and artisan's workshops. Oracle bones were also found here.

*ap*a*nage* region in the French Empire controlled by the younger brothers of the French king. Burgundy was an apanage until the Hundred Years' War.

apella Spartan meeting of all adult men with civil rights.

Aphrodite Greek goddess of love and beauty, daughter of Zeus.

apoikia Greek colony established as an independent settlement.

Apollo Greek god of the sun, oracles, music, poetry, and justice; son of Zeus. The god of medicine, he could also inflict disease as punishment.

apologias defenses by Christian scholars against pagan and Jewish philosophers.

apostles disciples of Jesus Christ, founders of the first Christian community after his death.

aqueduct literally, conductor of water; Roman system to transport water long distances in mains supported by high arched constructions. The water drained into large basins which led to public fountains.

Ara pacis Augustae altar on the Campus Martius built by Augustus after his return from Spain and Gaul. Consecrated in 9 BC, it was intended to serve as propaganda for Augustus's policy of peace.

Arabia desert peninsula lying between the Mediterranean Sea on the east, the Persian Gulf on the north, and the Red Sea on the south; populated by Bedouin people; most of the populace converted to Islam about 630.

Arabia Felix (Happy Arabia) empire in the south of present-day Arabia. It traded gold, spices and incense and formed a link in the caravan trade with India and the Far East.

Arabic crafts included woven cloth from Damascus and Mosul (damask and muslin), Spanish wrought ironwork, and Persian and Armenian hand-knotted carpets.

Aragon a Christian kingdom in northeastern Spain, south of the Pyrenees.

Aramaeans Semitic tribes who invaded southern Mesopotamia (Babylonia) from the west and the south beginning in 1100 BC. They slowly assumed the Babylonian culture and constituted a large part of the population.

Arcadius (c.337-408) son of Roman Emperor Theodosius I; Eastern Roman emperor in Constantinople at age eighteen.

Arcado Cyprian Greek dialect spoken in Arcadia (central

Peloponnisos) and on Cyprus.

Archaic colonization the establishment of settlements on the coasts of the Mediterranean and Black Seas from about 750 through the mid-sixth century BC.

Archaic period in Egypt from ca. 2900 to ca. 2650 BC in which two dynasties ruled from Memphis. During this era, Egypt was one kingdom, but the division between north and south was maintained.

Archaic period the era in Greek history from about 750 to 500 BC. Named for a concept drawn from Greek art history.

Archilochus (ca. 650 BC) Greek poet and satirist from the island of Paros.

Archimedes (287-212 BC) mathematician and physicist whose theories on natural forces in practice included the principle of displaced water: that a body submerged in a liquid at rest is acted upon by a force equal to the weight of the fluid displaced.

archives of Boghazköy (Hattusas) archives of clay tablets found in the ruins of the Hittite capital. They are written in Akkadian and Hittite in the cuneiform script and date from c.1350-1200 BC. They provide information on political history and organization, economy, and religion.

archons magistrates in Athens, beginning about the seventh century BC; elected annually. Their duties comprised legislation, justice, religion, and military affairs. After the reforms of Cleisthenes, they were selected by lot.

Ardashir I king of Persia (224-241).

arena literally meaning "the sand"; the part of the amphitheater where the audience sat around in tiered rows.

Areopagus the *Areos Pagos* (hill of the god Ares) next to the Athenian Acropolis, where the council of ex-archons of the same name were seated from the seventh century on.

arhats Hindu or Buddhist holy men.

Arianism doctrine of theologian Arius (fourth century); held that Jesus Christ was not of the same substance as God, but merely the best of created beings.

Aristophanes (c. 445-385 BC) Athenian comic dramatist who criticized current political, literary, and social views in fiercely satirical plays about democracy, the war with Sparta, and the Sophists.

Aristotle (384-322 BC) Athenian philosopher, disciple of Plato.

Arius (c.256-336) native of Libya, Alexandrian priest who articulated the Arian doctrine named for him.

Ark of the Covenant repository in which the Ten Commandments and Hebrew desert traditions were kept. It was originally located in Shiloh, but was stolen by the Philistines. Later the Ark was preserved in the Temple in Jerusalem built by Solomon.

Armagnacs supporters of Louis of Orléans who joined Bernard of Armagnac after the former's death and who started a bloody civil war with the Bourguignons.

Armenia a region in southwestern Asia south of the Caucasus Mountains.

Armenian emperors a succession of Byzantine emperors between 813 and 842, begun by Leo V.

Arnold of Brescia (d. 1155) popular preacher who criticized the Church's political power; his sermons caused a rebellion in Rome in 1146, after which the Senate regained its power; the pope was aided by Frederick Barbarossa in assassinating Arnold.

Artabanus V king of Parthia (213-224).

Artaxerxes I king of Persia (465-425 BC).

artifact any object once made or used by humans and recovered archaeologically.

Aryans Indo-European peoples who invaded the Indus Valley around 1800 BC and conquered the indigenous peoples. They initially mixed with these native inhabitants, but later dominated them by imposing a system of social stratification that became known as the caste system.

aryballos oil flask.

Ashikaga period (1338-1573) period during which the noble family of Ashikaga ruled Japan; after ousting emperor Go-Daigo (1333-1338), they conquered the shogunate.

ashram refuge.

Ashurbanipal king of the New Assyrian Empire from 669 to after 631 BC. He suppressed an uprising in Babylon and destroyed the city again.

Ashurnasirpal II king of the New Assyrian Empire from 684 to 669 BC. He defeated the Aramaean city-states in southern Mesopotamia and conquered Syrian and Phoenician cities.

askēsis (purity) Greek root of the word *asceticism*; part of the beliefs of the Pythagorean sect. He who does not succeed in keeping his body pure by following the rules of life also contaminates his soul.

Askia Mamadu Ture general and ruler of the Songhai Empire (1493-1528); he introduced Islam as a state religion.

Asoka (270-232 BC) king in northern India who contributed to the spread of Buddhism across India and beyond.

Assur Assyrian city-state named after the god Ashur, considered to be the creator and leader of the world.

Assyria ancient kingdom of the Near East, located in northern Mesopotamia. Assyria rose to great power in the early first millennium, established an empire, then collapsed in the seventh century BC.

Astarte Canaanite and Phoenician goddess of procreation, fertility, and love. She was equated with the Semitic Ishtar and later associated with the Greek goddess Aphrodite. She was also connected with Baal and was worshiped as the mother-goddess until Roman times.

asteroid belt orbit of asteroids between Mars and Jupiter.

Ataulf Visigoth king (410-415).

Athanasius, Saint (c.293-373) Christian bishop, theologian, and doctor of the Church; noted for his fourth-century opposition to the Arian heresy.

Athenians residents of Athens who had civil rights and belonged to the *demos*. All free adult men of Athenian origin were citizens. Women, slaves, and immigrants had no civil rights.

Athens Greek city-state in Attica; progressive, democratic cultural center with an economic basis in trade and an expansionist navy; controlled the Delian League during the Classical period.

Aton (or Aten) the Egyptian sun god Re was worshiped in the abstract image of the sun disk Aton. The name and image of Re was the only one kept on the monuments in addition to Aton.

Attic Delian Sea Alliance (477 BC) naval alliance, dominated by Athens, with the Greek cities in Asia Minor and the Aegean Islands, and the colonies in Thrace against Persia.

Attica Greek state and peninsula on which the polis of Athens lay.

Attila (c.406-453) king of the Huns (c.433-453); conquered Western Europe; defeated in Gaul by a coalition of Romans and Visigoths (451); plundered Italy (452).

Augustine of Canterbury, Saint archbishop of Canterbury (598-604); converted Anglo-Saxons in Britannia; founded Roman Catholic Christianity in Kent, competing with Irish Christianity; established Canterbury as the administrative center of the Anglo-Saxon Church.

Augustine of Hippo, Saint (354-430) Christian convert, bishop, and preeminent theologian, doctor of the Church; author of the apologia *De Civitate Dei (The City of God)*, the autobiography *Confessiones (Confessions), Epistles*, and treatises.

Augustus honorary title granted to Octavian by the Senate in 27 BC when he set aside the extraordinary qualifications inherent in his name. *Augustus* ("exalted") is a religious epithet for superhuman. His successors adopted Augustus as a fixed title.

Australopithecus upright-walking hominid from 4 million years ago, found in Africa.

Austrasia a Frankish kingdom in the seventh century, the eastern part of the original Merovingian Empire.

Avaris residence of the Hyksos kings in the eastern Nile Delta.

ayllu a small extended family in the Inca Empire, a landholding unit with social and administrative functions.

Aztec Empire pre-Columbian state in Central America that subjugated the Huastec to the north and the Mixtec and Zapotec to the south; under Motecuhzoma I (c. AD 1468) territory was won from the Mixteca; a composite civilization developed, based on Mixteca-Puebla heritage; agriculture and trade flourished; between AD 1519 and 1521 the Spaniards, under the leadership of Hernán Cortés, conquered the empire.

Aztec religion belief in a variety of gods with the ability to change character, who were worshiped with human sacrifices; the sun-god, Tonatiuh, and the earth monster, a devouring and nurturing goddess, were dual figures in this agricultural society; Tlaloc, the rain god and Huitzilopochtli, the war god, were among the several other gods.

Aztecs pre-Columbian culture in the Mexican Valley, established by nomads and Mexicans who founded the Aztec Empire in the fifteenth century, with Tenochtitlán as its primary city; engineering, architecture, art, mathematics, astronomy, sculpture, weaving, metalwork, music, and picture writing were advanced Aztec developments.

Baal Semitic god of storm and fertility. He was worshiped by the Canaanites and Phoenicians in fertility rites. The Israelites worshiped him as a fertility god.

Babylon city in southern Mesopotamia which constituted a centralist Amorite empire under Hammurabi. Later Babylon continued as the cultural and political capital of southern Mesopotamia. In 1594 BC, Babylon was destroyed by the Hittites. From 612 to 539, Babylon was the capital of the New Babylonian Empire.

Babylonian exile (1305-1376) period when the popes resided in Avignon because Italy was divided by feuds among noblemen; Avignon became a bureaucratic center of corrupt popes and prelates.

Babylonian exile period from c.587-536 BC in which the elite of Judah, after being conquered by the Babylonian king Nebuchadnezzar, lived in Babylon.

bacaudae armies of escaped coloni (tenant famers).

Baghdad (Syria) residence of the Abbasid caliphs, built by Al-Mansur to appease the Persian Muslims; center of trade, industry, and Persian culture; destroyed by Mongols.

Bajezid Lightning (c.1360-1402) (also known as Bayezid or Bajazet I, Thunderbolt) first Osman ruler to be given title of sultan; put down Balkan revolt, besieged Constantinople; in 1402 he was captured by the Mongols under Tamerlane (Timurlenk), and exhibited in a cage.

Baldwin (Boudewijn) with the Iron Arm first count of Flanders (863-879), he defended it against the Vikings. Abducting and marrying the daughter of Charles the Bald, he founded a dynasty of Baldwins in Flanders lasting through the eleventh century.

Baldwin I (of Jerusalem; Boudewijn of Bouillon) (1058-1118) king of Jerusalem (1100-1118), brother of Godfrey of Bouillon and a leader in the First Crusade. In 1098, he conquered Edessa and set up a Christian stronghold there.

Baldwin I (of the Latin Empire) (1172-1205) first Latin emperor of Constantinople (1204-1205), born in France.

Baldwin II (of Jerusalem) (?-1131) king of Jerusalem (1118-1131), cousin and successor of Baldwin of Bouillon.

Baldwin II (of the Latin Empire) (1217-1273) last Latin emperor of Constantinople (1228-1261).

Baldwin III (c. 1130-1162) Latin king of Jerusalem (1143-1162). He lost Damascus in 1154 to Nur ad-Din, Turkish ruler of Aleppo.

bandkeramik Neolithic culture of northern and central Europe dating from 5000 BC, recognized by its pottery decorations of distinct linear patterning.

Bantu black people of Africa, south of the equator, who speak related languages. After c.1000 BC they occupied large portions of Africa, leaving the area around Lake Chad and mixing with agricultural peoples.

baptism (Latin: dipping in) Christian ceremony admitting individuals into Christianity by immersion or sprinkling with water to symbolically wash away original sin.

Barsine (?-323 BC) also called Stateira; daughter of the Persian king Darius III; wife of Alexander the Great.

Basil II (c. 958-1025) Byzantine emperor (963-1025), called *Bulgaroctonus* (Killer of Bulgars), most powerful of the Macedonian dynasty.

Basil, Saint (c.329-379) Greek bishop of Caesarea; Cappadocian church father and eastern doctor of the Church; established monasticism in the east, emphasizing asceticism and obedience, spiritual growth, and the study of theological works.

basileus (king) title of the Byzantine emperor, regarded as the head of Christendom and God's representative on Earth.

basileus Mycenaean official, under the wanax, who ruled a small region. Possibly, he also supervised groups of artisans.

Batavians a German group from the region between the Rhine and the Meuse. They helped the Romans to subjugate the area and served in the Roman army. In AD 69 they revolted under Julius Civilis, but were quickly defeated.

Battle at Varna (1444) battle between an Osman army and a Polish-Hungarian army, during which the Christian army was slaughtered; this crusade had been called by the pope to counteract the successful Turkish conquests in the Balkans and Asia Minor.

Battle of Adrianople (Turkey) 20,000 Visigoths defeated and killed Roman Emperor Valens and most of his troops in 378.

Battle of Manzikert (1071) defeat marking the end of Byzantine imperial power in Asia Minor.

Battle of the Milvian Bridge (312) near Rome; victory of Constantine over his Italian rival, Maxentius.

1604　**Battle of the Spurs** (July 11, 1302) when an untrained

Flemish infantry army of civilians defeated armed French knights.

Becket, Thomas archbishop of Canterbury (1162-1170); opponent of Henry II Plantagenet, who took away the authority of the ecclesiastical courts; killed in 1170, after which the Church and the English people turned against Henry.

Bede the Venerable, Saint (c.673-735) English Benedictine monk and scholar, author of *Historia Ecclesiastica Gentis Anglorum (Ecclesiastical History of the English People)*, detailing English history from Roman occupation to 731.

Bedouin nomad people of the Arabian desert; converted to Islam about 622; dominated non-Islamic population under the Umayyads; forced to yield power to the Abbasid dynasty (c.750).

Belisarius (sixth century) general of Emperor Justinian; conquered the Vandal kingdom in North Africa (533-534); defeated the Ostrogoths in Italy (540).

Bell-beaker culture a group of Neolithic cultures between 2600 and 2000 BC that spread from Spain to northern Africa and over western and central Europe. It is named after its characteristic ceramic forms. These people are thought to have been the first in western Europe to process metals, particularly copper.

Benedict of Nursia, Saint (c.480-547) monk from Umbria (Italy); founder of the Benedictine monastic order and the monastery of Monte Cassino; the father of western monasticism.

Benedictine monastic order founded by Benedict; stresses communal living, obedience to an abbot, physical labor, study of the sciences, communal property and meals, and the avoidance of unnecessary speech.

Bernard of Clairvaux, St. (1090-1154) a Cistercian monk who summoned the French for the Second Crusade in 1146. Canonized in 1174.

Bhagavad-Gita Hindu poem composed around 200 BC and added to the *Mahabharata*, wherein the importance of action versus reflection is discussed during a meeting between Krishna and Arjuna.

Big Bang theory postulates the creation of the universe from the explosion of a quantity of very dense material and energy that formed atoms and thus the eventual universe.

bills of exchange IOU's substituting for money, enabling merchants to travel without fear of theft.

birdman a servant whose master was a king-priest on Easter Island who occupied a chosen position of godlike authority for the term of one year. It was the birdman's obligation to retrieve eggs from the Motu nui.

bishops seen by Christians as successors to the apostles; held the highest authority in the *ecclesia* (church), deriving their power from the support of emperors. The bishop of Rome is the pope.

black hole region in the universe with such a strong field of gravity that nothing can escape, created out of very heavy stars whose nuclei have collapsed during a supernova explosion.

Bleda (died 445) nephew of Hun king Roas who succeeded him with his brother Attila; murdered by Attila.

Blues political party in Constantinople that organized important horse races against the Greens. Despite the lack of a clear political program, they had great influence.

bodhisattva (Sanskrit: enlightened being) a potential Buddha, one who chooses to delay entering the state of nirvana in order to help all sentient beings; under the Mahayana doctrine, a bliss-bearing supernatural entity.

Boeotia (480-524) Roman philosopher and statesman; Theodoric's political advisor; executed for high treason.

His work on Greek scientific philosophers, notably Aristotle, had great influence on medieval scholastics.

Bohemund of Taranto (1052-1111) son of the Norman duke Robert Gestured and a leader in the First Crusade. In 1098, established a kingdom in conquered Antioch.

bojars Russian noblemen, major landowners whose feudal power had a detrimental effect on Kyyiv's (Kiev) central rule.

Boniface VIII pope (1294-1303); when he forbade Philip IV the Fair of France to tax the Church, the latter had him imprisoned in 1303 with the people's support.

boulē Council of 500 in Athens, comprising ten *phylae* (groups of fifty men each) annually selected to represent the entire city.

Bourguignons supporters of the Burgundian dukes John the Fearless and Philip the Good; they fought a civil war against the Armagnacs and obtained the support of the English king who occupied France in 1415 and 1436.

Brahma paramount Indian god, preacher of the *Vedas*, appears in Hinduism as part of a trinity of Brahman the Creator, Vishnu the Restorer, and Shiva the Destroyer.

Brahman divine absolute reality in Hinduism and the earlier Brahmanism.

Brahmanism ancient Indian religion; detailed in the scriptures called *Brahmanas* and *Vedas* of the sixth century BC.

Brahmans highest inherited social status in the Old Indian caste system, consisting of priests and learned men. They spent their time studying and writing the Vedas. They were qualified to perform offering ceremonies and teach the Vedas.

brahmin (Sanskrit: priest) highest Hindu caste.

Brasidas important Spartan general, killed with his Athenian enemy Cleon in 422 BC, clearing the way for the Peace of Nicias.

Britain area inhabited by the Celts, occupied and conquered after AD 43 under Claudius following attempts by Caesar in 55-54 BC. In 125, Hadrian's Wall was built as a northern border. The Romans left Britain around the year AD 400.

bronze copper-tin alloy widely used by 1700 BC.

Bronze Age period during which bronze became the most important basic material, varying from culture to culture; began about 5500 BC in the Near East and 3000 BC in Europe. The Mycenaean and Minoan civilizations flourished during this period.

Brutus, Iunius Roman statesman; relative of the last king Tarquinius Superbus; led the revolution against his tyrannical rule and instituted the republic.

Brutus, Marcus Junius (85-42 BC) Brutus supported Pompey in the civil war, was pardoned and became Caesar's favorite. In 44 BC, he led the plot against Caesar and killed him, together with Cassius. He committed suicide after being defeated by Antony in 42.

Buddha (the Enlightened One) the title of Siddhartha Gautama, founder of Buddhism; also anyone attaining enlightenment.

Buddhism religion founded by Siddhartha Gautama, called the Buddha; rejected much of Hinduism, including priestly authority, the Vedic scriptures, sacrificial practices, and the caste system. Its goal is *nirvana*, release from all desire and from the cycle of life, death, and rebirth; major schools are Theravada and Mahayana.

Buddhist era fourth to ninth centuries AD, when Buddhism spread from India to central, eastern, and southeast Asia.

Bulgaria constituted the strongest empire in eastern

Europe in the ninth and early tenth centuries. Incorporated into the Byzantine Empire in 1018, Bulgaria rebelled in 1185, forming another empire which collapsed over the fourteenth century.

Byblos first city in pre-Phoenician Levant to trade with Egypt. After c.1200 it was superseded as a Phoenician trading center by Sidon and later Tyre. Byblos was the center of the Astarte-Tammuz cult in Roman times.

Byzantine Empire eastern part of the Roman Empire that survived the disintegration of the Western Empire in the fifth century AD; named for the former capital city Byzantium (renamed Constantinople, now Istanbul); eastern Roman provinces included southeastern Europe and the Balkan Peninsula, southwestern Asia and the Middle East (modern Syria, Jordan, Israel, Lebanon, and Cyprus), and northeast Africa (Egypt and eastern Libya); war with Persians, Arabs, and Turks reduced the empire to Asia Minor and the Balkans; conquered by the Turks in 1453.

Byzantium city on the Bosporus which became the residence of Constantine; became known as Constantinople (present-day Istanbul) in AD 330. Byzantium was an important political and cultural center. In 395, it was made capital of the eastern Roman Empire and, later, of the Byzantine Empire.

C14 method a dating method based upon the radioactivity of the C14 isotope of carbon.

caesar title used by emperors after Augustus Caesar.

Caesar, Gaius Julius (100-44 BC) After setting up the First Triumvirate in 60 BC, he became governor of Gaul in 58; expanded Transalpine Gaul as far as the Rhine. Caesar conquered Italy with his army and started a civil war. In 46, holding power over the entire empire, he became dictator. He was murdered by a Republican conspiracy in 44.

Caesarea city in southern Syria expanded by Herod the Great into a fashionable metropolis with temples, amphitheaters, and a major trade center.

Caesaropapism the special relationship between church and state.

Cairo (Egypt) capital of the anticaliphate of the Fatimids; founded in 969; became an important metropolis that took over trade with India and China from Baghdad.

Calais port on the west coast of France, which was conquered by Edward III following the battle of Crécy in 1347 and which continued as an English bridgehead until the sixteenth century.

Caligula, Gaius Caesar (AD 12-41) Roman emperor 37-41, son of Gemanicus, Caligula (literally, little soldier's boot, a nickname from his youth) behaved like a Hellenistic sovereign, demanding divine adoration. After a four-year reign of terror, he was murdered by his bodyguard.

caliph (from *khalifah*, Arabic: successor) religious and political leader of Islam; successor to Muhammad. Competing caliphs divided the Islamic states.

caliphate office and realm held by a caliph.

Caliphate of Córdoba Islamic state in Spain (929-1031) first proclaimed by Emir 'Abd ar-Rahmon III.

calpixque Aztec official responsible for paying tribute owed to Tlatoani.

calpullis administrative units in the Aztec Empire drawn from a group of related families; each calpulli was given a plot of land to farm, a temple, and a school and, in turn, supplied soldiers and labor for public works.

camayos social groups in Inca society, comprising craftsmen, farmers, soldiers, and traders who devoted their services to the king; they were exempt from military service.

Cambyses king of the Medes and Persians who succeeded his father, Cyrus the Great of the Achaemenid dynasty in 529 or 528. He conquered Egypt in 525 and died in 522.

Campius Martius a field on the banks of the Tiber River, dedicated to Mars, where military exercises, sports, games and public meetings were held. Many temples and other public buildings were erected there during the Principate.

Canaanites Semitic tribes who settled in Palestine and the western Levant in the third millennium and mixed with the native population. They maintained separate city-states. By c.1200 their territory was infiltrated by Israelites and Philistines.

Cannae town in southeastern Italy; site of the worst defeat in Roman history; Hannibal surrounded a Roman army and decimated it (216 BC).

canticum a sung text.

Canute the Great king of England (1016-1035); united England, Norway, and Denmark into one kingdom; Church recognized him as a Christian king; after his death the kingdom fell apart and Edward the Confessor, son of Ethelred, became king.

capacochas ten-year-olds offered to the gods on the Inca altars at Cuzco; after death they were worshiped as divinities.

Capet, Hugh (c. 938-996) king of France (987-996). Founder of the Capetian dynasty that united France and lasted until 1328.

capitation tax in fixed amount payable by all adult men subjected by Muslims; imposed in addition to tax on landholdings. By the end of the seventh century, many men converted to Islam in order to avoid taxation.

Capua major Greek colony in southern Italy; first Greek colony to side with Hannibal in the Second Punic War.

Caracalla, Marcus Aurelius Antoninus (AD 188-217) Roman emperor 211-217.

caravans desert convoys using camels as pack animals to transport trade products from Arabia; organized along military lines.

Carchemish Hittite city on the Euphrates, an important trading center. After the fall of the Hittite Empire, c.1200, it became the most important Neo-Hittite separate state. Carchemish was conquered by the Assyrians.

Caroline minuscule a script introduced during the Carolingian Renaissance to replace the illegible Merovingian handwriting. It formed the basis for lower-case letters of the Latin alphabet.

Carolingian Renaissance a Frankish revival of Roman culture in the late eighth and ninth centuries, reorganizing education and reviving art and literature.

Carolingians Frankish dynasty of kings and emperors, called Carolingian after *Carolus*, the Latin form of Charlemagne.

Carthage Phoenician colony on the coast of North Africa (present-day Tunisia); important trading power; rival of Rome in the Punic Wars; conquered by Rome and made the central city of the Roman province named Africa in 146 BC.

Carthusians monastic order which stressed penance, solitude, and asceticism; founded at the end of the eleventh century.

Cassian, John also called Johannes Eremita or Johannes Massiliensis (360-435); spent fifteen years as a hermit in Egypt; brought eastern monasticism west; theological opponent of Augustine; wrote on monasticism.

Cassiodorus (c.490-583) Roman statesman and scholar; held high ministerial posts in the service of Theodoric; author of theological and literary textbooks; stimulated the copying of manuscripts in monasteries.

caste system social system introduced by the Aryans, who were originally divided into four hereditary strata based on occupation, each with its own rights and obligations: Brahmins (priests), Kshatriyas (warriors and kings), Vaishyas (landowners), and Shudras (servants). There was no possibility of contact or internal relocation among the castes. The native people were seen as below them and became the pariahs. This still-existing system evolved into numerous new castes and subcastes.

Castile originally a Christian kingdom in northern Spain, in the eleventh century it annexed León and spread Castilian culture throughout Spain.

castle fortified farmstead built by a feudal lord to protect himself and his serfs against raids. Originally wooden towers, by the thirteenth century, castles were commonly huge stone strongholds.

castra a specially fortified army camp, often permanent, surrounded by a moat and an earthen rampart; noted for its geometric organization plan. Permanent camps on the borders were built of stone.

catacombs underground corridors outside Rome where Christians buried their dead and assembled in secret during persecution.

Catherine of Siena fourteenth-century Dominican nun who persuaded the pope in 1376 to move back to Rome and led the popular movement against the antipapal Italian cities.

Catiline (Lucius Sergius Catilina) (108-62 BC) Roman politician and conspirator; executed in 62 BC.

Cato, Marcus Porcius (the Elder) (234-149 BC) Roman statesman and author; served as quaestor (204 BC), aedile (199 BC), praetor (198 BC), consul (195 BC), and most notably as censor (184 BC); combated Hellenism and senatorial corruption.

cavalry mounted soldiers.

cave paintings found throughout prehistory; especially noteworthy are hundreds of Paleolithic European examples.

Celts name given to a group of people occupying central and western Europe, from the British Isles to Hungary, from 1000 BC. Around 400 BC, they entered Spain and northern Italy, destroying Rome. Eventually subjugated by Caesar, those living in Gaul were Romanized. Bearers of the Celtic civilization are the Hallstatt culture and the La Tène culture, which share stylistic continuities. The Urnfield culture also shows Celtic characteristics.

cenobites hermits who sought personal solitude within a common monastic life, called *koinos bios* in Greek.

Cenozoic age 66 million years ago to the present.

censor office in the Roman Republic, to which two ex-consuls were elected for five-year terms; they estimated the number of citizens for purposes of categorization, taxation, and military service, and judged moral behavior.

centuria (century) Roman legion of 100 foot soldiers, originally composed of free Romans able to afford armor.

Cerberus mythological three-headed dog that guarded the passage to the underworld.

Chaldeans Aramaean tribe located in southern Mesopotamia. During the seventh century BC, the Chaldean chief Nabopolassar, aided by the Medes, brought Assyria down. This was the beginning of the New Babylonian Empire.

Châlons-sur-Marne site of massive battle between Romans, assisted by Visigoths and Attila the Hun in 451; Attila defeated.

chamber tombs Mycenaean graves of an underground chamber and an uncovered access road called *dromos*.

Charlemagne (Charles the Great) (742-814) Frankish king (768-814) and Holy Roman emperor (800-814). He established the Holy Roman Empire.

Charles II (the Bald) (823-877) Holy Roman emperor (875-877), king of France (as Charles I, 843-877), fourth son of Holy Roman emperor Louis I.

Charles Martel (the Hammer) (c.688-741) Carolingian Frankish *majordomo* (mayor of the palace) and ruler of Austrasia (modern northeastern France, southwestern Germany) (715-741); son of Pépin of Herstal; grandfather of Charlemagne; battled Alemanni, Bavarians, and Saxons; defeated an Islamic army, near Poitiers in 732, preventing the Muslim conquest of Europe.

Charles of Anjou king of Naples (1266-1285); with the pope's support he expelled the Ghibelline rulers from the Norman kingdom of Sicily; in 1282 he lost Sicily and moved to Naples.

Charles the Bold duke of Burgundy (1467-1477); expanded the Burgundian Empire; in 1476 he was defeated by the Swiss; in 1477 he died during the siege of Nancy, and Louis XI of France occupied Burgundy.

Charles V the Wise king of France (1364-1380); concluded the Peace of Bretigny in 1360 when he was still crown prince; restored and reorganized France and resumed the war in c.1370.

Charles VI king of France (1380-1422); concluded a truce with England in 1396; because of his madness, his relatives were fighting for power, especially his brother Louis of Orléans and his uncle Philip the Bold.

Charles VII king of France (1422-1461); thanks to Joan of Arc he was crowned king in 1429; concluded the Peace of Arras and caused the complete expulsion of the English from France (except for Calais) in 1453.

cheques (Arabic: bills) bonds used in lieu of currency, widely accepted in trading and banking centers like Baghdad and Córdoba.

Chibcha (Muisca) pre-Columbian culture in the South American Andes first established c.300 BC, existing to the sixteenth century AD; their two tribes, Zipas and Zaques, were divided into leaders and priests, people and slaves; they offered slaves to the sun-god.

Children of God term used by Mahatma Gandhi for the untouchables, lowest-ranking people of Hindu society.

Children's Crusade (1212) expedition of armies of children from France and Germany to Palestine; the French army largely fell into the hands of Islamic slave traders; the pope ordered the German army to return; many children died from exhaustion.

Chimú people who developed an ancient civilization on the desert coast of northern Peru that flourished after c.1200; used irrigation to turn desert land into fertile farming land, and had a complex social system and a well-planned capital, Chan Chan; surrendered to the Inca Empire c.1460.

Chin non-Chinese dynasty that ruled an empire in northern China (1115-1234); concluded a treaty with the Sung from the north against the Mongolian nomads, the Liao; in 1125 they forced the Sung to move south.

chinampas agricultural land skirted by trees to protect the raised soil from erosion; corn and beans were the first crops cultivated.

Chinese historiography first introduced by Ssu-ma (145-97 BC) and continued by Pan-ku (c. AD 92); Ssu-ma divided all narrations into components: the emperor; organization of the empire; culture, geography and economics; and biographies.

Chinese Stone Age China has been inhabited from the earliest times of humankind. From 7000 BC onward neolithic cultures lived in northern China, where the staple was millet, and in southern China, where rice was the staple. The northern areas were first to evolve into more complex societies.

Chinese walls earthen walls built on the northern and western borders of the Zhou states as protection against invading steppe-nomads. Walls were also built between the various Zhou states and around cities, made necessary by the continuous threat of war.

Chingiz Khan (Genghis Khan) Mongolian ruler (1167-1227); in 1190 he united the Mongols and was recognized as the great khan by the Kurultai (meeting of clan chiefs); established a Mongolian world empire by conquering China and some Islamic empires.

Chola early kingdom and maritime power, founded by former vassals, comprising much of southeast India, Kerala, Mysore, and Ceylon (Sri Lanka); kingdom existed from fourth century BC.

choregie Greek sponsors of theatrical productions and competitions.

chorus in Greek drama, the company of performers who explained and elaborated on the main action by singing, dancing, and narration.

Christ (Greek: Messiah) name accorded Jesus of Nazareth.

Christianity monotheistic religion founded by followers of Jesus Christ, who consider him the son of God, sent to earth to take on the sins of humankind through his death and resurrection. During Theodosius's reign Christianity became the state religion.

Christians followers of Jesus Christ; early Christians gathered for communal meals and to commemorate Jesus' death.

Chuang-tzu (c.369-286 BC) philosopher, teacher; important proponent of Daoism.

Cicero, Marcus Tullius (106-43 BC) famous Roman lawyer, orator, and author of philosophical and political works; challenged Catiline as consul in 60 BC, supported Pompey in the civil war in 49 BC, and took sides against Antony in 44. He was murdered in 43 BC on Antony's order.

Cimbrians a people who invaded southern France and Spain c. 111 BC; defeated by Marius in 102 and 101 BC.

Circus Maximus a large racecourse in Rome at the foot of the Palatine Hill, where chariot races were held as a source of amusement to the public. The circus was also used as a political safety valve; the public would applaud or jeer the charioteer favored by the emperor to indicate their support for the emperor himself.

Cistercians monastic order founded in 1098 in France near Citeaux; their emphasis was on austerity and simplicity.

city charter privileges granted by a liege lord to free cities in exchange for political support; privileges consisted of the administration of justice, toll exemption, city walls, and civil rights.

civil rights privilege of the city charter whereby fleeing serfs, who had lived in a place of refuge for one year and one day, became free citizens; usually the liege lords of a city stipulated that their own serfs were excluded.

civitas sine suffragio citizenship without the right to vote.

civitates self-governing autonomous communities.

Classical period period in Greek history (c. 500-334 BC); marked by Persian Wars (492-479 BC) and the Peloponnesian War (431-404 BC).

Claudius, Tiberius Claudius Drusus Nero Germanicus (AD 10-54) Roman emperor 41-54; started the conquest of Britain and the construction of the port at Ostia. His wife Agrippina murdered him to benefit her son Nero.

Cleisthenes reformer who introduced democracy to Athens in 508-507 BC.

Cleomenes (235-219 BC) king of Sparta; his forgiving of all debts and redistribution of land caused social unrest in Greece; defeated by Macedonia and the Achaean League.

Cleon (?-422 BC) extremist democratic Athenian politician; rose to power after Pericles's death in 429 BC.

Cleopatra (69-30 BC) Queen of Egypt 51-49; mistress of Julius Caesar and Mark Antony; defeated by Octavian at the battle of Actium in 31, she later took her own life.

clientes (clients) free, poor and noninfluential Roman citizens, supported financially and legally by rich patrician or plebeian patrons in exchange for votes and services.

Clotilda (470-545) daughter of Chilperic, king of Burgundy; married Clovis I (493); influential in his conversion to Christianity; canonized (c.549).

Clovis I (c.466-511) king of the Franks (481-511); conquered Gaul, except for Brittany and the south coast; defeated Alemanni and Visigoths; baptized in 496.

Cluny abbey in Burgundy founded by William of Aquitaine in 910 and put under direct papal authority to prevent influence by nobles and corrupt bishops; noted for church reform. Many monasteries were founded under its auspices.

clusters groups comprising dozens to thousands of galaxies held together through their mutual gravity. The Milky Way, the Magellanic Clouds, and the Andromeda nebula constitute a part of the local group. Clusters are grouped into superclusters.

collegia early forms of trade guilds.

colonia civilian settlement established to Romanize or control subjugated areas. The colonists were mainly ex-military and remained Roman citizens. Examples of such settlements are Carthage, Corinth, and Cologne.

colonization thirteenth-century claiming of hitherto uncultivated areas in Europe.

colonus the small tenant farmer of a great Roman estate. Always dependent on the large landowners, in AD 332, the coloni were forced by law to stay on the land as serfs.

Colosseum the great Roman amphitheater where the gladiators fought and the circus games took place. Named after the large statue of Nero, the Colossus.

comedy originally, any play or literary composition with a nontragic ending.

comet nebulous celestial body of small mass revolving around the Sun, composed of a relatively dense tenacious mass of dust, gas, or a mixture of each; often develops a tail when traveling in the part of its orbit nearest the Sun.

comitia centuriata (assembly of centuries) Roman assembly comprising thirty wealthy *centuriae iuniores* (junior centuries) and thirty *centuriae seniores* (senior centuries).

comitia tributa (assembly of tributes or districts) Roman assembly drawn from thirtyfive districts; each *tribus* (district) elected tribunes and aediles; introduced in the third and fourth centuries BC.

commune board of free cities that ruled independently of the liege lords; city aldermen, mostly rich merchants who had absolute power, were assisted by an advisory board of senators called consuls.

concilium plebis (council of plebs) Roman popular assembly of plebeians at the beginning of the republic. It elected tribunes able to veto patricians and the senate.

Concordat of Worms 1122 compromise between Pope Calixtus II and Holy Roman emperor Henry V on investiture. The church was accorded the right to elect and invest bishops but only in the presence of the emperor who retained the right to confer any land and wealth attached to the bishopric.

condottieri mercenary generals who conducted war by order of Italian cities; supported by the population; ruled the cities with military authority.

Confucianism Chinese philosophy founded by Kong-fu-tse; focused on human ethics within an ordered society; state ideology of the Han dynasty; spread to rest of Asia.

Conrad II of Swabia (c. 990-1039) king of Germany (1024-1039); Holy Roman emperor (1027-1039); king of the Lombards (1026). In 1033, he inherited the kingdom of Burgundy.

~~Constantine I, Flavius Valerius~~ (AD 280-337) called the Great, first Christian Roman emperor 306-337.

Constantine the Great, Flavius Valerius Constantinus (c.274-337) Roman emperor (306-337); initially emperor in the West, became absolute sovereign in 323; built Constantinople; legalized Christianity.

Constantine VI Byzantine emperor (780-797), son of Emperor Leo IV and Irene, who seized power and blinded him.

Constantine VII Porphyrogenitus (905-959) Byzantine emperor (908-959).

Constantinople (now Istanbul) founded by Constantine I in 324 as capital of the Byzantine (Eastern Roman) Empire and imperial residence; lying on both sides of the Bosporus Strait, separating Europe from Asia.

Constantius II Roman emperor (351-361), second son of Constantine the Great.

consul highest Roman official. Two consuls were appointed annually to govern the senate and the popular assembly.

Copernicus, Nicolaus (1473-1543) Polish astronomer who first conceived of a *heliocentric* (sun-centered) solar system.

copper reddish brown metallic element.

Córdoba (Spain) important in Phoenician and Carthaginian times, and a Roman settlement from the first century BC to its capture by the Visigoths in 572. Taken by the Muslims in 711, made capital of Muslim Spain in 756.

Corinth A Greek town destroyed in 146 BC for its resistance to Roman suppression. Rebuilt in 44 BC on Caesar's order as capital of the Roman colony Achaea.

corpse silhouette light discoloration in the ground left by a decomposed skeleton.

Corpus Iuris Civilis (Latin: *Body of Civil Law*) civil code composed by order of Emperor Justinian I under supervision of jurist Tribonian in the sixth century; classified and corrected all Roman jurisprudence to that time; referred to as the Justinian Code.

corvée the work carried out by serfs on feudal estates.

Council of Basel (1431-1449) council of the opponents of Pope Eugenius IV, who tried to abolish the council's authority and received an increasing amount of support among Christians who wanted a united Church; in 1437 the council appointed an antipope who abdicated in 1449, thus ending its authority.

Council of Chalcedon (451) convocation of church leaders near Constantinople leading to the first schism of the Christian Church over the relative status of the pope in Rome and the patriarch of Constantinople.

Council of Clermont the public meeting called by Pope Urban II in 1095 to announce the First Crusade.

Council of Constance (1414-1418) council that ended the Schism that had forced a number of popes to abdicate;

it constituted the Church's highest authority.

Council of Dad-Ishu (424) formally separated Eastern Christian church from Western.

Council of Nicaea (325) convocation of bishops of the Roman Empire, a forum to discuss church matters, including the nature of Jesus Christ. It rejected Arianism.

Council of Pisa (1409) Church's highest authority at this time; council of prelates that deposed the popes in Rome and Avignon and appointed a new one.

count loyal vassal who received land in fief from a Carolingian ruler.

cows the Aryans, who were pastoral nomads, considered cows sacred and offered them in sacrifice. The concept of vegetarianism known in the days of the Upanishads (c.600-300 BC) was elaborated on by Buddhists and Jains, who promoted the doctrine of ahimsa, or nonviolence.

Crécy town on the west coast of France where the French army, consisting of knights, was destroyed in 1346 by the English infantry and opened the way for Edward III to conquer Calais.

Cretaceous period in the Mesozoic age, from 144 to 66 million years ago.

Cro-Magnon outdated term for *Homo sapiens sapiens*, or modern human living some 200,000 years ago.

Croesus king of Lydia (560-546 BC); noted for his wealth; incorporated all Greece except Samos into the Lydian Empire; overthrown by Cyrus the Great of Persia, in 546 BC.

cromlechs. See henge monuments.

crusades military expeditions undertaken by Christians from the end of the eleventh to the end of the thirteenth century, primarily to recover the Holy Land from Muslim control.

Cryptozoic age in Earth history from 2 billion to 600 million years ago.

Ctesiphon capital of Persian Empire.

cuneiform a script consisting of characters pressed into clay with the use of styluses. It was used by the Sumerians and the Semites, though created by the native Mesopotamians. It started as images but evolved into a syllabic script.

curia group who ratified the king's election; an assembly with purely ceremonial function and thirty members called *curiae* in the republic of Rome.

curia regis Anglo-Saxon board of trusted men that advised the king, established by William the Conqueror; department of finance was called the exchequer after the cloth on which the monies were counted.

Cuzco capital of the Inca Empire, Tahuantinsuyu, located primarily in present-day Peru, founded by the legendary king Manco Capac; center for religion, temples, altars, and sacrificial offerings of capacochas.

Cycladian civilization Bronze Age civilization from ca. 3300 to 1000 BC on the Greek Cyclades Islands.

Cynics school of philosophy in fourth-century BC Greece founded by Diogenes of Sinope, nicknamed *Kyon* (cur or dog) for his ascetic lifestyle; considered civilization and the material world contemptible; advocated return to a simple, natural life to attain happiness through self-sufficiency and independence.

Cypselus seventh-century BC tyrant of the city of Corinth. His form of "affluence politics" was continued by Periander.

Cyrus the Great king of Persian Empire from 559 to 530 BC and member of the Achaemenid dynasty. In 558 he

obtained hegemony following an uprising against the Medes. In 547 he conquered Lydia and in c.539, the Neo-Babylonian Kingdom.

Dacia an area north of the Danube (present-day Rumania) subjugated by Trajan and made into a province after several wars in AD 106.

daimyo Japanese class of landowners, originally farmer leaders of humble origin, who introduced an efficient government of land and vassals; class developed during Period of Warring States.

Damascus ancient capital of a city-state in Roman times; conquered variously by David of Israel, Assyrian Tiglath-pileser III in 732 BC, and Alexander the Great in 333-332 BC; part of the Seleucid Kingdom until taken by Pompey the Great in 64 BC. Made a Christian bishopric in the first century AD, it was taken over by Muslims in 635 and Turks in 1056. Damascus was besieged but not taken by the Christians (in 1148). In 1154, it fell to the Egyptians. It was the headquarters of Saladin, sultan of Egypt and Syria, during the Third Crusade.

damnatio memoriae damned in memory; the removal from the official records of one's reign.

damos free Mycenaean men, peasants, merchants, and artisans. The damos owned communal land. Trade focused on metal and woodworking, shipbuilding, and textile manufacturing. There were also slaves who worked in the palace workshops.

danegeld a direct tax introduced by Aethelred the Unready, Anglo-Saxon king of England, paid as annual tribute to the Vikings (Danes).

Danelaw a Viking kingdom in northeast England.

Daode Jing (Tao-te-Ching, The Classic of the Way of Power), the earliest Daoist scripture, attributed to Laozi (Lao-tzu, c.500 BC), although written about 200-100 BC; probably his students record of his teachings.

Daoism (Taoism) Chinese philosophy originated by Laozi (Lao-tzu) about 500 BC; emphasizes inner harmony with nature and yielding to the Dao (Tao, the Way), the natural flow of things.

Darius king of the Persian Empire from 521 to 486 BC and member of the Achaemenid dynasty. He created political unity by dividing the empire into twenty satrapies, which were subject to central rule. He consolidated the borders, promoted trade, and developed an infrastructure. He was a follower of Zarathushtra. He started the First Persian War, annexed Thrace and Macedonia and undertook an expedition against Athens which ended in the Battle of Marathon.

Darius III (Codomannus) (c. 380-330 BC) last king of Persia (336-330 BC); great grandson of Darius II; handed rule by the eunuch Bagoas, whom he later killed; led the Persians against Alexander the Great; defeated at the battles of Issus (333 BC) and Gaugamela (331 BC); killed by one of his own satraps while fleeing Gaugamela.

Dark Age (ca. 1050-ca. 750 BC) period in Greek history so called because of the lack of information on it and because it formed an interim phase between the rich culture of the Bronze Age and the revival of culture in the Archaic Age.

Dark Continent Western concept from the nineteenth- and twentieth-centuries' study of African history. Because of prejudices and stereotypical ideas concerning the black African population, precolonial Africa was considered primitive and insignificant.

darshanas classical schools of Hinduism.

Darwin, Charles (1809-1882) English naturalist who postulated the theory of evolution.

David king of Israel and Judah, from c.1000 to 965 BC, successor to Saul. He defeated the Philistines, expanded the kingdom to its greatest size, seized Jerusalem from the Jebusites and made it his capital.

De Agri Cultura treatise on farming written by Hippocrates; the oldest surviving prose work in Latin.

De Temporum Ratione (*On the Reckoning of Time*, 725) written by Bede the Venerable; introduced the concept of dating events AD (*Anno domini*, the year of the Lord) and BC (before Christ).

deacons assistants to the apostles and bishops, usually prominent citizens who devoted their time to the followers of Christianity.

Dead Sea Scrolls rolls of parchment found in AD 1947 near the Dead Sea; contain the earliest biblical texts known, with Essene moral codes and theological comments; probably hidden by Essenes during Jewish revolt.

Decius (AD 201-251) emperor from AD 249 to 251. Systematic persecution of Christians took place for the first time under his reign. They refused to obey his edict making it compulsory for all Romans to worship the state deities.

Deir el-Medina place where the laborers working in the Valley of the Kings lived. The *ostraca* (potsherds or pieces of limestone) found here from the time of the Ramesside kings provide insights on Egyptian law, religion, economics, operations at the royal tombs, and daily life.

Dekkhan area in southern India ruled from sixth to the eighth centuries by the Chalukyo dynasty; Pulakesin II (608-642) expanded the region; Rashtrakutra dynasty (757-1190) was brought down by Muslim aggression.

Delian League (478-404 BC) voluntary alliance of Athens and Ionian city-states in Asia Minor, Aegean Islands, and colonies in Thrace to rid them of Persians remaining after the Persian War; dominated by Athens; dissolved after the Peloponnesian War.

Delphi city in central Greece, site of an Apollo sanctuary and an oracle. The utterances of Pythia, the priestess of the oracle, had great influence on personal and political life.

delta-cepheids pulsating stars that vary in surface temperature, color, and light intensity as they change size, alternately becoming smaller and larger.

Demetrius I (Poliorcetes) (?-283 BC) king of Macedonia (294 BC); son of Antigonus Monophtalmus. Defeated with his father at the Battle of Ipsus (Phrygia) by an alliance of diadochs in 301 BC; retained Macedonia and dependent Greek cities for the Antigonid dynasty; imprisoned by Seleucus in 286 BC.

democracy from the Greek *demos* (people) and *kratein* (to rule); government by the people, either directly or through elected representatives. This form of government arose at the end of the sixth century BC in Athens.

Democritus (fifth century BC) Greek philosopher.

demos (people) originally a designation for the nonaristocratic part of the Athenian population. After the reforms of Cleisthenes, the word was used to designate all Athenians with civil rights.

Demosthenes (384-322 BC) Athenian orator, logographer, and politician; led Athenian opposition to Macedonia; renowned for his Philippics, political oratories warning of the rising power of Philip II; urged Athenian alliance with Thebes against Macedonia.

dendrochronology dating method based on the comparison of annual rings of trees.

devas evil powers in Persian religion. The world was dominated by devas and ahuras, or good spirits, who constantly fought one another. People had to help the ahuras by way of magic formulas, predictions, and offerings.

dhamma (Sanskrit: the way to enlightenment) the teachings of Buddha.

dharma (Sanskrit: right social behavior) Hindu concept of correct behavior in line with the cosmic order.

diadochoi (successors) generals who succeeded Alexander the Great upon his death in 323 BC, dividing his empire; their vying dynasties included the Ptolemies, the Antigonids, and the Seleucids.

Diana Roman goddess of the moon and the hunt; identified with the Greek goddess Artemis; worshiped in the Latin League; given a sanctuary on the Aventine Hill in Rome in the late sixth century BC.

dictator a magistrate appointed by the consuls, given unlimited power in emergencies in state affairs and military matters, originally for a six-month term. As dictators during the civil wars, Sulla and Caesar held an unassailable position of power for an unlimited duration.

Diocletian, Gaius Aurelius Valerius Diocletianus (245-313); Roman emperor (284-305); last of the Illyrian dynasty; modernized administrative and military organization; established tetrarchy; divided the empire east and west; organized tax reforms and price controls.

Diogenes (ca. 400-325 BC) Greek philosopher and founder of Cynicism.

Dionysia Greek annual festival in honor of Dionysus, characterized by processions, poetry competitions, and theatrical performances.

Dionysus Greek god of wine, ecstasy, reproduction, life force, and of chaos and death.

dirham coin used in Constantinople.

Djenné town in the inner delta of the Niger River, famous for its clay architecture and peaceful society built around a variety of cultures; Djenné belonged to Mali and was conquered in 1473 by the Songhai.

dodeca polis twelve cities in Ionia.

dog dogs enjoyed great respect from the Persians because of their roles in the lives of nomadic cattlemen. They were placed on almost the same level as people.

Domesday Book land registry introduced during the reign of William the Conqueror in which all property of the inhabitants of England was registered for tax purposes.

dominate Roman imperial era starting with Diocletian; emperors were absolute rulers and the state despotic; compelled hereditary succession and increasing bureaucracy. Constantinople became the new government center and Christianity more important.

dominium mundi papal domination of the world; during the thirteenth century, dominium mundi reached the acme of its power, especially in the person of Innocent III.

Domitian (Titus Flavius Domitianus) (AD 51-96) Roman emperor AD 81-96. Noted for his reign of terror.

Donatio constantini (Donation of Constantine) eighth-century forged last will and testament of Constantine the Great, leaving the western part of his kingdom to the pope; basis for papal demand for authority over the rulers of Europe.

Doppler effect (red shift) change of wavelength frequency of objects by virtue of their relative distance from Earth. The same effect also occurs with sound (for example, a siren coming closer). Because space expands (constellations that are farther away move away from us faster than those nearer to us), this phenomenon can be used to measure distance.

Dorians Greek tribe that conquered parts of the Peloponnisos and Crete between 1200 and 1000 BC.

Doric Greek dialect spoken along the west side of Greece by the Dorians.

Draco Athenian statesman and lawgiver in the seventh century BC; drew up a harsh code of laws in 621 BC (Draconian Laws).

drag plow the oldest type of plow used for tilling land; an important technical innovation in agriculture; probably in general use about 2500 BC.

Druids Celtic priests in Gaul and Britain who held significant power due to their religious and medical knowledge and sorcery. They led the resistance against the Roman conquerors.

Dryopithecus tree ape living during the Miocene era (30 million years ago). There was an evolutionary relationship between this ape and later anthropod species, including hominid.

du Guesclin, Bertrand (1318-1380) nobleman from Gascony whom Charles V the Wise appointed supreme commander of the army; he trained unemployed mercenaries and fought a guerilla war against the army of Edward the Black.

dukka (Sanskrit: suffering) the underlying condition of existence, in Buddhism.

duumviri a provincial office comparable to the consulate in Rome. Shared by two members of the local aristocracy, they were in charge of a town for the period of one year.

Du'a (Arabic: private prayer) Islamic prayer.

earthenware vessels and containers made of baked clay, in widespread use for cooking and storage by Neolithic cultures.

Easter Island easternmost island of Polynesia, colonized around AD 500, the site of hundreds of enormous monolithic statues of mysterious origin.

Eastern Empire eastern part of the Roman Empire, divided after the death of Theodosius in 395. About the sixth century, it was called the Byzantine Empire, with Constantinople as its capital.

Eastern Frankish Empire acquired by Louis the German in 843, consisting of the tribal dukedoms of Bavaria, Saxony, Swabia, the Franks, and Lotharingia.

Eastern Roman Empire From the 6th to the 15th century AD, called the Byzantine Empire, it was the eastern segment of the Roman Empire, divided after the death of Emperor Theodosius (AD 395).

Ebro River river stipulated by treaty after the First Punic War as the border between the spheres of influence of Rome and Carthage.

ecclesia the tribal meeting of Athens open to all citizens that, after Cleisthenes's reforms, made the final political decisions on internal and foreign affairs.

ecclesiae Christian communities, governed by a bishop, where theological and liturgical issues were discussed; eventually met in special meeting halls (churches). *Ecclesiae* of the third century presented themselves as funeral societies to gain legal status.

Edessa a city in Syria conquered by Baldwin of Bouillon in 1098; established as a Christian principality; recaptured in 1145, leading to the Second Crusade.

edict an official order given by the emperor. Famous examples are Diocletian's price-control edict and Constantine's edict of Milan, which granted freedom of religion.

Edict of Milan (AD 313) proclaimed by Emperor Constantine in the west and Galerius in the east, it legalized Christian worship.

Edward III king of England (1327-1377); proclaimed himself king of France in 1337, thus unleashing the Hundred Years' War; reshaped the army into lance fighters and archers instead of heavily armed horsemen.

Edward, the Black Prince (1330-1376) son of Edward III and an important commander during the Hundred Years' War; destroyed regions of southern France and took John the Good prisoner at Poitiers.

Egyptian language from the end of prehistory (ca. 1000 BC); the Egyptians did not constitute a cultural unity but did develop a common language. The language is related to the Semitic African and Berber languages.

Egyptian temples sanctuaries for Egyptian gods kept by the pharaoh, who donated land, pastures, cattle, and valuable objects to the temples.

Eightfold Path Buddhist concept of the way to spiritual improvement: right views, right intention, right speech, right action, right livelihood, right effort, right mindfulness, and right concentration.

Eighth Crusade (1270) expedition led by Saint Louis IX to Tunis; Moors threatened Naples' trade position in the Mediterranean; during the siege of Tunis an epidemic broke out and Louis died.

Einhard (c. 770-840) Frankish scholar and monk, biographer of Charlemagne.

Einstein, Albert (1879-1955) German-American physicist who developed the theory of relativity.

El Cid (c. 1040-1099) *El Cid Campeador* (The Lord Champion), born Rodrigo Díaz de Vivar; Spanish legendary warrior.

Eleanor of Aquitaine heiress to the kingdom of Aquitaine and wife of Louis VII of France who had the marriage annulled in 1152; as revenge she married Henry II Plantagenet of England, giving him the western part of the French Empire.

elegy from *elegos* (lament); a poem of lament and praise for the dead.

elektron alloy of gold and silver used in the first coins minted in the seventh century BC.

Eleusis city on the Greek coast near Athens where mysteries were held between ca. 600 and ca. 400 BC.

emissary counts trusted men sent by Carolingian rulers to monitor the policy of regional counts and to hear the appeals of the people in the region.

Empire of the Golden Horde Mongolian empire comprising most of Russia whose name derives from its capital, the Mongol camp on the Volga; separated in 1240 from the Mongols in the east, it exploited Russian principalities by extracting annual taxes; internal warfare and attempts by Russian princes to end payment of taxes weakened the empire, and Tamerland (Timurlenk) defeated it in the late fourteenth century.

emporion early Greek trading post dependent on its founding metropolis.

Enki Sumerian god of the deep waters; creator of Earth and man and worshiped as the god of wisdom and culture.

Enlil Sumerian god of Earth and sky, responsible for prosperity and misfortune.

ensi head of the Sumerian city-state; a temple king and ruler of the city on behalf of the deity and the temple. In the Akkadian Empire, *ensis* became deputies ruling on behalf of the king.

Epamenondas (?-362 BC) Theban general; broke Spartan hegemony in 371 BC, making Thebes the predominant Greek power for ten years; noted for army reform and introduction of the diagonal phalanx.

ephors college of five magistrates elected annually from the general meeting *(apella)*, forming the highest administrative and judicial authority in Sparta.

Ephthalites also called White Huns; defeated Persian King Firuz II in 431.

epic a narrative poem about mythological heroes, written in hexameter verse. Best-known examples are Homer's *Iliad* and *Odyssey* (Greek) and Virgil's *Aeneid* (Latin).

Epictetus Greek Stoic philosopher.

Epicurus (c. 341-270 BC) Greek philosopher; taught that goal of life is pleasure regulated by moderation, morality, serenity, cultural development, and freedom from fear of death (since he postulated no afterlife).

epicycle theory obsolete theory that explained the geocentric conception of our solar system. It stated that a planet revolves in a circle (epicycle) around a central point, which moves in a large circle around the Earth.

equites the name of second-ranking Roman class, originally made up of cavalrymen, it also included traders and bankers.

Eratosthenes (c. 276-c.196 BC) Greek astronomer, mathematician, geographer, and poet in Alexandria, Egypt; noted for his measurement of the circumference of the earth to within 15-percent accuracy.

eremites hermits or recluses who lived solitary lives of asceticism. Many early Christians withdrew to such a life in the desert to acquire personal sanctity, a move that led to monasticism.

Ermanaric fourth-century Gothic king; with kingdom from Baltic to Black Seas.

Essenes Jewish religious brotherhoods that maintained a monastic way of life in communal settlements at the beginning of the first century BC. In all likelihood, Essenes wrote the *Dead Sea Scrolls*.

Ethelred the Unready king of England (979-1016); introduced danegeld as a direct tax to buy off the Norsemen; when he discontinued this practice, he was expelled by the Norsemen who founded an empire in England under Canute the Great.

Etruscans people thought to originate in Asia Minor who settled in central Italy about 800 BC; politically dominant in the sixth century BC.

eunuchs castrated men, often palace administrators, emperors' confidants.

eupatridae Athenian nobles whose rule between 683 and 621 BC was ended by Draco.

Euripides (c.485-406 BC) Athenian tragic dramatist; notable for realism and satire of traditional values; works include *Medea, Andromache*, and the *Bacchae*.

evangelists nominal authors of the gospels: Matthew, Mark, Luke, and John.

Evans, Arthur archaeologist and discoverer of the Minoan civilization. In AD 1900, he started excavating Knossos and reconstructed the palace in Knossos.

Evvoia an island in the Aegean Sea.

exodus departure of the Israelites from Egypt to Canaan under Moses' guidance around the thirteenth century BC as related in the Bible. It is said that for forty years they wandered in the desert to erase all Egyptian influences and develop their identity.

extragalactic systems galaxies outside the Milky Way, visible from the Earth as nebulae of gas.

Fabius, Quintus Maximus (Cunctator) (third century BC) Roman general, dictator in 217 BC; his tactic of avoiding direct confrontation led to Hannibal's defeat in the Second Punic War.

fairs annual commercial fairs at central rural locations in Europe in the thirteenth century.

Faiyum oasis lake in Egypt drained to provide fertile land; papyri found here contain text detailing the drainage and exploitation of the area by slaves and leaseholders.

fasces ax bound in a bundle of sticks; symbol of imperial authority in Rome; probably of Etruscan origin.

Fatimids Shiite dynasty of caliphs in North Africa (909-1177); descended from Muhammad's daughter Fatima; conquered Egypt and founded Cairo (c.950).

fauna term adopted by Linnaeus in 1746 to designate animals of a specifed region or time; often used with flora (plants).

feudalism the economic, political, and social system of medieval Europe in which power was based on land ownership and loyalty. Vassals held large landed estates, worked by serfs, in return for allegiance, military, and other services they paid the landowners or overlords.

Fifth Crusade (1217-1221) expedition during which Lisbon was conquered in 1217 and Damietta in Egypt in 1218; against the pope's wishes the crusaders tried to conquer Egyptian territory in exchange for Jerusalem, but this attempt failed.

Firdawsi, Abdul Kasim Hasan Persian poet who wrote *Shah-nama* (*Book of Kings*) (c.1000).

First Crusade (1096-1099) under Godfrey of Bouillon and Raymond of Toulouse, crusaders conquered Edessa, Tripoli, Antioch, and Jerusalem, making them Christian kingdoms.

First Interregnum period in Egyptian history from ca. 2150 to 2040 BC characterized by a decline of central royalty, economic decline, and starvation.

First Palace period period of the Minoan civilization from 1900 to 1700 BC. There are no palaces left from this period.

Five Pillars of Islam confession of faith, prayer, almsgiving, fasting, and pilgrimage.

flagellants groups of people who publicly flogged themselves as a way of doing penance, popular during the plague; banned by the Church when the movement demanded reforms.

Flamsteed, Sir John (1646-1719) first Royal Astronomer of England.

Flanders a region on the North Sea coast made part of his empire by Charlemagne in the ninth century. Under independent counts, it developed into a regional power. In the eleventh century, the courts of Flanders were vassals for both the French crown and the Holy Roman Empire. Duchy of the French king, beginning in the twelfth century, which was economically dependent on England for its textile manufacture; when Edward III prohibited the export of wool in 1337, Flanders rebelled against France; the uprising was crushed in 1340.

flint hard type of stone in calcium and chalk layers, easily chipped to make tools; widely used in the Paleolithic and Mesolithic ages.

flora term adopted by Linnaeus in 1745 to designate plants of a specified region or time.

flower wars fought for economic reasons and to expand land; prisoners of war were sacrificed to the Aztec gods during the many religious celebrations.

foederati (Latin: the federated) foreigners allied with the Romans; populated and patrolled land at imperial borders; provided troops for the Roman army.

forum marketplace and public square of an ancient Roman town or city; political, cultural, and commercial center.

fossils hardened remains or imprints of plants and animals, particularly skeletons or shells, preserved in layers of rock.

Four Noble Truths Buddhist concept that existence is suffering, and suffering is caused by ignorance of the true nature of reality, leading to attachment and craving for worldly pleasures; following the Eightfold Path can end suffering.

Fourth Crusade (1202-1204) expedition by French knights; they took Byzantium with the aid of Venice and founded a western-style empire.

Franks Germanic people, *foederati* (allies) along the Rhine River over the third century AD; divided into Ripuarian and Salian Franks; led by Clovis I, conquered territory between the Rhine and the Pyrenees Mountains, including Syagrius's Roman kingdom in Gaul (end of the fifth century); forced the Visigoths to Spain (507).

Fraunhofer, Joseph von (1787-1826) Bavarian optician and physicist, investigated spectra of planets and invented light-measuring instruments and ways to improve telescopes.

Frederick I Barbarossa Holy Roman Emperor of the German Empire (1152-1190); as a scion of the Hohenstaufen family he made peace with the Guelph leader, Henry of Saxony; strengthened his power and withdrew many privileges from the princes and dukes of his realm; fought against the rebellious Lombard League, the Guelphs, rebellious noblemen, and the pope; died during the Third Crusade.

Frederick II emperor of the Holy Roman Empire of Germany (1212-1250); was supported by Innocent III, but left the German noblemen to their own devices and harshly ruled the empire of Sicily; in 1228 he was crowned king of Jerusalem.

free city settlement populated by craftsmen and artisans who lived outside the feudal structure and had their own government and legal system; the liege lord granted these free areas privileges through city rights, such as toll exemption, the right to build walls, and citizenship for the inhabitants.

Friars minor (Franciscans) monastic order founded by Francis of Assisi in 1223; were mendicants who were not allowed to own anything; monasteries were also supposed to share their possessions with the poor.

Frisians Germanic tribesmen who settled on the Waddenzee and the North Sea coast in the sixth century. Defeated by Charles Martel; completely subjected by 785.

Fujiwara period (858-1160) period in which the Fujiwara-uji were the actual controlling power in Japan; they filled the offices of Sesshu, the emperor's regent, and Kampaku, head of civil authority; increasing power of the army diminished their control.

Funnel-beaker culture Neolithic culture around 2500 BC in northern and central Europe, named for the shape of their characteristic earthenware.

Gainas (died 400) Gothic mercenary general; appropriated power in Constantinople with his army; hated by the populace, especially because of his Arian beliefs; died in rebellion against him.

Gaiseric king of the Vandals (428-477).

Galerius Roman emperor (305-311); continued the Christian persecution Diocletian had begun, closing the catacombs and sacking churches. In 311 he issued an edict of tolerance, effectively legalizing Christianity.

Galla Placidia sister of Western Roman Emperor Honorius; taken hostage by Alaric I when he plundered Rome in 410.

Gallia (Gaul) land of the Gauls; Cisalpine Gaul (northern Italy) was conquered in 200 BC. Gallia Narbonensis (Provence) was colonized in 118 BC. Transalpine Gaul (France, Belgium) was conquered by Caesar (58-53 BC).
gamiko special vases made for weddings.

gau land given in fief to a loyal vassal, held by him in return for allegiance and services rendered to the landowner.

Gaugamela city in northern Mesopotamia where Alexander the Great defeated the Persians under Darius III in 331 BC.

Gauls Celtic people who moved westward from central Europe at the end of the sixth century BC; threatened the southern Mediterranean around 400 BC; conquered parts of Etruria, destroyed Rome; were paid ransom to settle in northern Italy.

Gautama, Siddhartha (c.480-400 BC) a prince of the Shakya clan; called the Buddha, founder of Buddhism.

Genghis Khan *See* Chingiz Khan.

gens (people) Roman clan led by chieftains, patres (fathers) with absolute authority over wives, children, and slaves; later, patres were members of the senate and called patricians.

geocentric concept of the world Earth-centered concept of the solar system, prevailing from antiquity until the sixteenth century AD.

geologic timescale timescale with which the developments of the Earth's crust are dated. By studying sedimentary and igneous rocks, relative dates can be established. By determining the half-lives of radioactive elements in minerals, geologic periods can be absolutely dated.

German Hansa alliance of North German and Dutch merchants and commercial towns founded in approximately 1150; had a monopoly on trade in the Baltic Sea and the North Sea; grew into a powerful alliance of cities, continuing into the fifteenth century.

Germania (Latin: *Germany*) written AD 98 by Roman Cornelius Tacitus; commentary on Germanic people.

Germanic kingdoms in fifth century; Europe ruled by Germans who let popular customs continue; influenced by Rome.

Germanic kings Germanic commanders in chief, initially chosen by tribesmen, who became absolute rulers.

Germanics people in northwestern Europe who migrated southward, beginning around 200 BC.

Germans European peoples from the north of the Rhine. Caesar drove out the Germans below the Rhine.

gerousia council of elders in Sparta, consisting of twenty-eight men aged sixty
and above, who were appointed for life.

Ghana West African empire established in the eighth century AD that dominated the savanna region around the year 1050; Soninke were the Islamic ruling class and they controlled the gold trade and endorsed organized commercial traffic in Africa; Ghana collapsed around 1200 under the emergence of other western African states; modern Ghana takes its name from the ancient empire.

Ghibellines supporters of the House of Hohenstaufen and proponents of the rule of a strong emperor over the Church; fought the Guelphs; in 1268, they were defeated for good.

Gilgamesh epic epic from Mesopotamian literature which was handed down in different versions from different eras. It describes the life of Gilgamesh, the king of Uruk, who searches for the herb of life together with his friend, Enkidu.

Gla city in Boeotia where a large fortress was built in the thirteenth century BC as a refuge for the local populace.

gladiator a man (often a slave or convicted criminal) in ancient Rome who fought to the death for public amusement in amphitheaters; opponents could be other gladiators or wild animals.

God State of Amon name for Thebes which evolved during the Third Interregnum when it became a separate state ruled by Amon's high priests.

Godfrey of Bouillon (1060-1100) duke of Lower Lotharingia and leader of the First Crusade. He took part in the capture of Jerusalem in 1099, ruling it as Protector of the Holy Sepulchre, refusing to be crowned king.

Gordian knot Greek legend; complex knot tied by King Gordius of Phrygia. According to oracle, he who untied it would rule Asia. Alexander the Great cut it with his sword. "To cut the Gordian knot" means quickly solving a difficult problem.

Gospels the first four books of the New Testament, named after and attributed to Matthew, Mark, Luke, and John; compiled after the crucifixion of Jesus Christ from the work of many people.

Goths a German group in the third century AD. Living in Dacia, they were feared plunderers threatening the Roman borders. In the 4th century AD, the West Goths were driven back by the Huns. The Romans granted them permission to settle below the Danube. About 400, they attacked Rome under the leadership of Alaric. The East Goths were conquered by the Huns and later moved to Hungary.

Gracchus, Gaius Sempronius (?-122 BC) Roman statesman; brother of Tiberius; tribune (123 BC); introduced social reforms; decreased grain prices. When he tried to grant civil rights to the *socii*, riots broke out in which he was killed.

Gracchus, Tiberius Sempronius (?-133 BC) Roman statesman; tribune (133 BC); pushed a land reform plan through the popular assembly. Landowners resisted, street fighting erupted. Gracchus was killed.

Graces the three Roman goddesses of beauty, joy, and charm; daughters of Zeus by the nymph Eurynome. Thalia was associated with good cheer; Aglaia with splendor; and Euphrosyne with mirth.

Granada a small mountain state in southern Spain where the last of the Muslims held out against the Christians until 1492.

Granicus River site of the battle in northwestern Asia Minor where Alexander the Great defeated a large Persian army in 334 BC, gaining control of Asia Minor.

Gratian (359-383) full name Flavius Gratianus, western Roman emperor (367-383); coemperor with his father Valentinian I until the latter's death in 375, then with his half brother Valentinian II.

Great Migration that of the Germanic peoples to the south and the west of Europe between the fourth and the sixth centuries AD; one of the causes of the decline of the Western Roman Empire in 476.

Great Moguls Mongolian Muslim dynasty established under Babur Shah (1526-1530) in India; authority of the Great Moguls extended to India, but diminished in the eighteenth century.

Greek fire secret Byzantine weapon against Arabs at sieges of Constantinople (674, 680, 717); burned when sprayed onto enemy ships; almost unquenchable.

Greek the language of Greece, used by the Byzantine Empire from the seventh century on.

Greenland island off the North American coast, discovered in 982 by the Viking Eric the Red; was colonized and had trade contacts with Norway and Iceland; politically tied to Norway in c.1260.

Greens influential party in Constantinople; organized horse races against the Blues party; comprised traders and working-class.

Gregorian calendar Pope Gregory XIII changed the Julian calendar in 1582, considering the years too long. He ordered leap year dropped at the turn of the century (with the exception of the millennium). In order to catch up, the days between the 4th and 15th of October, 1582, were canceled.

Gregorian chants ritual plain songs instituted by Pope Gregory I; used in the Roman Catholic Church; unharmonized, unaccompanied, and sung without meter.

Gregory I, the Great, Saint (c.540-604) pope (590-604); last of the four original doctors of the Church; defended Rome against the Lombards; had England Christianized, giving new momentum to Christianity in Europe.

Gregory VI pope (1045-1046). He bought the papal office from Benedict IX and subsequently used his wealth to repel corruption.

Gregory VII, St. (Hildebrand) (c. 1020-1085) pope (1073-1085), canonized in 1606. His effort to reform the medieval church is called Gregorian Reform. He insisted on the primacy of church over state, challenging lay investiture.

Gregory IX pope (1227-1241); excommunicated Frederick II because of his unwillingness to go on a crusade; supported the Lombard League against Frederick's expansion of power.

Guelphs supporters of the House of Guelph and proponents of a monarchy with little influence, powerful vassals, and an autonomous Church; from 1125 they fought the Ghibellines and defeated the last scion of the Hohenstaufen family.

guilds organizations of merchants and artisans who supervised the quality and price of manufacture and the working conditions; only guild members were allowed to exercise their craft in the cities.

gulf streams great currents of warm water in the ocean that affect the temperature of both the surrounding seas and the air above them.

Gupta Empire Indian dynasty (c.320-c.544) that ruled much of what is now modern India; brought down by the invasions of the White Huns; leading monarchs were Samudra Gupta (335-375), who made extensive conquests, and Chandra Gupta II (375-414).

guru a teacher, especially a Brahman in Hinduism who taught the *Vedas* and trained students to become pious Hindus.

Gutians Iranian mountain peoples who invaded the Akkadian Empire repeatedly between ca. 2230 and 2100 BC and plundered the cities. Shortly after 2200 they destroyed Akkad.

Hades god of the underworld and brother of Zeus; also the name of the underworld itself.

Hadith (Arabic: *Story*); companion book to the Koran; guide for Muslim daily life; details incidents in Muhammad's life.

Hadrian (Publius Aelius Hadrianus) (AD 76-138) adopted by Trajan. He consolidated the borders of the empire and surpressed a Jewish rebellion.

Hadrian's Wall masonry wall built by Hadrian (AD 120-123) to protect Roman Britain from northern peoples; runs from Solway Firth to the Tyne.

Hagar biblical second wife of Abraham, mother of Ismael.

Hagia Sophia great domed Church of the Holy Wisdom in Constantinople; built under Emperor Justinian (532-537).

hagiography biography of a saint; featured a moral message and visions, prophecies, and miracles testifying to the saint's piety.

hajib title of the highest ranking civil servant under the caliph in Córdoba; also used by rulers of the small states.

hajj (Arabic: pilgrimage) journey to Mecca.

Hallstatt culture central European culture of the late Bronze and early Iron Ages, from 1200-475 BC.

Hamilcar Barca (c. 270-228 BC) Carthaginian general; father of Hannibal; commanded Carthaginian forces in Sicily in the First Punic War; defeated by Rome in 241

BC; conquered much of the Iberian Peninsula (237-228 BC).

Hamites African peoples who speak related Hamito-Semitic languages but do not form a cultural or ethnic unit. The Hamites include, among others, the Hausa, Berbers, and Galla.

Hammurabi king of Babylon from 1792 to 1750 BC. He defeated the kings of Larsa and Assur and conquered Mari. He drew up a legal code and abolished the deification of kings.

Han dynasty dynasty in control of China (206 BC-AD 221); restored the agrarian economy and introduced Confucianism as the state religion; defeated the Huns and undertook expeditions across the Chinese borders; government tasks were fulfilled by state officials from the class of large landowners called mandarins.

hand-axe a Paleolithic tool originally made of flint; increasingly made of other stones, it was refined through the Paleolithic age.

Hannibal (?-183 BC) Carthaginian general; son of Hamilcar; during the Second Punic War, advanced from Spain to Italy, regularly defeating Roman armies; persuaded the socii to defect. In 203 BC, he was forced to defend Carthage against the Romans. After the peace in 201 BC, he fled from the Romans and committed suicide.

Hansa international league of merchants that arose from companies of travelers organized for safety reasons; the hansas protected their trade interests by acquiring product monopolies and controlling prices; the hansas grew into alliances of commercial towns.

Hansa of the Seventeen Towns alliance of Flemish and northern French commercial towns that controlled trade between western and southern Europe in the thirteenth century; textile products from Flanders were its focal point.

harmonia harmony produced by the movement of the heavenly bodies.

Harold Godwinson king of England in 1066; the personal advisor to Edward the Confessor; in 1066 he became king and fought the other pretenders to the throne: Norse king Harold Hardrada and Norman William the Conqueror; defeated Harold but died in the battle of Hastings while fighting William.

Harsha Buddhist leader heading an empire (606-647) in northern India comprising parts of the former Gupta Empire.

Harun ar-Rashid caliph (786-809) under him, the caliphate of the Abbasids peaked.

Hasidism Jewish religious movement in the eleventh and twelfth centuries that strictly adhered to the laws of the Bible and Talmud; especially influential in the Rhineland.

Hastings town on the English coast where William the Conqueror landed in 1066 and battled the army of King Harold; Normans defeated the Anglo-Saxons exhausted by the battle against the Norsemen; Harold died in battle and William became king of England.

Hatshepsut regent of Tuthmosis III; ruled from ca. 1484 to 1468 BC as king of Egypt, portrayed as a man. She sent commercial expeditions to, among others, the land of Punt, which was famous for its exotic wares.

Hattusas (Boghazköy) Hittite city founded in the early seventeenth century BC, which was the capital of the Hittite Empire from 1650 to 1200 BC. The king resided here. The archives found here contain a wealth of information about Hittite society and religion.

Hattusilis I Hittite king in the Old Hittite Kingdom from c.1650 to 1620 BC. He founded Hattusas and tried to protect Hittite power against the Hurrians in Syria and the mountain peoples of Asia Minor.

Hattusilis III Hittite king in the Hittite Empire from

c.1285 to 1265 BC. He made a peace agreement with Egypt around 1269 and was forced to defend his empire against the Anatolian mountain people, the Sea Peoples, and the rising Assyrians.

heaven Christian place where saved souls live eternally in the presence of God.

Hebrews *See* Israelites.

Hector Trojan hero killed by Achilles in a duel during the Trojan War.

hegira (Arabic: *flight*) journey of Muhammad from Mecca to Medina, September 20, 622; first date of Muslim calendar; considered starting point of Islam.

Helena, Saint (c.248-328) wife of the Roman emperor Constantius I and mother of Constantine the Great, emperor of Rome.

heliocentric concept of the world concept of the solar system as sun-centered, with the planets revolving around the Sun; first postulated by Copernicus in 1543.

hell place where souls of the damned live eternally, according to Christian belief; portrayed as eternal fire, ruled by the devil.

Helladic culture Bronze Age culture from ca. 3300 to 1000 BC on the Greek mainland.

Hellen the legendary ancestor of the Hellenes, or Greeks.

Hellenism Greek civilization especially as modified in the Hellenistic period by oriental influences; a body of humanistic and classical ideals associated with ancient Greece and including reason, the pursuit of knowledge and the arts, moderation, civic responsibility, and bodily development.

helots members of the original population of Laconia and Messenia in Greece, subjugated and enslaved by the Spartans.

henge monuments circles of megaliths or stone monuments (such as Stonehenge in England) whose purposes and origins are as yet unknown.

Henry II of Bavaria (973-1024) called Henry the Saint because of his piety; king of Germany (1002-1024), king of the Lombards (1004-1024), and Holy Roman emperor (1014-1024). Elected by German nobles to succeed Otto III, he was supporter of Cluniac reform. He was canonized in 1146.

Henry II Plantagenet king of England (1154-1189); through his marriage to Eleanor of Aquitaine, he acquired the western portion of the French Empire.

Henry III (The Black) (1017-1056) king of Germany (1028-1056) and Holy Roman emperor (1039-1056). Son and successor of Conrad II, he was an advocate of Cluniac reform but retained his authority over the church.

Henry IV (1050-1106) king of Germany (1056-1106) and Holy Roman emperor (1084-1106). He succeeded his father Emperor Henry III at age six; his mother ruled as regent. He was excommunicated by Pope Gregory VII in 1076 over the issue of lay investiture. In 1077, he did penance outside the castle at Canossa, was reinstated, and was excommunicated again in 1080. He deposed the pope in 1081.

Henry V king of England (1414-1422); defeated the Armagnacs in 1415 and occupied large areas of France, which enabled John the Fearless, duke of Burgundy, to obtain power in Paris.

Henry the Fowler of Saxony (c. 876-936) king of Germany (919-936). He united the German Empire.

Henry the Lion of Saxony duke of Saxony and Bavaria (1154-1180); vassal of Frederick Barbarossa; a Guelph, but made peace with Frederick in 1152; when Frederick fought the Lombard League in 1177, Henry refused to help him because of his own ambitions; Frederick deprived him of his dukedom as punishment, and Henry ended his life in exile in England.

Hera wife and sister of Zeus, goddess of birth and marriage.

Heraclitus (ca. 500 BC) Ionian natural philosopher.

Heraclius Byzantine emperor (610-641); began counteroffensive against Khosrow II (622); weakened the Persian Empire by his victories in the center of the realm (627).

Herakleopolis city in northern Egypt where a kingdom was founded by local administrators during the First Interregnum.

Herihor general at the end of the New Kingdom. He was to restore order in Thebes but took power as the high priest of Amon.

Hermes Greek god of travelers, shepherds, trade, and cunning. The son of Zeus and messenger of the gods, he also guided souls to the underworld.

hero brave mortal, often deified by the Greeks.

Herod the Great king of Palestine (37-4 BC) under the Romans.

Herodotus (ca. 484-424 BC) from Halicarnassus; father of Greek historiography; historian whose work *History* viewed the centuries-long battle between the Greeks and the Persians as a confrontation between Eastern and Western cultures.

Herophilus (c. 335-280 BC), Alexandrian physician, father of human anatomy; first to form conclusions from dissection; recognized that arteries pumped blood, that the brain is the center of the nervous system; identified motor and sensory nerves; described the eye, liver, and genitalia. His works have been lost.

Hesiodus (ca. 700 BC) epic poet from Boeotia. He wrote the didactic poems *Thegonia*, on religion and mythology, and *Works and Days*, a sort of manual for farmers.

hetairoi personal retinue of the Macedonian king, on equal footing with him and treated as friends; rebelled against Alexander the Great in 324 BC.

hexameter A form of verse used mainly in epic poems, consisting of six dactylic and spondaic feet. (A dactyl consists of one long and two short syllables; a spondee has two long syllables.)

heys title of high officials in the Osman Empire; they collected taxes in the provinces and recruited warriors.

Hezekiah king of Judah from c.727 to 698 BC and friend of Isaiah. He introduced reforms to placate Yahweh. He successfully defended Judah against the Assyrians.

hicma scientific center with a library built in Baghdad by order of Abbasid caliph Al Mamun; he had his scientists studied Greek culture and science; collected manuscripts.

hieratic simplified, quicker version of hieroglyphic writing written in ink on papyrus scrolls.

hieroglyphs oldest Egyptian script, originally based on images but later, as a result of the need to represent abstract concepts, it developed into a combination of ideograms, syllable signs, and letters.

high priests of Amon the priests in Thebes whose power increased in the New Kingdom due to the increasing wealth of the temples.

Hilary of Poitiers, Saint (c.315-367) pagan convert to Christianity, doctor of the Church, bishop of Poitiers; noted for his lifelong opposition to the Arian heresy.

Hinayana (the Lesser Vehicle) disparaging term for Theravada Buddhism.

Hinduism predominant religion in India, originating from Brahmanism; characterized by belief in many gods headed by Brahma, Shiva, and Vishnu.

hippeis (horsemen or knights) dominant social class in Athens, comprised aristocrats with large landholdings who were rich enough to own a horse.

Hippias (reigned 528-510 BC) son of Peisistratus; Athenian ruler with his brother Hipparchus until 514 BC, then alone until forced out; last Athenian tyrant.

Hippocrates of Kos (c. 460-c. 377 BC) Greek physician called the father of medicine; disassociated ancient medicine from superstition, basing it on diagnosis through clinical observation and logic. The Hippocratic Oath is attributed to him, as are some seventy medical works; he probably wrote six.

Hittite Empire period in Hittite history from c.1400 to 1200 BC when the empire reached its greatest expansion into Syria and northern Mesopotamia. Around 1200 the empire suddenly disappeared. Some Syrian and Anatolian cities preserved Hittite culture in separate Neo-Hittite states.

Hittite king leader of the Hittites who acted as king, commander of the army, supreme judge, and high priest. His staff consisted mainly of relatives. The queen mother also had a political function and was probably the high priestess.

Hittite legal code a hundred or so clay tablets from Boghazköy containing laws and rules having to do with the social organization. It shows that society consisted of aristocrats, serfs, and slaves. There was no wealthy middle class.

Hittite script from c.2000 on, the Hittites utilized the cuneiform script. Between c.1000 and 700 the Neo-Hittites used hieroglyphs consisting of pictographs and phonetic symbols. Though the cuneiform was deciphered, the hieroglyphs are still not well understood.

Hittite sun goddess Arinna, supreme goddess of the Hittites. She was queen of heaven and earth and leader of the kings. The queen mother was probably the high priestess of this national cult.

Hittites peoples from Asia Minor who spoke an Indo-European language and settled in Asia Minor around 2000 BC. They expanded their territory politically southward into Syria, Mesopotamia, and Canaan between 1650 and 1350. The Hittite Empire disappeared around 1200 after the rise of Assyria and invasions by the Sea Peoples.

Holocene era in the Quaternary period beginning 10,000 years ago, during which the temperature and the sea level rose; can be viewed as an interglacial period of the Pleistocene age that is still continuing.

Holy Roman Empire title adopted in the thirteenth century in an effort to reinstitute the Roman Empire. Mainly comprised of German states, its first emperor, Otto the Great, was crowned in 962. By 1100, the empire included the kingdoms of Italy, Bohemia, Burgundy, and Germany. It lasted until 1806.

Homer (ca. 800 BC) legendary Greek poet to whom the epics the *Iliad* and the *Odyssey* are attributed.

hominids a class of primates that includes *Homo habilis, Homo erectus, Homo sapiens,* and all *Australopithecus* species. This group also includes all the great apes, including humans, gorillas, orangutans, and chimpanzees.

homo novus the first in a Roman family to hold the offices of quaestor, aedile, praetor, and finally consul.

Homo erectus hominid who walked upright and lived from 150,000 to 500,000 years ago in Africa, Asia, and Europe; the first hominid species to be found outside Africa; includes Java man (*Pithecanthropus*) and Peking man; used tools, made shelters, and utilized fires.

Homo habilis hominid who walked upright; lived some 2 million years ago, at the same time as *Australopithecus*;

first hominid species found in association with manufactured tools.

Homo sapiens sapiens modern man; developed around 200,000 years ago; displaced Neandertals around 30,000 years ago.

homosexuality a sexual relationship between members of the same sex, acceptable in Greek society.

Honorius (384-423) son of Roman Emperor Theodosius I; Western Roman emperor at age twelve (395-423), under the guardianship of Stilicho.

hoplites soldiers in the Greek heavy infantry, armed with sword, lance, and the large, round shield called the hoplon.

hoplon large round shield first carried by Greek heavy infantry in the Archaic period.

Horace (Quintus Horatius Flaccus) (65-8 BC) Latin poet; his work, inspired by Greek poetry, includes odes, satires, the didactic poem on poetry *Ars Poetica*, and the chorus of *Carmen Saeculare*.

Horemheb pharaoh from 1333 to 1306 BC; had administrative and military experience and definitively restored the conditions that existed before the Amarna period.

Horus Egyptian sun god and son of Osiris, represented as a falcon. The pharaohs were considered his incarnation and represented his power on Earth.

Hosea Hebrew prophet (eighth century BC) who predicted the fall of the Israelites for not obeying Yahweh's commandments and worshiping other gods such as Baal. His prophecies are written in the Old Testament.

hospitium (Latin: guest right; English: hospice) Roman and foederati custom; eventually became a euphemism for landowners housing foreign soldiers; practice of claiming a third of land settled; adopted by Germanic rulers to establish large kingdoms.

huacas sacred objects of the Inca religion; objects, places, altars, and persons could be worshiped as huacas or were sometimes used as oracles; Incas would also worship as huacas the religious elements of conquered peoples.

hubris excessive pride.

Hugh Capet king of France (987-996); before he rose to power the French Empire had been fragmented as a result of the power of the county rulers; Hugh and his descendants, the Capetians, gained strength and slowly reunited the empire; dynasty ruled France until 1328 when the last Capetian king, Charles IV, died without a male heir.

Hulaku brother of the Mongolian rulers Mangu (1251-1260) and Kublai Khan (1260-1294), who conquered Baghdad, Aleppo, and Damascus; when Kublai Khan became chief khan, Hulaku officially recognized him, but continued to rule the Mongols in the west.

Hundred Years' War (1337-1453) war between France and England, which still possessed areas in France; immediate cause was a dispute about the succession to the French throne; by 1453, England had lost all territory in France except for Calais.

Huns central Asiatic people noted for horsemanship and ferocity in battle; drove the Visigoths from the Ukraine (c.370); conquered eastern and central Europe; seized western Europe under Attila (c.450).

hunters and gatherers nomadic communities based on the hunting of animals and the gathering of plant foods. They had to survive by unity, equality, and sharing. Due to changes in climate, meat became scarce, and by 8000 BC, the communities in Africa were gradually displaced by agricultural communities.

Hurrians tribe from the east which settled in northern Mesopotamia beginning ca. 1800 BC. They founded the Mitanni Empire ruled by a militarily superior Indo-

European elite. After 1200, the Hurrians settled in Urartu and from there conquered parts of Syria and Phoenicia.

Hussein (Husayn) son of Ali of Arabia; claimed the caliphate in Al-Kufa in 680; he and his clan were murdered by Umayyad armies of orthodox Muslims (Sunnites); adherents of Ali, called Shiites, seceded.

hydria a water jar.

Hyksos Asiatic rulers who settled in the Nile Delta during the Second Interregnum and ruled a large portion of northern Egypt. They were expelled ca. 1550 BC by Ahmose.

iambic verse a poetic style with a short (or unstressed syllable) followed by a long (or stressed) syllable.

Iberian culture non-Celtic Iron Age culture in Spain and southern France. High point of this culture was from the fifth to the third centuries BC. The Iberians survived on agriculture and animal husbandry.

ice ages (glacials) climatic episodes characterized by a great drop in temperature, the expansion of ice caps at regions of higher latitude (such as North America and northern and central Europe), and changes in flora and fauna. Between about 600,000 and 10,000 years ago there were four primary cold waves, corresponding to the cultures of the Paleolithic age.

Iceland island in the North Sea discovered and colonized by the Vikings in the ninth century; had commercial ties with Norway and was politically tied to the Norse king around 1260.

iconoclasm from the Greek *eikon* (image)and *kloein* (break); a movement originating in the Byzantine Empire in the eighth and ninth centuries that condemned the veneration of various forms of artwork called icons.

iconodouloi (icon defenders, or servants of images) supporters, including the Roman papacy, of the view that regarded icons as an acceptable form of Christian worship.

Iliad Greek epic poem attributed to Homer.

imam (Arabic: predecessor) Islamic priest or holy man. To Shiites, twelve imams, descended from Ali and Fatima, had the right to lead the Muslims, the last imam will return at the end of the world.

immersion technique boiling water by dropping red-hot stones into it; used since Paleolithic times.

immunity feudal independence from the authority of local civil servants.

imperator original title of a general after the victory that gave him the right to a triumphal procession. Augustus and his successors adopted this title as a first name, so that imperator became the title of the highest commander.

imperium originally, military authority given to Roman generals and consuls; later included the right to call together and speak before the Senate and the people's assembly; also denotes the sphere of power.

Inanna Sumerian fertility goddess, daughter of the god of heaven and ruler of the gods, Anu. She merged with the Semitic Ishtar during the Akkadian Empire and became the goddess of love and fertility.

Inca Empire (Tahuantinsuyu) pre-Columbian empire from the thirteenth century to 1532, stretching from the northern parts of Ecuador south to Argentina; fifteenth century saw a rapid expansion of the empire; conquered in 1532 by Pizarro.

Inca religion religion based on worship of a universal deity possessing a multitude of divine powers and personalities; personages of this one god included Viracocha, the creator, and Inti, the sun-god and the kings' forefather; Incas also worshiped their forefathers, their kings, huacas, and capacochas.
Inca Viracocha (c. AD 1438) king of the Incas in the fif-

teenth century and first to conquer land outside Inca territory; his successors, Pachacuti, Tupac Yupanqui, and Huayna Capac, expanded the Inca Empire by conquering in north and south.

Incas pre-Columbian civilization in South America that established the Inca Empire in the thirteenth century; they were an expansionist society controlled by a king; people lived in groups called ayllus and provided services to the state in the form of military service and labor on roads, buildings, and state-controlled farms; textiles were used for clothing but also were a status symbol.

Indian trade India traded with Rome, Persia, Greece, the Arab realm, and China; was a transit center for trade (including silk) with China and exported spices, precious stones, animals, and textiles; commercial trade spread Hinduism and Buddhism, Indian philosophy, and science.

Indo-European a common-language family of European and a few Asiatic (Indian) languages.

Indo-Iranian peoples nomadic peoples who lived between Mesopotamia and the Indus Valley and may have originated from Central Asia. They included the Persians and the Aryans (Indians) who shared related languages and religions. They separated during the second millennium BC.

Indra ancient Indian god of storms, war, and battle. He was portrayed as a warlike hero and is also the rain-giving god of fertility and vegetation. He originates from the prehistoric Indo-Iranian tradition and appears in the *Vedas*.

Indus River Valley (India) conquered by Alexander the Great (327 BC); the eastern border of his Macedonian empire.

infamia a bad public reputation.

inner planets planets with an orbit between Earth and the Sun, specifically Mercury and Venus.

Innocent III pope (1198-1216); restored papal authority in the papal states and established *dominium mundi* by playing foreign rulers against one another, granting political support.

insula (Latin: islands) lower-class housing; badly constructed apartment buildings packed into poor districts of Rome. Densely populated, they were often hit by large fires.

interdict papal sanction whereby citizens of the territory of a sinner are excluded from all religious ceremonies; in this manner the pope could pit the populace against the perpetrator.

interglacials episodes between the ice ages that were characterized by a mild subtropical climate, an elevated sea level, and consequent changes in flora and fauna.

interpluvials periods between pluvials. See pluvials.

interregnum (1256-1273) period of the German Empire without an emperor, because after the death of the Holy Roman emperor the electors were unable to agree on a new candidate.

interstellar material material consisting of gas and dust in the space between the stars.

investiture a ceremony in which the symbols of office are conferred on a prelate (church official).

investiture controversy a major dispute in the eleventh and twelfth centuries over lay investiture, the role played by secular nobility in the ceremonies putting church officials (prelates) in office. It was resolved in favor of the church at the Concordat of Worms in 1122.

Ionian natural philosophers philosophers of the sixth and fifth centuries BC who attempted to explain the cosmos through reference to nature and rationality, without recourse to mythology or religion. The first was Thales of Miletus.

Ionian Rebellion (499-495 BC) rebellion of the Ionian coastal cities in Asia Minor and the neighboring islands against Persia.

Ionians Greek tribe driven from the mainland (except Attica) by the Dorians; settled on the Greek islands and on the west coast of Asia Minor in the ninth century.

Ionic Greek dialect of the Ionians spoken in Attica and Evvoia, on the Greek islands of Chios and Samos, and in the central part of the west coast of Asia Minor.

Irene (752-803) empress of the Byzantine Empire (797-802). Married to Emperor Leo IV in 769, and regent for her son Constantine VI (780-790 and 792-797), whom she imprisoned and blinded. Deposed by Nicephorus and exiled to the island of Lésvos. She summoned the Council of Nicaea in 787 to restore image worship.

Irish Christianity founded by Patrick around AD 400, centered around monasteries that were also Celtic cultural centers.

iron metal that is obtained by heating iron ore and hammering it for a long period of time, after which it is shaped into objects. Iron was already being processed in western Asia in 2000 BC by Armenian tribes. It is more readily available and produced more easily than bronze.

Iron Age period after the Bronze Age during which the major weapons and tools were made of iron. The Hittites formed the first Iron Age culture, about 1500 BC. Between 1200 and 600 BC, ironworking spread over Europe and Asia.

Isaiah Israelite prophet (eighth century BC) who warned against Yahweh's wrath as manifested by the Assyrian threat. This could be averted by unconditional faith in Yahweh and a return to social righteousness. His prophecies are recorded in the Old Testament.

Isaurian dynasty founded by Leo III the Isaurian, it ruled the Byzantine Empire (717-802).

Isaurians mountain tribe from southern Asia Minor noted for military prowess; established a Byzantine imperial dynasty.

Ishmael biblical son of patriarch Abraham; progenitor of the Arabs.

Ishtar Semitic war goddess. She merged with Inanna into the goddess of love and fertility. Sargon I realized this Sumerian-Semitic mixture to promote the integration of the Sumerian and Semitic civilizations.

Isin Sumerian city-state founded ca. 2000 BC by Isbierra. Until ca. 1800 BC, the city comprised a large empire in southern Mesopotamia in addition to the other powerful city-state of Larsa.

Isis Egyptian goddess of fertility and, by extension, of the heavens and nature. The Romans became acquainted with the worship of Isis around 100 BC. During the Principate she had many followers, among them the Emperor Caligula.

Islam monotheistic religion worshiping Allah; founded by the Prophet Muhammad in the seventh century; its tenets, as revealed to him, are recorded in the Koran.

Islamic Empire expanded out of Arabia in the seventh and eighth centuries to Syria, Egypt, North Africa, Spain, and Asia to the Chinese border; despite religious unification, it did not become a single cultural entity; rebellions took place frequently.

Isocrates (436-338 BC) Athenian orator, logographer, and teacher of eloquence.

Israel Israelite kingdom occupying northern Canaan that split into two after Solomon's death (c.932 BC). The kingdom experienced an economic boom, but was characterized by dynastic instability and moral decay. In 720 Israel was conquered by Assyria.

Israelites Semitic tribes who infiltrated Canaan in the second millennium. They probably stayed in Egypt or in the border area between c.1650/1450 and 1214. After 1200 they conquered Canaan, according to the Bible. They lived in a loose alliance of tribes, and from c.1000, joined under a king.

Issus coastal city on the border between Syria and Asia Minor where Alexander defeated a large Persian army in 333 BC.

Ivan III the Great grand duke of Muscovy (1462-1505); subdued the Mongols and Lithuanians; after the fall of Constantinople, Muscovy was all that remained of the Christian Byzantine Empire, and Ivan took on the role of emperor over this reduced territory and established the Russian Czarist Empire; the word *Czar* is a Slavic word meaning "Caesar," or "Emperor."

Jacquerie farmers rebellion in 1358 by "Les Jacques," peasants around Paris, against their lords in response to years of oppression and the battle lost at Poitiers, crushed by Charles the Bad.

Janizaries (also Janissaries) army of slaves and Christian prisoners of war who were indoctrinated with Turkish culture and military discipline; they stood as the basis for the military successes the Turks enjoyed between 1360 and 1826; regular outbreaks of janizary revolts took place from the seventeenth century onward; their power ended in 1826 when Sultan Mahmud II had them massacred in their barracks.

Jeremiah Israelite prophet (seventh century BC). He predicted that Judah would fall as a result of the Assyrian threat. He also condemned social injustice as well as the superficial and material honoring of Yahweh. His prophecies are recorded in the Old Testament.

Jerome, Saint (c.345-c.420) father and doctor of Church; translated Bible into Latin version called the Vulgate; converted many aristocrats, including women; founded a monastery and a nunnery in Bethlehem.

Jerusalem capital of the Israelites in Canaan, founded by David around 1000 BC. Originally Jerusalem was a Jebusite city. After Solomon's death, Jerusalem became the capital of the kingdom of Judah. In 586 BC the city was destroyed by the Babylonian king Nebuchadnezzar.

Jesus Christ (c.6 BC-AD 30) Jewish religious leader crucified as a rebel; his followers were the first Christians.

Jewish Revolt uprising against the Roman procurator by radical Jewish factions, primarily zealots, from AD 66-70. Through a war of annihilation, the Roman armies restored order, captured Jerusalem in 70 and destroyed the Temple.

Jews in Medina Jewish community in Arabian town of Medina; rejected religion and politics of Muhammad; allowed to keep their faith, but obliged to pay capitation and recognize Islam.

jihad (Arabic: Holy War) Muslim duty to expand Allah's realm, to propagate Islam; led to the conquering of Mesopotamia, Syria, Egypt, North Africa, Central Asia, and Spain in the seventh and eighth centuries.

Joan of Arc (1412-1431) peasant girl, driven by visions, who broke the siege of Orléans and had Charles VII crowned king in Reims; her attack on Paris failed; was extradited to the English in 1430, who burned her at the stake as a heretic; became the symbol of French resistance against England.

John II the Good king of France (1350-1364); was taken prisoner at the battle of Poitiers in 1356; after paying ransom he was released but voluntarily returned when a French hostage escaped.

John Lackland king of England (1199-1216); slowly lost his French territories to Philip II Augustus; after his ally Otto IV had been defeated by Philip Augustus in 1214, he resigned himself to his loss.

John Orphanotropus eunuch who governed the Byzantine Empire from 1034 to 1042 through Emperor Michael IV and his cousin Michael V, adopted by Zoe. Their reign, characterized by extortion, was ended by popular revolt.

John the Baptist Jewish preacher who preached and baptized on the banks of the Jordan River; proclaimed the coming of the Messiah; executed by Herod Antipas.

John the Fearless duke of Burgundy (1404-1419); son of Philip the Bold; was probably responsible for having Louis of Orléans killed, whose supporters, the Armagnacs, then attacked John's followers, the Bourguignons; John entered an alliance with the English in 1415.

John XII (c. 937-964) pope (955-964). Called the boy pope because he was elected at eighteen, he crowned Otto the Great emperor in 962. He refused allegiance to Otto in 963 and was deposed.

Jovian Roman emperor 363-364.

Judah a southern region of the Hebrew kingdom that split from the northern kingdom of Israel after Solomon's death (c.925 BC). The kingdom suffered moral decay as the cult of Baal and Astarte expanded. In 586 BC Jerusalem, its capital, was destroyed by the Babylonian king Nebuchadnezzar.

Judas Maccabeus (?-161 BC) from the Hasmonaeans family of Jewish patriots. The Latin surname, probably derived from Aramaic maqqabē (the Hammerer), gave rise to the English *Maccabee*, applied to Judas's relatives. Notable for his defeat of much larger Syrian armies between 166 and 165 BC. His restoration of Jewish rites to the Temple of Jerusalem (December 165 BC), is commemorated by the Jewish festival Hanukkah.

judge prior to the united kingdom period, an Israelite leader who assumed military command of the loosely federated tribes in times of emergency. The Bible mentions twelve judges, including Samson.

Jugurtha (?-105 BC) African Numidian king in conflict with the Romans. When Italic merchants were killed during a civil war, Rome retaliated in the Jugurthian War (112-105 BC). Jugurtha was defeated by Sulla.

Julian (Flavius Claudius Julianus) (AD 331-363) called *Apostata* (the Unfaithful), Roman emperor 355-363, he favored the Roman gods and limited the rights of the Christians and the influence of the Church.

Julian calendar Introduced in 46 BC by Julius Caesar, this had a year comprised of 365 days with one extra day every fourth year. Before this, a year consisted of 355 days with a 22 or 23-day leap month every other year.

Julian the Apostate (Flavius Claudius Julianus) (c.331-363) Roman emperor (361-363); denounced Christianity; attempted to restore worship of the traditional Roman gods after the adoption of Christianity by Constantine the Great.

Jupiter god of the sky, thunder, and lightening; the highest of Roman deities, he controlled the universe; identified with the Greek god Zeus.

Jurassic period in the Mesozoic from 208 to 144 million years ago, named after the Jura mountains. During this period, flying reptiles and early ancestral birds evolved.

Justinian I the Great, Flavius Petrus Sabgatius Justinianus (483-565) Byzantine emperor (527-565); had the *Corpus Iuris Civilis* drawn up; built the great Hagia Sophia. Under his imperial renovation, he expanded Byzantine control of the West; recaptured North Africa, Italy, and the Spanish south coast; his generals Belisarius and Narses defeated the Ostrogoths.

Kaaba (Arabic: cube) black stone cube in Mecca originally considered holy by most Arabs for its more than 300 statues. Muhammad considered it a religious relic of Allah built by Ishmael and condemned the polytheism. Although driven away in 622, he returned to purge it in 628, making it the central temple of Islam.

kabbala Jewish secret mystic movement from the twelfth and thirteenth centuries which explained the Bible by way of numbers and mysticism.

kadi a government official in the caliphate of Córdoba charged with caring for the poor and public works in provincial capitals.

kalpis water pitcher.

Kamakura period (1192-1333) period in which Japan was ruled by shoguns of the Minamoto-uji (later followed by other clans) from Kamakura; the Minamoto defeated the Taira after a power struggle and Yoritomo Minamoto became the first shogun.

Kamares pottery refined Minoan pottery from the First Palace period, usually manufactured on potter's wheels and decorated with helical and plant designs in light colors on a blue-black background.

kampfio Germanic ritual duel; used to verify an accusation of witchcraft or prostitution.

kantharos vessel.

Kanun Nam collection of Osman Turkish laws and regulations based on Islamic law and the absolute supremacy of the sultan, recorded in the fifteenth century by order of Muhammad II.

karma (Sanskrit: fate, work) one's acts and their consequences in a subsequent existence. In Buddhism, karma is considered the result of actions which define kind of rebirth that occurs, not as punishment, but for evolution; in Hinduism, karma means cause and effect, bearing in this life the consequences of actions taken in previous lives.

Kassites mountain people who invaded Mesopotamia from the east after 1800 BC. They introduced the chariot. From 1600 onward the Kassites ruled Babylon until ca. 1200.

kehilla Jewish community in the Middle Ages; the religious and administrative authority; Jews were autonomous and based their government on the Talmud.

Kepler, Johannes (1571-1630) German astronomer who defended Copernicus's teachings. He wrote the laws of Kepler that account for the movement of the planets.

kernos ring-shaped vase.

Khadija (sixth century) first wife of Muhammad; a widow made wealthy through caravan trade. Their marriage enabled Muhammad to become a rich trader with ample time for mysticism and religion.

Khamose pharaoh in Thebes at the end of the Second Interregnum. He tried to expel the Hyksos from the north and thwarted their attempts to form an alliance with the Kushites.

Kharijites followers of Ali of Arabia who deserted him in 657 after his agreement to arbitrate his dispute over the caliphate with rival Mu'awiyah. The Kharijites assassinated Ali in 661.

Khosrow I (528-579) king of Persia (531-579); established a professional army; water supply; supported the poor; made palace a center of philosophy, primarily Indian.

Khosrow II king of Persia (590-628); seized Syria and Jerusalem from the Byzantines; continued conquest as far as Asia Minor and Egypt; defeated by Heraclius in 627.

Kiev *See* Kyyiv.

Kikuli Hittite at Hattusas's court who wrote a semiliterary work on the taming and care of horses. The horse trade was an important means of existence for the Hittites.

Kings Period era when Rome was ruled by kings: Romulus, Numa Pompilius, Tullus Hostilius, Ancus

Martius, and the Etruscans (616-509 BC): Priscus Tarquinius, Servius Tullius, and Tarquinius Superbus.

Kings' Peace treaty concluded in 387 BC between Sparta and other city-states including Thebes and Athens; written under Persian supervision, it ended Spartan imperialism and began Persian rule of the Ionian cities.

Kirchhoff, Gustav Robert (1824-1887) German physicist.

kitchen waste mounds huge garbage piles, mainly of mollusk shells, left by a Mesolithic culture on the North Sea and Atlantic coasts.

knightly order brotherhood of Christian nobleman who fought Muslims and were founded in the West; examples are the Knights Hospitaler and the Knights Templars; secular orders such as the Order of the Garter were honorary.

Knights Hospitalers society of Christian knights who fought Muslims; order grew out of the eleventh-century pilgrims' hospital in the Holy Land; when noblemen of the brotherhood became their leaders, the order took on a military character.

Knights of St. John Christian Hospitalers who ruled the eastern parts of the Mediterranean from 1310 to 1522 from the island of Rhodes; in 1481 they withstood an Osman siege; when Rhodes was conquered (1522) they moved to a new stronghold on Malta in (1530).

Knossos Minoan settlement housing a large palace from the Second Palace period until ca. 1300 BC.

Kojiki Japanese myth cycle centered around the creation of the world, including the narration of Jimmu Tenno, who established a Japanese state in the Yamato Plain in 660 BC; historians date this traditional first emperor to the third or fourth century AD.

Kong-fu-tse (Confucius) (551-479 BC) Chinese philosopher and founder of Confucianism.

Koran scripture of Islam, regarded by the faithful as revealed to Muhammad and recorded by scribes; written in verses organized into 114 chapters called *suras*; contains the history of Muhammad, references to the Bible, Islamic law.

kouros statue of a young man.

krater vessel in which water and wine are mixed.

krypteia random murder of helots (indigenous people made serfs) by young Spartans, possibly to prove their manhood. It intimidated the helots and reduced the risk of rebellion.

Kshatriyas second hereditary social status in the ancient Indian caste system consisting of princes and noble warriors. They possessed governmental and judicial power and were initially more respected than the Brahmans.

Kublai Khan Mongol ruler (1260-1294); established the Yuan dynasty in Khan Baug (Peking); his court was a center for Chinese culture; conquered land in the Far East and appointed Chinese and Islamic officials.

kurgans large burial mounds of the Scythians, used for kings and high officials.

kurieia (guardianship) especially the guardianship over women, considered inferior, by an adult male representative.

Kush kingdom south of Egypt. In the Late era the Kushites ruled Egypt and were expelled by the Assyrians in 664 BC.

Kyyiv (or Kiev) capital of the Russian empire of Vladimir and Yaroslav, who was formally in charge of the independent principalities after his death; Kyyiv was a flourishing trade center and seat of the Byzantine church; destroyed in 1240 by the Mongols.

La Tène culture Celtic Iron Age culture (475-40 BC).

Laconia the valley of the Eurotas River on the Peloponnisos Peninsula of Greece; original home territory of Sparta.

Lagash Sumerian city-state which constituted a dominant empire in southern Mesopotamia during the Gutian Interregnum (twenty-second century BC).

Land of the Queens Chinese name for Japan at the time of the Tombe civilization, indicating the existence of a political unity around the year 300 and possibly a matriarchal society; also known under the name of Wa.

Laozi (Lao-tze) (c.500 BC) Chinese philosopher, founder of Daoism. His philosophy is recorded in the Daoist scriptures called the *Daode Jing (Tao-te-ching, The Classic of the Way of Power)*.

Lares spirits of departed ancestors; guardian deities of private homes and estates. Each house had a chapel or altar for sacrifices to the Lares, who also protected roads and travelers. A *lararium* was a room containing statues of the house spirits.

Larsa Sumerian city-state which constituted a powerful kingdom in Sumer next to the empire of Isin during the Sumerian Renaissance between ca. 2000 and 1800 BC.

Late era period in Egyptian history from ca. 730 to 332 BC during which Egypt was ruled by foreign powers: the Kushites, the Assyrians, and the Persians.

Late Mycenaean era period from ca. 1250 to 1000 BC during which the decline of the Mycenaean civilization took place slowly due to invasions by unknown enemies, civil wars, natural disasters, overpopulation, and economic decline.

latifundia large, economically independent estates originally worked by slaves. When plantation size increased, they were developed using coloni who leased some land in exchange for part of the harvest.

Latin originally, the language of Latium and Rome. As Rome's power grew, Latin became the official language of the western Roman Empire. Greek continued to be spoken in the eastern part.

Latin America Central and South America as colonized by Latin people from Spain and Portugal from the sixteenth century onward; Spanish and Portuguese are now the main languages spoken in Latin America.

Latin Empire western rule of Constantinople (1204-1261); founded after the Christian conquest during the Fourth Crusade; empire was forced to fight border wars and rebellions; in 1261 Michael Paleologus restored the Byzantine Empire.

Latin League ethnic religious federation of Latin cities on the Italian Peninsula; fought the Etruscans in the sixth century BC; abolished in 338 BC, following rebellion against Roman domination.

Latini inhabitants of Latium; lived in small villages on the hills of the Italian Peninsula until the seventh century BC, when the Etruscans took over; thereafter, they lived in *oppida* (fortified towns); formed religious and political alliances, including the Latin League.

lawagetas Mycenaean official under the wanax. *Lawagetas* means leader of the people, most probably army commander.

Laws of the Twelve Tables Roman common law codified and engraved on twelve bronze plates by the *decemviri* (ten men), a commission of ten patricians, in 451 BC.

legalism pragmatic Chinese philosophy, strongest over the third century BC; absolute state rules supersede the individual.

legion Roman army division made up of 6,000 infantrymen and 300 cavalry, originally all Roman citizens. During the Principate there were approximately 25 legions. Non-Romans served with the *auxilia* (backup troops). Some soldiers received citizenship after serving in a legion.

Leo III, St. (c. 750-816) pope (795-816). In 800, he crowned Charlemagne emperor of the West, ending eastern influence on the western papacy. He retained religious control despite imperial intervention.

Leo III the Isaurian (c. 680-741) Byzantine emperor (717-741), restored government after near anarchy, deposing Emperor Theodosius III. Noted for his defense of Constantinople and his ban on icon veneration which led to his excommunication in 731.

Leo V the Armenian Byzantine emperor from 813 to 820.

Leo IX (1002-1054) pope (1049-1054). His exchange with Michael I Cerularius (patriarch of Constantinople) of anathemas and mutual excommunication in 1054 (called the Great Schism) was the culmination of long theological dispute between eastern and western Christians.

León tenth-century Christian kingdom in northwestern Spain; absorbed by Castile in the eleventh century.

Leonidas (d. 480 BC) Spartan king who died in the Battle of Thermopylae with hundreds of Spartans, covering the retreat of the main Greek army from the Persians.

Leukippus fifth-century BC Greek philosopher and student of Parmenides. He laid the foundation for atomic theory with his hypothesis that "being" consisted of innumerable small particles which cause diversity in the world through their infinite combinations.

Levallois technique a planned method of flint processing. Flakes struck from the original core of flint are worked into tools with precise retouching blows.

Libyans African tribes that threatened Egypt from the west. They were fought by Sethi but continued to be a threat. In the Third Interregnum they formed kingdoms in the Nile Delta and ended up usurping the pharaoh's power.

lineage (Africa) social group derived from one common ancestor.

Linear A script found on Minoan clay tablets in the palace complexes. Never deciphered, the script is probably a syllabic script and a simplified form of hieroglyphs.

Linear B script found on Mycenaean clay tablets on the Greek mainland and in Knossos. It is a syllabic script based on the characters of Linear A. The language of the Linear B tablets is Greek. It was deciphered in AD 1953.

Linear bandkeramik. See bandkeramik.

Linnaeus, Carolus (1707-1778) Swedish botanist who developed the system for classifying plants and animals by genus (always capitalized) and species.

Lithuanians people to the north of Russia who conquered parts of Russia and the Ukraine in the fourteenth century; Ivan the Great managed to confine their expansion.

liturgy prescribed form of Christian worship.

liturgy tax levy for rich Athenian citizens, consisting of a large sum spent on behalf of the state. This could involve financing the *gymnasium* (sports school) or a *choregie* (sponsors of theatrical productions), or equiping and commanding war ships.

Livy (Titus Livius) (59 BC-AD 17) Latin historian who wrote an extensive work, partially preserved, on the history of Rome from its foundation in 753 BC (*Ab Urbe Condita*).

logographers orators in Athens who wrote oratories (speeches) for others. During the classical era, orators strongly influenced politics. They were often *metoikoi* (foreigners) not allowed to hold political office.

Lombard League alliance of Italian cities that rebelled against Frederick I Barbarossa in 1167 after he revoked their royal privileges of coinage, tolls, and administration of justice, league defeated him in 1176.

1615

Lombards central European Germanic people; conquered most of Italy in 568, leaving Byzantine rule only on the coast and in the south. This Lombard Empire was subjected by Charlemagne in the eighth century.

Lothar I (c. 795-855) Holy Roman emperor (840-855), eldest son of Holy Roman Emperor Louis I, the Pious, and grandson of Charlemagne. Made coruler with his father in 817, he twice revolted against him with his brothers, Louis the German and Charles the Bald. He then battled them and lost at the Battle of Fontenay in 841. Lothar received Italy in 822, the eastern part of the empire in 839, and guarantee to the title of Holy Roman emperor and sovereignty over Italy, Burgundy, Alsace, Lorraine, and the Low Countries by the Treaty of Verdun in 843.

Louis of Orléans brother of Charles VI who assumed actual power of the French Empire between 1392 and 1407 due to Charles VI's madness; in 1407 he was assassinated, probably on the orders of his cousin John, duke of Burgundy.

Louis I the Pious (778-840) Holy Roman emperor (814-840), king of France (814-840), king of Germany (814-840), and king of Aquitaine (781-840). Son and sole successor of Charlemagne, as central authority in the kingdom disintegrated his sons Lothar I, Louis II (Louis the German), Pépin of Aquitaine, and Charles II (Charles the Bald, his son by a second marriage) struggled for power.

Louis II (c. 825-875) Holy Roman emperor (855-875) and king of Italy (844-875). First son of Holy Roman emperor Lothar I.

Louis II the German (c. 806-876) king of Germany (840-876), the third son of Holy Roman emperor Louis I. The Treaty of Verdun gave him absolute power over the Eastern Frankish Empire in 843. He went on to take eastern Lorraine in 870.

Louis VII Capetian king of France (1137-1180); by annulling his marriage to Eleanor he lost a large portion of his empire to Henry II Plantagenet; successfully pitted the French barons against Henry.

Louis IX the Saint king of France (1226-1270); during his rule peace and calm reigned; provided just legislation and abolished trial by judgment; in this manner he increased the popularity of the monarchy and the kingdom's unity.

Louis XI the Spider king of France (1461-1483); his intrigues slowly eroded the power of Burgundy; he bought off Edward IV, English ally to Charles the Bold, in 1475; following the latter's death in 1477 he occupied Burgundy.

Lower Egypt northern Egypt comprising the Nile Delta with its flat and fertile land.

Lower Paleolithic period from about 1.5 million to 180,000 years ago.

ludi magni Large games in honor of Jupiter, held annually from 366 BC. The festivities, originally religious in nature, included theatrical performances, circus games, and competitions.

lugal political leader (king) in the Sumerian city-states. He assumed the highest position of power from the ensis.

Lugalzaggesi king of the Sumerian city-state of Umma around 2350 BC. He defeated Urukagina of Lagash and destroyed the city. He also conquered Nippur and Uruk.

Lupercalia (wolves' feasts) Roman festival named for the wolves' skins worn by the participating priests.

Lycurgus ninth-century BC Spartan lawgiver and probable author of Spartan constitution.

lyric poetry originally written to be sung to the accompaniment of a lyre; one of two main types of poetry in ancient Greece. Lyric poetry was an independent genre but was also used in tragedies.

Lysias (459-380 BC) orator and *metoikos* (foreigner) logographer in Athens; expended his fortune on the revolutionary cause; renowned for his oratory against Eratosthenes, one of the Thirty Tyrants running Athens.

Maat Egyptian principle of order in the universe. As the son of Amon-Re the pharaoh was to uphold order. He was in charge of fertility and prosperity, and he protected gods and men against enemies and the forces of nature.

Maccabees Jewish movement fighting for political autonomy, founded in obtain freedom of religion; freed Palestine from Seleucid rule; established a monarchy of high priests in Jerusalem.

Macchu Picchu it is believed to have sheltered the last acllas after the Spanish conquest.

Macedonia ancient kingdom north of Greece. King Philip II expanded Macedonian rule to Greece. His son, Alexander the Great, conquered the Middle East and Egypt. Alexander's successors (the diadochs) fought for power in Macedonia until Antigonus Gonatas founded the dynasty of the Antigonids. Macedonia was divided in four sub-states in 167 BC; all were made a Roman province in 148 BC.

Macedonian Wars between Rome and Macedonia from c. 215 BC for power in Macedonia and Greece.

Macedonians dynasty of Byzantine emperors (842-1025) named after Basil I the Macedonian.

Macehualtin Aztec farmers, craftsmen, and traders who paid tribute to the Tlatoani.

Maecenas, Gaius Cilnius (70-8 BC) Roman statesman, friend, and employee of Augustus, especially known for supporting talented artists and writers, like Virgil and Horatius.

Magdalenian culture in Europe in the Upper Paleolithic between about 15,000 and 9000 BC, the end of the last ice age. The Magdalenian people mainly hunted reindeer, which were plentiful during this episode of the last Ice Age. They produced tools of bone and antler, rather than those exclusively of flint.

Magellan, Ferdinand (1480-1521) Portuguese navigator who circumnavigated the globe from 1519 to 1521. He was the first European to reach Oceania and was killed in battle in 1521 in the Philippines.

Magellanic Clouds star systems that accompany the Milky Way galaxy, divided into the Large and the Small Magellanic Clouds; irregular in shape.

magi mostly Median priests in Iran who adhered to the belief in devas and ahuras that was popular prior to Zoroastrianism. After the death of Zarathushtra, his teachings were modified with the addition of ritual and magical prescriptions.

Magna Carta manifest issued by John Lackland in 1215 under pressure from rebellious barons; rights and obligations of both king and barons were set forth in this document; taxation without approval by the barons was impossible.

Magna Grecia region in southern Italy (sometimes including Sicily) where many important Greek colonies were situated, such as Thourioi, Crotone, Naples, and Tarentum (Taranto). The area was pervaded by a strong Greek influence.

Magyars Hungarians; originally an Asiatic mounted people, they settled in the Danube region at the end of the ninth century and invaded the Eastern Frankish Empire; conquered in 955 by Otto the Great.

Mahabharata epic poem of Hinduism, composed between 400 BC and AD 200; describes cousins vying for control in the kingdom of the Kurus. The *Bhagavad-Gita* is included in the *Mahabharata*.

Mahayana (Sanskrit: great vehicle) the largest school of Buddhism; reveres the bodhisattva who has achieved enlightenment and Buddhahood and is reborn to help others find the Way (salvation); considers Buddha the incarnation of absolute truth.

majordomo (mayor of the palace) originally, the hereditary office of royal steward in the Frankish Empire. As Merovingian power weakened, they were used as royal ministers until 751.

Mali Sudan kingdom established in the eleventh century by the Mandinka along the Niger River; in the fourteenth century they controlled western Sudan and commercial traffic between Africa, Asia, and Europe; kingdom collapsed in the fifteenth century.

Mamelukes originally Turkish slaves hired as mercenaries by caliphs in Cairo to maintain order in the twelfth century; gained power in 1260; dominated Egypt until the beginning of the nineteenth century.

Mamertines Italian mercenaries and pirates on Sicily; their request for assistance from Carthage and Rome in a conflict with Hero of Syracuse was the immediate cause of the First Punic War.

mammals vertebrate warm-blooded animals, with skin more or less covered with hair, that dominated the Cenozoic age, evolved from mammallike predecessors in the Mesozoic age. Mammals normally bear and nurse live young, but egg-laying mammals also exist.

mammoth large woolly elephants with enormous tusks who lived in tundral areas during the cold periods of the Pleistocene era. They died out around 8000 BC.

Manetho priest who drew up a history of Egypt in the third century BC and divided the pharaohs in dynasties.

Mani (c.216-c.276) Persian prophet who founded Manichaeism. Mani considered himself the final prophet in a series that included Zoroaster, Buddha, and Jesus.

Manichaeism Persian philosophy named for its third-century founder, Mani. He saw himself as final prophet in line that included Zoroaster, Buddha, and Jesus. It postulated a world of perpetual conflict between good and evil, the transmigration of souls, and a celibate, vegetarian "elect" who could attain the Kingdom of Light after death. Lower "auditors" who served them could only attain possible rebirth as an elect.

Marathon city on the east coast of Attica, where the Persians suffered a devastating defeat in 490 BC by a small Athenian army under Miltiades.

Marcel, Etienne Parisian market superintendent who gained control of the administration of Paris in 1358; he wanted to limit royal authority and control the war finances; when the Jacquerie was suppressed, he was murdered.

Marco Polo Venetian merchant (1254-1324) who stayed in the Far East (1271-1295) and worked as a minister for Kublai Khan; in 1298 he was taken prisoner by Genoa; he dictated his memoirs from his prison cell.

Marcus Aurelius Antoninus (AD 121-180) Roman emperor 161-180, adopted by Antoninus Pius.

Marduk Babylonian sun god. He became god of the state under Hammurabi and was considered the creator of Earth and god of wisdom.

mare nostrum political and propaganda term for the Mediterranean ("our sea") and the surrounding area used by the Romans for their sphere of power.

Mari Semitic commercial center on the middle course of the Euphrates. Its first flowering ended with the conquest by Sargon I, after which Mari was ruled by Akkad, Ur, and Ashur. Between ca. 1780 and 1760 BC, Mari was again independent but was destroyed in ca. 1760.

Marius, Gaius (156-86 BC) Roman statesman; fought the African king Jugurtha (107 BC), the Cimbrians and Teutons (102-101 BC); led the opposition against the senate party and Sulla; his popular party exercised a bloody reign in Rome (87-83 BC); first to equip a professional army of plebeians.

market peace legal status of the annual fairs, which were outside of local law; annual fairs were autonomous and had their own administration of justice and were controlled by the superintendents.

market superintendents authorities appointed by the local lord during annual fairs; they granted licenses to notaries and money changers, appointed order troops, and administered justice.

marks (or marches) military districts on the borders of the Carolingian Empire to provide protection against invasion; governed by counts, with the title margrave or marquise. The Danish March became Denmark.

Mars god of war and the forces; father of the mythical founders of Rome, Romulus and Remus; protector of Rome; identified with the Greek god Ares.

Martin of Tours, Saint (316-397) bishop of Tours; one of the founders of monasticism in the west; patron saint of France for his conversion efforts in Gaul.

martyrs Christians who persisted in their faith despite persecution, torture, and death; believed to attain salvation upon death, they were often venerated.

Mary of Burgundy daughter of Charles the Bold; duchess of Burgundy (1477-1482); had to concede on many matters to the Netherlands States-General; married Maximilian II of Austria, and their kingdom became part of the Hapsburg Empire.

masterpiece proof of competence that an apprentice, a craftsman in training, had to complete to become a master and start his own business; in this manner the guilds were able to control the number of established businesses.

Matins of Bruges insurrection on May 18, 1302, by the Clauwaerts, the pro-English Flemish people against the French knights in Bruges, who had come to the assistance of the Francophile Flemish elite; many of the French aristocrats were killed during this insurrection.

Maui hero in Polynesian creation legend. The Polynesians considered him their patriarch. Under his guidance they left the overpopulated islands of Indonesia and settled in the Polynesian Islands.

Maurya major kingdom in India from c.320 to 185 BC. The Maurya dynasty was founded by Chandra Gupta Maurya. The empire reached its zenith and greatest expansion during the reign of Asoka (c.265-236 BC). During this period contact with the Hellenic Greeks increased.

mausoleum a monumental tomb. Augustus had a large mausoleum built in 28 BC for the imperial family at the Campus Martius. Hadrian had his built on the opposite bank of the Tiber in AD 130.

mawali (Arabic) term for non-Arabic converts to Islam.

Maya cities built according to a fixed pattern: all cities had a central square that served as a marketplace, with temples, Ulama fields, palaces, graves, and water reservoirs; temples were large buildings situated on a terraced pyramid.

Maya elite religious, military, and political leaders who governed the city-states; as a demonstration of their power they made conquests and had the people, craftsmen, and farmers build stone buildings such as pyramids; family history and the worship of forefathers played an important role.

Maya religion the most important Maya gods, among the great many worshiped, were Hunapuh and Xbalanque, the Hero twins, while the Popul Vuh and the Ulama ball game fulfilled a central role; Mayas also worshiped their leaders, forefathers, and supernatural creatures.

Maya script ideographic script of illustrations and hieroglyphics with a phonetic value; although certain parts are still undeciphered, this is undoubtedly the most developed script of all Central American civilizations, and relates family history and historical events.

Mayas pre-Columbian civilization in Central America from 2000 BC to the present day; from 500 BC it changed to a society of city-states ruled by a Maya elite; great Maya realms could be found in Petén and Yucatán.

Mecca Arabian caravan town; fled by Muhammad for Medina in 622 due to popular resistance to his crusade against polytheism; Mecca accepted Muhammad's authority in 628; geographical center of Islam.

Medes nomadic horsemen who settled in Iran during the second millennium. From c.700 they dominated a loose federation of tribes, including the Persians. Together with Babylon, they were responsible for the fall of the Assyrian Empire in 610 BC. In 559 the Persians assumed dominance.

medimner measure of wealth based on grain.

Medina Arabian oasis town to which Muhammad fled in 622; originally named Yathrib; renamed *Madinat al-Nabi* (the city of the prophet) or Medina. Muhammad converted its already largely monotheistic Jewish population. Medina waged war against Mecca until 628.

meditation deep and continuous concentration, used by a number of mystical traditions to bypass the mind and focus reflection on (divine) truth.

megaliths large prehistoric stone monuments. *See* alignments, henge monuments. and menhirs.

megaron center of the Mycenaean palace fortresses consisting of an oblong room with a hearth. The megaron also contained a forecourt with a row of columns.

Melanesia region in Oceania named by Europeans for the population's dark skin color. It includes, among others, New Guinea, New Caledonia, Vanuatu, the Solomon Islands, and the Fiji Islands. The cultures of the Melanesians vary greatly.

Melkart-Baal-Tsor Phoenician god of trade and shipping particularly worshiped in Tyre, where a large temple was dedicated to him; identified with the Greek god Hercules.

Memphis city in Lower Egypt and residence of the pharaoh during the Old Kingdom and during the time of the Ramesside kings.

Menander (?-293 BC) Greek playwright of comedy, representative of the new comedy. His plays were known only from imitations by Latin comedic dramatists until the nineteenth century AD, when Greek papyri with fragments of them were found.

Mengzi (Mencius) (327-289 BC) disciple of Confucius who considered peace and prosperity the result of kings acting in an ethical manner. Believing people inherently good, he insisted that government be exercised on their behalf. When it was not, subjects had the right to depose it.

menhirs pillarlike stone monuments or megaliths that apparently served as sacrificial sites.

Mercia Anglo-Saxon kingdom that once occupied most of southern England.

Mercury god of trade, merchants, and travelers; identified with the Greek god Hermes.

Merovingians rulers of the Frankish Empire from the fifth century, named after Meroveus, the grandfather of Clovis I.

Mésé main street of Constantinople; crafts and commercial center of the Byzantine Empire; many of the city's poor slept between its colonnades at night.

Mesolithic period from about 10,000 to 8000 BC, characterized by a warmer climate and a greater specialization in hunting by people who lived in semipermanent base camps. The age gradually ended as agriculture was introduced.

Mesopotamia area in the Near East surrounding the Tigris and Euphrates Rivers. Floods and irrigation made the land fertile, and around 4500 BC the first agricultural settlements were founded here.

Mesozoic period from about 248 to 66 million years ago. It is subdivided into the Triassic, Jurassic, and Cretaceous periods. During the Mesozoic age, Earth was dominated by dinosaurs. In addition, birdlike creatures and mammallike species developed.

Messenia basin of the Pamisos River in southwest Peloponnisos conquered by Sparta in the seventh century.

Messiah in Judaism, the savior sent by Yahweh (God); in Christianity, it is Jesus.

Metamorphoses poetical work (stories from Greek mythology) by Ovid.

meteor meteoroid that leaves a visible white trail as it hits Earth's atmosphere; a shooting star.

meteorite mass of metal or stone that has fallen on Earth or other planets from space.

meteoroid solid body traveling through outer space.

metoikoi (foreigners) inhabitants of Athens of foreign origin or descent who had no civil or voting rights and could not occupy government offices but were liable for taxes and army service.

metropolis mother city of a colony.

Mexica people from northern Mexico and creators of the Aztec Empire; after the fall of the Toltec Empire in the tenth century they settled in Texcoco and founded Tenochtitlán in 1345.

Michael II Byzantine emperor (820-829); an officer of the Armenikoi elite corps; planned the murder of Leo V.

Micronesia group of islands in Oceania, consisting of small coral islands north of Melanesia, such as the Carolines, Marshall Islands, and Gilbert Islands. The Micronesians display cultural similarities with the Melanesians and Polynesians.

Middle Ages period between AD 500 and 1500; characterized by cultural decline and the disappearance of money, trade, and cities. Large landowners on autonomic rural estates gained wealth and power through the institution of serfdom. Intellectual matters were left largely to priests.

Middle Assyrian period period in Mesopotamian history from the fourteenth century to ca. 1100 BC in which Assyria grew to become a major power. The kingdom fell into ruin as a result of invasions by the Aramaeans.

Middle Byzantine Empire former Eastern Roman Empire, from 843 (the reestablishment of the veneration icons) to 1204 (when the Crusaders occupied Constantinople).

Middle Egyptian language of the Middle Kingdom which continued to exist for approximately two thousand years as the written language of literary and religious texts.

Middle Egyptian literature literary texts from the Middle Kingdom characterized by criticism of society and disappointment with tradition and the hereafter.

Middle Kingdom period period in Egyptian history from ca. 2040 to 1640 BC during which unity was restored by the Theban kings. The period was characterized by a flowering of the economy, the arts, and literature.

Middle Paleolithic period from 180,000 to 34,000 years ago; its distinction is based on lithic technology. The range of tools was expanded and refined with the Levallois technique. The culture of the period is called the Mousterian, and tools from this period have been discovered with Neandertal remains.

Miletus major city in Ionia.

Milky Way galaxy star system of which our solar system is a part; in appearance, a flat disk with a spiral structure consisting of thin gas and hundreds of billions of stars.

milpa agriculture Maya agricultural method whereby plots of rain forest were cultivated and left fallow after soil depletion, thus forcing the Mayas to move regularly; with the introduction of other farming methods, such as canalization, larger towns slowly developed.

Mimamsa (inquiry) orthodox school of Hinduism that explained the *Vedas* and continued the Brahmanical offerings.

ministeriales vassals and trusted followers of the German emperor who fulfilled high offices in the emperor's service and could thus become free; Frederick I Barbarossa expanded his power by appointing ministeriales.

Minoan ceramics Bronze Age pottery. The Kamares pottery dates from the First Palace period. In the Second Palace period it was decorated with lively plants and marine animals in dark colors on a light background. The motifs were arranged in a more orderly fashion after the Third Palace period.

Minoan cities settlements with an urban character, paved streets, houses, and workshops. They were located near the palaces, but there were also separate cities such as Gournia on eastern Crete.

Minoan civilization Bronze Age civilization on Crete from ca. 3300 to 1000 BC, divided in the period before the palaces (3300-1900 BC), the palace periods (1900-1200 BC), and the period after the palaces (1200-1000 BC).

Minoan frescos colorful murals. Initially the palace walls were decorated with plants, later also with animals, such as birds and fish.

Minoan palaces Cretan building complexes which contained an inner court with storage rooms, living and work chambers, and representative areas during the Second Palace period.

Minoan religion probably consisted of fertility rites, usually in the open air, with processions and dances. Trees, snakes, bulls, and double axes were important elements. There are signs of human sacrifice.

Minoan villas small building complexes built on the same plan as the palaces. Possibly these were seats for officials representing central rule.

Minos legendary king of Crete for whom the Bronze Age Minoan civilization is named. He had the Minotaur, a monster, who was half bull, half man, locked up in the labyrinth. This myth is possibly reminiscent of the Cretan bull cult and the complex palaces.

Mitanni Kingdom Hurrian Kingdom from ca. 1500 to 1350 BC in northern Mesopotamia consisting of the Hurrians under an Indo-European elite. The Mitanni warred with Egypt and concluded an alliance with Tuthmosis III. They dominated Assyria but were assimilated into Assyria in ca. 1350.

Mithridates king of Pontus in northern Asia Minor (120-63 BC); led an uprising against Rome in 88 BC in Asia Minor and Greece; defeated by Sulla in 84 BC.

mitimas Inca subjects, both yanaconas and camayos, who were made to move from their original place of residence to work and live elsewhere.

monastery ascetic community of monks led by an abbot under permanent, strict regulations. In the east, Basil was the founder of monasticism, in the west, Benedict of Nursia.

money changers bankers who exchanged the various

currencies during annual fairs; booked a small percentage of profit on the transactions; also dealt in bills of exchange and IOU's and extended money loans at exorbitant interest rates; these practices were condemned by the Church.

Mongolian horde Mongolian army unit of 10,000 men set up by Chingiz (Genghis) Khan; army comprised separate units of ten men who would fight, hunt, and live together; hordes were all subject to the khan.

Mongolian religion Mongols practiced a monotheist religion inspired by the Nestorian Christians; they were never fully converted to Christianity; from the end of the thirteenth century the Mongols in the eastern parts of the empire were converted to Buddhism, western Mongols to Islam.

Mongols Asian tribes of horsemen to the north of China; Chingiz (Genghis) Khan united the Mongols in 1190 and became chief khan; in the twelfth and thirteenth centuries they conquered the Central Asian Islamic states, the sultanate of Delhi, Russia, China, and Japan.

Monophysitism (from Greek *monos*: single and *physis*: nature) a fifth- and sixth-century doctrine that contended Jesus Christ had only a single nature, which was divine, not human; conflicted with orthodox doctrine that Christ was at once divine and human.

moons celestial bodies orbiting planets through gravitational attraction.

moraines an accumulation of earth and stone that once formed at the edges and undersides of glaciers and was deposited after the ice melted.

Moscow (or Moscovy) Russian principality headed by a grand duke that became the seat of Byzantine Russian Christianity following the fall of Kyyiv (Kiev); Moscow separated from the Mongols in the late fourteenth century and stood at the head of all Russian principalities; after the conquest of Byzantium, Moscow became the new Christian center.

Moses Israelite lawgiver and leader who, according to the Bible, led the Exodus from Egypt at Yahweh's command; he probably lived during the thirteenth century BC. He is said to have written the Torah and received the Ten Commandments from God.

mosque Islamic place of prayer; worship meetings are held on Friday; first mosque was founded in Medina on a Friday, on the spot where Muhammad first prayed.

Mossi-Dagomba group African states and people who opposed the influence of Islam that was spread mainly by traders (djulas); they waged a guerrilla war against the Sudan Muslim states until the French occupation.

Mouseion (museum) founded in Alexandria by Ptolemy I as a temple to the Muses; center for the arts and sciences.

Mousterian Middle Paleolithic cultural period in Europe from 200,000 to 70,000 years ago.

muezzin (Arabic: singer) summons Muslim believers to prayer five times a day; first muezzin was the black slave Bilal in Medina.

Muhammad (c.570-632) founder of Islam; Arab prophet from Mecca; introduced monotheistic Islam as a reaction to Arab polytheism.

Muhammad of Ghur (?-1216) Muslim ruler who conquered an empire in northern India, where he ended the Delhi Hindu rule; his generals established the dynasty of Slave kings and the Delhi sultanate.

mundium (Latin: possession) Germanic concept of a man's right of possession over his wife and any other women he had, his children, his slaves, and his freedmen; women had no civil rights; could not inherit or administer property without approval from husbands, fathers, or eldest sons.

municipia (towns or municipalities) originally non-

Roman Italic cities granted Roman civil rights after being conquered; had local autonomy but no major political influence.

Mursilis I Hittite king in the Hittite Empire from c.1620 to 1590 BC. He conquered parts of Syria and razed Aleppo and Babylon.

Mursilis II Hittite king in the Hittite Empire from c.1350 to 1320 BC. He resided in Hattusas. He defended the empire against the surrounding states, conquered Asia Minor, and fought the Egyptians.

Muses in Greek mythology, nine goddesses who inspired philosophers, poets, musicians, and artists: Polyhymnia for sacred poetry, Calliope for epic poetry, Erato for love poetry, and Euterpe for lyric poetry. Terpsichore was in charge of choral singing and dance, Thalia of comedy, and Melpomene of tragedy. Clio presided over history and Urania over astronomy.

Muslim calendar counts the years from September 20, 622, date of Muhammad's *Hegira* or flight from Mecca to Medina.

Muslim from the Arabic, meaning one who surrenders to God; an adherent of Islam.

mustasib government official in the caliphate of Córdoba responsible for trade.

Muwatallis Hittite king in the Hittite Empire from c.1320 to 1285 BC. He fought the Egyptians in the battle of Qadesh (1285). The outcome of this battle is unclear, but it was probably a Hittite victory.

Mu'awiyah first Umayyad caliph (656-680); moved the capital of Islam from Medina to Damascus; opposed Ali and his followers; dominated Syria and Egypt. After Ali's death, he bought off Ali's son Hassan, to become sovereign of the Arabian Empire.

Mycale cape on the coast of Asia Minor, where the Persian fleet was defeated by the Greeks in 479 BC.

Mycenae Bronze Age settlement on the Peloponnisos where a palace fortress was built after 1450 BC. Schliemann discovered its rich royal tombs dating from the sixteenth century BC.

Mycenaean culture last stage of the Helladic civilization, starting in ca. 1600 BC with its golden age from 1400 to 1200. The Mycenaean world was divided into separate kingdoms which did not form one political unit but showed social, religious, and linguistic similarities.

Mycenaean palaces walled palace fortresses, containing the megaron, dwellings, storehouses, and workshops, and their economic function was comparable to that of the Minoan palaces.

mysteries secret rituals said to liberate believers from earthly bonds.

myth a story handed down from oral tradition about deities and supernatural beings, closely connected to the culture of a people.

Naramsin king of the Akkadian Empire from ca. 2260 to 2230 BC. He suppressed a rebellion by the Sumerian cities and conquered the areas surrounding Mesopotamia. He deified royal power in the Akkadian Empire.

Narses (sixth century) general of Emperor Justinian I; originally head of the palace guard; defeated the Ostrogoths, restoring Byzantine influence in Italy (552).

Natufian Mesolithic culture in the Near East; people lived by hunting, fishing, and the gathering of wild grains, which were processed with harvesting equipment and millstones.

Navarre Christian kingdom in northern Spain. Pushed into the Pyrenees over the eleventh century, it became increasingly involved in French politics. Its last king, Henry IV, was the founder of the French royal dynasty of the Bourbons.

Neandertal archaic branch of *Homo sapiens* classified today as *Homo sapiens Neandertalensis;* lived between 75,000 and 30,000 years ago in Europe and Asia, during the Mousterian culture.

Nebuchadnezzar II king of the New Babylonian Empire from 605 to 562 BC. Together with the Medes, his father had brought down the Assyrian Empire. Nebuchadnezzar conquered Syria, Phoenicia, and Judah. He built Babylon into an impressive capital.

Nehemiah Jewish governor who returned from exile in Babylon in 444 BC and, with Ezra, arranged for Jewish self-rule. He instituted a civil government, while Ezra introduced religious reforms. They drew up a set of Jewish laws, including the kosher rules on hygiene, diet, and the Sabbath.

Nekho pharaoh from 609 to 595 BC who threw off the Assyrian yoke. During his successors' reigns, Egypt developed again into an independent state until the Persians conquered Egypt in 525.

Neo-Hittite Empire period in Hittite history from c.1400 to 1200 BC, when the empire reached its greatest expansion into Syria and northern Mesopotamia. Around 1200 the empire suddenly disappeared. Some Syrian and Anatolian cities preserved Hittite culture in separate Neo-Hittite states.

Neolithic period from 8000 to 2000 BC, characterized by a shift from hunting to agriculture, animal husbandry, and permanent settlements.

Neolithic revolution the gradual transition from hunting and gathering to domestication of plants and animals.

Neolithical Japanese civilizations the Jomōn civilization (2500-250 BC) possibly comprised hunters and gatherers from eastern Siberia; economy of the Yayoi civilization (250 BC-AD 250) in the south of Japan was based on rice farming; bronze, and later also iron, were used for symbolic and ritual purposes; Yayoi civilization disintegrated as the result of immigrants who brought with them iron weapons and tools.

Nero (Nero Claudius Caesar Drusus Germanicus, originally named Lucius Domitius Ahenobarbus) (AD 37-68) Roman emperor (AD 54-69); noted for initiating the first major persecutions of Christians, the great fire of Rome that he was rumored to have set himself in 64, and a reign of malevolent disorder. Proclaimed a public enemy by the Roman Senate, he committed suicide on June 9, AD 68.

Nestorianism doctrine of Nestorius (382-451); archbishop of Constantinople (428-431); postulated that Jesus Christ did not have conjoined divine and human natures, being purely human on earth and purely god in heaven. Contended that Mary could not be called Mother of God; she begot the man Jesus, while God begot his divine aspect. This doctrine gained followers, against the orthodox Christian belief that Christ has two distinct natures, divine and human, joined in both person and substance. In the fifth century, Nestorianism spread throughout the Byzantine Empire; declared heretical by the Council of Ephesus (431). The Nestorian church became powerful where it sought refuge in Persia, India, China, and Mongolia in early medieval times.

Nestorius (died c. AD 451) Syrian monk who disputed the Greek title *Theotokos (Mother of God)* for Mary, insisting she was the mother of Jesus, not of God.

Neustria Frankish kingdom in the seventh century, consisting of the western region of the original Merovingian Empire; reunited with Austrasia in 687.

neutron stars formed from neutral particles of atoms; collapsed nuclei of atoms, with a strong magnetic field; those visible on Earth are called pulsars, because their rapid rotation can be seen as pulsating X rays.

new comedy genre of comedy from the Hellenistic era, characterized by stereotypes; did not satirize or offer political or social criticism; major representative was Menander.

New Assyrian Empire Assyrian Empire from ca. 900 to 612 BC that conquered Mesopotamia, Syria, Phoenicia, Palestine, and Egypt (in 671). After Tiglath-pileser III, conquered areas were no longer sacked but annexed, thus creating a worldwide empire. In 612 the empire was brought down by invasions from the Aramaeans in Babylonia and the Medes.

New Babylonian Empire rule by the Chaldeans over Mesopotamia out of Babylon. The empire arose in 612 BC after the fall of the Assyrian Empire and was conquered by the Persians in 539. Syria, Judah, and Phoenicia were annexed.

New Kingdom era era in Egyptian history from ca. 1550 to 1070 BC, when Egypt reached its greatest land area and became prosperous from agriculture, trade, and income from the conquered territories, such as western Asia (Syria-Palestine), Kush, and Nubia. The building of temples and the arts experienced a golden age.

New Persian Kingdom governed by Sassanid dynasty, founded by Ardashir (226); conquered by Arabs (651); notable for coexistence of many religions, including Christianity, Nestorianism, and Manichaeism.

New Testament the part of the Bible containing the teachings of Jesus Christ and his disciples, including the four Gospels, the Epistles of Paul, the Acts of the Apostles, and the Revelation of St. John.

Newton, Isaac (1642-1727) English mathematician, physicist, and astronomer. He postulated theories on the relationship between mass, velocity, and energy and studied the composition of sunlight.

Nicephorus I Byzantine emperor (802-811). He deposed Irene and restored iconoclasm.

Nicephorus II Phocas Byzantine emperor (963-969).

Nicias (?-413 BC) moderate democratic Athenian politician and strategist; negotiated the Peace of Nicias (421-418 BC); reluctantly took part in the Sicilian expedition which ended it; killed by the people of Syracuse.

Nicomedia capital of Roman Emperor Diocletian in northwestern Asia Minor.

Nika revolt (January 13-18, 532) uprising in Constantinople of the Greens and the Blues, who turned the population against Justinian; the population appointed a new emperor and destroyed the city center; Theodora barely prevented Justinian from fleeing; Belisarius repressed the revolt with mercenaries.

Nile river in Egypt forming a river delta on the Mediterranean Sea. During the annual rainy season in central Africa, the Nile floods its banks, rendering the Nile Valley fertile and suitable for agriculture and horticulture.

nirvana (Sanskrit: "blow out") the state of perfect inner peace and enlightenment, when desire is extinguished and the cycle of birth, death, and rebirth ends. In Hinduism, the word refers to blowing out the flame of life. To Buddha, it meant blowing out the fires of desire, hatred, and ignorance, reaching a condition of complete detachment.

Nithard Frankish scholar and monk at the time of the Carolingian Renaissance.

nobiles (nobles) class in the Roman Republic consisting of patricians and rich plebeians that arose after the equalization of patrician and plebeian power in 287 BC. Consuls and other magistrates were elected from it; it controlled the senate.

Normandy area in western Gaul given in fief to the Normans in 911 where they established a mighty empire. The Norman duke William the Conqueror conquered England in 1066. Norman nobles established a kingdom in southern Italy and on Sicily in 1029. In 1204 Normandy was incorporated in to the French Empire.

Normanist school historical school positing the theory that the first Russian states were created by Scandinavian tribes.

Normans "North men," or Vikings, Nordic people (Danes, Swedes, and Norwegians) who variously raided, traded, and settled on the coasts and rivers of Europe, Greenland, and North America in the eighth and ninth centuries.

Norsemen north Germanic tribes from Scandinavia who raided the coasts of Europe and undertook marauding expeditions; conquered England in 1013; between 1016 and 1035, Canute the Great, a Dane, was king of England; in 1066 the Norsemen were defeated by Harold.

nous eternal intelligence.

nova heavy star that explodes at the end of its life, collapsing into a neutron star or a black hole. Supernovas are very large novas.

Novgorod Russian trading post and manufacturing center for the German Hansa who monopolized trade in the North Sea and Baltic Sea; Novgorod came under Mongol threat in the thirteenth century; Ivan the Great conquered the city in 1471.

numen divine power, will, or function, not connected to a specific god. In Roman religion, divine expression of will was more important than divine personality.

Nyaya (analysis) Hindu philosophy of salvation achieved by true knowledge, logic, observation, and comparison.

Oaths of Strasbourg oaths of alliance sworn in 842 by Charles the Bald and Louis the German against Lothar I.

Oceania islands in the Pacific Ocean consisting of Australia, Melanesia, Indonesia, Polynesia, Micronesia and New Guinea.

Octavian (Gaius Julius Caesar Octavianus) (63 BC-AD 14) adopted son of Caesar, he defeated Caesar's murderers with the help of a triumvirate, taking power in the west. He defeated Antony at the battle of Actium in 31 BC. Granted extraordinary powers by the Senate to restore the Republic, he set them aside in 27 BC, but remained in power as princeps and, in fact, as the first Roman emperor. He restructured the empire, restored old norms and values, modernized Rome, and fostered a policy of peace.

Odo, St. (c. 879-944) second abbot of Cluny, he turned the monastery into a model community, abolishing simony and corruption. He sought to have the church share power in the empire with the secular rulers.

Odoacer (435-493) Herulian Germanic general; deposed last Roman emperor in 476, ending the Western Roman Empire; had himself proclaimed king of the first Germanic realm in Italy.

Odysseus Greek hero of the Trojan War.

Odyssey Greek epic poem ascribed to Homer, describing the journey of the Trojan War hero Odysseus to his home in Ithaca.

Offa king of Mercia (757-796). He controlled the Anglo-Saxon kingdoms in southern England, fostering English unification.

Ogodai Mongolian ruler (1229-1246); instructed his hordes to conquer Korea and the south of China and to raid Europe; after his death the Dnepr River became the far western border; assimilation of Mongols with the people they had overcome first started under his rule, and this led to the emergence of cultural differences.

oinochoe wine pitcher.

Old Babylonian era period in the history of Mesopotamia from ca. 1800 to 1600 BC, when the Amorite (Semitic) culture was dominant in southern Mesopotamia. Babylon was its economic, political, and cultural center.

Old Hittite kingdom period in Hittite history from c.1700 to 1500 BC in which the kingdom was established in Asia Minor.

Old Kingdom period period in Egyptian history from ca. 2650 to 2150 BC, also called the Pyramid period for the large number of pyramids built. The organization of manpower to build these illustrates the power of Egypt's central administration.

oligarchy government by a small elite.

Oligopithecus after the Greek *oligos* (small) and *pithekos* (ape); important findings of small ape fossils found in the Fayum depression in Egypt.

Olmec pre-Columbian people in Central America on the Caribbean coast (1200BC-AD 300), famous for its gigantic stone sculptures of heads and delicate jade objects; jaguar figure appears to have played an important role in Olmec religion.

Omar or Umar I second caliph (634-644) in Mecca; defeated Byzantines in Syria, Persians in Mesopotamia; conquered Egypt (641); introduced financial reforms of zakat (tax for the poor) and capitation (head tax).

oppida small fortified cities ruled by Latini aristocracy; grew from Latin hill towns during political and cultural domination by the Etruscans.

Optimates the conservative Senate party in the second and first centuries BC; opponents of the people's party (Populares), which favored reform.

oracle bone script Chinese script originally used in the late Shang period (c.1250-1050 BC) on oracle bones. It consisted of abstract symbols indicating words or portions of words. From these Shang characters current Chinese ideograms evolved.

oracle bones in China large bones that crack and split when heated, from which oracles were divined. During the Shang period the questions and oracular answers were written or engraved in characters on the bones.

orchestra semicircular floor in theaters where actors originally performed and later, the chorus danced and sang.

Orientalizing period part of the Archaic period dating from about 750 to 650 BC when the Greek world was strongly influenced by the East with regard to religion, architecture, pottery, and the use of bronze and iron.

Origen (c.185-254) Alexandrian Christian theologian.

Orléans city in the French duchy of Berry on the side of Charles VII and beleaguered by the English between 1427 and 1429; in 1429, the city was freed by a French army led by Joan of Arc.

Ormuz New Persian king (302-309); protected the poor against abuse of power by special protective courts; died in battle against the Bedouin.

Osiris Egyptian god of fertility and ruler of the Kingdom of the Dead. In the First Interregnum the cult of Osiris became popular. The Egyptians could reach the hereafter via Osiris; hence, the pharaoh became less important as a protector.

Osman Turks Turks under the dynasty of the Osmans who established the Osman (Ottoman) Empire in 1300 in Asia Minor (1300-1922); they fought the Serbs, Mongols, Christians, and Persians and conquered parts of Europe, the Balkans, and the Middle East.

Ostia port on the mouth of the Tiber River. Expanded under Emperor Claudius, Ostia became a international port and a transit harbor for the grain supplies to Rome.

ostracism banishment; Greek citizens could vote to banish a political leader for ten years in order to prevent tyranny.

Ostrogoths Germanic tribe from Ukraine, subjected by

the Huns; migrated to Hungary in the fifth century; established a kingdom in Italy under Theodoric (493); defeated under Totila (552).

Othman (Uthman I ibn Affan) Muhammad's son-in-law; third calpih (644-656)); founded Umayyad dynasty, appointing his clan members to important positions.

Otto I the Great (912-973) Holy Roman emperor (962-973), king of Germany (936-973). The son of German king Henry I, he became ruler of Italy by marrying Adelaide, the widowed queen of Lombardy. He deposed Pope John XII and had Leo VIII elected in 963.

Otto IV of Brunswick emperor of the German Empire (1198-1214); in 1214, Otto concluded an alliance with John Lackland, king of England, to jointly attack Philip Augustus of France, who supported the pretenders to the German throne; defeated at battle of Bouvines in 1214.

outer planets planets with an orbit outside Earth's, specifically Mars, Jupiter, Saturn, Uranus, Neptune, and Pluto.

Outremer name given to the Christian kingdoms in Palestine after the First Crusade.

Ovid (Publius Ovidius Naso) (43 BC-AD 18) Roman poet who wrote *Metamorphoses*; banished by Emperor Augustus in part because of his work.

Pachacuti-Inca (Cusi Yupanqui) king of Incas (1438-1471); drove out the raiding Chancas and conquered their territory to the north of Cuzco.

Pachomius (c.290-346) Christian hermit; founded monastic commune in Egypt.

Pala dynasty Buddhist dynasty controlling an empire from the eighth to the twelfth centuries in the Bengal region in northeastern India; Senas then took power, but they in turn were subjected by the Muslims.

Palatine oldest inhabited hill in Rome, home of the imperial palaces of Augustus, Tiberius, Domitian, and Septimius Severus. At the foot of the Palatine was the Forum Romanum.

Paleozoic period from about 600 million to 248 million years ago, subdivided into various periods. Characterized by the evolution of vertebrate animals, including amphibians, the first animals to live on land.

Palestine (named by the Greeks after Philistine) land along the Mediterranean Sea and to the Arabian desert, inhabited by Semitic tribes (Amorites, Canaanites, Israelites) as well as Hittites and Philistines. Beginning with Israelite kings, much of the area was politically united by c.1000 BC.

Pallas Athena Greek virginal goddess of wisdom, art and science, and handiwork, born from the head of Zeus.

Pallavas dynasty in southeast India from 500 to 800 that controlled the Hindu Tamils from the Dravida civilization; mostly followers of Buddhism and Brahmanism.

Panathenaea great festival in Athens for Pallas Athena, goddess of the city, involving a procession to the Acropolis, where sports, music, and poetry competitions were held.

panem et circenses (bread and circuses) term first used by Juvenal referring to the upperclass conviction that this was all the common people needed to remain content. Grain was distributed to the proletariat and the games were funded by the state.

Pantheon a round temple dedicated to all the gods of the empire. Originally built by Agrippa on the Campus Martius, it was destroyed several times and later rebuilt by Domitian, Hadrian, and Septimius Severus. Later, it was used as a Christian church.

paper writing material invented by Tsai-lun in AD 105, made from rags and plant fiber; was introduced to the Arab world in the eighth century by Chinese prisoners of

war; from there it spread to other parts of Europe; like silk, paper became an important export product.

papyrus writing material made by crisscrossing strips of papyrus reeds. These were shaped into rolls to be written on in ink.

paqana male descendants of deceased Sapa Inca who controlled the ayllu; according to ayllu tradition the authority and possessions of a deceased king would remain his; his worship would ensure the ayllu's fate after the Sapa's death.

parlementum civitatis town parliament or meeting of the people in free cities, where citizens could express their complaints and lodge requests; parliament exercised no influence on the town council because a few wealthy families were in power.

Parmenides fifth-century BC philosopher from Elea whose teachings contradicted the Ionian natural philosophy. The origin of the cosmos through the contraction of a protoplasm and movement and change implied a vacuum, according to Parmenides. This was the "nonbeing" which could not exist. Only the unchangeable, absolute "being" existed. Origin and perishing were illusion.

Parthenon temple on the Athenian Acropolis dedicated to Pallas Athena, built between 447 and 438 BC.

Parthia kingdom founded about 250 B.C., located in today's Iran and Afghanistan.

Parthians Persian horsemen who gained their independence from the Seleucids c. 250 BC and settled in northern Persia; conquered extensive territory east of the Seleucid Empire; later fought the Romans.

patriarch title accorded the heads (bishops) of the five main sections (called sees) of the Christian church: Rome (in the West) and Alexandria, Antioch, Constantinople, and Jerusalem (in the East). Those in the East viewed the pope as the patriarch of Rome, gave him primacy of honor, but did not accept Rome's claims for supremacy in church matters.

patricians a small group of families who held all management and religious functions at the beginning of the Republic. Gradually, they had to give way to the lower plebeians, indispensable to the defense of Rome. From 287 BC, plebeian decisions were regarded as equal to patrician laws.

patrimonium Petri (Peter's estate) tracts of land in Italy acquired by the popes to pay for papal living expenses.

Paul, Saint (c. AD 3-62) Saul of Tarsus, Jewish scribe, later disciple of Jesus Christ; first Christian theologian, his letters are part of the New Testament.

Paulus, Lucius Aemilius (c. 229-c.160 BC) Roman general who defeated Macedonia in 168 BC.

Pausanias (d. 467 BC) Spartan general and regent for a Spartan king. In 479 BC, he was commander in chief of the Greeks at Plataea. He later conquered Byzantium and was condemned in 467 due to connections with the Persians.

pax Augusta the peace Augustus glorified in propaganda, illustrated by his altar to it, the *ara pacis*. In reality, he carried out conquests in Europe to the banks of the Danube.

Peace of Arras (1435) peace treaty between Charles VII and Philip the Good, under which Philip agreed to withdraw in exchange for the region of Burgundy; Charles was then able to concentrate on the English and slowly expel them from French lands.

Peace of Bretigny truce concluded in 1360 between Charles V the Wise of France and Edward III of England in which Edward agreed to renounce his claims to the French throne in exchange for one third of France. In 1367, Charles declared the peace invalid.

Peace of God informal code of honor between the

church and medieval sovereigns to protect the people against plundering and murder.

Peace of Stralsund (1370) agreement between the German Hanseatic League and Denmark in which the cities of the Hanseatic League were exempted from tolls; Danish tolls to enter the Baltic Sea were the cause of war.

Peasants' Crusade popular response to the First Crusade in 1096. Urged on by Peter the Hermit and led by Walter the Penniless.

Peisistratus (d. 528 BC) Athenian tyrant who assumed power first in 561 BC. He was driven away twice, but established his government in 546 BC.

Peking man (*Sinanthropus pekinensis*) hominid belonging to *Homo erectus,* discovered in China in the 1930s by Franz Weidenreich, Pierre Teilhard de Chardin, and others. This hominid species were hunters and used fire; lived some 400,000 to 200,000 years ago.

Pithecanthropus erectus upright anthropoid whose thighbone and crown were reported to be the missing link between ape and man; discovered in Java in 1891 by Eugene Dubois.

Pelagianism Christian doctrine of Pelagius; considered human corruption not inborn, denying original sin and the need for infant baptism; humans could attain salvation by their own efforts; well accepted in southern Italy and Sicily but declared heretical by Augustine and the Church.

Pelagius (AD 400) Roman-British monk who denied the doctrine of original sin and the need for infant baptism; preached Christian asceticism and morality.

pelikē type of amphora, a vase with handles.

Peloponnesian League military alliance of Peloponnesian city-states between the sixth and fourth centuries BC, dominated by Sparta. In the Peloponnesian War, some members revolted because Sparta threatened their independence.

Peloponnesian War (431-404 BC) conflict of hegemony between Athens, generally allied with Ionians, and Sparta, allied with Dorians. The direct cause was a conflict about Corcyra. The army of Sparta annually destroyed Attica while the Athenian fleet plundered the Peloponnesian coasts. Sparta finally triumphed over Athens with the help of the Persians.

pentakosiomedimnoi (five hundred medimners) highest social class in Athens, introduced by Solon and based on annual income expressed in terms of grain.

Pépin of Herstal (c. 635-c. 714) majordomo (mayor of the palace) of Austrasia. In 687, he defeated his Neustrasian counterpart and gained power over the united Frankish Empire.

Pépin the Short (c. 714-768) mayor of the palace of Austrasia (741-751) and king of the Franks (751-768), son of Charles Martel, and grandson of Pépin of Herstal. In 751,Pépin deposed Childeric, becoming the first Carolingian king. Crowned by Pope Stephen II (III) in 754, he defeated the Lombards in northern Italy and gave the pope their territories, including Ravenna. Called the Donation of Pépin, it was the basis for the Papal States.

peregrination (wandering) practice by Irish monks of wandering the countryside and spreading Christianity, adopted by the Anglo-Saxon Church (notably the monks Willibrord and Boniface).

Periander (sixth century BC) son of Cypselus and tyrant of Corinth. He promoted the prosperity of Corinth by encouraging trade. According to Herodotus, his tyranny degenerated into a reign of terror.

Pericles (495-429 BC) Athenian leader of popular party and head of state (460-429 BC); led Athens to its greatest political, cultural, and architectural achievements.

Period of Warring States *See* Warring States period.

perioikoi (neighbors) original inhabitants living as freemen on the outskirts of the polis Sparta.

Persephone daughter of Demeter, the goddess of agriculture; her recurring abduction by Hades and return from the underworld symbolize growth and decay of life.

Persepolis important center of the Persian kingdom of the Achaemenids. From the reign of Darius it also was a major royal citadel with multicolumned halls. Persepolis was destroyed by Alexander the Great.

Perseus (c. 212-c. 166 BC) king of Macedonia; son and successor of Philip V; defeated by Rome in the Third (and final) Macedonian War (171-167 BC).

Persia ancient home of several tribes and great civilizations. In c.330 BC the Achaemenid Persian Empire was conquered by Alexander the Great.

Persian Wars wars between the Greek poleis and the Persians, instigated by the Greeks. The formal reason for the first war (492-490 BC) was the Greek support for the Ionian Rebellion. The second war (480-479 BC) marked the end of Persian power in the Aegean Sea.

Persians Indo-Iranian peoples who settled on the Persian plateau during the second millennium BC. They lived as a loose federation of tribes led by the Medes, against whom they rebelled in 558 BC. They then founded a large ancient world empire that was conquered by Alexander the Great around 330.

Petén region in Central America (Guatemala) where the Mayas lived in city-states in the Preclassical time (200 BC-AD 300); empire collapsed around 300, probably sparked by conflicts among the ruling classes; Mayas relocated to the Yucatán region.

phalanx battle array used by Greek and Macedonian infantry, consisting of eight rows of heavily armed soldiers. Thebans introduced the diagonal phalanx, with more rows on one side.

pharaoh Egyptian king portrayed as the incarnation of the falcon god, creator of the world. He was legislator, military general, and religious leader, and protected the Maat. Later he was considered the son of Re and incarnation of Horus. After his death he was deified.

Pharisees orthodox Jews, organized in the second century BC as the Hasidim; rigidly observed the written law but also accepted the validity of the oral law that had developed as scholars strove to interpret tradition.

Philip the Good duke of Burgundy (1419-1467); asked for English aid in his fight against the Armagnacs; finally acquired Burgundy and Flanders upon the Peace of Arras and annexed Holland, Brabant, Limburg, Namur, and Luxembourg.

Philip II (382-336 BC) king of Macedonia (359-336 BC); reorganized the army, conquered surrounding regions, and became involved in Greek politics. In 338 BC, he defeated the allied Athens and Thebes.

Philip II Augustus king of France (1180-1223); annexed the French territories that had been apportioned to the English king in 1152; expanded his powers by instituting a nonfeudal government system and forged the French kingdom into a powerful unity.

Philip IV the Fair king of France (1285-1314); his wars against England and Flanders caused a financial crisis; he confiscated the property of the Knights Templar, the Lombardian bankers, and the Jews, whom he expelled from his kingdom; he ended the secular power of the pope.

Philip VI Valois king of France (1328-1350); seized the French territories of Edward III, after which the latter proclaimed himself king of France; Hundred Years' War erupted not long after.

Philippics Demosthenes's orations against Philip of Macedonia in the fourth century BC.

Philistines Indo-European maritime people who settled in coastal Canaan at the end of the thirteenth century BC. They drove out the Israelites and Canaanites from the coastal areas, forcing the Israelite tribes to organize centrally. King David of Israel and Judah ended their expansion.

Philo Hebreus (c.25 BC-AD 45) Jewish scholar from Alexandria; contended Greek philosophers derived ideas from Jewish sources.

Phoenicia country north of Israel and the Palestinian areas (modern Lebanon) consisting of mountains and a narrow coastal strip. It was inhabited by local groups, mainly Canaanites. After Egyptian rule (c.1500-1350 BC) and Hittite rule (c.1350-1200 BC), Phoenicia became independent around 1000 BC. The Phoenician forests were used for shipbuilding and timber export.

Phoenician literature surviving Phoenician texts consist mainly of travel logs, ship journals, and manuals for sailing. They contain much information about navigation, the sea, and coastal areas. Much of the information was secret because the Phoenicians did not want to reveal their sources of income.

Phoenician trade settlements trade settlements founded by the Phoenician cities in strategic locations along the Mediterranean coast, such as Carthage, Marseilles, and Cádiz. They sometimes evolved into cities and had no colonial ties with the mother city.

Phoenician voyages Phoenician maritime voyages of discovery and colonization during the first half of the first millennium BC. They explored the West African coast, discovering native tribes and animals, including gorillas.

Phoenicians Semitic tribes in coastal Levant since c.1300 BC. They inhabited independent city-states and established trading partners throughout the Mediterranean, in Africa, and the Near East. Around 1000 BC they became the most important navigators in the Mediterranean.

phylae ten divisions of the Athenian citizenry chosen as part of the 510 BC reforms of Cleisthenes. The ten phylae were each drawn from one urban, one coastal, and one rural district.

Picts ancient people of Great Britain, driven into Scotland by Romans and Britons.

Pindar (520-440 BC) Greek lyricist from Thebes.

pipiltin Aztec nobility comprising political advisors, governors, priests, and military leaders who supported the Tlatoani.

plague disease of humans and rats spread by parasitic insects, usually fleas, biting humans when their rat hosts died; buboes (egg-sized swellings) formed in lymph nodes of victims; also spread by infection and contact; final septicemic phase caused dark purple skin color, which led to name Black Death; killed a third of Europe's population in the fourteenth century.

planet any celestial body revolving around a star.

planetes (wanderer) planets; name given by the ancient Greeks to the celestial bodies they saw "wandering" among the fixed stars.

planetesimals small heavenly bodies created from the coalescence of dust particles remaining after star formation; planets are formed through their collision.

planetoids planetesimals that have not formed into planets.

Plataea city in Boeotia where the Persians were defeated by the Greeks in the Second Persian War in 479 BC.

Plato (c. 429-347 BC) Athenian philosopher and disciple of Socrates; wrote philosophical dialogues in which he had Socrates express his own theories.

plebeian member of the ancient Roman lower class; originally, the masses of Rome had no influence but were put on the same level as the patricians in 287 BC. Rich plebeians shared power with patricians beginning in the fourth century BC.

Pleistocene era in the Quaternary during which the ice ages occurred; dated from 1.8 million to 10,000 years ago.

pluvials climate changes in northern Africa and the Middle East characterized by greater quantities of precipitation. These are associated with the growth of ice caps on the northern hemisphere during the ice ages. The periods between pluvials are called interpluvials.

Pnyx hill in Athens where the tribal meeting, called the *ecclesia*, convened after the end of the sixth century BC. The hill was large enough to accommodate around 6,000 citizens.

pochtecas a special class of traders in Aztec society who enjoyed a higher status, due to their economic importance and spying capacities in enemy territory.

podesta dictator who ruled Italian cities as an absolute ruler representing the interests of the aristocracy; usually appointed at the request of cities that were divided by the disputes between aristocrats.

Poitiers city in central France where Edward the Black Prince of England destroyed the French army in 1356 with an English army of archers and lancers; John the Good, the French king, was taken prisoner.

polis (city) independent Greek city-state (plural: *poleis*).

pollen method dating method based upon the identification of pollen grains; plant species correspond to specific climatic changes.

Polycarpus of Smyrna earliest recorded Christian martyr, burned to death c.AD 156.

Polynesia a group of islands named by Europeans in Oceania east of Melanesia, including Hawaii, Samoa, Tahiti, the Society Islands, New Zealand, and Easter Island. The inhabitants were able navigators.

Polynesian epics heroic epics handed down orally that described voyages, discoveries, wars, and revenge. They illustrate Polynesian creation myths, culture heroes, and colonization movements, and the far-advanced Polynesian art of navigation. To these were added supernatural phenomena and lyrical hymns.

Pomerium sacred precinct of Rome; burial of the dead took place outside it.

Pompeii a southern Italian city which was covered by ash and lava when Mt. Vesuvius erupted in AD 79. Never rebuilt, the city was excavated beginning in 1860. It offers a picture of Roman daily life.

Pompey (Gaius Pompeius Magnus) (106-48 BC) Roman general and statesman; set up the First Triumvirate with Caesar and Crassus in 60 BC.

pontifex maximus head of the college of priests responsible for the state religion. During the Principate, the emperor was also *pontifex maximus*.

Pontius Pilate (Pilatus) procurator of the province of Judaea AD 26-36 when Jesus was crucified.

pope bishop and patriarch of Rome, head of the Roman Catholic Church.

Popul Vuh oral Maya version of the myth of the creation of the world; it was recorded in writing in the sixteenth century, depicting the nobility as semigods; in order to enhance their position of power.

Portugal the region given to Henry of Burgundy and his wife, Theresa, in 1093 by King Alfonso I of Castile. Their son Alfonso Henriques rebelled against Theresa in 1128 and was granted the throne as Alfonso I by the dominant Portuguese nobility in 1143. The kingdom gained papal recognition in 1179.

Poseidon god of the sea, earthquakes, and volcanic phenomena, creator of the horse, brother of Zeus.

praefectus urbi (Latin: prefect of the city) the official assigned by the Byzantine emperor to head the administration of Rome.

praetor Roman official charged with jurisprudence for one year; competent to lead the army; originally appointed as provincial governor.

Praetorian Guard imperial bodyguard.

Prajnaparamita Sutra Mahayana Buddhist addition to the *Theravada* text, the *Tripitaka*.

pratityasamutpada (Sanskrit: dependent origin) Hindu doctrine; each link in chain of existence is determined by previous one and becomes prerequisite for next.

pre-Columbian age period preceding the discovery of America in 1492 and the Spanish and Portuguese colonization; Latin America was inhabited by different pre-Columbian civilizations, including the Mayas, Aztecs, and Incas; there is evidence for the first migrations at least 17,000 years ago, and the first settlements date from around 10,000 BC.

pre-Columbian civilization a collective name for the multitude of civilizations living in Central and South America prior to the fifteenth-century invasions from European countries; primary among them are the Olmec, Maya, Teotihuacán, Inca, and Aztec.

predestination concept that everything that happens is foreordained by God, including the soul's salvation or damnation.

prehistory period of human history before the development of writing; knowledge of this time is based on archaeological sources and scientific dating methods.

primate any member of the most highly developed order of mammals, including humans, apes, monkeys, and lemurs.

Prince of Princes title of Baghdad official (not caliph) ruling Shiite-dominated Arab Empire (945-1050); Seljuks restored the caliphate.

princeps "first citizen," originally the name for senators holding most power; adopted as an imperial title.

printing first invented during the Tang dynasty, when texts were printed on paper using loose wooden letters; this encouraged the distribution of texts and made possible the first paper money notes.

private traders African trading class that developed under the influence of foreign trading posts established from the seventh century AD; private traders reorganized regional and local trade networks and laid the foundations for the Sudan kingdoms.

proconsul Roman official with consular authority who commanded an army and frequently served as governor of a senatorial province.

proletariat lowest class in ancient Roman society; people who did not own property.

prophets Israelite wise men who transmitted Yahweh's messages and commandments and predicted the future, as recorded in the Old Testament. They warned against social injustice and worshiping gods other than Yahweh. Only collective piety might avert the people's destruction, they taught.

propraetor former Roman praetor sent to govern a province.

proscription list system of terror introduced by Sulla (82-78 BC); opponents of his senate party were listed for public persecution. They were exiled or murdered and their possessions were confiscated.

prosimians half-apes that developed strongly over the

Oligocene epoch (about 40 million years ago).

protohistory period in the history of humans that lies between prehistory and history; knowledge of this period is based upon archaeological materials and the few historical resources left by other peoples who already used writing.

Protruding-foot beaker culture (single-grave culture) Neolithic culture around 2500 BC in northern Europe, named after its typical earthenware forms.

provincia (provinces) territory conquered by Rome outside of Italy; governed and often exploited by (pro)consuls or (pro)praetors. The first provinces were Corsica, Sardinia, and portions of Sicily won from Carthage.

Prusias II king of Bithynia (192-148 BC).

prytanes the fifty *boulē* (or Council of 500) members from one *phylae* who formed the daily administration of Athens for one-month periods.

Ptolemy (c. AD 100-c.170) astronomer and mathematician of Alexandria; dominated scientific thought until sixteenth century AD; used geometry to model an earth-centered universe described in the *Almagest*, originally written in Greek. His works include *Optics* , *Harmonica*, *Geography*, and *Tetrabiblos* (on astrology).

Ptolemy I. *See* Ptolemy I Soter

Ptolemy I Soter (preserver) (c. 367-285 BC) king of Egypt (323-285 BC), founder of the Ptolemic dynasty; a general of Alexander and one of the diadochs who succeeded him; proclaimed himself king of independent Egypt in 305 BC, expanding it to Palestine and Cyrenaica. His dynasty ruled Egypt until the arrival of the Romans (31 BC).

Ptolemy II Ptolemy Philadelphus (brotherly); king of Egypt (285-246 BC); son of Ptolemy I.

Ptolemy V Epiphanes (Illustrious) (c.210-181 BC) king of Egypt (205-181 BC).

publicani (publicans) Roman tax collectors.

Punic War, First (264-241 BC) war between Rome and Carthage for supremacy in the western Mediterranean. Rome adopted seafaring armies to defeat the Carthaginian power at sea. By introducing grappling, they defeated the Carthaginians. Carthage then ceded Sicily.

Punic War, Second (218-201 BC); between Rome and Carthage (under Hannibal) for supremacy in the western Mediterranean.

Punic War, Third (150-146 BC) between Rome and Carthage for supremacy in the Mediterranean; the Romans destroyed Carthage in 146 BC.

Puranas (ancient stories) extensive Hindu texts composed between the first centuries AD and the Middle Ages.

Pylos Mycenaean settlement on the Peloponnisos where a palace fortress was built after 1450 BC. It was not walled, but was probably protected by fortresses along the coast. Pylos was destroyed around 1200. Many Linear B clay tablets were found here.

pyramid an architectural structure often of stone, having a rectangular base and four triangular sides; used as the foundation for temples and priest accommodations by many pre-Columbian societies, especially the Maya, Teotihuacán, and the Aztec.

pyramids Egyptian royal tombs consisting of a stone pyramid which symbolized the original mountain of the creation. An extensive complex of buildings was also part of it. The first pyramid was a step pyramid. The height of pyramid building took place in the fourth dynasty (2600-2460 BC) when the pyramids became larger and had smoother surfaces.

Pyrrhus (318-272 BC) king of Epirus (319-272 BC);

supported Tarentum against the Romans; defeated the Romans albeit with great losses on his side (280-279 BC), leading to the phrase *Pyrrhic victory*.

Pythagoras (ca. 582-ca. 500 BC) Greek philosopher and mathematician, whose religious, political, and philosophical doctrines strongly influenced Plato. His work is known only from the philosophic sect he established in Crotone, the movement called Pythagoreanism, which believed in immortality and a concept of numerical mystery. It adopted an ascetic style of living.

Pythia priestess of the oracle at Delphi. She made her oracular utterances while in a trance; priests translated them into understandable language.

Qin state in western China which existed from 256 to 206 BC. It gradually conquered the Zhou states and politically unified all of northern China in 221. A central government was established, and the feudal system was exchanged for direct government by officials.

quaestor originally, a Roman official who judged certain criminal cases; later, a civil servant in charge of finances. The quaestorship was the beginning of a political career.

quasar (quasi-stellar object) a name for galaxies located far away that, viewed from the surface, look like stars and have a bright nucleus.

Quaternary period in the Cenozoic from about 1.5 million years ago to the present.

quipu pieces of knotted string used for administrative purposes in the Inca Empire; *quipucamayoc*, officials who knew how to arrange the knots, were in charge of such matters as recording public works and the distribution of excess food.

rabbi (Hebrew: my master) ordained teacher of Jewish law; authorized to perform marriages and decide questions of ritual and law.

radio-astronomy study of the radio rays of celestial bodies.

Rajputas warrior tribe in northwest India, with clans dominated by a military nobility; they are assumed to have arrived from the north as a marauding people; after 975 the empire disintegrated and was divided into states, to be finally defeated by the Muslims.

Ramayana short Hindu epic concerning the adventures of Rama, king of Ayodha, also considered an avatar of Vishnut, and a Hindu deity.

Ramesside kings period in Egyptian history from 1306 to 1070 BC named after the nineteenth and twentieth dynasties when the name of most pharaohs was Ramses.

Ramses II pharaoh from 1290 to 1224 BC. Among his numerous building projects were his own temple, the Ramesseum, and the expansion of the residence in Avaris.

Rashi eleventh-century Jewish rabbi; lived in Troyes, France; wrote commentaries on the Bible and the Talmud still in use today.

Ravenna Italian seaport conquered by Theodoric (493); recaptured by the Byzantines (540); made Byzantine center in Italy; conquered by Lombards.

Raymond of Toulouse (1042-1105) a southern French nobleman and one of the leaders in the First Crusade.

Re (or Ra) Egyptian sun god. His most important temple stood in Heliopolis. The pharaoh was considered his son and ascended to his heavenly empire after death. Re was later associated with Amon.

Reconquista (Spanish: reconquest) Christian reconquering of occupied Spain from the Muslims (tenth to thirteenth centuries).

Red Eyebrows secret Chinese fellowship that established its authority in AD 8 under Wang Man and planned to introduce land reforms; their defeat by the Han fourteen

years later ended in anarchy, which eventually brought down the Han dynasty.

Remus legendary founder of Rome. *See also* Romulus.

renovatio imperii (Latin: imperial renovation) Justinian's plan to restore Roman prestige and return the western provinces to Byzantine rule. He reconquered the south coast of Spain, Italy, and North Africa.

res publica (public thing) republic; Roman state (c. 509-31 BC) governed by two annually elected consuls; citizens exercised influence through popular assemblies and the Senate.

rhetors orator-politicians in Athens. With their rhetorical gifts, they had great influence on Athenian politics.

Rhine River in Germany and the Netherlands, this formed the northern border of the Roman Empire from the time of Augustus on.

Richard I the Lion Heart king of England (1189-1199); participated in the Third Crusade and warred against Philip II Augustus, who undermined Richard's position by supporting his brother John Lackland.

Rig-Veda earliest sacred document of the Aryans, composed around 1200 BC, which consists of hymns to the gods and incantations of various poets. It mentions thirty-three gods.

Roas or Rugilas (died c. 433) Hun king.

Robert Guiscard (1015-1085) Norman conqueror of Calabria and Apulia in southern Italy. A vassal of the pope, he was appointed duke. His brother Roger I conquered Sicily.

Roger I (c. 1031-1101) Norman conqueror of Sicily, he took from 1061 to 1091 to win the region from the Byzantines.

Roger II (1095-1154) first king of Sicily (1130-1154). Second son of Roger I, he pieced together a kingdom from inherited titles as count of Sicily (1103) and duke of Apulia (by 1129). Claiming sovereignty in 1130 over the southern Italian regions of Calabria, Capua, and Naples, he established a realm that would last seven centuries. He encouraged religious diversity and peace.

Roman Catholic Church term now used for the Christian church governed by bishops and the pope in Rome; became the center of western Christianity in the Middle Ages.

Roman king designation of the emperor of the German or Holy Roman Empire before he was crowned emperor.

Romance languages any of the languages derived from vernacular or Low Latin; originating in the Germanic kingdoms, they developed into separate languages; include French, Spanish, Italian, Portuguese, Catalan, Provençal, and Romanian.

Romanus IV Diogenes Byzantine emperor (1068-1071), betrayed by his own officers at the Battle of Manzikert in 1071, he was defeated and taken prisoner by the Seljuks.

Rome capital of the Roman Empire, located on the Tiber River in Latium; according to legend, founded in 753 BC by Romulus and Remus.

Romulus legendary founder of Rome. *See also* Remus.

Romulus Augustulus last Western Roman emperor; deposed in 476.

Roncaglia town in Italy and site of a diet or council in 1158 during which Frederick I Barbarossa demanded all royal privileges, such as levying of tolls, coinage, and jurisdiction, which resulted in a major rebellion by the nobility and the cities.

routiers mercenaries during the Hundred Years' War who were dismissed after the Peace of Bretigny and proceeded to raid the countryside; Bertrand du Guesclin assembled

them and after 1370 they conducted a successful guerilla war against the English in southern France.

Roxana (?-c. 311 BC) daughter of Oxyartes of Sogdiana; a Persian wife of Alexander the Great.

Royal Zhou central authority during the Zhou dynasty to which all feudal states were initially subject. Gradually the feudal states grew and became more independent, eventually making the king of Zhou a merely symbolic head of these states.

Rudolf of Hapsburg emperor of the German Empire (1273-1291); elected by the elective monarchs; increased his power by defeating the Bohemian king Ottokar and by annexing his territories in Austria, Carinthia, and Styria.

Sabbath seventh day of the week and day of rest according to the Ten Commandments of the Israelites. The Sabbath lasts from Friday night to Saturday night. The Sabbath was originally a Mesopotamian institution and was probably given a different religious significance by the Israelites.

Sadducees from the name Zadok, Old Testament priest under Kings David and Solomon (2 Samuel 15:24-29); aristocratic school of religious thought and political party in the first century BC in the Jewish state; accepted only the written Torah as binding law; did not believe in personal immortality or the existence of spirits.

Saguntum Spanish city south of the Ebro River; its request for Roman assistance was the direct cause of the Second Punic War.

Sahara desert region between North Africa and Sudan; the many commercial routes that ran through the region were controlled between 1000 and 1600 by Sudan kingdoms; introduction of the camel as a beast of burden encouraged the development of trade and the authority of the Sudan states.

saint individual recognized by the Christian Church as having lived or died in an exemplary manner, distinguished by piety; venerated by some Christians and considered able to intercede for faithful and effect miracles; each saint has fixed day of commemoration.

salah (Arabic: ritual prayer) Islamic prayer performed, facing Mecca, five times daily.

Salamis island on the west coast of Attica where the Persian fleet, under Xerxes, was defeated by the Greeks in 480 BC.

Salic Law rule in some noble families of Europe forbidding the succession of females or descendants through the female line to titles or offices.

Samaritans inhabitants of Samaria in central Palestine; came into conflict with the Jews returning from the Babylonian captivity starting in 536 BC.

Samnites mountain people of the southern Apennines; fought Rome and the Latin League (343-341 BC); later supported Rome against the league. After another two wars (326-304 BC, 298-290 BC), they were made allies of Rome.

samsara (Sanskrit) cycle of birth, death, and rebirth, taken from the *Upanishads*.

Samson one of the judges of the Bible. According to biblical stories, Samson possessed enormous power, the source of which was his long hair. He successfully fought the Philistines until he was betrayed by a Philistine woman, Delilah.

sangha (Sanskrit) community of Buddhist mendicant monks, founded by Buddha's first disciples, who achieve own nirvana through asceticism and teach the *dharma*.

Sanhedrin the Jewish state council of 71 priests and religious leaders responsible for all religious and civil functions; presided over by the high priest; abolished with the destruction of Jerusalem in AD 70.

Sankhya (count) school of Hindu philosophy based on dualism, the theory that reality is divided into matter (*prakrit*) and the soul or spirit (*purusha*).

Sapa Inca king of Incas, *Inca* being the title for Inca rulers; every ruler founded a new ayllu, for which he needed to conquer new territory and riches; he was worshiped after his death and continued his rule by way of the paqana.

Sappho (ca. 600 BC) poetess from Lésvos who ran a school for girls from the aristocracy. Her verses to them are generally regarded as erotic.

Saracens Like *Moors*, a pejorative term for Arab Muslims, in medieval texts. They set up the caliphate of Córdoba and were seen by the Christians as a continuous threat.

Sarah biblical first wife of Isaac.

sarcophagi Egyptian wooden coffins in which the dead were conserved, swathed in linen and buried. Thus, the deceased could join Osiris. The coffin was decorated with magical sayings to simplify access to the Kingdom of the Dead.

Sargon I founder and king of the Akkadian Empire from ca. 2340 to 2290 BC. Sargon based his power on the state monopoly in raw materials, and he was the largest landowner.

Sargon II king of the New Assyrian Kingdom from 722 to 705 BC. He subjugated the Syrian and Phoenician coastal cities, defeated the Hurrians from Urartu, and defeated the Aramaean king Merodachbaladan who had conquered Babylon. He then became the new king of Babylon.

Sassanids dynasty of kings (226-651); captured Mesopotamia and East Syria from the Byzantines (fourth century); conquered Jerusalem (614); defeated by Alexius (628).

satellite anything, man-made or natural, that is in orbit around a central body, including Earth.

satrap governor of a Persian Empire satrapy. Satraps largely continued the original government and managed the collection of taxes, road maintenance, and security. They were supervised by royal secretaries. Army commanders in satrapies were controlled by the Persian king. When the empire declined, their power increased.

satrapies autonomous provinces governed by the satraps in the ancient Persian Empire that were formed from conquered kingdoms. They largely retained their original government, but paid taxes to the empire and supplied troops in time of war.

Saturn god of agriculture; also worshipped by the Romans as the bringer of culture and affluence; identified with the Greek god Cronus.

satyr play Greek dramatic work with a heroic mythological theme like the tragedies, but with a humorous tone and a chorus of satyrs. It formed the last part of a tetralogy and was thus always performed after three tragedies.

Saul Israelite king, c.1025-1000 BC, who was the first to centrally govern the Israelite tribes in Canaan. His rule was not universally recognized. He fought the Philistines and died in battle against them.

Saxons ancient people of northern Germany; conquered parts of England in the fifth and sixth centuries.

Schism (1378-1417) division in the Church which occurred when the cardinals elected Clement VII as pope because they were dissatisfied with Urban VI; during this time there were two popes, one in Avignon and one in Rome; both were supported by competing secular rulers who expanded their influence in this manner.

Schliemann, Heinrich amateur archaeologist who conducted excavations after AD 1871 in Troy (Asia Minor) and near Mycenae after 1876. He considered the *Iliad*

and *Odyssey* by the eighth-century BC epic poet Homer as historically correct.

Scipio Africanus the Elder (Publius **Cornelius Scipio Africanus Maior**) (c. 234-183 BC) Roman general; hero of the Second Punic War against the Carthaginians; made commander of Roman forces in Spain (210 BC); consul (205 BC); defeated Hannibal and the Carthaginians at the Battle of Zama (North Africa) in 202 BC.

Scipio Africanus the Younger (Publius **Cornelius Scipio Aemilianus Africanus Numantinus**) (c. 185-129 BC) Roman general; adopted grandson of Scipio the Elder; military tribune to Spain (151 BC); commander in the Third Punic War; consul (147 BC) captured and destroyed Carthage (146 BC).

script of Easter Island type of script consisting of ideograms found on Easter Island on boards dating from c. AD 1500. It may be a type of stenography with key words representing long tales. It is possibly of non-Polynesian origin.

Scythians western Asian and Russian herdsmen from the eighth century BC, north of the Black Sea; nomadic horsemen, they plundered the Near East and eastern Europe.

Sea Peoples groups who threatened the coasts of the eastern Mediterranean, including the Nile Delta, during the time of the Ramesside kings. The Philistines were one of the Sea Peoples.

seal stones Minoan jewelry which served as a personal seal and amulet. They were decorated with geometric animal and human figures. After 1900 BC they also show hieroglyphic characters, the precursors of the Linear A script.

Second Crusade (1147-1149) authorized by the pope and preached by Bernard of Clairvaux in 1146, after the Turks had conquered Edessa and threatened Jerusalem. The Christians unsuccessfully besieged Damascus and returned home empty-handed.

Second Interregnum period in Egyptian history from ca. 1783 to 1550 BC when central power broke down due to the arrival of foreigners and foreign rulers in Lower Egypt, such as the Hyksos.

Second Palace period flowering era of Minoan civilization from 1700 to 1450 BC. During this time the palaces at Knossos, Phaistos, and Mallia were rebuilt. Intensive trade with the east, Egypt, the Aegean Islands, and the Greek mainland were maintained.

Seleucid Empire eastern portions of Alexander the Great's empire governed by descendants of Seleucus.

Seleucus I (355-280 BC) king of Babylon (312-280 BC); general of Alexander the Great; as one of the diadochs, gained power in Mesopotamia and areas east; expanded west to Syria and Asia Minor; founder of the Seleucid dynasty.

Selim I Osman sultan (1512-1520) who planned to conquer the Muslim empires in the east; he conquered the Persian Empire and Syria and attacked the Mamelukes in Egypt; he appointed himself caliph.

Seljuks Turkish clan converted to Islam in the tenth century; major dynasty in the Middle East over the eleventh and twelfth centuries. Under Sultan Togrul Beg, protector of the Sunni Muslim caliph of Baghdad, they established an empire in Persia between 1040 and 1055. Opposed by Shia Muslims and Christian Byzantines, Seljuks Alp Arslan and Malik Shah entered Syria, Palestine, and Anatolia. This and Alp Arslan's victory at the Battle of Manzikert (1071) was rationale for the First Crusade.

Semites people residing in northern and southern Mesopotamia. They spoke a language different from the Sumerians and were largely rural dwellers. After 2400 BC, they dominated and founded the Akkadian Empire. The Akkadian and Sumerian civilizations rapidly became one.

Senate the supreme council of ancient Rome; originally comprised of patricians only, it came to include the lower plebeians.

Senate of Rome commune of Rome elected in 1144, after a popular uprising; after a power struggle with the popes, the Senate ultimately was given authority in local matters.

Seneca, Lucius Annaeus (4 BC-AD 65) Latin writer and Stoic philosopher, Seneca was a teacher and advisor to Nero between 49 and 62. He retired in 62 and was ordered to commit suicide by Nero in 65. Noted for his tragedies; his philosophical works include *De Ira, De Clementia,* and *Epistulae Morales.*

Sennacherib king of the New Assyrian Kingdom from 705 to 681 BC. He defeated the Aramaean king Merodach-baladan in 703, who again took power in Babylon. When Babylon rebelled again under Merodach-baladan, Sennacherib razed Babylon to the ground in 689. His successor rebuilt the city.

Septuagint (Latin: 70) the 72 scholars who produced the Greek translation of Jewish religious writings; commissioned by Ptolemy Philadelphus; customarily abbreviated LXX, the roman numerals for seventy.

Serbs central European Christian people who formed a strong state in the fourteenth century and posed a threat to the Osman Empire; they were defeated by the Osmans in 1389; Serb Empire was finally subjected in the late fifteenth century.

serfs peasant farmers dependent on their feudal lords, they performed unpaid labor (*corvée*) and exchanged their personal freedom and part of their harvest for a small plot of land and protection.

Sesostris III pharaoh from ca. 1880 to 1840 BC. He ended the power and independence of the local administrators and established a centralized system of royal supervisors. He expanded Egypt with territory in Palestine.

sesterces monetary unit used by the Romans.

Seth Egyptian god of aggression, chaos, and darkness. He killed Osiris whose life was restored by the goddess Isis. He was associated with the Hyksos god Baal.

Sethi I pharaoh from ca. 1302 to 1290 BC. He conquered the Libyans and had temples built, including a temple in Abydos dedicated to the gods and the pharaoh. He built palaces in Memphis and near Avaris.

Sethnakht pharaoh from ca. 1184 to 1182 BC. He ended domestic unrest during the era of the Ramesside kings, caused by internecine fighting for succession of the throne. He became the founder of the twentieth dynasty.

Seventh Crusade (1248-1254) expedition led by Louis IX the Saint to Damietta in Egypt where the Muslims took him prisoner; his alliance with the Mongols against the Muslims failed.

Shah-nama (Book of Kings) Persian epic poem composed by Firdaws (c.1000).

Shakti (power) Hindu female creative and destroying energy of God; embodied as mother goddess and bride of Shiva; pre-Arian religion of the Mother Goddess had a resurgence during the fifth century AD when the feminine creative principle was worshiped with a great variety of rituals.

Shang culture Bronze Age culture in northern China from c.1800 to 1050 BC. The area under the influence of the Shang culture was not politically united, even though a Shang state existed within the territory of the Shang civilization from c.1500 on. The Shang were the first royal historical dynasty. They built cities and produced bronzeware and weapons.

Shang dynasty state governed by Shang kings from c.1600 to 1050 BC. Anyang was the last capital of Shang from the mid-thirteenth to the eleventh centuries BC. Shang kings moved their capitals for reasons not fully understood; the earlier capitals have not yet been archaeologically located. There was a centralized government and cities governed by autonomous vassals in the outlying areas. The populace were generally peasants who leased land from the rulers in the cities and from the king in exchange for labor.

Shankara (c.788-820) Indian philosopher who believed in monism or nondualism, called *Advaita Vedanta*. He insisted on the identity of atman (soul) and Brahman.

Shapur I king of Persia (241-272); expanded the New Persian Kingdom to the Himalayas; conquered Armenia; defeated the Byzantines in Antioch, taking many Syrian prisoners of war; Christianity spread throughout his realm.

Shapur II king of Persia (309-379); captured parts of eastern Syria and Mesopotamia from the Eastern Roman Empire; defeated Julian (363); brought the New Persian Kingdom to its height.

Sharia the religious and moral principles of Islam, considered law in Islamic states.

sheikh (Arabic: leader) leader of the Bedouin people; chosen to solve conflicts; did not have absolute power.

Shiites (from *shi'ah*, Arabic: partisan) supporters of Muhammad's son-in-law Ali; seceded from orthodox Islam after the murder of Hussein in 680; they venerate their leaders (imams) as divinely guided.

Shintoism indigenous Japanese religion based on the worship of forefathers; the sun goddess, Amaterasu, the first mother, was the most prominent of the goddesses; the emperor was revered as her leading priest and mythological son; Japan's national symbol became the rising sun.

Shiva Hindu god of destruction and reproduction; member of the Hindu trinity with Vishnu and Brahma; his worshipers are known as *shaivas*. He frequently manifests in his female aspects: Parvati and Kali.

shogun military Japanese commander, since 1192 the hereditary title of honor for the actual rulers of Japan; emperor was the virtual head of state; office continued to exist until 1868; shoguns belonged to the class of large landowners who exercised a feudal rule.

Shudras fourth and lowest rank in the caste system of India, consisting of servants and laborers whose chief duty was to serve the three higher classes. They were considered second-class citizens with few rights, and not allowed to read the *Vedas*. Some groups were avoided by other castes.

Sicilian expedition (415-413 BC) unsuccessful Athenian military campaign to gain hegemony in the Mediterranean.

Sicilian Vespers rebellion in 1282 by the Sicilians against the French rule of Charles of Anjou; during this uprising, all Frenchmen in Palermo were killed; Sicily offered the crown to Peter of Aragon.

Sicily Mediterranean island where Muslims established a center of Islamic culture in the ninth century; ousted by the Normans in 1061.

Sidon city on the Phoenician coast that was a powerful trading center c.1400-700 BC. Phoenicians were often called Sidonians.

silk fine material made from the threads spun by the silkworm; this product was only produced in China, and Persian traders made huge profits on the silk trade; in 522 silkworm eggs were shipped to Byzantium and the Persian monopoly was opened up.

simony the buying and selling of Christian ecclesiastical offices for money.

Six dynasties period in Chinese history (316-589) in which six dynasties fought for power; increased trade

resulted in cultural and economic bloom; there were many Buddhist influences.

Sixth Crusade (1228) expedition led by Frederick II, during which he obtained Jerusalem by negotiating with the Muslims; he was crowned king of Jerusalem; in 1244 the Muslims reconquered Jerusalem.

skēnē a raised platform, precursor of scenery.

Skeptics Greek school of philosophy founded around 300 BC; from *skeptikos* (inquiring); denied the possibility of real knowledge; considered inquiry to be always a process of doubting and judgments to have only relative value.

Slave Kings Muslim dynasty of the Delhi sultanate, an empire in northern India (1206-1526); its rulers tyrannized the Hindu population, leading to many revolts; their authority came under severe threat by Tamerlane's (Timurlenk) plundering raids in 1398 and they eventually lost it to the Great Moguls.

smiths specialized metalworkers.

socii (allies) Italian cities subjugated by the Romans and granted limited civil rights and local autonomy. In 91 BC they revolted, gaining full civil rights in 88 BC.

Socrates (c. 470-399 BC) the most famous Athenian philosopher, his ideas were passed down primarily through the writings of Plato. He stressed virtue as knowledge, believing that if one knew the good, one would perform it rather than evil. Noted for his logic and style of questioning dialogue, he was condemned to death because of his alleged undermining of the democratic order.

Sogas uji in the Yamato Empire who ruled Japan between 592 and 645 and who introduced Buddhism and related Chinese and Korean influences in technology, art, script, and philosophy; by introducing a Chinese hierarchy, Shotoku Taishi (573-622) planned to confine uji authority.

Soghai kingdom Sudan kingdom (1450-1540) centered around the capital of Gao, initially controlled by the Sunni dynasty and later, following a rebellion, by the Askia; Songhai controlled the Sahara's commercial routes, the salt mines, the tax system, and the commercial trade with northern Africa.

solar system any system of a central star with celestial bodies in orbit around it.

soldier-emperors Roman emperors drawn from the military, particularly between AD 235 and 270.

Solomon king of the united kingdom of Israel and Judah from c.965 to 925 BC and son of David. He brought peace and prosperity, promoted trade through foreign relations and infrastructure, and built the Temple of Yahweh in Jerusalem.

Solon sixth-century BC Athenian law reformer who abolished debt slavery in 594 BC; expanded participation of all free citizens in government.

Song of Roland an epic poem among the first literary works in many European languages about the death of Roland, one of Charlemagne's commanders.

sophia Greek word for wisdom, or knowledge and insight.

Sophists itinerant teachers of philosophy, politics, and rhetoric in fifth-century Greece; noted for skill in clever but fallacious argument and persuasive rhetoric; provided instruction for a fee; most considered truth and morality relative; first to systematize education; notable Sophists were Hippias of Elis, Protagoras, Gorgias, and Prodicus of Ceos.

Sophocles (496-406 BC) famous Greek tragedian. Only seven of his works have survived: *Ajax*, *Antigone*, *Electra*, *Oedipus Rex*, *Trachinea*, *Philoctetus*, and *Oedipus in Colonos*. (There is also a large part of a satyr play he wrote, called the *Sleuth Hounds*.) He introduced the third actor in drama.

soteriology Christian doctrine of saving through healing.

Spaniards South European people who colonized Africa and conquered pre-Columbian civilizations in South and Central America; spread European diseases such as smallpox and influenza, thereby weakening the Incas, Mayas, and Aztecs.

Sparta city-state in the southern Peloponnisos; isolated agricultural land power, resistant to external influences; oligarchy; fought Athens in the Peloponnesian War.

Spartacus (?-71 BC) Thracian gladiator who led a slave rebellion against Rome in 73 BC.

Spartan upbringing education based on the austere lifestyle of Sparta; individuals were of secondary importance to the state and its army.

spectral analysis analysis of the electromagnetic radiation of heavenly bodies through which one can determine their chemical compositions, movements, and temperatures; temperature also gives an indication of such factors as the size and longevity of stars, which are therefore classified on the basis of their spectra.

spectroscopy study of the spectra of starlight.

spectrum a band of colors ranging from red through orange, yellow, green, blue, and indigo to violet, created by the passage of white light through a prism, a rainbow is a visible spectrum; not all spectra can be seen.

speed of light speed with which a light particle travels through a vacuum; is also the greatest speed with which a signal can travel.

star gaseous heavenly body consisting mostly of hydrogen and helium, which emits energy caused by internal nuclear fusion processes; universe consists of huge numbers of stars, the nearest of which is the Sun.

Stephen Langton archbishop of Canterbury (1206-1228); a mediator between John Lackland and rebellious vassals; added rights of the Church and the people to the *Magna Carta*.

steward administrator in France having a fixed salary who was directly supervised by the king; in this manner, an administrative apparatus loyal to the king was created, increasing his power.

Stilicho, Flavius (359-408) Roman general who acted as regent and power behind the throne of Western Roman Emperor Flavius Honorious; ambassador to Persia (383); married niece of Emperor Theodosius I, with whom he was appointed joint guardian of Honorius; had his daughter married to Honorius (398); made consul (400); battled Visigoth King Alaric I (401, 403); defended Italy against Germanic/Celtic invaders led by Radagaisus (405); executed by order of Honorius under suspicion that he wanted to make his own son emperor.

stoa sheltered promenade.

Stoicism Greek school of philosophy founded by Zeno in 308 BC; holds that all happenings are the free result of divine will and that man should, therefore, calmly accept his fate, free of passion, joy, or grief. Self-control and austerity are emphasized. Stoicism was fashionable in the first century BC and during the first centuries of the Principate.

strategist one of ten commanders in chief in Athens, elected annually by the tribal meeting on the basis of his qualities.

Suche Bator (1893-1923) founder of the Mongolian Peoples Republic and leader of the Mongolian independence fighters during World War I; created a communist state in the Gobi Desert, the Mongolian ancestral land.

Sudan savanna region wedged between the Sahara and the tropical rain forests on the west coast; between 1000 and 1600 it saw the emergence of Islamic states that controlled the commercial routes through the Sahara and formed important trading posts for gold, salt, and trading with Asia and Europe.

Süleyman I sultan of the Osman Empire (1520-1566); conquered Rhodes and Belgrade and controlled the Mediterranean, frustrating trade; reorganized the state and tolerated different religions in the empire.

Sulla, Lucius Cornelius (Felix) (138-78 BC) Roman general and statesman; led the optimates (aristocratic party) during the civil war of 88-86 BC; praetor (93 BC); propraetor in Cilicia (92 BC); leader in the Social War (90-88 BC) against the northern Italian allies; consul (88 BC). In 83 BC, he defeated Marius's popular party, became dictator, instituted constitutional reform, restored senatorial power. He reorganized Rome's criminal procedures; resigned (79 BC).

sultan Islamic ruler of a Muslim state; rulers from the Osman state selected their successors from among their sons, who were then permitted to kill or lock up their brothers to prevent civil wars.

Sumerian language which died out as a spoken language around 2000 BC as the Amorites reinforced the Semitic cultural element in Mesopotamia. It continued as a religious language until the second century BC.

Sumerian Renaissance period in Mesopotamian history from ca. 2200 to ca. 1800 BC when the Sumerian civilization flowered again. Major centers of the Sumerian Renaissance were Lagash, Ur, Isin, and Larsa. Invasions by the Amorite nomads ended the renaissance.

Sumerians people who were settled in southern Mesopotamia (Sumer). They lived in independent city-states dominated by a temple economy. Lugalzaggesi tried to create a Sumerian unified state, but the rise of the Akkadian Empire (ca. 2340 BC) prevented this.

Sun star in the Milky Way galaxy and central point of our solar system. It was born 4.6 billion years ago and will expand, over a period of 6 billion more years, to become a red giant star. After that it will gradually blow off its outer layers, become a white dwarf star, and go out.

Sung dynasty dynasty that controlled China (960-1271); Sung Empire of the north (960-1125) was characterized by reinstatement of central authority, prosperity, and cultural bloom; were driven south by the Chin; Sung Empire of the south (1125-1271) quickly crumbled despite their use of gunpowder in weapons.

Sunnites (from *sunnah*, Arabic: custom or law) orthodox Muslims who follow the Sunna or body of Islamic custom.

Suppiluliumas Hittite king of the Hittite Empire from c.1380 to 1335 BC. He expanded the kingdom to its greatest size, conquered Syria with an organized army of charioteers, and fought the Mitanni.

Susa city in southwest Iran that was the winter residence of the Achaemenids in the ancient Persian Empire. Together with Babylon, they formed the administrative and political center of the empire.

svadharma (Sanskrit: personal dharma) Hindu concept that holds the individual is born to a certain social level and occupation and should work within it to the best of his ability in order to fulfill his dharma.

symposium drinking feast.

Syracuse Corinthian colony on Sicily; flourished culturally and commercially in the fifth century BC and dominated the other Sicilian colonies. Syracuse resisted Athenian siege and defeated Athens with the help of Sparta (415-413 BC).

Taika reforms period of reforms in Japan (645-702) introduced by Emperor Kotoku, who became absolute ruler and landownership was abolished; in 710 the construction of Nara was begun, which was to be Japan's capital until 794.

talent ancient unit of weight and money.

Talmud Jewish document, continuously revised, encompassing all legal and religious discussions which were handed down orally by the Jewish people until they were written down in 500; constituted the basis for the government of Jewish communities in Europe.

Tamerlane (Timurlenk) Mongolian ruler (1370-1405); around 1370 he subjected the Mongols in the west; conquered territory in Persia, India, Syria,and the Osman Empire and spread Islam; Mongolian power gradually disintegrated after his death.

Tang dynasty dynasty ruling China (618-907); arts and literature flowered during this period and Confucianism was reinstated; China became a world power through its conquests in Turkestan, Korea, Pomu, and Tibet; from the eighth century large landowners engaged in border conflicts and power struggles.

Tannenberg (1430) a place in Poland where the battle between the Teutonic Order and the Polish and Lithuanian armies took place; German knights were defeated.

tantras (Sanskrit: warp, as in weaving) esoteric Indian texts used in both Buddhist and Hindu Tantric sects; concern symbolism, ritual, and magic, presented as dialogue between Shiva and his consort Parvati.

Tantrism religious sects in Hinduism and Buddhism based on tantras; followers sought unity of matter and soul, male and female principles, through magic, ritual, and yoga.

Tao-te-Ching See *Daode Jing*.

Taoism *See* Daoism.

Tarentum major Greek colony in southern Italy. After a conflict with Thurii, which called for Roman aid, Tarentum hired Pyrrhus. He defeated the Romans in 280 and 279 BC. In 275 BC, Tarentum was again beleaguered. It surrendered in 272 BC.

Tarik (eighth century) African Berber Muslim general; occupied Gibraltar in 711; took Spain from the Visigoths; *Gibraltar* means Tarik's rock.

telestai Mycenaean officials under the wanax. They probably performed religious tasks and possibly were landowners.

Telestrion mystery temple, initiation building.

tell artificial mound made up of the waste layers and ruins of older cultures, upon which new cultures were established.

temple economy Sumerian administrative form where temples owned and operated most of the land and cattle. The highest power was in the hands of so-called ensis. Later the lugal became the highest commander.

Ten Commandments Israelites considered these ethical and religious provisions to be Yahweh's commandments after Yahweh was said to have given them to Moses on Mount Sinai in the desert. They were probably written down at a later time. The first commandment concerned monotheism.

Tenochtitlán (Mexico City) capital of the Aztec Empire founded around AD 1345 by the Mexica; town boasted roads, a sewage system, water supply system, and a variety of temples; was divided into districts inhabited by people of the same profession and status.

Teotihuacán pre-Columbian society in Central America centered around their town of Teotihuacán from 600 BC to AD 750; around 200 BC Teotihuacán grew from a collection of villages to an influential city-state and economic center.

terps mounds primarily consisting of kitchen waste and earth, dating from 400 BC, particularly in low coastal areas along the North Sea. They provide useful evidence of human occupation.

terra-cotta armies thousands of life-sized terra-cotta statues of soldiers and horses found since 1974 near the tomb of the first emperor of Qin (or King Zheng of Qin).

Tertiary period in the Cenozoic from about 66 to 1.5 million years ago, divided into the Paleocene, Eocene, Oligocene, Miocene, and Pliocene eras when mammals and hominids developed.

Tertullian (c.160-230) Quintus Septimius Florens Tertullianus; Latin church father.

Teshup Hurrian storm god who was adopted by the Hittites and worshiped as the god of storms and war. He was the husband of the Hittite sun goddess Arinna and was considered the king of the heavens.

tetralogy four-part Greek play consisting of three tragedies and a satyr play.

tetrarchy The rule of four emperors put into effect by Diocletian in AD 293; divided imperial power between two primary leaders called Augustus, assisted by two Caesars who were also their successors.

Teutonic Order order of knights who founded a powerful state in the thirteenth century in northern Germany and the Baltic States; knights were defeated in the battle of Tannenberg; by the end of the fifteenth century, they had lost their political influence.

Teutons a people who invaded southern France and Spain c. 111 BC; defeated by Marius in 102 and 101 BC.

Thales of Miletus (ca. 625-ca. 546 BC) Ionian founder of Greek philosophy.

Thebes (Egyptian) city in Upper Egypt, religious center and residence during the Middle Kingdom and New Kingdom until ca. 1300 BC. From ca. 1070 onward, Thebes became an independent kingdom ruled by the high priests of Amon. In and around Thebes there are many temples and royal tombs in the Valley of the Kings.

Thebes Greek city-state; dominant under Epamenondas (371-362 BC); razed by Alexander the Great (335 BC).

Themistocles (ca. 525-ca. 460 BC) Athenian statesman who evacuated Athens in 480 BC; led the fleet in the Battle of Salamis.

Theodora (c.508-548) Byzantine empress (527-548); originally a dancer and an actress, became wife of Emperor Justinian I; had considerable influence over his policy, due in part to her Monophysite convictions; saved Justinian's position during the Nika revolt.

Theodoric the Great (c.454-526) Ostrogoth king (474-526); founded Ostrogoth Kingdom in Italy with the permission of the Eastern Roman Empire of Odoacer; tried to restore Western Roman Empire politically and militarily.

Theodosius I, the Great, Flavius Theodosius (c.346-395) Eastern Roman emperor (379-395); Western Roman emperor (394-395); made peace with the Visigoths; prohibited all religions but Christianity; last ruler of a united Roman Empire. After his death, it was divided east and west between Arcadius and Honorius.

Thera volcanic island north of Crete where a Minoan-like civilization existed during the Bronze Age. A volcanic eruption destroyed Thera around 1500 BC. This possibly affected the destruction of the Minoan palaces (ca. 1450 BC).

Theravada (the Way of the Elders) Buddhist school of *Sravakayana* (vehicle of the disciples); disparagingly called *Hinayana* (little vehicle) by advocates of Mahayana Buddhism; emphasizes self-reliant striving against desire; emphasizes monasticism.

thermae public gathering places with cold, lukewarm and hot baths, sport schools, training fields and sometimes libraries. Most famous are the Baths of Caracalla, built between AD 212 and 216 in Rome.

Thermopylae mountain pass between Thessaly and central Greece where Leonidas and hundreds of Spartans died covering the retreat of the Greek army from the Persians in 480 BC.

thetes social class in Athens, comprising small farmers and day laborers.

Third Crusade (1189-1192) following the taking of Jerusalem in 1187, Frederick Barbarossa, Philip II Augustus, and Richard I the Lion Heart traveled to Palestine; Christians conquered the fortress of Acre, but Jerusalem remained in Turkish hands; mutual strife forced the Christians to return.

Third Interregnum period in Egyptian history from ca. 1070 to 730 BC during which Egypt was divided into the pharaoh's territory and the divine state of Amon. Finally the pharaoh's power was usurped by Libyan principalities.

Third Palace period period in the Minoan civilization from 1450 to 1200 BC in which Mycenaeans ruled Crete after a number of palaces were destroyed due to internal fighting, invasions, and earthquakes. Knossos again became the administrative center and trade became more international.

Thirty Tyrants thirty oligarchs who ruled Athens (404-403 BC) following the Peloponnesian War; noted for their unrestricted use of power.

tholos Mycenaean domed grave for the elite occurring after ca. 1600 BC, consisting of a round hole in the ground, covered with a dome of stone blocks covered with soil and flagstones as reinforcement. A grave stone was placed on top.

Thomas the Slav (?-823) a Slavic officer who led an army of discontented farmers and adventurers against Byzantine emperor Michael II. He laid siege to Byzantium, with Muslim support. He was captured and killed while fleeing a Bulgarian attack.

Thourioi colony founded by Athens in southern Italy in 443 BC, intended as a cultural model by Pericles.

three-course rotation agricultural system introduced in the tenth century; land was cultivated two years and lay fallow the third year, preventing exhaustion of the soil.

Three Kingdoms period in Chinese history (220-280) in which three kingdoms were in perfect balance: Wu (221-280), Wei in the north (221-265) and Shu in the southwest (221-263); chaotic period followed in 280, during which no ruling power emerged.

Thucydides (c. 460-c. 400 BC), early Greek historian; wrote *History of the Peloponnesian War* as it occurred.

thyrsus a staff with a pine cone on top, usually carried by the bacchants.

Tiber River flows southward through central Italy and Rome to the Mediterranean Sea at Ostia.

Tiberius Claudius Nero (42 BC-AD 37) Roman emperor AD 14-37.

Tibet country north of India; developed its own form of Buddhism (Lamaism) in the eighth century AD.

Tiglath-pileser III king of the New Assyrian Kingdom from 745 to 727 BC. He created a professional army with chariots and cavalry as its center. He defeated the Aramaean and Syrian city-states, annexed their territory, and deported some of the population. He conquered Babylon and was crowned its king.

Tihuanaco pre-Columbian civilization that survived for several centuries from around 300 BC in the mountain regions of what is known today as Bolivia; a major temple is near Lake Titicaca; including the Incas and others, were influenced by its religion.

timocracy according to Aristotle, a state in which political power is in direct proportion to property ownership.

Timurlenk *See* Tamerlane.

Tiryns Mycenaean settlement on the Peloponnisos where a palace fortress was built after 1450 BC. Like the other fortresses, it was surrounded by Cyclopean walls consisting of large limestone blocks, containing vaulted galleries.

Tlatoani Aztec king chosen by the aristocracy from among the most eligible members of the royal family; candidates were healthy in body and mind and possessed knowledge of religious and military affairs.

Toltecs pre-Columbian empire in Central America centered around the city of Tula, north of present-day Mexico City, from the ninth until the twelfth centuries; their religion and architecture influenced other cultures, especially the Aztecs.

Tombe civilization civilization (AD 300-800) in the Kinki region (China), characterized by enormous burial hills with symbols such as the magatama, or comma-shaped jewelry; it was possibly established by northeastern tribes of horsemen.

Torah an aggregate of civil, religious, and ritual laws and rules used by the Israelites. They are ascribed to Moses, but do not reflect nomadic life in the desert; they were probably written down later by priests in Jerusalem.

Totila Ostrogoth king (541-552); initially successful in driving the Byzantines out of Italy; defeated by Emperor Justinian's General Narses (552).

tragedy dramatic work originating from choral songs at the Dionysia festivals in Greece. Most tragedies had a mythological subject. They consisted of dramatic scenes with a maximum of three actors and the choir, alternated with choral songs.

Trajan (Marcus Ulpius Trajanus) (AD 52-117) Roman emperor 98-117.

transmigration Hindu concept of the atman moving through the cycle of phenomenal existence.

treasury term used for royal lands used to finance a Carolingian king's policy.

Treaty of Meerssen (870) divided the northern part of Lothar I's empire between Charles the Bald and Louis the German.

Treaty of Verdun (843) following the Battle of Fontenay in 841, it divided up the Carolingian Empire. Charles the Bald received the West, Louis the German the East, and Lothar I guarantee to the title of Holy Roman emperor and sovereignty over Italy, Burgundy, Alsace, Lorraine, and the Low Countries.

Tree of Enlightenment the bo tree under which Siddhartha Gautama attained enlightenment.

trepanation prehistoric surgery to remove a piece of skull.

trial by ordeal Germanic tradition whereby God would indicate the guilty party in legal disputes by way of trials and ritual duels; the Church considered this practice superstitious; Saint Louis attempted to abolish the custom.

Triassic period in the Mesozoic from 248 to 208 million years ago, characterized by the development of reptiles into a wide range of dinosaur species.

tribal dukedoms the territories of Bavaria, Saxony, Swabia, and the Franks in eastern Francia where ancient tribal traditions inhibited feudalism.

tribal houses Neolithic structures housing several families.

tribune of the people Roman representative of the plebeians introduced in 494 BC to protect the lower class against the patricians and the senate, later represented all the people.

tribunus plebis (tribune of the plebeians) any of several Roman magistrates appointed after 494 BC to protect the rights of the plebeians from the power of the patricians. After these two groups were given equal status (287 BC), the tribunus plebis became the representative of all the people and was closely involved with political decision-making. Caesar and Augustus derived their constitutional authority mainly from function as tribunus plebis.

tribus (district) division where Roman citizens were registered on the basis of landholdings and assessed taxes called *tributum*.

Tripitaka (Sanskrit: three baskets) the scriptures of Theravada Buddhism; refers to the baskets used by first-century BC Sri Lankan Buddhist monks to hold palm-leaf scrolls.

triumvirate a Roman three-man state commission with a special task. In 60 BC, Pompey, Crassus, and Caesar formed the first; in 43 BC, Octavian, Lepidus, and Antony formed the Second Triumvirate.

Trojan War legendary war between Greek princes and Troy, provoked by the abduction of the Greek queen Helen.

Troy legendary city in Asia Minor near the entrance to the Dardanelles, besieged and destroyed by the Greeks during the Trojan War. Its ruins were discovered through the archaeological work of Heinrich Schleimann in the nineteenth century AD.

tumuli Neolithic burial mounds of the Protruding-foot beaker culture and the Funnel- beaker cultures.

Turkestan region and modern country in central Asia; conquered by Arabs (beginning of the eighth century); their expansion was halted by Chinese border armies.

Turks Asian peoples north of Persia who converted to Islam, but retained their own language and customs. Their leaders, sultans, became more and more powerful from the ninth century onward and limited the power of the caliphs to religious issues.

Tutankhamen pharaoh from ca. 1345 to 1335 BC. He left the residence at Akhetaton and began restoring the chaos and dissatisfaction created by Akhenaton by resuming the cult of deities. His grave was left untouched and contained precious funerary treasures.

Tuthmosis III pharaoh from ca. 1490 to 1438 BC. He ruled together with Hatshepsut who reigned as king from ca. 1484. After her death (1468), he undertook major military campaigns conquering western Asia up to the Euphrates River. He allied himself with the Mitanni.

Tyler, Wat (d. 1381) led a peasant uprising in 1381 in England which erupted after tax increases; Richard II acceded to Tyler's demands, but the mayor of London killed Tyler and the rebellion was crushed forcibly.

tyranny government seized unjustly by an absolute ruler. Between 650 and 500 BC in Greece, tyrants (absolute rulers) were often benign, receiving popular support.

Tyre Phoenician city situated on an island off the coast of Lebanon. Tyre was a booming trading city in the tenth to seventh centuries BC that founded many colonies, including Carthage. Power was largely in the hands of noble families.

Ugarit northern Canaan (Levant) trading town, a Semitic city-state from the third millennium BC. After reaching its height of power (1550-1360 BC), Ugarit was controlled by the Hittites, but was destroyed around 1200 by the Sea Peoples. Clay tablets from the second millennium BC contain information about Semitic languages and religions. Artifacts pre-figure the Phoenician culture to follow.

uji Japanese clans forming a Japanese tribal society worshiping their own god; the emperor stood at the head of all clans and political battles between clan leaders caused unrest.

ulama religious ball game organized by the Mayas; several playing fields have been discovered; intended for the nobility, the game's players symbolized themes from Maya religion; kings used the game to legitimize their power; losers often sacrificed.

ulemas Osman lawyers and consultants to the sultans and beys; they used their knowledge of the Turkish, Arab, and Persian languages and the Koran to consult the imperial government; also lectured on the Koran.

Ulfilas Christian bishop who translated the Bible into Gothic, enabling large-scale Gothic conversions to Christianity.

Umayyad dynasty dynasty of caliphs in Damascus from the Umayyad clan that dominated the Arab world, including non-Islamic population (c.661-750); engaged in power struggle with the Shiites; ousted by the Abbasids.

Umayyads clan of Arab tribes based in Mecca who founded the first Muslim dynasty (661-750) of Córdoba. They established an Islamic kingdom in Spain in 756. In 929, they set up the caliphate of Córdoba and ruled until 1031.

Ummah Arabic tribal brotherhood forged by Muhammad.

Union of Kalmar (1397) union of Norway, Denmark, and Sweden forged by Margaretha, regent of Denmark and Norway, and acknowledged by the Swedes in 1389, the kingdoms remained autonomous; in 1523, Sweden became independent.

universe approximately 15 billion years old; continues to expand.

Untouchables lowest social group in the Indian caste system, which probably originally consisted of indigenous non-Aryan inhabitants. They were placed below and outside the caste system and were considered inferior and, therefore, untouchable. They carried out slave labor and lived on the edge of Aryan settlements.

Upper Egypt southern Egypt with the desert area and the elongated, narrow and fertile Nile Valley. The southerners were more isolated and conservative than the residents of the delta. A king from Upper Egypt probably conquered Lower Egypt around 3000 BC.

Upper Paleolithic period from 34,000 to 10,000 BC, characterized by technical innovations in lithic processing and symbolic representation; tools became increasingly specialized; four overlapping cultural periods within this era are identified as the Aurignacian, the Gravettian, the Solutrean, and the Magdalenian.

Ur Sumerian city-state which constituted a centralized empire in Mesopotamia from ca. 2100 to ca. 2000 BC. Ur assumed the dominant position of Lagash. The Sumerian renaissance is called the Ur III Period after the successful third dynasty in Ur.

Urban II (1040-1099) pope (1088-1099). His 1095 proclamation at Clermont initiated the First Crusade.

urbs Latin word for city, but also a reference to Rome as the capital of the Roman Empire.

Urnfield culture late Bronze Age culture between 1600 and 800 BC found throughout central Europe in which the ashes of the cremated deceased were buried in urns.

ushebtis Egyptian figurines serving as funerary equipment in addition to food and other objects. They were supposed to perform the tasks which were given to the deceased in the kingdom of the dead, e.g., answering questions posed by the gods.

usurper one who unlawfully assumes the throne.

Vaipulya Sutras Mahayana Buddhist addition to the *Tripitaka*.

Vaishesika (the school of individual characteristics) school of Hindu philosophy that complements the *Nyaya*; classifies the forms of reality.

Vais(h)yas third inherited social status in the caste system of India, consisting of merchants and farmers.

Valens (c.328-378) Eastern Roman emperor (364-378); offered Visigoths land south of the Danube River; made them *foederati* (allies). They revolted due to lack of food, killing Valens in battle.

Valentinian I (321-375) Western Roman emperor (364-375).

Valentinian II (371-392) Western Roman emperor (375-392).

Valentinian III (419-455) Western Roman emperor (425-455).

Valerian Publius Licinius Valerianus (died in Persian captivity AD 260) emperor of Rome (253-260).

Valley of the Kings western bank of the Nile opposite Thebes where the New Kingdom's pharaohs were buried. They were placed in wooden human-shaped mummy cases in burial tombs hewn from the rocks. The royal funerary temples were built separately on the shore of the Nile.

van Artevelde, Jacob (d. 1340) aristocrat from Ghent, leader of the Flemish rebellion against France; tried in vain to create an alliance of towns under the English king who was recognized as the king of France; was murdered in 1340.

Vandals eastern Germanic people; migrated to Gaul and Spain at the beginning of the fifth century; under Geiserik, founded a kingdom in North Africa (429); plundered Rome (455); defeated by Emperor Justinian I (534).

Varro, Gaius Terentius (?-c. 200 BC) consul with patrician Lucius Aemilius Paulus; favored an offensive against Hannibal.

vase painting style of earthenware decoration in the period following the Bronze Age. Attican black-patterned pottery of the sixth century was replaced by red-patterned pottery about 525 BC. The art of vase painting disappeared in the third century BC.

vassals men who swore allegiance to a patron landowner and owed him services in exchange for protection and land.

Vedanta (end of the *Vedas*) school of Hindu philosophy; focused on union with Brahman and salvation of the material world.

Vedas earliest sacred Hindu scriptures; four collections of sacrificial hymns taken over from oral tradition of Brahmanism and prescriptions for ritual: the *Rig-Veda*, the *Samaveda*, the *Yajurveda*, and the *Atharvaveda*. Vedic literature also includes the *Brahmanas* that define the rituals and mythology, the *Aran-yakas* (*Forest Treatises*), and the *Upanishads* (later theological and more mystical interpretation of the earlier works).

Venice lagoon in Italy which grew into Europe's first commercial settlement; in the tenth century, Venice became an independent political entity, which looked to Byzantium for trade and cultural interchange.

Venus goddess of fertility, love, and spring; identified with the Greek goddess Aphrodite. During the Principate, Venus was honored as ancestress of the Julian line of emperors because she was the mother of Aeneas, the forefather of Rome.

Vespasian (Titus Flavius Sabinus Vespasianus) (AD 9-79) Roman emperor 69-79: under his rule, both the Jewish uprising and the Batavian rebellion were crushed.

Vestal virgins six female priests of the goddess Vesta, goddess of hearthfire and symbol of the Roman state; these were required to take vows of chastity and look after the sacred fire in the Temple of Vesta.

Via Appia oldest and most important Roman road, constructed by Appius Claudius Caecus in 312 BC, it ran from Rome to Capua and insured success in the battle against the Samnites.

Virgil (Publius Vergilius Maro) (70-19 BC) Latin poet, author of *The eclogues* (The Pastoral) and *Georgica*, his didactic poem on agriculture, and the epic *Aeneid*. It tells the story of the legendary Aeneas, illustrating predestination in Rome's growth to a world power.

Vishnu Hindu god called the Preserver; forms a trinity with Brahma and Shiva; takes human form as Krishna.

Vishtaspa Persian king c. sixth century BC who was converted to the faith of Zarathushtra. Responsible for spreading the faith, he was probably a local ruler who fought the nomadic Tatar (Tartar) tribes.

Visigoths (Latin: *Visigothi* or noble Goths) Germanic people from the Ukraine, driven out by the Huns; settled south of the Danube as *foederati* (allies) of Rome; rebelled in 378; plundered Rome under Alaric (410); established a kingdom in Spain conquered by the Arabs (711).

vizier high Egyptian administrative official, usually a close relative of the pharaoh. He controlled the levying of taxes, the lower officials, the court and the royal treasuries, and granaries. Like other officials, he was buried in a *mastaba*, a rectangular decorated grave near the pyramids.

Vladimir I king of the Kyyivan (Kievan) Russian kingdom (980-1015); spread eastern Christianity in his kingdom to unite the many culturally diverse Slavic peoples; his son Yaroslav extended the kingdom from the Black Sea to the Gulf of Finland.

Vulgate (Latin: popular or common) fourth-century Latin translation and organization of the Bible by Jerome; the authorized version in the Roman Catholic Church.

Wallia Visigoth king (415-418).

wanax a Mycenaean ruler. He was commander of the army and the administrative officials, and he owned much land which he rented out in part. In his palace the administration was kept for land use, manufacture and trade, agriculture, the artisans, and industry. Most likely these rulers were independent but in contact with one another.

Warring States Period (China) last period of the Zhou dynasty through the unification of China, from the early fifth century to 221 BC. War was a constant fact of life, yet trade, agriculture, and urbanization evolved simultaneously. Legislation and philosophy, such as Confucianism, legalism, and Daoism developed.

Warring States period (Japan) period (1467-1568) in which the leading ujis fought for control; Ashikagas and Fujiwaras gradually lost their political power; revolts broke out against the feudalism of the Japanese landowners.

water culture African culture between 9000 and 2000 BC in northern Africa in the Nile-Sahara territory. Because of the wet climate at that time, many lakes, marshes, and rivers developed. The population subsisted on marine animals and plants and lived in permanent settlements.

wergeld (German: fine) under Germanic criminal law, required to be paid by the killer of a person or an animal. People and animals were assigned values, depending on importance. This arrangement ended the Germanic *faidas* (feuds).

Western Roman Empire western part of the Roman Empire divided after Theodosius's death in 395. With Rome as its capital, it remained in existence until 476, when the last emperor was deposed by Odoacer.

White Huns nomadic horseman from Central Asia who raided India after 470 and brought down the Gupta Empire; empire later fell apart into small states; White Huns were driven from India around 500; they were also known as Heftakites.

William the Conqueror king of England (1066-1087); a Norman duke who defeated King Harold at Hastings in 1066 and conquered England; established a centralized monarchy, granting estates to loyal followers but retaining power; it took a full century before the Norman occupiers merged with the Anglo-Saxons.

Wu-ti ruler of the Han dynasty (140-86 BC) who reinforced China's position of power by entering into pacts with people from Central Asia and providing support against the Huns.

Xenophanes (580-480 BC) itinerant Ionian philosopher and poet.

Xerxes I king of Persia (485-465 BC); destroyed Athens in 480 BC during the Second Persian War.

Yahweh God of the Israelites, initially a war god who led the movement into Canaan, later a protective god. The Yahweh cult was monotheistic and prohibited other cults, such as that of the fertility god Baal. According to the prophets, Yahweh would punish the people for social injustice and impiety, thus avenging the poor and the oppressed.

Yamato Empire uji empire controlled by the uji of the sun goddess, who made sun worship the state religion; controlled other Japanese ujis from the fifth century.

yanaconas social group within the Inca society; appointed from the aristocratic classes, they acted as personal assistants to the king and his noblemen; were released from the ayllu obligations of common citizens.

Yathrib Arabian city renamed *Madinat al-Nabi* (the city of the prophet) or Medina.

Yazdegerd III last Sassanid king of Persia (632-641).

Yazid I caliph (680-683); son and successor of Mu'awiyah.

Yüan dynasty Mongol dynasty established by Kublai Khan that ruled China (1271-1368); in 1368 the Chinese Ming dynasty subjected the Mongol Khans; Kublai Khan promoted the integration of Chinese and Mongol civilizations.

yoga (Sanskrit: yoke) Hindu school of philosophy and practice involving physical and mental discipline to restore the balance of spiritual energy; intense concentration attained by prescribed postures and exercises, including controlled breathing, to gain mystical union with Brahman.

Yucatán region in Central America (Mexico) where the Mayas lived in city-states in the Classical period (300 BC-AD 900) and the Postclassical period (900-1500); Mayas fought many wars to expand their territory.

zakat income tax paid by Muslims, intended for poor relief and charity; one of the religious duties for the exaltation of Allah.

Zarathushtra (Zoroaster) founder of the ancient Persian religion Zoroastrianism. A social-religious reformer who lived between the seventh and the sixth centuries BC, his teachings were based on what he saw as the battle between the good Ahura Mazda and the evil Angra Mainyu. By acting, thinking, and speaking properly one supported Ahura Mazda.

zealots first-century AD orthodox Jewish sect that resisted Roman domination in Palestine and demanded social reforms; some took guerilla action.

Zen Buddhism Buddhist school originally developed in China (Ch'in in Chinese), later in Japan; a blending of Mahayana Buddhism and Daoism.

Zend-Avesta the holy book of Zarathushtra's religion. It contained stories of creation, liturgical writings, and the history of Persia and its religion. *Avesta* is the part containing the writings, *Zend* is the commentary.

Zenon of Elea (fifth century BC) Greek philosopher and student of Parmenides.

zeugitai social class of economically independent farmers in Athens; owners of *zeugos* (yoke of oxen). The zeugitai served as foot soldiers in the army and, after Solon's reforms, could hold minor political offices.

Zeus supreme deity of the Greek gods.

Zheng of Qin king of Qin (221-207 BC) who proclaimed himself Qin Shihuangdi (first emperor of Qin) in 221 BC after all Zhou states had been conquered. He expanded the empire to the north and the south.

Zhou dynasty Chinese culture c.1050-256 BC. Around 1050 the Zhou people, part of the Shang culture from the northwest, overtook the Shang and created many feudal states in northern China. From the sixth century on, their armies relied particularly on infantry and cavalry made up mostly of peasants. The peasants also worked as construction laborers and maintained dikes and irrigation works.

Zhuangzi (Zhuang-tse) (369-268 BC) Chinese Daoist philosopher who reinterpreted the Daode Jing (Tao-te-ching) to make Daoism accessible to a wider audience.

ziggurat Sumerian temple tower built on terraces. It was decorated with stylus mosaics, whereby colored styluses were affixed to the clay temple walls. The temples played a central role in the life of the Sumerians.

Zion (City of David) one of the two hills on which Jerusalem was built. It was the religious site of the city where the Temple of Yahweh, with the Ark of the Covenant, was located. It was also the source of the sole water supply.

Zoroastrianism traditional religion of Persians prior to conversion to Islam; founded by Zoroaster; posited competing spirits of good and evil.

Bibliography

Volume 1 Origins of Humanity

The Universe
Audouze, J. *The Cambridge Atlas of Astronomy*. Cambridge, 1985.
Gingerich, O. *The Eye of Heaven*. New York, 1993.
Kovalesky, J. *Modern Astronomy*. Berlin, 1995.
Krauss, J. D. *Radio Astronomy*. Powell, OH, 1986.
Mitton, J. *A Concise Dictionary of Astronomy*. Oxford, 1991.
Mitton, S. and Mitton, J. *Astronomy*. Oxford, 1994.
Newton, J. *The guide to Amateur Astronomy*. Cambridge, 1988.
O'Meara, D. J. *Pythagoras Revived*. Oxford, 1989.
Pasachoff, J. M. *Astronomy*. Philadelphia, 1987.
Zombeck, M. V. *Handbook of Space Astronomy and Astrophysics*. Cambridge, 1994.

The Universe Today
Hayashi, C. *Origin of the Solar System*. Kyoto, 1988.
Jones, B. W. *The Solar System*. Oxford, 1984.
Macfarlane, I. *The Black Hole*. London, 1975.
Meadows, J. *Space Garbage*. London, 1985.
———. *Guest Star*. London, 1985.
Sharov, A. *Edwin Hubble, the Discoverer of the Big Bang Universe*. Cambridge, 1993.
Siwel, L. *The Magic of Physics*. Basingstoke, 1987.
Thomas, W.A. *The Big Bang*. Oxford, 1986.

Our Place in the Universe
Browne, J. *Charles Darwin: a Biography*. London, 1995.
Colbert, E. H. *The Dinosaur Book*. New York, 1945.
Denett, D. C. *Darwin's Dangerous Idea*. New York, 1995.
Emiliani, C. *Planet Earth*. Cambridge, 1992.
Erwin, D. H. *The Great Paleozoic Crisis*. Columbia, 1993.
Wilford, J. N. *The Riddle of the Dinosaur*. London, 1986.

Human Evolution
Andersen, B. C. *The Ice Age World*. Oslo, 1994.
Bendall, D.S., ed. *Evolution from Molecules to Man*. Cambridge, 1980.
Gooch, S. *The Neanderthal Question*. London, 1977.
Juritzky, A. *Prehistoric Man as an Artist*. Amsterdam, 1953.
Knight, C. R. *Prehistoric Man: the Great Adventurer*. New York, 1949.
Matthews, J., ed. *Man's Place in Evolution*. Cambridge, 1980.
Nilssen, T. *The Pleistocene*. London, 1983.
Sutcliffe, A. J. *On the Track of Ice Age Mammals*. London, 1985.

The Paleolithic Period
Bordes, F. *The Old Stone Age*. London, 1968.
Clark, G. *The Stone Age Hunters*. London, 1967.
Davis, D. M. *Journey into the Stone Age*. London, 1969.
Osborn, J. R. *Stone Age to Iron Age*. London, 1978.
Quennel, M. *Everyday Life in the Old Stone Age*. London, 1955.
Sahlins, M. *Stone Age Economics*. London, 1974.
Wymer, J. *The Paleolithic Age*. London, 1982.

The Mesolithic and Neolithic Periods
Bender, B. *Farming in Prehistory*. London, 1975.
Clark, G. *World Prehistory in New Perspective*. Cambridge, 1977.
Cunliffe, B., ed. *Oxford Illustrated Prehistory of Europe*. Oxford, 1994.
Gebauer, A.B., ed. *Transitions to Agriculture in Prehistory*. Madison, WI, 1992.
Mellars, P., ed. *Emergence of Modern Humans*. Edinburgh, 1990.
Price, T. D., ed. *Prehistoric Hunter-Gatherers*. Orlando, 1984.
Rindos, D. *The Origins of Agriculture*. New York, 1983.
Szelag, Tadeusz. *New Stone Age Archaeology*. Warsaw, 1987.

Wenke, R. J. *Patterns in Prehistory*. New York, 1990.

The Neolithic Period
Bradley, R. J., ed. *Neolithic Studies*. Oxford, 1984.
Burgess, C. *The Age of Stonehenge*. London, 1980.
Cole, S. *The Neolithic Revolution*. London, 1970.
Hodder, I. *The Domestication of Europe*. Oxford, 1990.
Quennel, M. *Everyday Life in the New Stone, Bronze and Early Iron Ages*. London, 1955.
Whittle, A. W. R. *Neolithic Europe*. Cambridge, 1985.

Prehistoric Humans
Barker, G. *Prehistoric Farming in Europe*. Cambridge, 1985.
Brumfield, E. M., et al. *Specialisation, Exchange and Complex Societies*. Cambridge, 1987.
Croes, D. R. et al. *Long-Term Subsistence Change in Prehistoric North America*. Greenwich, CT, 1992.
Jochim, M. A. *Hunter-Gatherer Subsistence and Settlement*. New York, 1976.
Killion, T. W. *Gardens of Prehistory*. Alabama, 1992.
Lemonier, P. *Technological Choices*. London, 1993.
Wheeler, M. *Civilisations of the Indus Valley and Beyond*. London, 1966.

The Bronze Age
Burgess, C. *Bronze Age Hoards*. Oxford, 1979.
Coles, J.M., and Harding, A.F. *The Bronze Age in Europe*. London, 1979.
Immerwahr, S. A. *The Neolithic and Bronze Ages*. Princeton, 1971.
Thompson, T. L. *The Settlement of Palestine in the Bronze Age*. Wiesbaden, 1979.

Developing Use of Metals
Adouze, F. *Towns, Villages and Countryside of Celtic Europe*. London, 1992.
Collis, J. *Oppida*. Sheffield, 1984.
———. *The European Iron Age*. London, 1984.
Finlay, I. *Celtic Art: An Introduction*. London, 1973.
Hedeager, L. *Iron-Age Societies*. Oxford, 1992.
Powell, T.G.E. *The Celts*. London, 1980.
Rankin, H.D. *Celts and the Classical World*. London, 1987.

The Iron Age
Goffart, W. *Barbarians and Romans*. Princeton, 1980.
Gurney, O. R. *The Hittites*. Harmondsworth, 1980.
Hoffner, H. A. *Hittite Myth*. Atlanta, 1990.
Piotrovsky, B., et al. *Scythian Art*. Oxford, 1987.
Todd, M. *The Northern Barbarians*. London, 1975.
———. *The Early Germans*. Oxford, 1992

Volume 2 Egypt and Mesopotamia

Ancient Egypt
Aldred, C. *Egyptian Art*. London, 1980.
Baines, J., and Málek, J. *Atlas of Ancient Egypt*. Oxford, 1984.
James, T. G. H. *Pharaoh's People: Scenes from Life in Imperial Egypt*. London, 1984.
Lichtheim, M. *Ancient Egyptian Literature*, 3 vols. Berkeley, Los Angeles, London, 1973-1980.
Málck, J., and Forman, W. *In the Shadow of the Pyramids*. London, 1986.
Spencer, A. J. *Death in Ancient Egypt*. Cambridge, 1992.

The Minoan Civilization
Buchholz, H.-G., ed. *Aegäische Bronzezeit*. Darmstadt, 1987.
Buchholz, H.-G., and Karageorgis, V. *Prehistoric Greece and Cyprus: an Archaeological Handbook*. London, 1973.
Castleden, R. *Minoans: Life in Bronze-Age Crete*. London, 1992
Dickinson, O. T. P. K. *The Aegean Bronze Age*. Cambridge, 1994.

Myers, J. W., Myers, E. E., and Cadogan, G. *An Aerial Atlas of Ancient Crete*. Berkeley, 1992.

Mycenae
Chadwick, J. *Linear B and Related Scripts*. Berkeley, 1987.
McDonald, W. A., and Thomas, C. G. *Progress into the Past: The Rediscovery of Mycenean Civilization*. Bloomington, 1990.
Sachermeyer, F. *Die Levante im Zeitalter der Wanderungen: vom 13. bis zum 11. Jahrhundert v. Chr.* Wien, 1982.

The Sumerians
Kramer, S. N. *The Sumerians*. Chicago, 1964.
Oates, J. *The Rise of Civilization*. London, 1976.
Parrot, A. *Sumer*. New York, 1961.
Postgate, J. N. *Early Mesopotamia: Society and Economy at the Dawn of History*. London, 1992.
Roux, G. *Ancient Iraq*. Harmondsworth, 1972.
Woolley, C. L. *The Sumerians*. New York, London, 1965.

Akkad and the Sumerian Renaissance
Kramer, S. N. *The Sacred Marriage Rite*. Bloomington, 1969.
Kuppers, J. R. *Les nomades en Mesopotamie au temps des rois de Mari*. Paris, 1957.
Oppenheim, A. L. *Letters from Mesopotamia*. Chicago, 1967.
Postgate, J. N. *The First Empires*. Oxford, 1977.
———. *Early Mesopotamia: Society and Economy at the Dawn of History*. London, 1992.

Hammurabi and Gilgamesh
Heidel, A. *The Gilgamesh Epic and Old Testament Parallels*. Chicago, 1976.
Lambert, W. G. *Babylonian Wisdom Literature*. Oxford, 1960.
Oberhuber, K., ed. *Das Gilgamesj-Epos*. Darmstadt, 1977.
Saggs, H. F. W. *The Greatness That Was Babylon*. London, 1962.
———. *Ancient Near Eastern Religion*. London 1995.
Sandars, N. K. *The Epic of Gilgamesh*. Harmondsworth, 1970.

Babylon
Jacobson, T. *The Treasures of Darkness: A History of Mesopotamian Religion*. New Haven, 1976.
Lambert, W. G. *Babylonian Wisdom Literature*. Oxford, 1960.
Oates, J. *Babylon*. London, 1979.
Oppenheim, A. L. *Ancient Mesopotamia*. Chicago, 1964.
Saggs, H. F. W. *Everyday Life in Babylonia and Assyria*. London, 1965.

Assyria
Andrae, W. *Das wiedererstandene Assur*. Munich, 1977.
Cardascia, G. *Les loi assyriennes*. Paris, 1969.
Contenau, G. *Everyday Life in Babylon and Assyria*. London, 1954.
Laessoe, J. *People of Ancient Assyria*. London, 1963.
Mallowan, M. E. L. *Nimrud and Its Remains*, 2 vols. London, 1966.
Oded, B. *Mass Deportations and Deportees in the Neo-Assyrian Empire*. Wiesbaden, 1979.
Saggs, H. F. W. *The Might That Was Assyria*. London, 1984.

Volume 3 Ancient Cultures

The Phoenicians
Baumgarten, A. I. *The Phoenician History of Philo of Byblos: A Commentary*. Leiden, 1981.
Cary, M., and Warmington, E. H. *The Ancient Explorers*. Harmondsworth, 1963.
Harden, D. B. *The Phoenicians*. London, 1962.

The Influence of the Phoenicians
Craigie, P. C. *Ugarit and the Old Testament*. Grand Rapids, 1983.
Diringer, D. *The Alphabet: A Key to the History of Mankind*. London, 1968.
Hooker, J. T., ed. *Reading the Past: Ancient Writing from Cuneiform to the Alphabet*. London, 1990.
Kloos, C. *Yhws's Combat with the Sea: A Canaanite Tradition in the Religion of Ancient Israel*. Leiden, 1986.
Sass, B. *The Genesis of the Alphabet and Its Development in the Second Millennium BC*. Wiesbaden, 1988.

The Israelites and Neighboring Peoples
Bright, J. *A History of Israel*. Philadelphia, 1972.
de Geus, C. H. J. *Early Israel: Anthropological and Historical Studies on the Israelite Society before the Monarchy*. Leiden, 1985.
Rappaport, A. S. *Ancient Israel: Myths and Legends*. London, 1987.
Van Seters, J. *Abraham in History and Tradition*. New Haven-London, 1975.
Thomas, D. Winton. *Documents from Old Testament Times*. London, 1958.

Kings and Prophets
Anderson, G. W. *The History of the Religion of Israel*. Oxford, 1966.
De Vaux, R. *Ancient Israel, Its Life and Institutions*. London, 1973.
Robinson, T. H. *Prophesy and Prophets in Ancient Israel*. London, 1979.
Talmon, S. King. *Cult and Calender in Ancient Israel*. London, 1986.
Yeivin, S. *The Israelite Conquest of Canaan*. London, 1971.

The Hittites
Gurney, O. R. *The Hittites*. Harmondsworth, 1966.
Macgueen, J. G. *The Hittites and Their Contemporaries in Asia Minor*. London, 1986.
Neufeld, E. *The Hittite Laws*. London, 1951.

The Early History of China
Barnes, G. L. *China, Korea and Japan: The Rise of Civilization in East Asia*. London, 1993.
Blunden, C., and Elvin, M. *Cultural Atlas of China*. Oxford, 1988.
Fairbank, J. K., and Reischauer, E. O. *China: Tradition and Transformation*. Sydney, 1989.
Gernet, J. *A History of Chinese Civilization*. Cambridge, 1987.
Ramsey, S. R. *The Languages of China*. Princeton, 1989.

The Persians
Frye, R. N. *The Heritage of Persia*. New York, 1963.
Gerschevitsch, I., ed. *The Cambridge History of Iran: From the Third Millennium BC to the Death of Alexander in 323 BC*. Cambridge, 1983.
Ghirshman, R. *Iran, from the Earliest Times to the Islamic Conquest*. London, 1954.
Nyberg, H. *Die Religionen des alten Iran*. Liepzig, 1938.

Zarathushtra
Boyce, M. *A History of Zoroastrianism*. 2 vols. London, 1975-1982.
Dandamacv, M. A. *Persien unter den ersten Achameniden (6. Jahrhundert)*. Wiesbaden, 1976.
Dawson, M. M. *The Ethical Religion of Zoroaster*. New York, 1969.
Olmstead, A. T. *History of the Persian Empire*. Chicago, 1984.
Schlerath, B., ed. *Zarathrusta*. Darmstadt, 1970.
Zaehner, R. C. *The Teachings of the Magi: A Compendium of Zoroastrian Beliefs*. London, 1975.

Indo-Europeans in India
Marshall, I. *Mohenjo-Daro and the Indus Civilization*. London, 1931.
Smith, V. *History of India*. Oxford, 1958.

Cultures of the Pacific
Barclay, G. *A History of the Pacific*. London, 1978.
Burney, J. *Chronological History of Voyages and Discoveries in the South Seas*. London, 1967.
Layard, L. *Stone Men of Malekula*. New York, 1942.
Mead, M. *Coming of Age in Samoa*. New York, 1929.
Reund, P. *Easter Island*. New York, 1947.

Ward, G., ed. *Man in the Pacific Islands*. London, 1972.

Africa
Davidson, B. *The Story of Africa*. London, 1984.
De Graft-Johnson, C. *African Glory*. London, 1954.
Gann, L. H., and Duignan, P. *Burden of Empire*. London, 1967.
Murdock, J. P. *Africa*. New York, 1959.
Oliver, R. *The Dawn of African History*. London, 1961.

Volume 4   The Ancient Greeks

The *Iliad* and the *Odyssey*
Heubeck, A. *Die homerische Frage: Ein Bericht über die Forschung der letzten Jahrzehnte*. 2nd ed. Darmstadt, 1988.
Kirk, G. S. *Homer and the Oral Tradition*. Cambridge, 1976.
McDonald, W. A., and Thomas, C. G. *Progress into the Past: The Rediscovery of Mycenaean Civilization*. 2nd ed. Bloomington, 1990.
Naerebout, F. G. "Male-Female Relationships in the Homeric Epics," *Sexual Asymmetry: Studies in Ancient Society*, J. H. Blok and P. Mason, eds., pp. 109-146. Amsterdam, 1987.
Patzek, B. *Homer und Mykene: mündliche Dichtung und Geschichtsschreibung*. München, 1992.
Siebler, M. *Troia-Homer-Schliemann: Mythos und Wahrheit*. Mainz, 1990.
Ulf, C. *Die homerische Gesellschaft: Materialien zur analytischen Beschreibung und historischen Lokalisierung.* Vestigia Bd. 43. München, 1990.
Wace, A. J. B., and Stubbings, F. H., eds. *A Companion to Homer*. London, 1963.

Crisis and Renaissance
Haegg, R., ed. *The Greek Renaissance of the Eighth Century BC: Tradition and Innovation*. Stockholm, 1983.
Jeffery, L. H. *Archaic Greece: The City-states c. 700-500 BC*. London, 1976.
Murray, O. *Early Greece*. Fontana History of the Ancient World. Glasgow, 1983.
Snodgrass, A. M. *The Dark Age*. London, 1971.
———. *Archaic Greece: The Age of Experiment.* London, 1980.

The Greek Expansion
Boardman, J. *The Greeks Overseas: Their Early Colonies and Trade*. London, 1980.
Dover, K. J. *Greek Homosexuality*. New York, 1980.
Fränkel, H. *Early Greek Poetry and Philosophy*. New York, London, 1973.
Graham, A. J. *Colony and Mother City in Ancient Greece*. Manchester, 1964.
Lesky, A. *A History of Greek Literature*. New York, 1966.
Malkin I. *Religion and Colonization in Ancient Greece*. Leiden, 1987.
Mosse, C. *La colonisation dans l'antiquité*. Paris, 1970.
Ridgway, D. *The First Western Greeks*. Cambridge, 1992.

Sparta and Athens
Cartledge, P. *Sparta and Lakonia: A Regional History, 1300-362 B.C.* London, 1979.
Clauss, M. *Sparta: Eine Einführung in seine Geschichte und Zivilisation*. München, 1983.
Hignett, C. *A History of the Athenian Constitution to the End of the Fifth Century B.C.* Oxford, 1952.
Link, S. *Der Kosmos Sparta: Recht und Sitte in klassisch-er Zeit*. Darmstadt, 1994.
MacDowell, D. M. *Spartan Law*. Scottish Classical Studies 1. Edinburgh, 1986.
Powell, A., ed. *Classical Sparta: Techniques Behind Her Success*. London, 1989.
Stockton, D. *The Classical Athenian Democracy*. Oxford, 1990.
Welwei, K.-W. *Athen: Vom neolitischer Siedlungsplatz zur archaischen Grosspolis*. Darmstadt, 1992.

The Greek Tyrants
Austin, M., and Vidal-Naquet, P. *Economic and Social History of Ancient Greece: An Introduction*. London, 1977.
Berve, H. *Die Tyrannis bei den Griechen*. München, 1967.
Finley, M. I. *The Ancient Economy*. London, 1985.
Kloft, H. *Die Wirtschaft der griechisch-römischen Welt. Eine Einführung*. Darmstadt, 1992.

Salmon, J. B. *Wealthy Corinth: A History of the City to 338 BC*. Oxford, 1984.
Stahl, M. *Aristokraten und Tyrannen im archaischen Athen*. Stuttgart, 1987.
Starr, C. G. *The Economic and Social Growth of Early Greece, 800-500 BC*. New York, 1977.

Greek Religion and Philosophy
Burkert, W. *Greek Religion: Archaic and Classical*. London, 1985.
———. *Orientalizing Revolution: Near Eastern Influence on Greek Culture in the Early Archaic Age*. Cambridge, MA, 1993.
———. *Ancient Mystery Cults.* Carl Newell Jackson Lectures, 1982. Cambridge, MA, 1987.
Burnet, J. *Greek Philosophy: Thales to Plato*. London, 1968.
Easterling, P. E., and Muir, J. V., eds. *Greek Religion and Society*. Cambridge, 1985.
Geyer, C.-F. *Einführung in die Philosophie der Antike*. Darmstadt, 1992.
Graf, F. *Greek Mythology*. München, 1987.
Guthrie, W. K. C. *A History of Greek Philosophy*. Cambridge, 1962-1981.
Kirk, G. S., and Raven, J. E. *The Presocratic Philosophers*. Cambridge, 1960.
Mylonas, G. E. *Eleusis and the Eleusinian Mysteries*. Princeton, 1961.
Parke, H. W. *Greek Oracles*. London, 1967.
West, M. *Early Greek Philosophy and the Orient*. Oxford, 1971.

Cleisthenes
Bleicken, J. *Die Athenische Demokratie*. Paderborn, 1994.
Farrar, C. *The Origins of Democratic Thinking: The Invention of Politics in Classical Athens*. Cambridge, 1988.
Jones, A. H. M. *Athenian Democracy*. Oxford, 1957.
Stockton, D. *The Classical Athenian Democracy*. Oxford, 1990.
Welwei, K.-W. *Die griechische Polis: Verfassung und Gesellschaft in archaischer und klassischer Zeit*. Stuttgart, 1983.

The Persian Wars
Bengtson, H., ed. *Die Mittelmeerwelt im Altertum 1: Griechen und Perser*. Frankfurt am Main, 1965.
Burn, A. R. *Persia and the Greeks: The Defense of the West 546-478 BC*. London, 1962.
Cook, J. M. *The Persian Empire*. London, 1983.
Walser, G. *Hellas und Iran: Studien zu den griechisch-persischen Beziehungen vor Alexander*. Darmstadt, 1984.

The Age of Pericles
Connor, W. R. *The New Politicians of Fifth Century Athens*. Princeton, 1971.
Connor, W. R. et al. *Aspects of Athenian Democracy*. Copenhagen, 1990.
Davies, J. K. *Democracy and Classical Greece*. Glasgow, 1978.
Meiggs, R. *The Athenian Empire*. Oxford, 1972.
Osborne, R. *Demos: The Discovery of Classical Athens*. London, 1984.
Schubert, C. *Perikles*. Darmstadt, 1994.

Greek Theater
Blume, H.-D. *Einführung in das antike Theaterwesen*. Darmstadt, 1978.
Else, G. F. *The Origin and Early Form of Greek Tragedy*. Cambridge, MA, 1967.
Herington, J. *Poetry into Drama: Early Tragedy and the Greek Poetic Tradition*. Berkeley, 1985.
Pickard-Cambridge, A. W. *Dithyramb, Tragedy and Comedy*. 2nd rev. ed. by T. B. L. Webster. Oxford, 1966.
———. *The Dramatic Festivals of Athens*. 2nd rev. ed. by J. Gould and D. M. Lewis. Oxford, 1988.
Stoessl, F. *Die Vorgeschichte des griechischen Theaters*. Darmstadt, 1987.
Winkler, John J., and Zeitlin, Froma I., eds. *Nothing to Do with Dionysos? Athenian Drama in Its Social Context*. Princeton, 1990.

From Pythagoras to Diogenes
Guthrie, W. K. *A History of Greek Philosophy*. Cambridge, 1962-1981.
Kirk, G. S., Raven, J. E., and Schofield, M. *The*

Presocratic Philosophers: A Critical History with a Selection of Texts. Cambridge, 1983.

Lloyd, G. E. M. *Early Greek Science: Thales to Aristotle.* London, 1970.

McKirahan, R. D. *Philosophy before Socrates: An Introduction with Texts and Commentary.* Indianapolis, 1994.

Vander Waerdt, P. A. *The Socratic Movement.* Ithaca, 1994.

Vlastos, G. *Socrates: Ironist and Moral Philosopher.* Ithaca, 1991.

The Greek City-States and The Peloponnesian War

Connor, W. R. *Thucydides.* Princeton, 1987.

Ellis, W. *Alcibiades.* London, 1989.

Kagan, D. *The Outbreak of the Peloponnesian War.* Ithaca, 1969.

———. *The Archidamian War.* Ithaca, 1974.

———. *The Peace of Nicias and the Sicilian Expedition.* Ithaca, 1982.

Meiggs, R. *The Athenian Empire.* Oxford, 1972.

Volume 5 Greece and Rome

Greece after the Classical Period

Cartledge, P. *Agesilaos and the Crisis of Sparta.* London, 1987.

Ellis, J. R. *Philip II and Macedonian Imperialism.* London, 1976.

Hansen, M. H. *The Athenian Democracy in the Age of Demosthenes: Structure, Principles and Ideology.* Oxford, 1991.

Alexander the Great

Bosworth, A. B. *Conquest and Empire: The Reign of Alexander the Great.* Cambridge, 1988.

Engels, D. W. *Alexander the Great and the Logistics of the Macedonian Army.* Berkeley, 1978.

Lane Fox, R. *Alexander the Great.* London, 1973.

Tarn, W. W. *Alexander the Great.* Cambridge, 1948.

Hellenism

Bowman, A. K. *Egypt after the Pharaohs, 332 B.C.-A.D. 642.* Oxford, 1990.

Cary, M. *A History of the Greek World, 323 to 146 B.C.* London, 1951.

Ellis, W. M. *Ptolemy of Egypt.* London, 1993.

Fraser, P. H. *Ptolemaic Alexandria.* Oxford, 1972.

Green, P. *Alexander to Actium: The Historical Evolution of the Hellenistic Age.* Berkeley, 1993.

Heckel, W. *The Marshals of Alexander's Empire.* London, 1992.

Kincaid, C. A. *Successors of Alexander the Great.* Princeton, 1985.

Kuhrt, A., and Sherwin-White, S. *From Samarkand to Sardis: A New Approach to the Seleucid Empire.* Berkeley, 1993.

The Greek Legacy

Barker, E. *Greek Political Theory: Plato and His Predecessors.* London, 1918.

Farrington, B. *Greek Science.* Harmondsworth, 1961.

———. *The Faith of Epicurus.* New York, 1967.

Guthrie, W. K. C. *A History of Greek Philosophy.* Cambridge, 1962-1981.

Lesky, A. *A History of Greek Literature.* New York, 1966.

Long, A. A. *Hellenistic Philosophy: Stoics, Epicureans, Sceptics.* London, 1986.

Mohr, R. D. *Platonic Cosmology.* Leiden, 1985.

Neugebauer, O. *The Exact Sciences in Antiquity.* Princeton, 1952.

Pollitt, J. J. *Art in the Hellenistic Age.* Cambridge, 1990.

Taylor, A. E. *Plato: The Man and His Work.* London, 1926.

Ancient Rome

Alfoldi, A. *Early Rome and the Latins.* Ann Arbor, 1965.

Galinsky, G. K. *Aeneas, Siciliy, and Rome.* Princeton, 1969.

Gjerstadt, E. *Legends and Facts of Early Roman History.* Lund, 1962.

Grant, M. *Roman Myths.* London, 1971.

Patricians and Plebeians

Crawford, M. *The Roman Republic,* Fontana History of the Roman World. Glasgow, 1978.

Ferenczy, E. *From the Patrician State to the Patricio-plebeian State.* Amsterdam, 1976.

Ogilvie, R. M. *Early Rome and the Etruscans,* Fontana History of the Ancient World. Glasgow, 1976.

Raaflaub, K. A., ed. *Social Struggles in Archaic Rome: New Perspectives on the Conflict of the Orders.* Berkeley, 1986.

From City to State

Crawford, M. *The Roman Republic,* Fontana History of the Ancient World. Glasgow, 1978.

Harris, W. V. *Rome in Etruria and Umbria.* Oxford, 1971.

Keaveney, A. *Rome and the Unification of Italy.* London, 1987.

Pallottino, M. *Etruscologia.* Milan, 1975.

Salmon, E. T. *Samnium and the Samnites.* Cambridge, 1967.

Duel for the West

Bagnall, N. *The Punic Wars.* London, 1990.

Caven, B. *The Punic Wars.* London, 1980.

Conolly, P. *Hannibal and the Enemies of Rome.* London, 1978.

Errington, R. M. *The Dawn of Empire: Rome's Rise to World Power.* Ithaca, 1972.

The Roman Revolution

Astin, A. E. *Scipio Aemilianus.* Oxford, 1971.

Badian, E. *Foreign Clientelae.* Oxford, 1958.

Gruen, E. S. *The Hellenistic World and the Coming of Rome,* 2 vols. Berkeley, 1984.

Keaveney, A. *Sulla: The Last Republican.* London, 1982.

Stockton, D. *The Gracchi.* Oxford, 1979.

Volume 6 The Roman Empire

The End of the Republic

F.E. Adcock, *Marcus Crassus, Millionaire,* Cambridge 1966.

M. Gelzer, *Caesar, Politician and Statesman,* Oxford 1968.

P. Greenhalgh, *Pompey,* 2 vols. London 1980-81.

A. Keaveney, *Lucullus, a Life,* London 1992.

A.W. Lintott, *Violence in Republican Rome,* Oxford 1968.

D.C.A. Shotter, *The Fall of the Roman Republic,* London 1994.

D.L. Stockton, *Cicero: a Political Biography,* Oxford 1971.

From Caesar to Augustus

E. Bradford, *Julius Caesar: The Pursuit of Power,* London 1984.

M.L. Clarke, *The Noblest Roman: Marcus Brutus and His Reputation,* London 1981.

E. Gruen, *The Last Generation of the Roman Republic,* Berkeley 1974.

E. Huzar, *Mark Antony, a Biography,* Minnesota 1978.

D.C.A. Shotter, *Augustus Caesar,* London 1991.

R. Syme, *The Roman Revolution,* Oxford 1939.

L.R. Taylor, *Party Politics in the Age of Caesar,* Berkeley 1944.

Dictatorship

G.W. Bowersock, *Augustus and the Greek World,* Oxford 1965.

D. Earl, *The Age of Augustus,* London 1968.

D. Kienast, *Augustus, Prinzeps und Monarch,* Darmstadt 1982.

G. Rickman, *The Corn Supply of Ancient Rome,* Oxford 1980.

D.C.A. Shotter, *Augustus Caesar,* London 1991.

R. Syme, *The Roman Revolution,* Oxford 1939.

C.M. Wells, *The German Policy of Augustus,* Oxford 1972.

The First Emperors

J.P.V.D. Balsdon, *The Emperor Gaius,* Oxford 1934.

A. Barrett, *Caligula: the Corruption of Power,* London 1989.

B. Levick, *Tiberius the Politician,* London 1976.

B. Levick, *Claudius,* London 1989.

A. Momigliano, *Claudius: the Emperor and His Achievement,* Oxford 1961.

R. Seager, *Tiberius,* London 1972.

Z. Yavets, *Plebs and Princeps,* Oxford 1969.

Consolidation of Power

P.A.L. Greenhalgh, *The Year of the Four Emperors, Galba, Otho, Vitellius and Vespasian,* London 1975.

M. Griffin, *Nero: the End of a Dynasty,* London 1984.

L. Homo, *Vespasien, l'empereur du bon sens,* Paris 1949.

B.W. Jones, *The Emperor Titus,* London 1984.

E.M. Smallwood, *The Jews under Roman Rule,* Leiden 1976.

K. Wellesley, *The Long Year AD 69,* London 1975.

Romanization of the Empire

A. Birley, *Marcus Aurelius,* London 1966.

B.W. Jones, *The Emperor Domitian,* London 1992.

F.A. Lepper, *Trajan's Parthian War,* Oxford 1948.

F. Millar, *The Emperor in the Roman World,* London 1977.

B. d'Orgeval, *L'Empereur Hadrien,* Paris 1950.

H.M.D. Parker, *A History of the Roman World from AD 138 to AD 337,* London 1958.

S. Perowne, *Hadrian,* London 1986.

Life in Rome

K.R. Bradley, *Slaves and Masters in the Roman Empire,* Brussels 1984.

R.P. Duncan-Jones, *The Economy of the Roman Empire,* Cambridge 1974.

B.W. Frier, *Landlords and Tenants in Imperial Rome,* Princeton 1980.

J. Liversidge, *Everyday Life in the Roman Empire,* London 1978.

R. MacMullen, *Roman Social Relations, 50 BC - AD 284,* New Haven 1974.

G. Rickman, *The Corn Supply of Ancient Rome,* Oxford 1980.

Z. Yavets, *Slaves and Slavery in Ancient Rome,* Oxford 1987.

Bread and Games

J.P.V.D. Balsdon, *Life and Leisure in Ancient Rome,* Bodley Head 1969.

A. Cameron, *Circus Factions: Blues and Greens at Rome and Byzantium,* Oxford 1966.

J. Carcopino, *Daily Life in Ancient Rome,* Harmondsworth 1956.

L. Friedländer, *Roman Life and Manners under the Early Empire,* Leipzig 1920.

M. Grant, *Gladiators,* Harmondsworth 1967.

J. Humphrey, *Roman Circuses and Chariot Racing,* London 1986.

P. Veyne, *Le pain et le cirque,* Paris 1976.

Decline in Power

G.C. Brauer Jr., *The Age of the Soldier Emperors,* Park Ridge N.J. 1975.

A.R. Birley, *The African Emperor Septimius Severus,* London 1988.

W.H.C. Frend, *Martyrdom and Persecution in the Early Church,* New York 1966.

M. Grant, *The Climax of Rome: the Final Achievement of the Ancient World, AD 161 - 337,* Boston 1968.

R. MacMullen, *Roman Government's Response to Crisis,* New Haven 1976.

J. Vogt, *The Decline of Rome,* New York 1967.

The Late Empire

T.D. Barnes, *Constantine and Eusebius,* Cambridge Mass. 1981.

D. van Berchem, *L'armée de Dioclétien et la réforme constantinienne,* Paris 1952.

R.L. Fox, *Pagans and Christians,* London 1986.

A.H.M. Jones, *The Later Roman Empire,* 3 vol. Oxford 1964.

A.H.M. Jones, *The Decline of the Ancient World,* London 1966.

W. Seston, *Dioclétien et la tétrarchie,* Paris 1946.

S. Williams, *Diocletian and the Roman Recovery,* London 1985.

Allies and Enemies

J.P.V.D. Balsdon, *Romans and Aliens,* London 1979.

L. Casson, *The Periplus Maris Erythraei,* Princeton 1989.

J.I. Miller, *The Spice Trade of the Roman Empire, 29 BC - AD 641,* Oxford 1969.

J.S. Romm, *The Edges of the Earth in Ancient Thought: Geography, Exploration and Fiction,* Princeton 1992.

J.W. Sedlar, *India and the Greek World,* Totowa N.J. 1980.

N.H.H. Sitwell, *Outside the Empire: the World the Romans Knew,* London 1984
M. Todd, *The Northern Barbarians, 100 BC-AD 300,* London 1975.

Volume 7 Religions of the World

The Buddha
Carrithers, M. *The Buddha.* Oxford, 1986.
Herbert, P. M. *The Life of the Buddha.* London, 1993.
Holy Places of the Buddha. Berkeley, 1994.
Kalupahana, D. J. *The Way of Siddharta.* Lanham, 1987.
Klimkeit, H. J. *Der Buddha.* Stuttgart, 1990.
Morup, S. *The Date of the Buddha's Mahaparinirvana.* New Delhi, 1991.
Seth, V. *Study of Biographies of the Buddha.* New Delhi, 1992.
Withshire, M. G. *Ascetic Figures before and in Early Buddhism.* Berlin/New York, 1990.

Buddhism
Frederic, L. *Buddhism.* Paris, 1995.
Gombrich, R. *Theravada Buddhism.* London, 1988.
Reat, N. Ross. *Buddhism: A History.* Berkeley, 1994.
Swearer, D. *The Buddhist World of SE Asia.* New York, 1995.
Thurman, R. A. F. *Essential Tibetan Buddhism.* San Francisco, 1995.
Zwalf, W., ed. *Buddhism: Art and Faith.* London, 1985.

Hinduism
Basham, A. L. *The Origins and Development of Classical Hinduism.* Boston, 1989.
Cross, S. *The Elements of Hinduism.* Shaftesbury, 1994.
Dange, S. A. *Rigveda Hymns and Ancient Thought.* New Delhi, 1992.
Daweewarn, D. *Brahmanism in SE Asia.* New Delhi, 1987.
Gonda, J. *A History of Indian Literature.* Wiesbaden, 1975.
———. Visnuism and Sivaism. London, 1970.
Kanitkar, V. P., and Cole, W. O. *Hinduism.* London, 1995.
Klostermaier, K. K. *A Survey of Hinduism.* New York, 1994.
Van Nooten and Holland. *Rig Veda.* Cambridge, 1994.
Shirvastava, V. S. *Hinduism in SE Asia.* New Delhi, 1989.

Early Chinese Thinkers
Girardot, N. J. *Myth and Meaning in Early Taoism.* Berkeley, 1980.
Kohn, L., ed. *The Taoist Experience.* Albany, NY, 1993.
Kohn, L. *Early Chinese Mysticism.* Princeton, 1992.
Nikkilae, P. *Early Confucianism.* Helsinki, 1992.
Rozman, G., ed. *The East Asian Region.* Princeton, 1990.
Schipper, K. *The Taoist Body.* Berkeley, 1993.
Seidl, A. *Taoismus.* Tokyo, 1990.

The Jewish People
Avi-Yonah, M. *The Jews under Roman and Byzantine Rule.* Jerusalem, 1984.
Bickerman, B. *The God of the Maccabees.* Leiden, 1979.
Cantor, N. *The Sacred Chain.* London, 1995.
Grant, M. *Herod the Great.* London, 1971.
Harrington, D. *The Maccabean Revolt.* Wilmington, 1988.
McCullough, W. S. *The History and Literature of the Palestinian Jews.* Toronto, 1975.
Modrzejewski, J. Meleze. *The Jews of Egypt.* Edinburgh, 1995.
Schurer, E. *The History of the Jewish People in the Age of Jesus Christ.* Edinburgh, 1973.
Smallwood, E. M. *The Jews under Roman Rule from Pompey to Diocletian.* Leiden, 1981.

The Beginning of Christianity
Bornkamm, G. *Paul.* New York, 1971.
Gager, J. G. *Kingdom and Community.* Englewood Cliffs, 1975.
Hering, J. *The First Epistle of St. Paul.* London, 1962.
Meeks, W. A. *The First Urban Christians.* London, 1983.
Sanders, E. P. *Jesus and Judaism.* Philadelphia, 1985.
Van der Loos, H. *The Miracles of Jesus.* Leiden, 1968.
Zeitlin, I. M. *Jesus and the Judaism of His Time.* Cambridge, 1989.

Christianity Comes of Age
Barnes, T. D. *Early Christianity and the Roman Empire.* London, 1984.
Droge, A. J., and Tabor, J. D. *A Noble Death.* San Francisco, 1992.
Frend, W. *Martyrdom and Persecution in the Early Church.* New York, 1967.
———. The Rise of Christianity. London, 1984.
Grant, R. *Augustus to Constantine.* San Francisco, 1990.
Fox, R. Lane. *Pagans and Christians in the Mediterranean World.* London, 1986.
Markus, R. A. *Christianity in the Roman World.* London, 1974.
MacMullen, R. *Christianizing the Roman Empire.* New Haven, 1984.

The Fall of Paganism
Barnes, T. *Athansius and Constantine.* Cambridge, 1993.
Chadwick, H. *The Early Church.* Harmondsworth, 1967.
Frend, W. *The Rise of Christianity.* London, 1984.
Hillgarth, J. *Christianity and Paganism.* Philadelphia, 1986.
Laistner, M. L. W. *Christianity and Pagan Culture in the Late Roman Empire.* New York, 1951.
MacMullen, R. *Christianizing the Roman Empire.* New Haven, 1984.
———. Constantine. London, 1967.

Christian Theology and Popular Belief
Brown, P. *Augustine of Hippo: A Biography.* London, 1967.
Chadwick, H. B. *Augustine: Past Masters.* Oxford, 1986.
Evans, G. R. *Augustine on Evil.* Cambridge, 1982.
Gregory, P. T. E. *Vox Populi.* Columbus, 1977.
Markus, R. A. *The End of Ancient Christianity.* Cambridge, 1990.
———. Saeculum. Cambridge, 1988.
———. Augustine. New York, 1972.
Marrou, H. I. *Décadence Romain.* Paris, 1977.

Monasticism
Bims, J. *Ascetics and Ambassadors of Christ.* New York, 1994.
Brown, P. *The Cult of the Saints.* Chicago, 1981.
———. The Body and Society. New York, 1988.
Cameron, A., and Kuhrt, A. *Images of Women in Late Antiquity.* Detroit, 1983.
Chitty, D. W. *The Desert a City.* Oxford, 1966.
Meinardus, O. F. A. *Monks and Monasteries of the Egyptian Deserts.* Cairo, 1989.
Prinz, F. *Askese und Kultur.* Munchen, 1980.
Rousseau, P. *Ascetics, Authority and the Church in the Age of Jerome and Cassian.* Oxford, 1978.
———. Pachomonius. Berkeley, 1985.

The Church in the West
Barley, M. *Christianity in Britain.* Leicester, 1968.
Chaney, W. A. *The Cult of Kingship in Anglo-Saxon England.* Berkeley, 1970.
Corse, T. *St. Patrick and Irish Christianity.* Minneapolis, 1979.
Harting, H. Mayr. *The Coming of Christianity to Anglo-Saxon England.* London, 1972.
Herrin, J. *The Formation of Christendom.* Princeton, 1987.
Houwen, L. *Beda venerabilis.* Groningen, 1996.
Myrtum, H. *The Origins of Early Irish Christianity.* London, 1992.
Straw, C. *Gregory the Great.* Berkeley, 1988.
Talbot, C. H. *The Anglo-Saxon Missionaries in Germany.* London, 1981.

Volume 8 Christianity and Islam

The Fall of Rome
Garnsey, P. D. A., and Saller, R. P. *The Roman Empire: Economy, Society and Culture.* London, 1987.
Heather, P. J. *Goths and Romans, 332-489.* Oxford, 1991.
Marasovic, J. *Diocletian's Palace.* Split, 1972.
Millar, F. *The Roman Empire and Its Neighbours.* London, 1957.
Starr, C. G. *The Roman Empire, 27 BC-AD 476: A Study in Survival.* Oxford, 1982.
Thompson, E. A. *The Goths in Spain.* Oxford, 1969.
Wells, C. M. *The Roman Empire.* London, 1984.
Williams, S. *Diocletian and the Roman Recovery.* London, 1985.

The Changing Face of Europe
Briggs, M. S. *Goths and Vandals: A Study of Destruction, Neglect and Preservation.* London, 1952.
Ferreiro, A. *The Visigoths in Gaul and Spain.* Leiden, 1988.
Holmqvist, W. *German Art during the First Millennium AD.* Stockholm, 1955.
Kurth, G. *Clovis.* Brussels, 1929.
Murray, A. C. *Germanic Kinship Structure: Studies in Law and Society in Antiquity and the Early Middle Ages.* Toronto, 1983.
Owen, F. *The Germanic People: Their Origin, Expansion and Culture.* New Haven, 1966.
Sherk, R. K. *The Roman Empire, Augustus to Hadrian.* Cambridge, 1993.
Thompson, E. A. *The Visigoths in the Time of Ulfila.* Oxford, 1966.

The Culture of the Germanic Empires
Dunbabin, J. *France in the Making.* Oxford, 1985.
Goffart, W. *The Narrators of Barbarian History.* Princeton, 1989.
Herrin, J. *The Formation of Christendom.* Princeton, 1988.
Jarrett, M. G., and Dobson, B. *Britain and Rome.* Kendal, 1965.
Nelson, J. L. *Politics and Ritual in Early Medieval Europe.* London, 1986.
Philip, R. *Britain: A Granary for Rome?* Amsterdam, 1982.
Reuter, T. *Germany in the Early Middle Ages.* London, 1991.
Wallace-Hadrill, J. M. *Early Medieval History.* Oxford, 1976.

Constantinople
Barth, H. *Constantinople.* Paris, 1953.
Byron, R. *The Byzantine Achievement: A Historical Perspective, AD 330-1453.* New York, 1964.
Clogan, P. M. *Byzantine and Western Studies.* Totowa, 1984.
Dalton, O. *Byzantine Art and Archaeology.* Oxford, 1961.
Downey, G. *Constantinople in the Age of Justinian.* Norman, 1968.
Herrin, J. *Constantinople in the Early Eighth Century.* Leiden, 1984.
Rice, D. *Byzantine Art.* Harmondsworth, 1968.
Sherard, P. *Constantinople: Iconography of a Sacred City.* London, 1965.

The Rule of Justinian
Barker, J. W. *Justinian and the Later Roman Empire.* Madison, 1966.
Birks, P. *Justinian's Institutes.* New York, 1987.
Browning, R. *Justinian and Theodora.* London, 1971.
Bridge, A. *Theodora.* München, 1980.
Kolbert, C. F. *Justinian: The Digest of Roman Law.* Harmondsworth, 1979.
Moorhead, J. *Theoderic in Italy.* Oxford, 1992.
———. Justinian. London, 1994.
Ure, P. N. *Justinian and His Age.* Greenwood, 1979.

The New Persian Empire
Benveniste, E. *Persian Religion According to the Chief Greek Texts.* Paris, 1959.
Colledge, M. *The Parthians.* London, 1967.
———. The Parthian Period. Leiden, 1986.
Cook, J. M. *The Persian Empire.* London, 1983.
Matheson, S. A. *Persia: An Archaeological Guide.* London, 1979.
Ort, L. J. R. *Mani: A Religio-Historical Description of His Personality.* Leiden, 1967.
Ross, E. D. *Persian Art.* London, 1938.
Widengren, G. *Mani and Manichaeism.* London, 1965.

Muhammad
Hodges, R. *Mohammed, Charlemagne and the Origins of Europe.* New York, 1983.
Rodinson, M. *Mohammed.* Brussels, 1982.

Islam
Azzam, S. *Islam and Contemporary Society.* London, 1982.
Hitti, P. K. *Islam: A Way of Life.* Minneapolis, 1971.
Kateregga, B. D. *Islam and Christianity: A Muslim and a Christian in Dialogue.* Nairobi, 1985.

Martin, R. A. *Islam: A Cultural Perspective*. Englewood Cliffs, 1982.

Peters, R. *Islam and Colonialism: The Doctrine of Jihad in Modern History*. The Hague, 1979.

Rahman, F. *Islam: The History of a Religion*. London, 1966.

Roberts, D. S. *Islam: A Westerner's Guide*. London, 1981.

———. *Islam: A Concise Introduction*. San Francisco, 1982.

Sjadzali, M. *Islam and Governmental Systems: Teachings, History and Reflections*. Jakarta, 1991.

Williams, J. A. *Islam*. New York, 1967.

Jihad
Cudsi, A. S. *Islam and Power*. London, 1982.

Dekmejian, R. H. *Islam in Revolution: Fundamentalism in the Arab World*. New York, 1985.

Von Grunebaum, G. E. *Islam: Essays on the Nature and Growth of a Cultural Tradition*. London, 1969.

———. *Islam and Medieval Hellenism: Social and Cultural Perspectives*. London, 1976.

Lewis, B. *Islam in History: Ideas, Men and Events in the Middle East*. La Salla, 1973.

———. *Islam: From the Prophet Muhammad to the Capture of Constantinople*. London, 1976.

Makdisi, G. *Islam and the West in the Middle Ages*. Paris, 1977.

Semaan, K. I. *Islam and the Medieval West: Aspects of Intercultural Relations*. New York, 1980.

Verhoeven, F. R. J. *Islam: Its Origin and Spread in Words, Maps and Pictures*. Amsterdam, 1962.

Vryonis, S. *Islam and Cultural Change in the Middle Ages*. Wiesbaden, 1975.

The Caliphs
Ashtiany, J. *Abbasid Belles-lettres*. Cambridge, 1990.

Bosworth, C. E. *The Islamic Dynasties*. Edinburgh, 1980.

Frye, R. N. *Islamic Iran and Central Asia, 7th-12th Centuries*. London, 1979.

Knappert, J. *Islamic Legend: Histories of the Heroes, Saints and Prophets of Islam*. Leiden, 1985.

Lewis, A. R. *The Islamic World and the West, AD 622-1492*. New York, 1970.

al-Qulanisi, Ibn. *The Damascus Chronicle of the Crusades*. New York, 1980.

Seddiqui, A. H. *Caliphate and Kingship in Medieval Persia*. Philadelphia, 1977.

Shaban, M. A. *The Abbasid Revolution*. Cambridge, 1979.

Sykes, M. *The Caliphs' Last Heritage*. New York, 1973.

Walker, A. T. *The Caliphate*. Oxford, 1924.

The Riches of Islam
Atl, E. *Islamic Art and Patronage: Treasures from Kuwait*. New York, 1990.

Brandenburg, D. *Islamic Miniature Painting in Medieval Manuscripts*. Basle, 1982.

Brend, B. *Islamic Art*. Cambridge, MA, 1991.

Burns, R. I. *Islam under the Crusaders*. Princeton, 1973.

Ettinghausen, R. *Islamic Art and Archaeology*. Berlin, 1984.

Glick, T. F. *Islamic and Christian Spain in the Early Middle Ages*. Princeton, 1979.

King, D. A. *Islamic Astronomical Instruments*. London, 1987.

Kuhnel, I. *Islamic Art and Architecture*. London, 1966.

Schimmel, A. *Islamic Calligraphy*. Leiden, 1970.

Spuhler, F. *Islamic Carpets and Textiles*. London, 1978.

Volume 9 The Middle Ages

The Frankish Empire
Bachrach, B. S. *Merovingian Military Organization 481-751*. Minneapolis, 1972.

Geary, P. J. *Before France and Germany: The Creation and Transformation of the Merovingian World*. Cambridge, 1988.

James, E. *The Franks*. Oxford, 1988.

Leyser, K. J. *The Ascent of Latin Europe*. Oxford, 1986.

Reuter, T., ed. *The Medieval Nobility:Studies on the Ruling Classes of France and Germany from the Sixth to the Twelfth Century*. Amsterdam/New York/Oxford, 1979.

Wallace-Hadrill, J. M. *The Barbarian West*. New York, 1962.

———. *The Long-haired Kings and Other Studies in Frankish History*. London, 1962.

Wood, I., and P. Sawyer. *Early Medieval Kingship*. Leeds, 1977.

Wood, I. *The Merovingian Kingdoms, 450-751*. London/New York, 1993.

Charlemagne
Collins, R. *Early Medieval Spain*. London, 1983.

Ganshof, F. L. *The Carolingians and the Frankish Monarchy*. London, 1971.

Halphen, F. L. *Charlemagne and the Carolingian Empire*. Amsterdam/New York/London, 1977.

Hodges, R., and D. Whitehouse. *Mohammed, Charlemagne and the Origins of Europe*. London, 1983.

McKitterick, R. *The Frankish Kingdoms under the Carolingians*. London/New York, 1983.

———, ed. *Carolingian Culture: Emulation and Innovation*. Cambridge, 1994.

Nelson, J. L. *Politics and Ritual in Early Medieval Europe*. London, 1986.

Pirenne, H. *Mohammed and Charlemagne*. London, 1939.

Reuter, T. *Germany in the Early Middle Ages, 800-1056*. London/New York, 1991.

The Western Empire
Bullough, D. *The Age of Charlemagne*. London, 1965.

Cabaniss, A. *Son of Charlemagne: A Contemporary Life of Louis the Pious*. Syracuse, 1961.

Duckett, E. S. *Alcuin, Friend of Charlemagne*. New York, 1951.

Godman, P. *Poetry of the Carolingian Renaissance*. London, 1985.

Godman, P., and R. Collins, eds. *Charlemagne's Heir: New Perspectives on the Reign of Louis the Pious*. Oxford, 1986.

Hodges, R. *The Anglo-Saxon Achievement*. London, 1989.

Laistner, M. L. W. *Thought and Letters in Western Europe, AD 500-900*. London, 1931.

Nelson, J. L. *Charles the Bald*. London/New York, 1992.

McKitterick, R. *The Carolingians and the Written Word*. Cambridge, 1989.

Sawyer, P. *The Age of the Vikings*. London, 1962.

Ullmann, W. *The Carolingian Renaissance and the Idea of Kingship*. London, 1969.

Wallach, L. *Alcuin and Charlemagne*. Ithaca, 1959.

Feudalism
Beeler, J. *Warfare in Feudal Society*. Ithaca, 1971.

Brønsted, J. *The Vikings*. Harmondsworth, 1960.

Cheyette, F. L. *Lordship and Community in Medieval Europe*. New York, 1968.

Duby, G. *The Three Orders: Feudal Society Imagined*. Chicago, 1980.

Herlihy, D. *The History of Feudalism*. New York, 1971.

Odegaard, C. *Vassi and Fideles in the Carolingian Empire*. Cambridge, 1945.

Sawyer, P. *Kings and Vikings: Scandinavia and Europe, AD 700-1100*. London, 1982.

Southern, R. W. *The Making of the Middle Ages*. London, 1953.

The Feudal Society
Boch, M. *Feudal Society*. London, 1961.

Ganshof, F. L. *Feudalism*. London, 1952.

Hamilton, B. *Religion in the Medieval West*. London, 1986.

Knowles, D. *Christian Monasticism*. London, 1969.

Lawrence, C. H. *Medieval Monasticism*. London/New York, 1989.

Rosenwein, B. *Rhinocerous Bound: Cluny in the Tenth Century*. Philadelphia, 1982.

Southern, R. W. *Western Society and the Church in the Middle Ages*. Harmondsworth, 1970.

Strayer, J. R. *Feudalism*. New York, 1965.

Ullmann, W. *The Growth of Papal Government in the Middle Ages*. London, 1955.

Early Medieval Politics
Blumenthal, U. *The Investiture Contest*. Philadelphia, 1988.

Hallam, E. H. *Capetingian France, 987-1328*. New York, 1980.

Kantorowicz, E. *The King's Two Bodies*. Princeton, 1957.

Leyser, K. J. *Rule and Conflict in an Early Medieval Society: Ottonian Saxony*. Bloomington, 1979.

Painter, S. *The Rise of the Feudal Monarchies*. Ithaca, 1951.

Robinson, I. S. *Authority and Resistance in the Investiture Contest*. New York, 1978.

Tellenbach, G. *Church, State and Christian Society at the Time of the Investiture Contest*. Oxford, 1940.

Tierney, B. *The Crisis of Church and State, 1050-1300*. Toronto, 1988.

Williams, S., ed. *The Gregorian Epoch*. Boston, 1964.

The Muslims
Collins, R. *Early Medieval Spain: Unity and Diversion*. New York, 1983.

Jackson, G. *The Making of Medieval Spain*. London, 1972.

MacKay, A. *Spain in the Middle Ages. From Frontier to Empire, 1100-1500*. Basingstoke, 1977.

Russell, F. H. *The Just War in the Middle Ages*. Cambridge, 1975.

O'Callaghan, J. F. *A History of Medieval Spain*. Ithaca, 1975.

Vicens Vives, J., and J. Nadal Oller. *An Economic History of Spain*. Princeton, 1969.

The Reconquista
Brooke, R., and C. Brooke. *Popular Religion in the Middle Ages: Western Europe 1000-1300*. London, 1984.

Duby, G. *Rural Economy and Country Life in the Medieval West*. London, 1968.

Fossier, R. *Peasant Life in the Medieval West*. Oxford, 1988.

Heaton, H. *Economic History of Europe*. New York, 1948.

Hyde, J. K. *Society and Politics in Medieval Italy: The Evolution of Civil Life, 1000-1350*. London, 1973.

Postan, M. M., ed. *The Agrarian Life of the Middle Ages*. Cambridge, 1966.

White, L. *Medieval Technology and Social Change*. New York, 1966.

Wickham, C. *Early Medieval Italy: Central Power and Local Society*. London, 1981.

Byzantium
Attwater, D. *The Christian Churches of the East*. London, 1961.

Chitty, J. *The Desert: A City*. n.p., 1966.

Every, G. *The Byzantine Patriarchate*. London, 1962.

———. *Understanding Eastern Christianity*. London, 1980.

Hussey, J. M. *The Orthodox Church in the Byzantine Empire*. Oxford, 1986.

Lawrence, C. H. *Medieval Monasticism*. London/New York, 1984.

Painter, B., and S. Tierney. *Western Europe in the Middle Ages*. New York, 1985.

Rousseau, P. *Ascetics, Authority and the Church in the Age of Jerome and Cassian*. Paris, 1978.

The Middle Byzantine Empire
Hussey, J. M. *Church and Learning in the Byzantine Empire*. n.p., 1963.

Lemerle, P. *Byzantine Humanism*. Canberra, 1986.

Noble, T. F. X. *The Birth of the Papal State*. Philadelphia, 1984.

Vasiliev, A. A. *History of the Byzantine Empire*. London, 1963.

Ware, T. *The Orthodox Church*. Harmondsworth, 1963.

The Crusades
Atiya, A. S. *Crusade, Commerce and Culture*. New York, 1966.

Bradford, E. *The Great Betrayal*. London, 1967.

Mayer, H. E. *The Crusades*. London, 1972.

Powell, J. *The Anatomy of a Crusade, 1213-1221*. Philadelphia, 1977.

Prawer, J. *The Latin Kingdom of Jerusalem: European Colonialism in the Middle Ages*. London, 1972.

Queller, D. E. *The Fourth Crusade: The Conquest of Constantinople*. Leicester, 1978.

Runciman, S. *A History of the Crusades*. Cambridge, 1967.

Smail, R. C. *Crusading Warfare*. Cambridge, 1956.

Volume 10 Medieval Polities and Life

Growth and Prosperity
Duby, G. *The Early Growth of the European Economy*. London, 1974.

Lopez, R. J. *The Commercial Revolution of the Middle*

Ages, 950-1350. New York, 1976.
Pounds, N. J. G. *An Economic History of Medieval Europe.* New York, 1975.

Towns and Cities
Hilton, R. H. *English and French Towns in Feudal Society.* Cambridge, 1992.
Little, L. K. *Religious Poverty and the Profit Economy of Medieval Europe.* Ithaca, 1983.
Mundy, J. H. *The Medieval Town.* Princeton, 1985.

Rivalry Along the Channel
Fawtier, R. *The Capetian Kings of France.* London, 1982.
Hallam, E. M. *Capetian France, 987-1328.* London, 1980.
Hallam, H. E. *Rural England, 1066-1348.* London, 1981.
Stafford, P. *Unification and Conquest: A Political and Social History of England in the Tenth and Eleventh Centuries.* London, 1989.

Popes and Emperors
Bartlett, R. *The Making of Europe: Conquest, Colonization and Cultural Change, 950-1350.* London, 1993.
Gillingham, J. B. *The Kingdom of Germany in the High Middle Ages.* London, 1971.
Hyde, J. K. *Society and Politics in Medieval Italy.* London, 1983.
Munz, P. *Frederick Barbarossa: A Study in Medieval Politics.* London, 1983.

Rulers in Europe
Abulafia, D. *Frederick II: A Medieval Emperor.* London, 1988.
Davies, R. R. *The British Isles, 1100-1500: Comparisons, Contrasts and Connections.* Edinburgh, 1988.
Haverkamp, A. *Medieval Germany, 1056-1273.* Oxford, 1988.
Hyde, J. K. *Society and Politics in Medieval Italy.* London, 1983.
Runciman, S. *The Sicilian Vespers: The History of the Mediterranean World in the Later Thirteenth Century.* Cambridge, 1982.
Strayer, J. R. *The Reign of Philip the Fair.* Princeton, 1980.
Warren, W. L. *The Governance of Norman and Angevin England, 1086-1272.* London, 1987.

The Late Middle Ages
Dykema, A. and Oberman, H. A., eds. *Anticlericalism in Late Medieval and Early Modern Europe.* Leiden, 1991.
Given-Wilson, C., and Curteis A. *The Black Death: Natural and Human Disasters in Medieval Europe.* London, 1984.
Gottfried, R. S. *The Black Death.* London, 1983.
Hale, J. R. *Renaissance Europe.* London, 1985.
Miskimin, H. A. *The Economy of Early Renaissance Europe.* Englewood Cliffs, 1969.
Schildhauer, J. *The Hansa: History and Culture.* Leipzig, 1985.

Jewish Culture in the Middle Ages
Ashtor, E. *The Jews and the Mediterranean Economy, 10th-15th Centuries.* London 1983.
Cohen, J. *The Friars and the Jews: The Evolution of Medieval Anti-Judaism.* Ithaca, 1983.
Cohen, M. R. *Under Crescent and Cross: The Jews in the Middle Ages.* Princeton, 1994.
Katz, J. *Tradition and Crisis: Jewish Society at the End of the Middle Ages.* London, 1985.
Stow, K. R. *Alienated Minority: The Jews of Medieval Latin Europe.* Cambridge, 1992.

The Hundred Years' War
Brown, A. L. *The Governance of Late Medieval England 1272-1461.* London, 1989.
Davies, R. R. *The British Isles, 1100-1500: Comparisons, Contrasts and Connections.* Edinburgh, 1988.
Fowler, K. *The Age of Plantagenet and Valois.* London, 1980.
Lander, J. R. *The Limitations of English Monarchy in the Later Middle Ages.* Toronto, 1988.
Ormrod, W. M. *The Reign of Edward III: Crown and Political Society in England, 1327-1377.* London, 1993.
Warner, M. *Joan of Arc: The Image of Female Heroism.* London, 1983.

Emperors, Princes, and Dukes
Du Boulay, F. R. H. *Germany in the Later Middle Ages.* London, 1983.
Jones, P. J. *The Malatesa of Rimini and the Papal State.* London, 1974.
Martines, L., ed. *Violence and Civil Disorder in Italian Cities, 1200-1500.* Los Angeles, 1973.
Waley, D. *The Italian City-republics.* London, 1969.

Central Europe During the Middle Ages
Christiansen, E. *The Northern Crusades: The Baltic and the Catholic Frontier, 1100-1525.* London, 1980.
Fennell, J. *The Crisis of Medieval Russia, 1200-1304.* London, 1983.
Halperin, C. J. *The Mongol Impact on Russian History.* London, 1987.
Schildhauer, J. *The Hansa: History and Culture.* Leipzig, 1985.

Burgundy
Vaughan, R. *Valois Burgundy.* London, 1975
———. *Philip the Good: The Apogee of Burgundy.* London/New York, 1970.

Volume 11 Empires of the Ancient World

Pre-Columbian Cultures
Berrin and Pasztory. *Teotihuacán.* London, 1993.
Coe, M. D. *Mexico.* London, 1994.
Davies, N. *The Toltecs.* Norman, 1987.
Diehl and Berlo., eds. *Mesoamerica After the Decline of Teotihuacan.* Washington, 1989.
———. *Tula.* London, 1983.
Guthrie, J., ed. *The Olmec World.* Princeton, 1995.
Miller, M. E. *The Art of Mesoamerica from Olmec to Aztec.* London, 1986.
Sharer and Grove. *Regional Perspectives on the Olmecs.* Cambridge, 1989.

The Maya
Antochiw, M. *Route of the Mayas.* London, 1995.
Goetz and Morley. *Popol Vuh.* Norman, 1991.
MacAnay, P. A. *Living with the Ancestors.* Austin, 1995.
de Montmollin, O. *Settlement and Politics in Three Classic Maya Polities.* Madison, 1995.
Sabloff, J. A. *The New Archaeology and the Ancient Maya.* New York, 1994.
Sharer, R. J. *The Ancient Maya.* Stanford, 1994.
Taube, K. *Aztecs and Maya Myths.* Austin, 1993.
Wearne, P. *The Maya of Guatemala.* London, 1994.
Weaver, M. P. *The Aztecs, Maya and Their Predecessors.* San Diego, 1993.

The Aztecs
Bierhorst, J. *History and Mythology of the Aztecs.* Tucson, 1992.
Coe, M. D. *Mexico.* London, 1994.
Gillespie, S. D. *The Aztec Kings.* Tucson, 1989.
Glendinnen, I. *Aztecs.* Cambridge, 1991.
Grusinski, S. *The Aztecs: Rise and Fall of an Empire.* London, 1992.
Hassig, R. *Aztec Warfare.* Norman, 1988.
Hodge and Smiths. *Economies and Politics in the Aztec Realm.* Albany, NY, 1994.
Leon-Portilla, M. *The Broken Spears.* Boston, 1993.
Moctezuma, E. M. *The Aztecs.* New York, 1989.
———. *The Great Temple of the Aztecs.* London, 1994.
Taube, K. *Aztec and Maya Myth.* Austin, 1993.
Townsend, R. F. *The Aztecs.* London, 1992.
Weaver, M. P. *The Aztecs, Mayas and Their Predecessors.* San Diego, 1993.

The World of the Incas
Bauer, B. S. *The Development of the Inca State.* Austin, 1992.
Bauer and Dearborn. *Astronomy and Empire in the Ancient Andes.* Austin, 1992.
Cobe, B. *Inca Religion and Customs.* Austin, 1995.
Davies, N. *The Incas.* Niwat/Colorado, 1995.
Hemming, J. *The Conquest of the Incas.* London, 1993.
Kent, M. *Kinship and Labor in the Structure of the Inca Empire.* Michigan, 1989.
Malpass, M. A., ed. *Provincial Inca.* Iowa City, 1993.
Moseley, M. E. *The Incas and Their Ancestors.* London, 1992.
Paerssinen, M. *Tawantinsuu.* Helsinki, 1992.
Patterson, T. C. *The Inca Empire.* New York, 1991.

Protzen, J. P. *Inca Architecture and Construction at Ollantaytambo.* New York, 1993.
Stone-Miller, R. *Art of the Andes.* London, 1995.
Zuidman, T. *Inca Civilization in Cuzco.* Austin, 1990.

India in the Middle Ages
Ahir, D. C. *Buddhism in South India.* Delhi, 1992.
Bhattacharyya, N. N. *Buddhism in the History of Indian Ideas.* New Delhi, 1993.
Cook, E., ed. *Light of Liberation.* Berkeley, 1992.
Gonda, J. *A History of Indian Literature.* Wiesbaden, 1984.
Ilangasinha, L. B. *Buddhism in Medieval Sri Lanka.* Delhi, 1992.
Khandalavala, K. *The Golden Age.* Bombay, 1991.
Kulke and Rothermund. *A History of India.* London, 1990.
Pyysiaeninen, J. *Beyond Language and Reason.* Helsinki, 1993.
Sharma, T. R. *A Political History of the Imperial Guptas.* New Delhi, 1989.
Sinor, D., ed. *The Cambridge History of Early Inner Asia.* Cambridge, 1990.
Strong, J. S. *The Legend and Cult of Upagupta.* Princeton, 1992.
Thapar, R. *A History of India, Vol. 1.* Harmondsworth, 1966.

The March of Progress
Brook, T. *Praying for Power.* Cambridge, MA, 1993.
Chan and de Bary, eds. *Yuan Thought.* New York, 1982.
Cotterell, A. *China.* London, 1988.
Ebrey, P. B. *Confucianism and Family Rituals in Imperial China.* Princeton, 1991.
Gernet, J. *Buddhism in Chinese Society.* New York, 1995.
Hyme and Schirokauer. *Ordering the World.* Berkeley, 1993.
Loewe, M. *Crisis and Conflict in Han China.* London, 1974.
Serruys, H. *The Mongols and Ming China.* London, 1987.
Twitchett and Fairbank. *The Cambridge History of China.* Cambridge, 1994.
Twitchett and Wright, eds. *Perspectives on the Tang.* London, 1973.
Waldron, A. *The Great Wall of China.* Cambridge, 1992.
Zurcher, A. *The Buddhist Conquest of China.* Leiden, 1959.

From Kiev to Moscow
Alef, G. *The Origins of Muscovite Autocracy.* Wiesbaden, 1986.
Baron, S. H. *Explorations in Muscovite History.* Hampshire, 1991.
Crummey, R. O. *The Formation of Muscovy.* New York, 1987.
Fennell, J. *The Crisis of Medieval Russia.* New York, 1983.
———. *A History of the Russian Church to 1448.* London, 1995.
Halperin, C. J. *The Tatar Yoke.* Columbus, 1986.
———. *Russia and the Golden Horde.* Bloomington, 1985.
de Hartog, L. *Russia and the Mongol Yoke.* New York, 1996.
Martin, J. *Medieval Russia.* Cambridge, 1995.
Presniakov, A. E. *The Tsardom of Muscovy.* Gulf Breeze, 1978.
Schapov, Y. N. *State and Church in Early Russia.* New York, 1993.

The Emergence of Japan
Bottomley and Hopson. *Arms and Armor of the Samurai.* New York, 1993.
Grossberg, K. A. *Japan's Renaissance.* Cambridge, 1981.
Hall and Takeshi, eds. *Japan in Murumachi Age.* Berkeley, 1977.
Hall, J. W., ed. *The Cambridge History of Japan.* Cambridge, 1988.
Kashiwahara and Sonoda. *Shapers of Japanese Buddhism.* Tokyo, 1994.
Kyohan and Petzold. *The Classification of Buddhism.* Wiesbaden, 1995.
Mass, J. P. *Lordship and Inheritance in Early Medieval Japan.* Stanford, 1989.
———. *The Development of Kamakura Rule.* Stanford, 1979.

Mass, J. P., ed. *Court and Bakufu in Japan.* Princeton, 1982.

Meyer, N. W. *Japan: A Concise History.* Lanham, 1992.

Sansom, G. *A History of Japan.* Stanford, 1982.

The Mongols

DeFrancis, J. *In the Footsteps of Genghis Khan.* Honolulu, 1993.

Halkovic, Jr., S. A. *The Mongols of the West.* Bloomington, 1985.

de Hartog, L. *Genghis Khan, Conqueror of the World.* London, 1989.

Hoang, M. *Genghis Khan.* London, 1990.

Kahn, P. *The Secret History of the Mongols.* San Francisco, 1984.

Morgan, D. *The Mongols.* Oxford, 1986.

Nicolle, D. *The Mongol Warlords.* Poole, 1990.

Onon, U. *The History and the Life of Chinghis Khan.* Leiden, 1990.

Ratchenevsky, P. *Ghenghis Khan.* Oxford, 1991.

Riasanovsky, V. A. *Customary Law of the Mongol Tribes.* Westport, 1979.

Rossabi, M. *Khubilai Khan.* Berkeley, 1988.

The Kingdoms of Africa

Agbodeka, F. *An Economic History of Ghana from the Earliest Times.* Accra, 1992.

Carmichael, J. *African Eldorado.* London, 1993.

Elfasi, M. *Africa from the Seventh to the Eleventh Century.* Berkeley, 1988.

Fage and Oliver. *The Cambridge History of Africa, Vol. I-IV.* Cambridge, 1982.

Levtzion, M. *Ancient Ghana and Mali.* London, 1973.

MacNaughton, P. R. *The Mande Blacksmiths.* Bloomington, 1988.

McKissack and McKissack. *The Royal Kingdoms of Ghana, Mali, and Songhay.* New York, 1994.

Mokhtar, G. *Ancient Civilizations of Africa.* Berkeley, 1990.

Niane, D. T. *Africa from the Twelfth to the Sixteenth Century.* Berkeley, 1984.

Owusu-Ansah and McFarland. *Historical Dictionary of Ghana.* Metuchen, NJ, 1995.

The Advent of the Ottoman Empire

Brummett, P. *Ottoman Seapower and Levantine Diplomacy in the Age of Discovery.* New York, 1994.

Cunt and Woodhead. *Süleyman the Magnificent and His Age.* London, 1995.

Goodwin, G. *The Janissaries.* London, 1994.

Hourani, A. *History of the Arab People.* London, 1991.

Inalcik and Quataert, eds. *An Economic and Social History of the Ottoman Empire.* Cambridge, 1994.

Kortepeter, C. M. *The Ottoman Turcs.* Istanbul, 1991.

Levy, A., ed. *The Jews of the Ottoman Empire.* Princeton, 1994.

Mansfield, P. *A History of the Middle East.* London, 1991.

Pritcher, D. E. *An Historical Geography of the Ottoman Empire from the Earliest Times to the End of the Sixteenth Century.* Leiden, 1972.

Shaw, S. *Empire of the Gazis.* New York, 1970.

Stiles, E. *The Ottoman Empire.* London, 1991.

Thematic indexes

ARTS and CULTURE

Academy, an institute for philosophical and scientific teaching and research **5:** 607, 644, 648
Abbevillian culture (700,000 years ago) **1:** 126
About Nature, title of writings of Anaximander of Miletus **4:** 503
Acharnians, Greek play of Aristophanes, produced in 425 BC **5:** 600. *See also* Aristophanes
Acheulean culture **1:** 45, 50-51
Acropolis **4:** *456*, 476, 483, 485, *503*, 521, *526-527*, 534, 537, 553, 565, 567 **5:** 587, 591, *594-595* **11:** 1451
Aedesius, Greek philosopher (d.355) **11:** 1544
Aeneid, epic work by Virgil **5:** 650 **6:** 733, *752-753*, 853-854, 856
Aeolic dialect, Greek dialect **4:** 448, 565
Aeschylus (525-456 BC), Greek writer of tragedies **4:** 521, 534, 537, 542-544, *542*, 546, *546*, 565 **5:** 587, 591, 600, 615, 709
Agora **4:** *506*, 508, 537, 565
Agriculture **1:** 66-70, 72-76, 78, 80, 84, 97, 100, 119-120, 133-135 **2:** *151*, 152, 175, 248, 279-280 **3:** 308, 349, 355, 362, 365-366, 405, 407, 408, 409 **4:** 489-490, 567 **7:** 889, 901, 970 **8:** 1044, 1084, 1110, 1125-1126 **9:** 1231, 1250 **10:** 1303-1304, 1309-1310, 1359, 1422
Ahmad Baba, writer (1556-1627) **11:** 1548
Al-Akhtal, Arab poet **8:** 1113
Alcaeus, lyric poet from Lésvos (620-580 BC) **4:** 466, 565
Alcestis, Greek play by Euripides **5:** 600
Alcman (Alcmaeon), Greek poet **4:** 464, 468
Alcuin (or Albinus) (735-804), Anglo-Latin poet, educator and cleric **9:** 1178-1180, 1182, 1185, *1186*
Alphabet **3:** 301, 308 **4:** 449-450, 457, 498, 565 **6:** 766, 836
Amphitheater **6:** 772, 778, 782, 801-803, *802*, 807, 812, *819*, 853-854, 801-803
Amphitheatrum Flavium. *See* Colosseum
Amratian (Naqada I), Egyptian predynastic culture phase **2:** 152
Anaxagoras, Greek philosopher (c.500-428 BC) **4:** 534, 547-548, 553, 565
Anaximander of Miletus, Ionian natural philosopher (610-c.547 BC) **4:** 503-504, 565
Anaximenes of Miletus, Ionian natural philosopher (585-525 BC) **4:** 503-504, 547, 565
Andromache, work by Athenian tragic dramatist Euripides **5:** 600, 710
Annalum Regium Francorum (Annals of the Franks) **9:** *1182*
Aphrodite of Auxerre **4:** *446*
Apocolocyntosis Divi Claudi **6:** 809
Aqueduct(s) **6:** 749, 751, 766, 826, 853 **8:** 1034, 1044, *1049*, 1064, 1066 **11:** 1466, 1472
Ara Pacis Augustae (Altar of Peace) **6:** *745*, 754, 853, 855
Arabian culture **8:** 1121
Archilochus, Greek poet and satirist (c.600 BC) **4:** 461-462, 465-466, 565
Archimedes (287-212 BC), mathematician and physicist **5:** 641-642, 690, 709 **8:** 1119
Architecture **4:** 447, 449, 534, 567
Aristarchus of Samos, Greek astronomer (c.310-230 BC) **1:** 8 **5:** 642
Aristophanes (c.445-385 BC), Athenian comic dramatist **4:** 534, 542, 546, 558 **5:** 587, 591, 598, 600, 709.
Aristotle (384-322 BC), Greek philosopher, logician, and scientist **4:** 480, 536, 547-548, 553-554, 568 **5:** 602, 606-607, *607*, *613*, 614-615, *615*, 644, 648, 709 **8:** 1080, 1119, 1129, 1141 **9:** *1238* **11:** 1548
Arithmetica **9:** 1179
Ars Poetica **6:** 854
Art of poetry **4:** 474
Assyrian culture **2:** 260
Astrology **2:** 251

Astronomia **9:** 1179
Asuka, period in Japanese history and art (552-645) **11:** 1530

Babylonian culture (c.4000-331 BC) **1:** 106
Bacchae Greek play by Euripides **5:** 600, 710
Badarian, Egyptian predynastic cultural phase **2:** 152
Bandkeramik **1:** *73*, 75-78, 80, 95, 133-134
Baths of Caracalla **6:** 810, *810*, 856
Bell-beaker culture **1:** 88, 90, 98, 105, 108, 133; - pottery **1:** 88
Black-patterned pottery **4:** 568
Bronze Age culture (c.fourth millennium-c.1000 BC) **1:** 108, 136
Bronze Gate **9:** 1248, 1254
Bronze Palace **7:** 980 **9:** 1168

Cambrian Period (570-505 million years ago) **1:** 33-34
Canaanite culture **1:** 69
Canossa, tenth-century castle in Italy **9:** 1218-1219, 1286
Carmen Saeculare **6:** 752, 854
Castilian culture **9:** 1285
Castle of Canossa. *See* Canossa
Castrum amphitheater **6:** *802*
Cathedral **9:** *1170*, *1191*, *1211*, *1219*, *1241*
Cathedral of Monza **8:** 1040
Cave paintings **1:** 56-57, 60, *62*, 64, 92, 99, 133 **11:** 1450
Celtic sculpture **1:** 124
Chrysippus of Soli (c.280 BC-c.206), Greek philosopher **5:** 648
Chuang-tzu (c.369-286 BC), philosopher, teacher; important proponent of Daoism **7:** 909, 911, 997
Church of Holy Wisdom **8:** 1052, 1068. *See also* Hagia Sophia
Church(es) **8:** 1017-1018, 1044, 1046, 1048, 1050, 1054, 1063, 1098, 1107
Cicero, Marcus Tullius (106-43 BC), Roman greatest orator, statesman, scholar and writer **4:** 515 **5:** 647, 673 **6:** *730*, 731-732, 734, 736-737, 743, 767, 802, 808, 853 **7:** 960, 962
Circus Maximus **6:** *770*, 806-807, 853 **8:** 1066
Circus of Nero **6:** 772
Circuses **6:** 774, 799, *802*, 807, 855
Civis romanus sum **6:** 772
Civitas sine suffragio **6:** 836, 853
Clay tablets **2:** 177, 183, 206, 209, 214, 216, 218, 222, 234, 253, 270, 277-279
Cleanthes of Assos (331/330-232/231 BC), Stoic philosopher **5:** 648
Codex Aureus, tenth century manuscript (Echternach) **7:** 944 **9:** *1220*, *1224*
Codex Cortesianus **11:** 1459
Codex Dresdensis **11:** 1459
Codex Mendoza **11:** 1460
Codex Perez **11:** 1459
Codex Tro **11:** 1459
Colonnades **6:** 793
Colosseum **6:** 772, 778, *778*, 801, *802*, 807, 854 **7:** 981
Colossus **2:** 177 **6:** 778, 854
Comedy **4:** 534, 537, 539-541, 546, 565 **5:** 587, 591, 598, 600, 638-639, 711
Confucius (551-479 BC), philosopher of ancient China **3:** 356-357 **7:** 902-905, *904-905*, 907, 909-910, 997 **11:** 1502
Cultures of Mexico **11:** 1450
Curvilinear art **11:** 1450
Cyrillic alphabet **9:** 1264

Damnatio memoriae **6:** 774, 783, 812, 854
Dante Pyramid **11:** 1457
De Administrando Imperio **9:** 1261
De Bello Gallico **6:** 736, 738
De Ceremoniis Aulae Byzantinae **9:** 1261
De Clementia **6:** 856

De Germania **9:** 1171
De Ira **6:** 856
De Temporum Ratione **7:** 997
De Thematibus **9:** 1261
Delatores maiestatis **6:** 761
Democritus, Greek philosopher (c.460-c.370 BC) **4:** 552, 565
Didactic poem **4:** 462, 550
Diocles (fourth century BC), philosopher and pioneer in medicine **6:** 827
Diogenes, Greek philosopher (c.400-325 BC) **4:** 547, *556*, 558, 565
Dravida culture **11:** 1493, 1574
Duomo (Cathedral of Milan) **10:** 1397

Earthenware **1:** 68, *68*, 70, 75-76, 78, 80, 82, *85*, *92*, *94*, 100, 102, *108*, 112, 117, *125*, 133, 135 **4:** 447, *456*, 483, *534*, 567-568
Einhard (c.770-840), Frankish scholar and monk, biographer of Charlemagne **9:** 1170, 1172, 1182, *1182*, 1286
El Argar Culture (peak: 1700-1000 BC) **1:** *92*, *105*, 107-108
El cantar de mío Cid **9:** 1238
Elegy, poem of lament **4:** 464, 565
Elp culture **1:** 110
Enmerkar, Sumarian epic tale **2:** 222
Enuma Elish, Babylonian epic **2:** 251
Epic poem **4:** 439, 566 **7:** 997; - style **4:** 441
Epic poetry **5:** 638
Epic verses **8:** 1079
Epictetus, Greek Stoic philosopher **5:** 710 **6:** 808
Epicurus (c.341-270 BC) Greek philosopher **5:** *642*, 646-647, 710
Epistula de litteris colendis **9:** 1179
Epistulae Morales **6:** 856
Eratosthenes (c.276-c.196 BC) Greek astronomer, mathematician, geographer, and poet **5:** 604-605, 643, 710-711
Erechtheum **4:** *503*, *526*, *531*, 534 **5:** 587, 591, *595*
Euripides, Athenian poet, playwright (c.484-406 BC) **4:** 534, 542, 546, 548 **5:** *586-587*, 587, 591, 598, 600, 615, 710

Fabius Pictor (fl. c.200 BC), one of the first Roman prose historians **5:** 650
Fibulae **1:** 112
Flavian amphitheater **6:** 778. *See also* Colosseum
Floor mosaic **6:** *732*
Florus, Publius Annius (late first and early second century), historian of Rome and poet **6:** 810
Forum **6:** 729, 735, 746, 749, *749*, *754-755*, 766, *781*, 787, 793-794, *794*, 796, 805, 808, 814, *842*, 854-855
Forum Boarium **5:** 697 **6:** *729*
Forum of Augustus **6:** *746*
Forum Romanum **5:** 684, 693 **6:** *735*, *749*, *754-755*, *781*, 794, 814, *842*, 855 **7:** 946, 981
Four Books **3:** 356
Frescoes **2:** *197*, 201-203 **4:** 497 **6:** 772, *773*, 805 **8:** 1018, 1031 **10:** 1313, 1341, 1344, 1368; house of the - **2:** 201
Funnel-beakers **1:** 83-84; - culture **1:** 80, 87, 92, 98, 133

Galileo Galilei, astronomer, mathematician, and physicist (1564-1642) **1:** 10-11
Gemma augustea cameo **6:** *750*
Glassware **1:** 118
Golden Gate **8:** 1052
Graffiti **6:** 805 **8:** 1134
Greco-Roman **3:** 387 **6:** 845-846 **7:** *883*, 892, 948-951
Gregorian calendar **6:** 854

Hagia Sophia (St. Sophia, Church of the Holy Wisdom) **8:** 1050, 1052, *1054-1055*, 1056, *1057*, *1063*, 1142-1143 **9:** *1243*, 1247, 1251, *1260*, 1263, 1266, 1274 **11:** 1559, *1563*

GOVERNMENT and POLITICS

173-175, *179*, 277, 280

Hattusilis I (reigned c.1650-1620 BC), Hittite king in the Old Hittite Kingdom **3:** 344

Hattusilis III (reigned c.1285-1265 BC), Hittite king in the Hittite Empire **1:** 116 **2:** 186 **3:** 339, 345, 347

Hekau-Chasut, desert kings (Thirteenth dynasty) **2:** 168

Henry I (the Fowler) of Saxony (876?-939), German king (925-939) **9:** 1202, 1221, 1286-1287

Henry I, byname Henry Beauclerc (Good Scholar), king of England (1100-1135) **10:** 1322

Henry II (1133-1189), byname Henry of Anjou, duke of Normandy (from 1150), count of Anjou (from 1151), duke of Aquitaine (from 1152), and king of England (from 1154) **10:** *1321-1322*, 1325-1326, 1352, 1379

Henry II (the Saint) of Bavaria (973-1024), king of Germany (1002-1024), king of the Lombards (1004-1024) and Holy Roman emperor (1014-1024) **9:** *1211*, 1213, 1286

Henry III (1207-1272), king of England (1216-1272) **10:** 1344, 1352-1353

Henry IV (1050-1106), king of Germany (1056-1106) and Holy Roman emperor (1084-1106) **9:** 1215-1216, 1218-1219, *1221-1222*, 1286-1287

Henry IV, also called Earl of Derby (1377-1397); or Duke of Hereford (1397-1399); byname Henry Bolingbroke, or Henry of Lancaster (1366?-1413), king of England (1399-1413) **10:** 1338, 1363, *1380*, 1381

Henry V (1086-1125), German king (from 1099) and Holy Roman emperor (1111-1125) **9:** 1219-1221, 1285 **10:** 1333, 1381, 1383, *1385-1386*, 1412

Henry VI (1165-1197), German king and Holy Roman emperor of the Hohenstaufen dynasty **10:** 1330, 1335, 1338, 1340, 1342, 1383, 1386

Henry of Burgundy, Count of Portugal (twelfth century) **9:** 1237, 1288

Henry the Lion, duke of Saxony (1142-1180) and of Bavaria (as Henry XII, 1156-1180) **10:** 1334, *1337*, 1338, 1340

Heraclius, Byzantine emperor (610-641) **8:** 1078, *1078*, 1099-1100, 1142-1143 **9:** 1244, 1246, 1248

Herod the Great, Roman-appointed King of Judaea (37-4 BC) **1:** 68-69

Hezekiah (reigned c.727-698 BC), king of Judah and friend of Isaiah **3:** 335

Hippeis, dominant social class in Athens **4:** 476, 480, 566

Hippias, Athenian ruler (reigned 528-510 BC) **4:** 487-488, 505, 517, 566

Hiram, Phoenician king of Tyre (reigned 969-936 BC) **3:** 297, 300, 308, 332

Hisham II, Hisham ibn'abd al-Malik (691-743), tenth caliph **9:** 1227

Hisham III (?-1036), last Umayyad **9:** 1230

Hojo Yasutoki, regent of Japan (1183-1242) **11:** 1529

Honorius, Flavius, Western Roman emperor (reigned 393-423) **7:** 954

Horemheb, general and later king of Egypt (1319-1307 BC) **2:** 180-182, *180*, 278

Hortensius, Quintus, dictator of Rome in 287 **5:** 666 **7:** 962

Hunneric, Vandal king **8:** 1031

Husayn ibn Al, king of the Hejaz **8:** 1122

Ibbi-Sin, Sumerian king (fl. third millennium BC) **2:** 233

Imperial laws **8:** 1067

Internal administration **2:** 161

Irene (752-803), Byzantine empress (797-802), married to Emperor Leo IV in 769 and regent for her son Constantine VI (780-790 and 792-797) **9:** 1170-1171, 1180, 1255-1256, 1285-1287

Isaac I Comnenus (c.1005-1061), Byzantine emperor (1057-1059) **9:** 1269

Isaac II Angelus (c.1135-1204), Byzantine emperor (1185-1204) **9:** 1276

Isabel of Castile (1451-1504), queen of Castile and Aragon **9:** 1236

Ishbi-Erra, king of Isin (c.2017-c.1985 BC) **2:** 233

Ishme-Dagan I, king of Assyria (fl. second millennium BC) **2:** 247, 260

Ismail I, Persian ruler who founded Safavid dynasty in 1501 **11:** 1564

Ivan III the Great, grand duke of Muscovy (1462-1505) **11:** 1518, *1518*, 1538, 1574

Ivan IV Vasilyevich (Ivan the Terrible, reigned 1533-1584) **11:** 1518

Jacob van Artevelde (c.1295-1345), Flemish leader who played a leading role in the preliminary phase of the Hundred Years' War (1337-1453) **10:** *1370*, 1377

Jadwiga (of Anjou), original Hungarian Hedvig (1373/74-1399), queen of Poland (1384-1399) **10:** 1410

Jagiello, Vladislav, grand duke of Lithuania (as Jogaila, 1377-1401) and king of Poland (1386-1434), who joined two states that became the leading power of eastern Europe **10:** 1410

Jimmu, emperor of Japan (c.607 BC) **11:** 1523, 1574

John, byname Lackland (French Jean Sans Terre) (1167-1216), king of England (1199-1216) **10:** *1328*, 1330, 1332, *1342*, 1344, *1348*, 1352, *1360*, 1367-1368, *1377*, 1378-1379, 1381, *1383*, 1386, 1383, 1403, 1406-1407, *1407*, 1412, 1413

John I Tzimisces (925-976), Byzantine emperor (969-976) **9:** 1264

John of Brienne (c.1148-1237), count of Brienne, king of Jerusalem, Latin emperor of Constantinople **9:** 1276

John VI Cantacuzene, Byzantine emperor in 1347 **11:** 1556

Jovian, Flavius Jovianus (c.331-364), Roman emperor 363-364 **6:** 833

Jugurtha (c.160-104 BC), king of Numidia (118-105 BC) **5:** 699-700, 710-711 **6:** 840

Julian, Flavius Claudius Julianus (331/332-363), Roman emperor 361-363, byname Julian the Apostate **6:** 733, 742, 833, *834*, 853-854, 856 **7:** *945*, 947, 949-950, 960, 972, 997

Justinian I, Flavius Petrus Sabbatius Justinianus (483-565), Byzantine emperor (527-565) **9:** 1239, *1243-1244*, 1243, 1251, 1266 **11:** 1500

Kammu, emperor (reigned 781-806) **11:** 1526

Kamose, king of Egypt (1555-1550 BC) **2:** 170-171

Kao-tsu, first Tang emperor **11:** 1501, 1508

Khamose, king of Egypt at end of Second Interregnum **2:** 278

Khan, Chingiz. *See* Chingiz Khan

Khan, Genghis. *See* Chingiz Khan

Khan, Kublai. *See* Kublai Khan

Kublai Khan, Mongol ruler (1260-1294) **11:** 1512, 1529, 1537, *1537*, 1540-1542, 1574

Law of the Burgundians **8:** 1035

Laws of the Twelve Tables, Roman common law codified and engraved on twelve bronze plates by the decemviri (ten men) in 451 BC. **5:** 607, 661-662, 664, 711

Leo III the Isaurean (c.675/680-741), Byzantine emperor (717-741) and founder of the Isaurean dynasty **8:** 1110 **9:** 1180, 1254-1256, *1256*, 1259, 1286-1287

Leo IV (749-780), Byzantine emperor **9:** 1255-1256, 1285-1286

Leo V the Armenian (?-820), Byzantine emperor (813-820) **9:** 1257-1258, *1261-1262*, 1285, 1287

Leo VI (866-912), Byzantine co-emperor from 870 and emperor from 886 to 912 **9:** 1260

Leonidas I, king of Sparta (?-480 BC) **4:** 475, 520-521, *520*, 523, 566, 568

Lepidus, Marcus Aemilius (?-13/12 BC), Roman statesman **6:** 743, 856

Lex frumentaria (grain law), enacted by Gaius Sempronius Gracchus (c.153-121 BC) **5:** 696

Lex Hortensia Hortensia, dictator of Rome in 287 **5:** 666

Li Su (280-208 BC) Chinese statesman **3:** 358 **7:** 910

Li Yuan, emperor of the Tang dynasty (566-635) **11:** 1508

Licinian-Sextian Laws **5:** 664

Licinius (c.270-325) Roman emperor **6:** 831-832 **7:** 942, 944, 949, 997 **8:** 1017-1018, 1045, 1142

Liu Pang, first Han emperor (256-195 BC) **11:** 1501

Lombard law **8:** 1040

Lothar I (795-855), Frankish emperor **9:** 1182, 1184, *1184*, *1186*, 1187, 1190, 1199, 1213, 1287-1288

Lothar III (1075-1137), German king (1125-1137) and Holy Roman emperor (1133-1137) **10:** 1328

Louis I the Pious (778-840), Holy Roman emperor (814-840), king of France (814-840), king of Germany (814-840) and king of Aquitaine (781-840) **9:** 1285, 1287

Louis II, king (1845-1886) **11:** 1563

Louis II the German (c.806-876), king of Germany (840-876) **9:** 1184, 1187, 1190-1191, 1199, 1240, 1286-1288

Louis IV, byname Louis d'outremer (Louis from Overseas) (921-954), king of France (reigned 936-954) **10:** 1349, 1391

Louis IX, also called Saint Louis (1214-1270), king of France (reigned 1226-1270) **9:** 1278 **10:** *1350*, *1352-1354*, 1354

Louis the Child (893-911), king of Germany (899-911) **9:** 1202

Louis VI, byname Louis the Fat, (1081-1137), king of France (reigned 1108-1137) **9:** 1221 **10:** 1328

Louis VII, byname Louis the Younger (c.1120-1180), Capetian king of France **9:** 1273, *1273*, 1276 **10:** 1328

Louis XI, king of France (reigned 1461-1483) **10:** 1420, 1422

Lucius Septimius, Roman emperor **8:** 1046, 1069

Lycurgus, Spartan lawgiver (ninth century BC) **4:** *471*, 472-473, 478, 485, 566

Maccabees, Jewish movement that fought for political autonomy **7:** 918-919, 997

Macrinus, Marcus Opellius (c.164-218), Roman emperor (217-218) **6:** 815-816

Maecenas, Gaius Cilnius (c.70-8 BC), Roman diplomat **6:** 750, *751*, 855

Magnentius, in full Flavius Magnus Magnentius (d. 353), usurping Roman emperor **7:** 948

Magnus Clemens Maximus, usurping Roman emperor who ruled Britain, Gaul, and Spain (reigned 383-388) **7:** 951 **8:** 1020, 1066

Mahatma Gandhi **3:** 384 **7:** 893, 997. *See also* Gandhi

Mahmud II, Ottoman sultan (1785-1839) **11:** 1574

Mahmud of Ghazni, sultan (reigned 998-1030) **8:** 1080 **11:** 1492, 1494, 1496

Mai Idris Alooma (reigned 1580-1617) **11:** 1549

Malik Shah (1055-1092), third Seljuq sultan **9:** 1288

Marcus Aurelius Antonius (121-180) Roman emperor (161-180) **6:** 730-731, 789, *790*, 792, 802, 808, 812, 814, 816, 819, 824, *836*, 853-855 **8:** 1016, 1069

Marcus Porcius Cato (234-149BC), Roman statesman **5:** 693

Margaret of Denmark (1353-1412), regent of Denmark (from 1375), of Norway (from 1380), and of Sweden (from 1389) **10:** 1401

Marius, Gaius (c.156-86 BC), Roman general and politician **1:** 126 **5:** 699-702, *700*, 709, 711-712 **6:** 855 **7:** 950

Marjorian, Roman emperor **8:** 1030

Masinissa (c.240 BC-148), ruler of the North African kingdom of Numidia **5:** 690 **6:** 839

Mauricius, Flavius Tiberius (c.539-602), general and Byzantine emperor (582-602) **9:** 1244

Maxentius, Marcus Aurelius Valerius (?-312), Roman emperor (306-312) **6:** 831 **7:** 943, *946* **8:** 1017, *1017*, 1141

Maximian, Marcus Aurelius Valerius Maximianus (?-310), Roman emperor with Diocletian 286-305 **6:** 827-828, *827*, 830-831, *831* **7:** *946*

Maximinus Daia, Galerius Valerius (?-313), Roman emperor 310-113 **6:** 830-831

Meerssen, Treaty of (870), divided the northern part of Lothar I's empire between Charles the Bald and Louis the German **9:** 1199, 1288

Mehmed I (Muhammad, reigned 1413-1421) **11:** *1558*, 1559, *1561*, 1561-1562, *1563*, 1564, 1566

Mehmed II, Sultan of Ottoman Turkey (reigned 1444-1446 and 1451-1481) **11:** 1559, *1561*, 1561-1562, *1563*, 1564, 1566, *1566*

Menander (c.160 BC-c.135 BC), Indo-Greek king **6:** 798

Menes, first king of unified Egypt (c.3100 BC) **2:** 153 **3:** 413

Menkaure, king of Egypt (c.2613-2494 BC) **2:** 156, 158

Mentuhotep II, king of Egypt (2010-1998 BC) **2:** 158-159, *158*, 162

Mentuhotep III, king of Egypt (1998-1991 BC) **2:** 160

Merneptah, king of Egypt (1224-1214 BC) **2:** 186-187 **3:** 320, 322

Merodach Baladan II, king of Babylonia (721-710 BC) **2:** 267-268, 270, 279-280

Meroveus (c.450), king of the Salian Franks **9:** 1287

Michael I Cerularius, patriarch of Constantinople (1043 to 1057) **9:** 1263, 1287

Michael II (?-829), Byzantine emperor (820-829) **9:** 1259, *1259*, 1287

Michael III (838-867), Byzantine emperor **9:** 1259, 1264

Michael IV (?-1041), Byzantine emperor **9:** 1263, 1265, 1287

Michael Paleologus (1261), king of Nicaea **10:** 1339, 1384

RELIGION

Gregory VI (?-1048), pope (1045-1046) **9**: 1215, 1286
Gregory VII, original name Hildebrand (c.1020-1085), pope (reigned 1073-1085) **9**: 1215, 1219, 1221, *1222*, 1232, 1268, 1286 **10**: 1333-1334, 1348
Gregory VIII (?-c.1137), antipope (1118-1121) **9**: 1220-1221, 1273, 1276
Gregory IX, original name Ugo, or Ugolino, di Segni (c.1170-1241), pope (reigned 1227-1241), founder of the papal Inquisition **9**: 1278 **10**: 1347
Gregory XI, original name Pierre-Roger de Beaufort (c.1329-1378), pope (reigned 1370-1378) **10**: 1365
Gregory XIII (1502-1585), pope from 1572-1585 **6**: 854

Hadad, Semitic god of storms **2**: 250
Hades, Greek god of the underworld **4**: 444, 500, 566-567
Hadith, companion book to the Koran **8**: 1089-1090, 1142
Haggai, prophet (fl. sixth century BC) **7**: 916
Hajj, journey to Mecca **8**: 1090, 1142
Harley Gospels **9**: *1180*
Hathor, Egyptian goddess of the sky **2**: 177, 186
Heaven **7**: 902, 905, 912, 956
Helios, Greek god of the sun **4**: 497 **6**: *816*
Hera, Greek goddess of birth and marriage **4**: *450*, 496-497, *496*, *499*, *501*, *547*, 558, 566 **5**: 690
Hermes, Greek god of commerce, invention, travel **4**: 496, 566 **6**: 855
Hestia, Greek goddess of the hearth **4**: 496
Hierarchy of gods **4**: 461
High priest **2**: 191, 277 **7**: 916-918, 920, 930, 932
Hilary of Poitiers, Saint (c.315-367), pagan convert to Christianity, doctor of the Church, bishop of Poitiers **7**: 997
Hindu **3**: 363, 380, 384, 388, 390 **7**: 879, *889-893*, 890-891, 893-894, *896*, 897, *898*, 900, 997
Hinduism **3**: 380, 383, 384, *386*, 388, 390 **7**: 871, 878, 886, 888-893, 889, 896-897, 900, 997 **11**: 1497, 1500, 1574
Holy of Holies **6**: 731
Holy City **3**: 329 **9**: 1276 **10**: 1348, 1364, 1366; - Communion **7**: 930 **9**: 1224 **10**: 1357; - cross **8**: 1078; - Father **9**: 1241 **10**: 1364; - Land **9**: 1267-1268, *1272*, 1273, 1277-1278, *1278*, 1286 **10**: *1333*, 1339, *1344*, *1350*, 1374, 1406-1407; - Mass **7**: 959 **9**: 1179; - period **8**: 1093; - Road **4**: 500; - Spirit **7**: 946, 956, 974, *979* **8**: *1029*, 1035 **9**: 1223, 1266
Honorius, pope (625-638) **11**: 1561
Horus, Egyptian sky god in form of falcon **2**: 155, 278-279
Hosea, Hebrew prophet (eighth century BC) **3**: 333-334
Huitzilopochtli (war god) **11**: 1469, *1470*, 1471-1472, 1573; - temple of **11**: 1469
Human sacrifice **11**: 1464, 1469-1470

Iconoclasm **8**: 1110 **9**: 1168, 1180, 1252-1256, *1256*, *1258*, 1259, *1262*, 1286-1287
Icons **8**: 1110 **9**: 1180, 1250, 1252-1256, 1259, *1261*, 1265, 1286-1287
Illapa (god of thunder and weather) **11**: 1483
Imam **8**: 1106, 1142
Inanna, city goddess of Uruk **2**: 221, 223, 225, 227, 245, 250, 251, 278
Indra, ancient Indian god of storms, war, and battle **3**: *384*, 388
Inquisition **9**: 1236 **11**: 1561
Inti (sun god) **11**: 1483, *1487*, 1573-1574
Investiture controversy, power struggle between papacy and Holy Roman Empire (eleventh-twelfth century) **9**: 1215-1216, 1218-1221, 1285-1286 **10**: 1340
Irish Christianity **7**: 997
Isaiah, Israelite prophet (eighth century BC) **3**: 334-335, *334* **7**: 930
Ishtar, Canaanite deity of war 327, 347. *See also* Astarte, Shauska
Ishtar, goddess of the Sumero-Akkadian pantheon **2**: 223, 225-226, 230-231, *234*, 245-246, *247*, 250, *257-258*, 258, *263*, 278
Ishvara (Sanskrit: Lord) in Hinduism, the personal, or immanent, god, as distinct from the absolute, or transcendent, supreme being (Brahman) **7**: 900
Isis, Egyptian goddess **2**: *188*, 280 **5**: 633 **6**: 752, *764*, 767, 801, 854
Islam **3**: 362-363, 378 **7**: 888 **8**: 1078, 1082, *1082-1083*,

1087-1088, 1090, 1092, 1095-1096, *1098*, 1103, 1105, *1105*, 1107, 1113-1114, 1118, 1120-1121, 1123, 1126, 1129-1130, 1132, 1141-1144 **9**: 1226-1227, *1229*, *1238*, 1288 **10**: 1345, 1348 **11**: 1494, 1496, 1539, 1544, *1544*, 1549, 1555, 1557, 1562, 1566, 1573-1574
Islamic holy men **8**: 1106
Itzamna (Mayan deity) **11**: 1462

Jason, high priest in Jerusalem in 168 **7**: 918
Jehovah, Judeo-Christian name for God **3**: 322
Jeremiah, Israelite prophet (seventh century BC) **3**: 335-336, 335 **7**: 914
Jerome, Saint (c.345-c.420) father and doctor of Church; translated Bible into Latin version called the Vulgate **7**: 975-976, 987, 997 **9**: *1178*
Jester God **11**: 1462
Jesus Christ (Jesus of Nazareth or Jesus of Galilee) (c.6 BC-AD 30) **6**: 730, 758, 771-772, 817, 855 **7**: 920, 925-934, 938, 944, 948, 955-956, 960, 962-963, 972, 974, 980, 997 **8**: 1017, 1035, 1053-1054, *1057*, 1060, 1072, 1076, 1088, 1090, 1100, 1113, 1141, 1143 **10**: *1365*, 1369 **11**: 1516
Jewish Bible **8**: 1088; - sect **7**: 934, 997; - temple **6**: 762 **7**: 921
Jezebel (c.843 BC), in the Old Testament (Kings I and II), the wife of King Ahab **7**: 913
Jihad **8**: 1096, 1098-1099, 1113, 1141-1142 **9**: 1230 **11**: 1566
Jizo (Japanese god) **11**: 1526
Job, biblical figure related to human suffering **7**: 986
John the Baptist, Jewish preacher who baptized on the banks of the Jordan **7**: *914*, 918, 926, *926*, 956, 997 **8**: 1043, 1066, 1105
John XII (c.937-964), pope (955-964) **9**: 1206, 1208, 1231, 1240, 1287
Joshua, Old Testament figure **1**: 68 **7**: 925
Judas (c.AD 30) one of the Twelve Apostles, notorious for betraying Jesus **7**: 918, *930*, 931
Juno, Roman goddess **4**: 512
Jupiter, Roman god **4**: 497 **5**: 642, 652 **6**: 762, 785, 806, 828, 854-855. *See also* Zeus

Kalkin, apparition of Vishnu, as rider on a white horse, who will appear to destroy the universe and inaugurate the new **7**: 894
Kauravas, cousins of the god Krishna **7**: 891
Khadijah, wife of Muhammad **8**: 1085-1086, 1091-1092
Ki, Sumerian goddess of earth **2**: 220
Koran, scripture of Islam **8**: 1084, 1086, 1088, 1090-1091, *1093*, 1101, 1103-1106, 1111, 1113-1114, 1119, 1142-1143 **9**: 1227, 1253 **11**: 1562, 1566, 1574
Krishna, one of the most widely revered and most popular of all Indian divinities, worshiped as the eighth incarnation (avatar, or avatara) of the Hindu god Vishnu **7**: 891, 894, *894*, 897, 997
Kurma, appearance of Vishnu, as turtle **7**: 894

Lakshmi, wife of Hindu god Vishnu **7**: 897
Latin League, ethnic religious federation of Latin cities **5**: 664, 670, 709-711
Leo I the Great, Saint (?-461), pope (440-461) **8**: 1028-1029, 1031, *1031*, 1054 **9**: 1250
Leo III, Saint (?-816), pope (795-816) **9**: *1165*, *1168*, 1170, *1170*, 1287
Leo IV, Saint (?-855), pope (847-855) **9**: 1240
Leo IX, Saint (1002-1054), pope (1049-1054) **9**: 1287
Leo VIII (?-965), pope (963-965) **9**: 1206, 1287
Liturgy **4**: 566 **7**: 938, 959, 988, 997
Lucifer, "bearer of light," fallen angel **7**: 956

Maat, Egyptian goddess of truth and justice **2**: 278-279
Mahendra, Buddhist monastery founded in the late third century BC in Anuradhapura, the ancient capital of Sri Lanka **7**: 888
Maize god **11**: 1462
Manetho, Egyptian priest who wrote a history of Egypt (c.300 BC) **2**: 154, 157, 160, 168, 180, 192, 278
Mani (216-274?) Iranian founder of the Manichaean religion **7**: 963-964, 997 **8**: 1072, 1074, 1143
Mara, evil god who tempted Buddha **7**: 873
Marduk (Bel), chief god of Babylon, national god of Babylonia **2**: 236, 251, 254, 258, 270, 278
Mars, Roman god **5**: *622*, 642, 650, *691* **6**: *746*, 853, 855
Mars Ultor **6**: *746*

Martin of Tours, Saint (316-397), bishop of Tours; one of the founders of monasticism in the West **7**: 954, 975, 978, 997
Martin V, original name Oddo, or Oddone, Colonna (1368-1431), pope (reigned 1417-1431) **10**: *1366*, 1368, *1368*
Martyrs **7**: 938, *942*, 955, 982, 997 **10**: 1372
Mattathias, Jewish priest, head of the Hasmonaean dynasty **7**: 918
Matthew, first in order of the four canonical Gospels and often called the "ecclesiastical" Gospel **7**: 926, 930-931, 933, 933, 970, 997
Matthew, Saint, the Evangelist, one of the twelve apostles **9**: 1222, 1263
Maurice Bourdin, archbishop of Braga, later antipope Gregory VIII **9**: 1220
Maximianus, bishop of Ravenna **8**: 1063
Melkart-Baal-Tsor, Phoenician god of trade and shipping. Also known as Moloch **3**: 299
Mentu, Egyptian god **2**: 159-160, 166
Mercury, in Roman religion, god of merchandise and merchants **5**: 642, *654* **6**: 855
Michael, archangel **7**: 956, *965*, 972
Min, Egyptian god of fertility **2**: 159
Mithras, Eastern god **5**: 664 **6**: 767
Mnemosyne, the goddess of memory **5**: 638, 711
Mohammed. *See* Muhammad
Mohammedans. *See* Muhammadans
Monasteries **7**: 875, 877, 879, 881, 886, 928, *967*, 969, 971-972, 975-976, 978, 984, 988, 990, 997 **8**: 1044, 1133, 1141 **10**: 1307, 1314, 1407
Monastery of San Pedro **9**: *1240*
Monks **8**: 1044, 1100 **10**: 1307, 1314, 1406
Monotheism **2**: 177, 179, 181 **3**: 322 **4**: 502 **7**: 913 **8**: 1090, 1092 **10**: 1369
Moon god **11**: 1462
Moses, Israelite lawgiver and leader **2**: 223 **3**: 313, *313*, 320-323, *322*, *324*, 325 **7**: 917, 964 **8**: 1088, 1090 **10**: 1345, 1374
Mosque **8**: *1055*, 1068, 1092, 1101, *1102*, *1105-1107*, *1109-1110*, *1112*, 1113, *1115-1117*, *1120*, 1143
Muhammad (c.570-632), founder and prophet of the religion of Islam **3**: 368, 375 **8**: 1081, *1081*, *1083-1085*, 1084-1088, *1090-1092*, 1090-1096, *1094-1098*, 1099-1101, 1103, *1105*, 1105-1106, 1111-1114, 1119, 1121-1122, 1128, 1132, 1141-1144 **9**: 1194, 1225, 1227, 1230 **11**: 1566
Muhammadans **9**: 1162, 1167
Muslim **3**: 363 **8**: *1055*, 1072, 1080, *1086*, 1088-1089, *1090*, 1092, 1092-1093, 1095, 1095-1096, 1098, 1101-1102, 1104-1105, 1104-1108, 1108, 1111-1114, 1112-1114, *1113-1114*, 1116, 1118-1119, 1122-1123, 1125-1126, 1129-1130, 1132-1133, 1141-1144 **10**: 1308, *1311*, *1338*, 1346, 1357
Mystery cults **4**: 498-500, *502*, 566

Nabu, Assyro-Babylonian god of writing and vegetation **2**: 268
Nanna (Sin), Sumero-Akkadian god of the moon **2**: 221, 225, 250 **3**: 315
Nanshe, Sumerian city goddess of Nina **2**: 228
Narasimha, appearance of Vishnu as the demon-defeating man-lion **7**: 894
Nataraja, four-handed dancing Hindu god **7**: 896
Neferti, Prophecy of **2**: 160, 164, *183*
Nestorian monasteries **8**: 1133
Nestorius (d. c.451) Syrian monk who disputed the Greek title Theotokos (Mother of God) for Mary **7**: 956, 997
Nestorius, archbishop of Constantinople (428-431) **8**: 1076, 1133, 1143
New Monastic Orders **10**: 1306, 1314, 1406
New Testament **1**: 68 **7**: 926, 933-934, 937, 946, 964, 974, 997
Nike, Greek goddess of victory **4**: 534
Ningirsu, Mesopotamian city god of Girsu **2**: 228, 232, *237*, *246*, 258
Ninurta and Gula, temples of **2**: 258
Nisiba, goddess of Umma **2**: 222
Noah, hero of the biblical story of the flood in the Old Testament book of Genesis **7**: 894 **8**: 1088

Odo (Eudes), Saint (c.879-944), Cluny abbot **9**: 1192, 1209, 1211-1212, 1224, 1287
Odudua (goddess) **11**: 1551

TRADE and ECONOMY

Solidus **8:** 1018, 1040 **9:** 1168, 1250
Spice Route **11:** 1497
Spices **3:** 305 **8:** 1130, *1132*

Talents, ancient units of weight and money **5:** 591, 634, 682, 690, 702
Tax collection **6:** 828, 833 **9:** 1250
Tax system **9:** 1228
Taxes **3:** 356, 365, 378 **9:** 1206, 1228, 1249-1250, 1256, 1262 **10:** 1308, *1325*, 1327, 1337, 1344, 1347, 1354, 1356, 1363, 1397, 1420
Temple economy **2:** 218, 280
Textile factories **8:** 1016; - production **4:** 490 **9:** 1232 **10:** 1304
Three-field system **10:** 1304
Toll collection **9:** 1198
Toll rights **9:** 1184
Trade **4:** 454, 461, 472, 483-484, 487, 489-490, 492, 512, 525-526, 566-567
Traders **8:** 1084, 1121, 1126, 1128, 1142 **10:** 1305, 1388
Trading routes **4:** 448
Trans-Saharan trade **11:** 1550
Treadmills **8:** 1131
Tremis (one-third of a denarius) **8:** 1044

Via Appia **6:** *732*, 737, 784, 856
Via Biberatica **6:** *794*
Via Traiana **6:** 784

Weavers **10:** 1304
Wine **4:** 461

WARS and BATTLES

Aemilius Paulus (Lucius) (c.229-160BC), Roman general **5:** 688
Africanus the Elder (Publius Cornelius Scipio Africanus Maior) (c.234-183 BC), Roman general **5:** 687, 690, 712
Agricola, Gnaeus Julius (40-93 BC), Roman general **6:** 783
Alcibiades (c.450-404 BC), Athenian general (420 BC) **5:** *591*, 594-598, 709
Antipater, (c.398-319 BC) Macedonian general **5:** 615, 617, 630, 709 **7:** 920
Arbogast (394), barbarian general of the Roman Empire **7:** 954
Areobindus, general (fl. sixth century) **8:** 1056
Ascalon, Battle at (1153) **9:** 1274
Ashanti-British War (1873-1874) **11:** 1550
Ashikaga, warrior statesman (1305-1358) **11:** 1529-1530, 1573

Basel, Peace of (Sept. 22, 1499) **10:** 1390
Battle-ax **1:** 86, 110
Battle of the gods **2:** 251
Battle tactics **5:** 588
Battlefields **5:** 590
Belarius, Byzantine general **8:** 1065
Belisarius, Roman general **8:** 1050-1051, 1061, 1063-1065, 1141, 1143 **9:** 1239
Bonifacius, Roman General **8:** 1029
Brasidas, Spartan general **5:** 594, 709

Callias, Peace of (449 BC) **4:** 525
Cannae, Battle of (216 BC) **5:** 688 **7:** 953
Cavalry **3:** 352, 354 **4:** 518, 522, *523* **5:** 590, 617, 621, 658, 678, 684-685, 690 **9:** 1162-1163, 1166, 1200, *1233*, 1244, 1285 **10:** *1323*, 1378, 1381
Cavalrymen **2:** 264
Centuria (century) Roman legion **5:** 658, 660-661, 709
Chang Chien, Chinese general (first century BC) **11:** 1504
Charioteers **2:** 176, 264-265
Civil war **11:** 1505, 1528, 1558-1559
Clodius Albinus (?-197), Roman general **6:** 813
Cohorts **6:** 751, 755, 759
Colline, Battle of the (82 BC) **5:** 702
Commander of the Roman army **8:** 1019
Conquistadores **11:** 1465, 1469, 1472, 1476
Corbulo, Gnaeus Domitius (?-67), Roman general **6:** 772, 773

Daimyo **11:** 1530, 1573

Diadochoi (successors), generals who succeeded Alexander the Great **5:** 625, 710
Diadochs, Battle of the **5:** 625
Duilius (fl. third century BC), Roman commander **5:** 681-682

Eastern Roman armies **8:** 1031
Epamenondas (?-362 BC) Theban general **5:** 609-610

Fabius, Quintus Maximus (Cunctator), third century BC, Roman general, dictator in 217 BC. **5:** 650, 687-688, 710
Flavius Stilicho, Roman military commander **8:** 1023, 1057, 1141
Flower wars **11:** 1470, 1574
Fontenay, Battle at (841) **9:** 1187, 1287-1288
Foot soldiers **5:** 590, 612, 616-617, 658, *679*, 709-710
Fortifications **5:** 588

Gallic Wars (58-50 BC) **6:** 736, 738
Gaugamela, Battle of (331 BC) **5:** 621
Granicus River, Battle of (334 BC) **5:** 617
Great Attack **8:** 1100
Great War, The Peloponnesian War (431-404 BC) **5:** 587

Hamilcar Barca (c.270-228 BC) Carthaginian general; father of Hannibal **5:** 680, 682, 684, 710
Hannibal (247-183 BC), legendary Carthaginian general; son of Hamilcar **5:** *679*, 682, 684-685, *686-688*, 687-691, 709-710, 712 **6:** 799, 838-839 **7:** 952-953
Hasdrubal (221 BC), Carthaginian general, the son-in-law of Hamilcar Barca **5:** 684, 689-690
Hegira, Battle at **8:** 1095
Heiji War (1159-1160) **11:** 1528
Helot rebellion **4:** 472
Holy war **9:** 1230
Hoplites, Greek foot soldiers **4:** 453, 506, *509*, 518, 522, 553, 566-567 **5:** 590, 596, 710
Hoplon, round shield **4:** 453, 506, 566
Hormuz, Battle of (224) **8:** 1070
Hundred Years' War (1337-1453) **10:** 1308, 1358, 1362, 1364, 1375-1376, 1381, 1412, 1418, 1422

Ionian rebellion (499-495 BC) **4:** 515, 517, 519, 566-567
Issus, Battle of (333 BC) **5:** 619

János Hundayi, Hungarian general (c.1407-1456) **11:** 1559
Jewish Revolt (first, 66-70) (second, 132-135) **6:** 773, 776, 854 **7:** 997
Jugurthine War **5:** 700

Kadesh, Battle at (1275 BC) **1:** 116
Kirina, Battle of (c.1235) **11:** 1545
Knights **5:** 600, 685, 692, 710
Kortrijk, Battle of, also called Battle of Courtrai (July 11, 1302) **10:** 1362
Kosovo, Battle of (1448) **11:** 1559, *1559*
Kukikovo, Battle at (1380) **11:** 1518

Lamachus, Athenian commander **5:** 596
Lamian War (323-322 BC) **5:** 630
Las Navas de Tolosa, Battle at (1212) **9:** *1232*, 1237
Lechfield, Battle at (955) **9:** 1231
Legion soldiers (legionnaires) **6:** 755, 792
Legions **5:** 658, 678, 688, 690, 709, 711 **6:** *732*, 738, 748, 755, *774-775*, 774-776, 783, 790, 792, 814, 820, 824, 787-788, 854-855 **8:** 1015
Legnano, Battle of (1176) **10:** 1338
Leuctra, Battle of (371 BC) **5:** 610
Liegnitz (or Legnica), Battle of (April 15, 1241) **10:** 1404
Lonkoping, Battle of **10:** 1409
Lysandrus, Spartan general **5:** 601

Macedonian Wars **5:** 691, *695*, 697, 711 **6:** 838, 837-838
Mantinea, Battle of (362 BC) **5:** 610
Manzikert, Battle at (1072) **9:** 1266, 1268, 1285, 1288
Mardonius, Achaemenian Persian general (?-479 BC) **4:** 517, 522 **5:** 584
Meccan rebellion **8:** 1113
Mercenaries, hired soldiers **4:** 482, 487, 492 **5:** 590, 616-617, 619, 681, 684, 711
Metellus (c.91 BC), Roman general **5:** 700
Militarism **4:** 473
Military coups **4:** 482

Miltiades, general who led the Athenian forces to victory over the Persians at the Battle of Marathon (490 BC) **4:** 518-519, 518-519, 566
Minamoto, Yoshiyo, Japanese warrior (1039-1106) **11:** 1530; - family **11:** 1528, *1530*
Munda, Battle of (45 BC) **6:** 742

Navas de Tolosa, Battle of (1212) **9:** *1232*, 1237
Neustadt, Siege of (1275) **11:** 1536
Nicias, Peace of **5:** 587, 589, 595, 709, 711
Nika revolt **8:** 1050-1051, *1055*, 1056, 1061, 1065, 1068, 1143-1144
Nisibis, Peace of (298) **6:** 833

Onin War (1467-1477) **11:** 1530

Partakes, Macedonian general **5:** 630
Paulus, Lucius Aemilius (c.229-c.160 BC) Roman general **5:** 688
Pausanias, Spartan general (?-467 BC) **4:** 522, 567
Pelopidas, Theban general **5:** 609
Peloponnesian League, military coalition **5:** 590, 711
Peloponnesian War, war between the two leading Greek city-states Athens and Sparta (431-404 BC) **4:** 472, 525-526, 528, 553, 568 **5:** 587, 589-590, *590*, *595*, 600-601, 604, 607, 634, 709-712
Perdiccas (c.365 BC-321), general under Alexander the Great **5:** 625
Persian armies **8:** 1064, 1078
Persian Wars, wars between Greek poleis and the Persians; First Persian War (492-490 BC), Second Persian War (480-479 BC) **4:** 475, 511, 515-518, *519*, *522*, *524*, 565, 567-568 **5:** 584, 587
Phalanx, battle array used by Greek and Macedonian infantry **4:** 453, 567 **5:** *609*, 610, 617, 658, 710-711; - formation **5:** 610, 617
Pharsalus, Battle of (48 BC) **6:** 737, 740
Pizarro, Francisco, Spanish conquerer (c.1475-1541) **11:** 1477, 1479, 1574
Poitiers, Battle of, also called Battle of Tours (732) **9:** 1163 **10:** *1377*, 1378
Postumus, Marcus Cassianus Latinius (?-268), Roman general **6:** 820, 824
Praetorian Cohort (*Cohors praetoria*) **6:** 755, 759
Praetorian Guard (22 BC-AD 312) **6:** 764, 768, 770-771, 774-775, *774*, 781, 784, 809, *811*, 814, 816, 820, 855
Praetorian prefect **6:** 815
Punic War, First (264-241 BC) **5:** *683*, 687, 689, *691*, 710-711
Punic War, Second (218-201 BC) **5:** 689, 695-696, *696*, 709-710, 712
Punic War, Third (150-146 BC) **5:** 703-704, 712
Punic Wars (264-241 BC, 218-201 BC, 149-146 BC) **6:** 837, 839, 855
Pydna, Battle of (168 BC) **5:** 698

Qadesh, Battle of (1285 BC), in Syria **2:** 186 **3:** 337, 339, 345

Rebellion **8:** 1050, 1056, 1061, 1068, 1102, 1113, 1142 **10:** 1329, 1337, 1377, 1379, 1381
Reconquista **8:** 1107, 1108, 1122, 1144 **9:** 1227, *1229*, 1231, *1231*, 1234, 1237, 1239, *1239-1240*, 1288
Reconquistadores **8:** 1131
Religious battles **8:** 1067
Revolution **8:** 1103, 1113 **10:** 1320, 1359
Rhineland army **6:** 775
Río Barbate, Battle at (711) **9:** 1226
Robert Guiscard (c.1015-1085), military adventurer **9:** 1219, 1242, 1268, 1270
Roncesvalles, Battle at (788) **9:** 1172, *1173*

Salamis, Battle of (480 BC) **4:** 534, 544, 567 **5:** 585
Samnite Wars (343-341 BC, 316-304 BC, 298-290 BC) **6:** 836
Scipio Africanus the Elder (Publius Cornelius Scipio Africanus Maior) (c.23-183 BC) Roman general **5:** 699, 712
Scipio Africanus the Younger (Publius Cornelius Scipio Aemilianus Africanus Numantians) (c.185-129 BC), Roman general **5:** 695, 712 **6:** 739, 838-839
Sind, conquest of (711) **11:** 1491, 1494
Slave rebellion (73-71 BC) **6:** 730
Social War **5:** 701, 712

Index

Ainu **11:** 1520

Airyana Vaeja **3:** 362-363, 367

Aisha **8:** 1103, 1141

Ajax, in Greek mythology, Greek hero in Trojan War **4:** *439, 447,* 544, *548,* 567

Akhetaton (Tel el-Amarna) **2:** 177, 179-180, 182-183, 277, 280 **3:** 321. *See also* Amenhotep IV

Akhthoes (Cheti III), king of Egypt (ninth dynasty) **2:** 158

Akkad **2:** 217, 219, 223-227, *226-228,* 230, 233-234, 236, 247, 259, 277-278; - dynasty **2:** 226, *227;* - period **2:** 247

Akkadian **2:** 177, 218-221, 223-225, *226,* 227, 233-234, 237, 244, 247-248, 250-251, 259-260, 265, 270, 277-280 **3:** 315, 321, 339; - cuneiform **2:** 177, 218, 225; - empire **2:** 226, 227, 250, 277-280; - language **2:** 233, 259, 277; - period **2:** 224-225; - religion **2:** 250

Akkadians **2:** 222, 224-225, 227, 233

Akragas **4:** 458

Aksum, Kingdom of (50-1100) **11:** 1544

Al-Akhtal, Arab poet Al-Akhtal **8:** 1113

Al-Arish **8:** 1102

Al-Fustat **8:** 1102

Al-Hakam, caliph **9:** 1228

Al-Hakim (985-1021), sixth ruler of the Egyptian Shi'i Fatimid dynasty **9:** *1238*

Al-Hariri **8:** 1099, 1101, 1104, 1109, 1126-1127, 1131, 1134

Al-Hijaz **8:** 1081

Al-Hudabija **8:** 1095

Al-Iskander. *See* Shah-nama

Al-Kamil (1180-1238), last sultan (1218-1238) of the Ayyubid line **9:** 1278

Al-Kufa **8:** *1095,* 1102-1105, *1105, 1107,* 1111, *1113,* 1113-1114, *1115, 1119, 1132,* 1142

Al-Majisti Arabic translation of Ptolemy's *Almagesti* (Great Work) **5:** 642, 712. *See also* Almagesti

Al-Mamun, Caliph (813-830) **8:** 1119-1120

Al Mansūr **8:** 1116-1118, 1133-1134

Al Mawsil **9:** 1272, 1276

Al-Medina **8:** 1092

Al Mina **4:** 457

Al-Mustasim **8:** 1120

Al-Nasir li-din Allah **9:** 1226-1227

Al-Qurnah **2:** 217

Al-Zahra **9:** *1227*

Alans **8:** 1024-1026

Alaric, (c.370-410) chief of the Visigoths from 395 and leader of the army that sacked Rome in 410 **6:** 853-854 **7:** 966 **8:** *1023,* 1023-1024, *1025, 1027,* 1032, 1039, 1059, 1141-1142, 1144

Alaric II (d. 507) **8:** *1027,* 1032

Alaska **1:** 42

Alba Longa, city in southern Latium, considered the mother city of Rome **5:** 650-651, 709, 712

Albania **8:** 1056 **11:** 1559

Albans, St. (?-c. AD 304), first British martyr **6:** 772

Albert of Mecklenburg, overthrew King Haakon of Sweden in 1363 **10:** 1409

Albertus Magnus, Saint (d.1280) **11:** 1561

Albi **9:** 1277

Albigenses, heretical Christian sect in southern France (twelfth-thirteenth century) **9:** 1277 **11:** 1560

Albigensian Crusade (1208-1213), crusade against heresy in southern France **9:** 1277

Albigensian heresy **11:** 1560

Albinus. *See* Alcuin

Alcaeus, lyric poet from Lésvos (620-580 BC) **4:** 466, 565

Alcestis Greek play by Euripides **5:** 600

Alcibiades (c.450-404 BC) Athenian general (420 BC) **5:** *591,* 594-598, 709

Alcmaeonides family, Athenian family (sixth-fifth century BC), ancestors of Pericles **4:** 485-486, 488

Alcman (Alcmaeon), Greek poet **4:** 464, 468

Alcuin (or Albinus) (735-804), Anglo-Latin poet, educator and cleric **9:** 1178-1180, 1182, 1285, *1186*

Alemanni(ans), Germanic people **6:** 820, 853 **7:** 950 **8:** 1032, 1141 **9:** 1162, 1167

Aleppo **3:** 331, 339, *339,* 345, 346 **8:** 1105-1106, 1119, 1128, 1132 **9:** 1285 **11:** 1539, 1574

Alexander **5:** 607, 609, *610,* 611-628, *613-617, 620-624, 627,* 630, 633-634, *639,* 709-712. *See also* Alexander the Great

Alexander III, pope (1159-1181) **10:** 1337-1338

Alexander IV, Alexander the Great's posthumous son by Roxana **5:** 625-626. *See also* Roxana

Alexander Nevsky, king (reigned 1236-1263) **10:** 1403-1404

Alexander Severus. *See* Severus Alexander

Alexander the Great (356-323 BC) king of Macedonia (336-323 BC); son of Philip II **2:** 192 **3:** 297, 365, 378 **4:** 457, *556* **5:** 607, 609, *610,* 611-613, *613-614, 616-617, 620-622,* 624, 628, 630, *639,* 709-712 **6:** 731, 733, *812,* 815-816, 831, 845, 855 **7:** 925, 997 **8:** 1016, 1065, 1069, 1072, 1074, 1080-1081, 1098, 1108 **9:** 1286

Alexander, the Scissors **8:** 1065

Alexandria, city founded by Alexander the Great **5:** 620, *620,* 624, 626-629, 633, *635,* 636-638, *637,* 641, 643, *647,* 685, 709-712 **6:** 740-741, 743-744, 762, 794, 822, *840,* 846 **7:** *917, 947,* 948, 954, 959, 968-970, 974, 997 **8:** *1029, 1078,* 1080, 1102, *1105, 1132* **9:** 1263, 1287

Alexandrian **5:** 626, 629, 637-639, 642, 710; - library **5:** 626. *See also* Alexandria

Alexianus **6:** 816

Alexius I Comnenus (1048-1118), Byzantine emperor (1081-1118) **9:** 1268-1269, 1272, 1274, 1285

Alexius IV, Byzantine emperor (reigned 1203-1204) **10:** 1339

Alfandega (customs) **8:** 1128

Alfonso II the Chaste (Alfonsus Castus) (c.759-842), king of Asturias (791-842) **9:** *1234*

Alfonso III (c.838-c.910), king of Asturias (866-910) **9:** 1226, 1233-1234, 1237

Alfonso VI (1040-1109), king of Castile and Leon **9:** 1238

Alfonso Henriques, king of Portugal (1143) **9:** 1237, 1288

Alfonsus Castus. *See* Alfonso II the Chaste

Alfred Jewel **9:** *1193*

Alfred the Great (849-899), Saxon king of Wessex, England (871-899) **9:** *1193,* 1206, 1285

Algeciras **3:** 300

Algeria **3:** 403-404, 414 **6:** 839 **7:** 962 **8:** 1122

Ali, fourth caliph (reigned 656-661) **11:** 1548-1549, 1564

Ali Ghaji **11:** 1549

Ali, son-in-law of Muhammad 1080, *1088,* 1091, *1098, 1100,* 1103-1106, *1105,* 1111, 1113-1114, 1121-1122, 1141-1144

Aljafaria **9:** *1228-1229*

Alkinoös, mythological king **4:** 442

Allada **11:** 1551

Allah **8:** 1087-1091, 1093-1094, 1096, 1098-1099, 1106, 1121, 1141-1144 **9:** 1226 **11:** 1566

Allahabad **7:** 875

Allia River **5:** 668

Allyus **11:** 1483

Almagest **1:** 9

Almagesti, Ptolemy's Great Work **5:** 642, 712. *See also Al-Majisti*

Almeria **1:** 92, 107

Almohads (Berber confederation that created an Islamic empire in North Africa and Spain (1130-1269) **9:** 1230, 1237, *1237,* 1239, 1285; - armies **9:** *1232;* - decline **9:** *1232*

Almoravids **11:** 1545. *See also* Almohads

Alodia **11:** 1544

Alp Arslan (c.1030-1072), second of the first three great sultans of the Seljuq Turks **9:** 1288

Alpaca **11:** 1449, 1485, 1487; - wool **11:** 1485, 1487

Alphabet **3:** 301, 308 **4:** 449-450, 457, 498, 565 **6:** 766, 836

Alps **1:** *36,* 41, 90, *98,* 99, 113, 116, 123 **5:** 669, 684, 687, 690 **6:** 738 **7:** 980 **8:** 1027 **9:** 1166, 1170, 1206, 1232 **10:** 1305, 1316-1318, 1335, 1337, 1346, 1349, 1368, 1404

Alsace **9:** 1187, 1287-1288

Alta Germania **6:** *777*

Altamira **1:** *48,* 56, 60

Altar of Peace. *See* Ara Pacis Augustae

Altiplano **11:** 1452

Amalfi **9:** 1222

Amarna (Tel el-Amarna) **2:** *176,* 177, 178, 179-180, 183, *183,* 277-278; *See also* Akhetaton; -letters **2:** 177, 180, 183, 277 **3:** 329; - period **2:** 177, 180, 183, 278

Amaterasu (sun goddess) **11:** 1523, 1574

Amazons **3:** 347 **8:** 1080

Ambracia, Corinthian colony **4:** 526

Ambrose (c.339-397), bishop of Milan **7:** *948,* 953-954, 997

962, 987, 997

Amen. *See* Amon

Amenemhet I (Ammenemes I), king of Egypt (1991-1962 BC) **2:** 160-161, 164, *167,* 277

Amenemhet III (Ammenemes III), king of Egypt (1844-1797 BC) **2:** 167

Amenhotep I, king of Egypt (1525-1504 BC) **2:** *169, 171,* 172-173, 173, 175, 177, 179, 183

Amenhotep II, king of Egypt (1427-1401 BC) **2:** *173,* 175

Amenhotep III, king of Egypt (1391-1353 BC) **2:** *171,* 175, 177, 183

Amenhotep IV (Akhenaton), king of Egypt (1353-1335 BC) **2:** 171, *176,* 177, *178,* 179-183, *183,* 277, 280

Ameni. *See* Amenemhet I

Amenmesse, king of Egypt **2:** 189

America **1:** 41, 64, 67, 75, 92, 96-97, 102, 134 **11:** 1447-1448, 1453, *1454, 1456,* 1462, 1464, 1474, 1476-1478, 1573-1574

American continent **11:** 1476

American Old West **1:** 102

Amhara **11:** 1544

Amidism **7:** 886, 997

Amiens **7:** 975 **9:** 1187

Aminiso. *See* Amnissos

Ammenemes I. *See* Amenemhet I

Ammisaduga, Babylonian king (1646-1626 BC) **2:** 247

Amnissos (Aminiso) **2:** 209

Amon (Amen), Egyptian deity, king of the Egyptian pantheon **2:** 159-161, 172, 174, *174-175,* 176-177, 179, 181, 184, *184,* 186, *186,* 191, 277-280; divine state of - **2:** 191, 280; high priest of - **2:** 191, 277; priests of - **2:** 177, 191, 278, 280; temple of - **2:** 176, *179,* 186

Amon-Re, Egyptian god of the sun **5:** 620. *See also* Amon

Amoretto **6:** *747*

Amorite **2:** 233-234, 247, 250, 277, 279-280; - dynasty **2:** 233-234; - empire **2:** 247, 277

Amorites **2:** 183-184, 226, 233-234, 247, 277, 280 **3:** 315, 316

Amos, Israelite prophet (eighth century BC) **3:** 333

Amphibians **1:** 35, 135

Amphipolis **5:** 589, *620, 639*

Amphitheater **6:** 772, 778, 782, 801-803, *802,* 807, 812, *819,* 853-854

Amphitheatrum Flavium. *See* Colosseum

Amphora **4:** *441, 458, 473, 480, 496, 512, 529, 548, 552,* 558, 565, 567 **6:** 800

Amratian (Naqada I), Egyptian predynastic culture phase **2:** 152

Amsterdam **11:** 1516

Amu Darya River **8:** 1069

Amulets **2:** 199 **6:** 806

Amulius, younger brother of Numitor, king of Alba Longa **5:** 650

Amurru. *See* Amorites

An, god of the heavens **2:** 220, 222

An Nafud **8:** 1083

Anagni **10:** 1356, 1366

Anarchy **4:** 532

Anastasia Romanovna, duchess of Russia, daughter of Nicholas II (1901-1916/17) **11:** 1518

Anastasius I **8:** 1050, 1053-1054, 1056, 1141

Anatman **7:** 878, 997

Anatolia **2:** 262, 268 **3:** 345 **4:** 445, 498 **8:** 1082, 1110, 1131 **9:** 1268-1269, 1272, 1276, 1288 **11:** 1556-1559, 1562

Anatomically Modern Humans (AMH) **1:** *39, 47,* 49-50, 133

Anatomy **1:** 38 **2:** 156

Anaxagoras, Greek philosopher (c.500-428 BC) **4:** 534, 547-548, 553, 565

Anaximander of Miletus, Ionian natural philosopher (610-c.547 BC) **4:** 503-504, 565

Anaximenes of Miletus, Ionian natural philosopher (585-525 BC) **4:** 503-504, 547, 565

Ancestor worship **11:** 1481

Ancien Régime **10:** 1359

Ancient uyi **11:** 1526

Ancus Marcius, fourth king of Rome (642-617 BC) **5:** 651

Andes **11:** 1452, 1477-1478, 1573

Andromache, in Greek legend, wife of Hector **4:** 442-444

Andromache work by Athenian tragic dramatist Euripides **5:** 600, 710

Andromeda galaxy **1:** 16, *20*
Anemospilia **2:** 204
Angels **7:** 920, 956, *980*, 982, 986-987, 997
Angers **9:** 1186
Angiosperms **1:** 35
Angles, Germanic people **8:** 1039, 1141 **9:** 1285
Anglo-Frisian **8:** 1043
Anglo-Saxon **9:** 1161-1162, 1164, 1178-1179, 1190, 1206, 1285-1287 **10:** 1323-1325, 1327, 1332
Anglo-Saxons **7:** 988, 990, 997
Angola **11:** 1554
Angra Mainyu, evil spirit in religion of Zarathushtra **3:** 363, 370-371
Angular momentum **1:** 9
Anguttara **7:** 881
Anima **6:** 752, 767
Animal husbandry **1:** 70, 72, 75-76, 78, 84, 97, 120, 135
Anitya **7:** 878
Anjou **9:** 1209, 1231 **10:** *1322*, 1327, 1329, *1348-1349*, 1349-1350, 1410
Ankara **11:** 1542
Ankhesenamen, queen of Egypt (1362-1351 BC) **2:** 180, 182
Ankhtifi, king of Egypt **2:** 158
Ankole **11:** 1553
Annalum Regium Francorum (*Annals of the Franks*) **9:** *1182*
Annam **11:** 1504
Annealing **1:** 104
Antarctica **1:** 30, 41
Anthemius of Tralles (?-472), Western Roman emperor (467-472) **8:** 1068 **9:** 1251
Anthony (of Egypt) (c.251-356) religious hermit and one of the earliest monks **7:** *963*, 968-971, *971*, *974*, 997
Anthropoid **1:** 44, 48, 135
Anti-Arian **8:** 1037, 1054, 1060
Anti-Lebanon **3:** 297
Anti-Semitism **9:** 1270
Antigonids, dynasty of Macedonian dynasty (306-168 BC) **5:** 627-628, 630, 709-711
Antigonus Gonatas (320-239 BC) son of Demetrius Poliocretes, king of Macedonia **5:** 628, 709, 711
Antigonus I (382-301 BC) called Monophthalmus (one-eyed) or Cyclops; king of Macedonia (306-301 BC) **5:** 627, 709
Antinoupolis **6:** 788
Antinous (c.110-130), favorite of Hadrian **6:** 788, 800
Antioch, metropolis in Asia, built by Seleucus, who named it after his father Antiochus **5:** *625*, 628-629, *689*, 690, 709 **6:** 794, *817*, 846 **7:** 918, 937, 945, 948, 959 **8:** 1019, 1071, 1077, *1078*, 1113, *1132*, 1144 **9:** 1263, 1272, 1274, 1276, *1276*, 1285-1287
Antioch III the Great (242-187 BC) king of Syria (223-187 BC) **5:** *689*, 690, 709
Antiochus I Soter (the Preserver), king of Syria (c.280-262 BC) son of Seleucus I **7:** 888, 917-918, 997
Antiochus III (242-187 BC), Seleucid king **5:** 691
Antiochus IV Epiphanes (the Mad) (c. 215-164BC) Seleucid king of the Hellenistic Syrian kingdom **5:** 629, *636* **6:** 806 **7:** 918, 997
Antipater (c. 398-319 BC), Macedonian general left in charge of Macedonia in 334 BC when Alexander the Great went to conquer the Persian Empire **5:** 615, 617, 630, 709 **7:** 920
Antiseptics **2:** 156
Antisuyu **11:** 1480
Antonia **7:** 921, 930
Antonine constitution of citizenship **6:** 815
Antonine dynasty **6:** 814
Antonine, either of the Roman emperors Antonius Pius and Marcus Aurelius **6:** 781, 784, 789, 811, 814-815
Antonine wall **6:** 789
Antoninus Pius, Titus Aelius Hadrianus Antonius Augustus Pius (86-161), Roman emperor (138-161) **6:** 784, *787*, 789, 835, 855
Antony, Mark (Marcus Antonius) (82-30 BC) **6:** *741*, 742-745, *743-744*, 853, 855-856
Antrustions, member of the personal guard of the Frankish Merovingian rulers (481/2-751) **9:** 1172
Antwerp **10:** 1306
Anu, Sumero-Akkadian god of the sky, father of all the gods **2:** 222, 236, 246, 278
Anum, god **2:** 220, 236
Anunaki **2:** 236

Anushirvan, one who has a soul **8:** 1077
Anyang **3:** 351-352
Apakura **3:** 402
Apella, Spartan assembly **4:** 472-473, 498, 565-566
Apennines **5:** 654, 670, 688, 712 **6:** 836
Aphrodite, Greek goddess of love and beauty **4:** *446*, 498, 500, 546, 565 **5:** 606, 642 **6:** 856
Aphrodite of Auxerre **4:** *446*
Apocolocyntosis Divi Claudi **6:** 809
Apoikia, Greek colony **4:** 457-458, 461, 565
Apollo, deity in Greek religion **4:** *477*, *484*, 498, *499-500*, *504*, *514*, *516*, *524*, 565 **5:** *583*, *630*, 638
Apollonius **5:** 636
Apologias **7:** 997
Apophis **2:** 170
Apostata. *See* Julian
Apostate **10:** 1386
Apostle James **9:** *1236*
Apostle Paul **7:** *933*, 937, 955, 961, 967 **9:** *1168. See also* Paul
Apostle Peter **7:** 933, 938, 954 **9:** 1222, 1263. *See also* Peter
Apostles **7:** *930*, 932-934, 936, 955-956, 960, 972, 997
Apostolic life **9:** 1224
Appenzell **10:** 1390
Appius Claudius (48 BC), Roman politician **5:** 673, 680, 695
Appius Claudius Caecus. *See* Claudius
Apso, Sumerian god **2:** 221
Apulia **5:** 1241-1242, 1270, 1288
Aquae Sulis **6:** *810*
Aqueduct(s) **6:** 749, 751, 766, 826, 853 **8:** 1034, 1044, *1049*, 1064, 1066 **11:** 1466, 1472
Aquila **6:** *823*
Aquileia **8:** 1027
Aquitaine **9:** 1160, 1162, 1166, 1182, 1184, 1211, 1231, 1285, 1287 **10:** *1321*, 1327, 1329
Aquitania **6:** 820 **8:** 1025, 1028, 1108
Ara Pacis Augustae (Altar of Peace) **6:** *745*, 754, 853, 855
Arab conquest **3:** 378
Arabia **2:** 218 **3:** 297, 300, 332, 413 **5:** *620*, 629 **6:** 787, 844, 853 **7:** 917 **8:** 1081-1086, *1082-1083*, 1095, 1122, 1126, 1141-1143 **11:** 1500, 1562; deserts of - **2:** 218 **8:** 1117, 1141
Arabia Felix (Happy Arabia) **6:** 853
Arabia Petraea **6:** 787
Arabian (or eastern) desert **2:** 151, 253
Arabian Peninsula **3:** 414 **11:** 1544. *See also* Arabia
Arabian; - culture **8:** 1121; - desert **2:** 218 **8:** 1117, 1141; - Empire **8:** 1126, 1143 **9:** 1226; - language **8:** 1086; - numerals **8:** 1131; - Sea **6:** 845
Arabic **2:** 152, 192 **8:** *1087*, 1087-1088, 1091, 1106, 1114, 1117-1118, 1120, 1128-1129, 1134, 1141-1144 **10:** 1345, 1422
Arabs **3:** 315, 319, 392 **8:** 1068, *1078*, 1078-1080, 1082-1083, 1088, 1091, 1093-1094, 1098, 1101-1102, 1104, 1106-1110, *1108*, 1114, 1118, 1124, *1126*, 1126-1127, 1130-1132, 1134, 1141-1144 **9:** 1164, 1166, 1193, 1227, *1238*, 1244, *1255*, *1264* **11:** 1491, 1494, 1500, 1544, 1548, 1551, 1566
Aradus **3:** 312
Aragon **9:** 1233, 1236, 1239, 1285 **10:** 1350, 1354, *1356*, 1366, 1368, 1394, 1422; kingdom of - **9:** 1236
Aram **2:** 263
Aramaean tribes **2:** 256, 262, 267
Aramaeans **2:** 256, 262-263, 266-268, 277-279
Aramaic **2:** 265 **5:** 629, 632, 710 **7:** 927 **8:** 1106
Aranyakas **3:** 387 **7:** 891, 897
Arbogast (394), barbarian general of the Roman Empire **7:** 954
Arcadia, central Peloponnisos region **4:** 448, 565
Arcadius (c. 377-408), Eastern Roman emperor **7:** 954 **8:** 1020, *1020*, *1022*, 1023, 1044, 1057-1058, 1141, 1144
Arcado-Cyprian, Greek dialect **4:** 448, 565
Arch **6:** *761*, *781*, *784-785*, *787-788*, 814, *828*, *834*, 839, *842*
Archaeologists **2:** 152, 167, 180, 195, 212, 218, 258, 268 **4:** 439, 445, 461
Archaeology **1:** 74, 87 **2:** 218 **6:** 733, 805 **11:** 1519
Archaeopteryx **1:** 36
Archaic Colonization **4:** 454, 457
Archaic period (3100-2755 BC) **2:** 153-154, 277
Archaic Period, era in Greek history from c.750 to 500 BC **4:** 445, 449, *449*, 453-454, 460, 466, 476, 481-482,

490, 492, 565, 567; - tyrannis **4:** 483
Archanes **2:** 200
Archbishop of Canterbury **10:** 1326, 1344
Archelaus, king of Macedonia (reigned 413-399) **7:** 921
Arches **8:** 1048, 1068
Archidamus, king of Sparta **5:** 591
Archilochus, Greek poet and satirist (c.600 BC) **4:** 461-462, 465-466, 565
Archimedes (287-212 BC), mathematician and physicist **5:** 641-642, 690, 709 **8:** 1119
Architecture **4:** 447, 449, 534, 567
Archons, magistrates in Athens **4:** 477-478, 480, 487, 519, 527, 539, 565
Archontate **4:** 527
Arctic Ocean **11:** 1513, 1536
Ardashir I **8:** 1069-1070, 1141
Ardashir II **8:** *1074*
Ardennes **1:** 86, 120
Arena **6:** 801-803, 806, 853
Areobindus, general (fl. sixth century) **8:** 1056
Areopagus, meeting place of Athenian aristocratic council **4:** 477, 480, 527, 565
Areos Pagos (hill of the god Ares). *See* Areopagus
Ares, Greek god of war **5:** 622 **6:** 855. *See also* Mars
Areta, Queen, mythological figure **4:** 442
Argentina **11:** 1478, 1574
Argiletum **6:** 794
Argive Plain **2:** 211
Argolis **4:** 445, 453; Plain of - **2:** 205 **4:** 445
Argos **2:** 216 **4:** 444, 452-453, 544 **5:** 609, *664*, 674, *695* **8:** 1023, 1141
Arhats **7:** 882, 997
Ariadne, Greek mythological figure **2:** 195
Arian **7:** 945-948, 974, 982, 997 **8:** 1019, 1023, 1025, 1031, 1035, 1053-1054, 1058, 1063, *1066*, 1142; - heresy **7:** 997 **8:** 1019
Arian Baptistry **8:** 1066
Arian Christians **6:** 834
Arianism **7:** 945, 974-975, 997 **8:** 1035, 1037, 1054, 1141
Aricia **5:** *668*
Aridaeus **5:** 625-626
Aristarchus of Samos, Greek astronomer (c.310-230 BC) **1:** 8 **5:** 642
Aristides the Just (fifth century BC), Athenian statesman, founder of the Delian League **4:** 524
Aristocracy **3:** 381 **4:** 453-454, 459-460, 480, 482-485, 527, 567 **5:** 630, 634, 676, 702, 711 **7:** 949 **9:** 1160, 1163, 1171, 1175, 1178, 1183, 1196, 1213, 1255 **10:** 1308, 1310, 1354, 1377, 1381, 1412. *See also* Nobility
Aristogeiton, legendary Greek hero (fifth century BC). *See also* Harmodius **4:** 487-488, *490*
Aristolaides family **4:** 485
Aristophanes (c.445-385 BC) Athenian comic dramatist **4:** 534, 542, 546, 558 **5:** 587, 591, 598, 600, 709. *See also* Acharnians
Aristotle (384-322 BC), Greek philosopher, logician, and scientist **4:** 480, 536, 547-548, 553-554, 568 **5:** 602, 606-607, *607*, *613*, 614-615, *615*, 644, 648, 709 **8:** 1080, 1119, 1129, 1141 **9:** *1238* **11:** 1548
Arithmetica **9:** 1179
Arius (c. 256-336), native of Libya, Alexandrian priest **7:** 944-945, 974, 997 **8:** 1035, 1053-1054, 1141
Arizona **1:** *21*, *26*, *34*
Arjuna, one of the five Pandava brothers, who are the heroes of the Indian epic the *Mahabharata* **7:** 891, 997
Ark (of the Covenant), repository in which the Ten Commandments and Hebrew desert traditions were kept **3:** 322, 327, 329-330, 332
Armenia **1:** 116 **4:** 513 **6:** 731, 755, 773, 787, 833 **8:** 1071-1072, 1078, 1095, 1144 **9:** 1248, 1264, 1285 **11:** 1539, 1542
Armeniakoi, regiment **9:** 1256-1257, 1259
Armenian emperors, succession of Byzantine emperors (813-842) **9:** 1285
Arminius (18 BC-AD 19), German tribal leader **6:** 755
Arno River **10:** 1310
Arnold (of Brescia) (c.1100-c.1155), radical religious reformer noted for his outspoken criticism of clerical wealth and corruption and for his strenuous opposition to the temporal power of the popes **10:** 1316-1317
Arpad **2:** 265, 267
Arrian, Flavius Arrianus (second century AD) governor of Capadocia (131-137) **5:** 614, 709
Ars Poetica **6:** 854

Clodius Albinus (?-AD 197), Roman general **6:** 813

Clodius Pulcher, Publius (c.93-52 BC), politician in Late Republican Rome **6:** 736-737, 799, 813

Clotilda, wife of Clovis I **8:** 1032, 1141

Clouds **5:** 600

Clovis I (c.466-511), king of the Franks (481-511) **8:** *1027, 1029*, 1032, 1034, 1141-1142 **9:** 1287

Clunaic; - model **9:** 1224; - pope **9:** 1268; - reform **9:** 1286

Cluny, abbey in Burgundy founded by William of Aquitaine in 910 **9:** 1211-1212, *1214, 1221*, 1232, 1239, 1268, *1269*, 1285, 1287

Clusium **5:** 668

Clytemnestra, tomb of **2:** 210

Cnut. *See* Canute

Coastal party **4:** 485-486

Coatlicue (goddess of the earth) **11:** 1467

Code of Ur-Nammu **3:** 315

Codex Albendensis **8:** 1044

Codex Aureus, tenth century manuscript (Echternach) **7:** 944 **9:** *1220, 1224*

Codex Cortesianus **11:** 1459

Codex Dresdensis **11:** 1459

Codex Mendoza **11:** 1460

Codex Perez **11:** 1459

Codex Tro **11:** 1459

Codices **11:** 1448, 1459

Coelenterates **1:** 35

Coemperor **6:** 789 **8:** 1016-1017, 1020, 1069, 1142

Coemptio **6:** 797

Cohorts **6:** 751, 755, 759

Coimbra **9:** 1237

Coins **4:** 474, 492, 512, *524*, 566

Colchester **6:** 772

Colima **11:** 1450

Collective education **4:** 474

Collegium (pl. *collegia*) **6:** 796, 800, 853; - of millers and bakers **6:** 800; - of musicians **6:** 800

Cologne **1:** 76 **6:** 854 **10:** 1307, 1372, 1391

Colombia **11:** 1447, *1450*, 1452

Coloni. See Colonus

Colonia (pl. *coloniae*) **6:** 790, 853

Colonial era **4:** 461

Colonists **4:** 458-460

Colonization **4:** 454, 457, 460-461, *460*, 481, 483, 490, 565 **6:** 741, 837 **11:** 1574

Colonnades **6:** 793

Colonnas **10:** 1394

Colonus (pl. *coloni*) **6:** 826-828, 853-854

Colony **3:** 300, 303, 306, 409 **4:** 457-462, *460, 466*, 484, 488, 490, *496*, 515, 526, 534, 547, *547*, 550, *558*, 565-566, 568 **5:** 590, 604, 667, 672, 678, 709, 712 **10:** 1408

Colophon **4:** 462, 504

Colosseum **6:** 772, 778, *778*, 801, *802*, 807, 854 **7:** 981

Colossus **2:** 177 **6:** 778, 854

Columbus **11:** 1447

Column **6:** *782, 786*, 787, *790, 841*

Comedies **5:** 587, 591, 598, 600, 638-639, 711

Comedy **4:** 534, 537, 539-541, 546, 565

Comes **9:** 1175, 1234, 1237

Comets **1:** 11, 23

Comitatenses **6:** 831

Comitatus **9:** 1171-1172, 1174, 1185

Comitatus Portaculenis **9:** 1237

Comitia centuriata (assembly of centuries) Roman assembly **5:** 658, 664, 666, 690, 709

Comitia curiate, Romulus, Rome's founder, divided the people into three tribes and thirty curiae **5:** 658, 664

Comitia tributa (assembly of tributes or districts) Roman assembly drawn from thirty-five districts **5:** 661, 666, 700, 709

Comitium **8:** 1038

Commander of the Roman army **8:** 1019

Commercial routes **11:** 1456, 1574

Commodus, Lucius Aulius Aurelius (161-192), Roman emperor 177-192, sole emperor after 180 **6:** 811-812, 815, 824

Commoner(s) **3:** 351 **8:** 1015 **10:** 1325, 1392

Communal government **10:** 1312-1313, 1315

Commune **10:** 1310, 1313-1314, 1317, 1335

Concilium plebis (council of plebs), Roman popular assembly of plebeians **5:** 660-661, 666, 709 **6:** 728

Concordat of Worms (1122), compromise between Pope Calixtus II and Holy Roman emperor Henry V on investi-

ture **9:** 1220-1221, 1285-1286 **10:** 1335. *See also* Worms

Concordia ordinum **6:** 732

Condottieri (mercenaries) **10:** 1395-1396

Confederation of Delos. *See* Delian League

Confessor **10:** 1324, 1328

Confucianism **3:** 356-357, 360 **7:** 902, 907-908, 910, 912, *912*, 997 **11:** 1502, 1504, 1508, 1510, 1512, 1524, 1541, 1574

Confucians **7:** 908, 910-912

Confucius (551-479 BC) philosopher of ancient China **3:** 356-357 **7:** 902-905, *904-905*, 907, 909-910, 997 **11:** 1502

Congo Musa **11:** 1547

Congregation **11:** 1563

Coniuratio **10:** 1310

Conquistadores **11:** 1465, 1469, 1472, 1476

Conrad **10:** 1333, 1349

Conrad I of Franconia (?-918), German king (911-918) **9:** 1214

Conrad II of Swabia (c.990-1039), king of Germany (1024-1039), Holy Roman emperor (1027-1039), king of the Lombards (1026) **9:** 1214, *1224*, 1285-1286

Conrad III (1093-1152), German king (1138-1152) **9:** 1272, *1273*, 1276

Conrad IV, German king from 1237 and king of Sicily from 1251 **10:** 1349

Conrad of Franconia. *See* Conrad I

Conscripti **5:** 657

Conservatism **4:** 473

Consilium principis **6:** 817

Consolation (*Consolamentum*) **9:** 1277

Consonants **4:** 450

Constance, heiress of the Norman kingdom of Sicily **10:** 1338, *1366*, 1368, 1392

Constans, Flavius Julius (323-350), Roman emperor (337-350) **6:** 832

Constantine **8:** 1016, *1057*, 1068, 1141-1142 **9:** 1168, 1170-1171, 1180, 1208, 1212, 1245-1247, 1250, 1254, 1256-1257, 1260-1261, *1262*, 1263-1265, 1285-1286

Constantine I, Flavius Valerius (c.280-337) (Constantine the Great), first Christian Roman emperor (306-337) **6:** *828*, 830-832, *831-832, 834*, 853-854 **7:** 975 **8:** 1035, 1054, 1141-1142

Constantine II (317-340), Roman emperor (337-340) **6:** 832

Constantine IV (?-685), Byzantine emperor (668-685) **9:** 1170

Constantine V Copronymus (718-775), Byzantine emperor (741-775) **9:** 1180, 1254, 1256-1257

Constantine VI, Byzantine emperor (780-797) **9:** 1180, 1256, 1285-1286

Constantine VII Porphyrogenitus (905-959), Byzantine emperor (908-959) **9:** 1260-1261, 1285

Constantine VIII (c.960-1028), Byzantine co-ruler with Basil II (976-1025), sole ruler (1025-1028) **9:** 1264

Constantine IX Monomachus (1000-1055), Byzantine co-ruler with Zoë and Theodora (1042-1055) **9:** *1262*, 1263

Constantine XI Paleologus, last Byzantine emperor (1404-1453) **11:** 1559

Constantine the Great (c.274-337 AD), Roman emperor **3:** 369 **7:** *944*, 949, 956, 997 **9:** 1168, 1246, 1285-1286. *See also* Constantine I

Constantinople **6:** 831, 834, 853-854 **7:** 945-946, 948, 951, 954, 954, 972, 976, 979-982, 988, 997 **8:** *1016, 1018*, 1018-1019, 1023, 1025-1026, 1028, 1030, 1033-1035, 1044-1046, *1045-1046*, 1048, *1049-1050*, 1050, *1052*, 1052-1054, *1054-1057*, 1056-1058, 1060-1061, 1063-1065, *1064*, 1076, *1078*, 1078-1079, 1081, 1099-1101, *1105*, 1107-1110, 1112-1113, *1113*, 1119, *1119*, 1124, *1132*, 1141-1143 **9:** 1164, 1168, 1180, 1211, 1222, 1224, 1227, 1245-1247, *1247*, 1249, *1249-1250*, 1251, 1254, 1256, 1259-1265, 1269-1270, 1272, 1274, 1276, 1278, 1285, 1287 **10:** 1339, *1339*, 1344-1345, *1350*, 1387 **11:** 1500, 1513, 1516, 1518, 1558-1559, 1561, *1561-1562*, 1573-1574. *See also* Byzantium

Constantius Chlorus **8:** 1016

Constantius I, original name Flavius Valerius Constantius, Roman emperor **7:** 943, 997 **8:** 1016

Constantius II **6:** 828, 830, 832, *834* **7:** 945-946, 948, 950, 997 **8:** 1019, 1035, 1037, 1054

Constitutio Antoniniana de Civitate **6:** 815

Construction projects **2:** 154

Consul **5:** 664, 672, 678, 681-682, 687-688, 690, 693,

696, 699-701, 709, 712 **6:** 727, 730, 732, 735, 737, 739, 741, 745, 768, 782, 838, 853-855

Consulate **5:** 657, 666

Consuls **5:** 657, 661, 664, 671, 678, 688, 697, 709, 711-712 **10:** 1313, 1316

Continental Drift **1:** 30; - plates **1:** 30

Copán (Honduras) **11:** 1456, 1461-1462

Copenhagen **10:** 1402

Copernican **1:** 9-10

Copernicus, Nicolaus, astronomer (1473-1543) **1:** 9, 133-134

Copper **1:** 88, 90, 98-100, 102-107, 133, 136; - Age (early phase of the Bronze Age) **1:** 106; - oxide **1:** 104-105

Coptic **2:** 152, 192 **3:** 412 **7:** 959, 968 **8:** 1054, 1106-1107

Corbulo, Gnaeus Domitius (?-67), Roman general **6:** *772*, 773

Corcyra, island (Corfu) **4:** 526 **5:** 590-591, 597, 711

Córdoba **6:** 808 **8:** 1095, 1113, 1119, 1132, 1141 **9:** 1166, *1191*, 1194, 1225, *1225-1227*, 1227-1230, 1234, 1238, 1241, 1285-1288 **11:** 1545

Core axes **1:** 51

Corfu. *See* Corcyra

Corinth **4:** 452, 454, 458, 482-484, *483-484*, 519, 521, 525-526, 537, 565, 567 **5:** 588, 590, 609, 615, *620*, 685, *695*, 698, 709 **6:** 839, 854 **7:** 933 **8:** 1023, 1141; tyranny in - **4:** 483

Corinthian; - Canal **4:** 484; - Gulf **4:** 526; - Isthmus **4:** 476; - pottery **4:** 483; - War **5:** 609

Cornelius Tacitus **8:** 1021, 1038, 1142

Cornwall **1:** 107

Coromandel coast **11:** 1497

Corona (atmosphere of the sun) **1:** 14

Coronation **9:** 1171, 1178, 1207-1208, 1219, 1256, 1276 **10:** 1343, 1348, *1379*, 1392, 1418, 1421

Corpus Iuris Civilis, civil code **8:** 1067

Corsica **5:** 667, 684, 712 **6:** 837 **8:** 1029, 1031, 1064 **9:** 1242 **10:** 1312

Cortés, Hernán **11:** 1469, 1476, 1573

Corvée **9:** 1286, 1288

Cos **4:** 448

Cosmology **1:** 19-20, 80 **4:** 503

Cosmos **5:** 647

Costa Rica **11:** 1447

Cotrone **9:** 1213

Council of 500 (500 *Medimnoi*) **4:** 480, 506-507, 527, 565, 567

Council of Basel, held in 1431; Pope Martin tried to sabotage it in vain **10:** 1368

Council of Chalcedon (451), Pope Leo I tried to accommodate the issue of Monophysitism **7:** 980, 997 **8:** 1054 **9:** 1250

Council of Clermont (1095), called by Pope Urban II to announce the First Crusade **9:** 1267-1269, 1286, 1288

Council of Dad-Ishu **8:** 1076, 1142

Council of Elders **3:** 299 **5:** 655-656 **8:** 1102, 1112

Council of Ephesus **7:** 956, 997

Council of Ferrara, ecumenical council of the Roman Catholic church (1438-1445) in which the Latin and Greek churches tried to reach agreement on their doctrinal differences and end the schism between them **10:** 1368

Council of lords **9:** 1164-1165

Council of Lyons **10:** *1347*

Council of Muslim elders **8:** 1112

Council of Nicaea (787), ecumenical council of the Christian Church **7:** 946, *953*, 954, 974, 997 **8:** 1017 **9:** 1180, 1256, 1260-1261, 1286

Council of Orthodoxy (843), iconoclasm condemned **9:** 1180, 1259

Council of Pavia, called by Pope Martin in 1423, asserting papal supremacy in all matters ecclesiastical **10:** 1368

Count **9:** 1175-1176, 1183, 1196, 1198, 1211, 1237, 1242, 1266, 1269, 1285-1286, 1288

Countersenate **6:** 729

Counterearth **1:** 8

Court of Justice **4:** 480

Courtrai **10:** 1317

Covenant **3:** 322, 327, 329. *See also* Ark

Cows **3:** 388, 410

Coya **11:** 1481

Cracow **10:** 1402, 1410

Crassus, Dices Marcus Licinius (c.115-53 BC), Roman

Flavius Claudius Julianus, Roman emperor (reigned 361-363) **7**: 997. *See also* Julian the Apostate

Flavius Constantius. *See* Constantius II

Flavius Stilicho, Roman military commander **8**: 1023, 1057, 1141

Flavius Theodosius. *See* Theodosius I

Flavius Valerius Constantinus. *See* Constantius I

Flax **1**: 91, 97

Flemish **10**: *1319*, 1330, *1358*, 1362, 1377, *1404*

Flint **1**: *49-50*, 49-52, *52*, 56, 64, *67*, *76*, 77-80, *84*, 90, 97-99, 110, 133-134; - industry **1**: 80; - processing **1**: 50, 134

Florence **10**: 1312, 1364, *1368*, 1395-1396, 1414, 1422

Florus, Publius Annius (late first and early second century), historian of Rome and poet **6**: 810

Flower wars **11**: 1470, 1574

Foederati, federates **6**: 776, 836, 841 **8**: 1020, 1024-1026, 1028, 1032, 1034, 1037, 1060, 1142, 1144

Foliated Cross **11**: 1456

Foljungar dynasty **10**: 1402

Fontenay, Battle at (841), Lothar I battled against his brothers Louis the German and Charles the Bald **9**: 1187, 1287-1288

Foot soldiers **5**: 590, 612, 616-617, 658, *679*, 709-710

Fora **8**: 1066

Forging Trade **1**: 105

Form **5**: 606, 644

Fortifications **5**: 588

Forum (pl. *Fora*) **5**: 661-662, *684*, *692-693*, *697* **6**: *729*, *735*, *746*, 749, *749*, *754-755*, 766, *781*, 787, 793-794, *794*, 796, 805, 808, 814, *842*, 854-855 **7**: *946*, *981*, 997 **8**: 1044

Forum Boarium **5**: 697 **6**: *729*

Forum of Augustus **6**: *746*

Forum Romanum **5**: 684, 693 **6**: *735*, *749*, *754-755*, *781*, 794, 814, *842*, 855 **7**: 946, 981

Fossils **1**: 29, 33, 35, 38-39, 44, 92, 133, 135

Four Books **3**: 356

Four Noble Truths **7**: 874, 877, 997

Fourteenth dynasty (c.1715-1650 BC) **2**: 168

Fourth Crusade (1202-1204) **9**: 1276-1277 **10**: 1339, 1344

Fourth Lateran Council, held in 1215; an elaborate crusade plan repeating earlier prohibitions on the transport of military supplies to Muslims **10**: 1369

France **1**: 7, 9, 46, *51*, 52-54, *56*, *59*, 60, 64, *65-66*, *72-73*, 74, 76, 78, 80, *80-81*, *86*, 87, 99, *101*, *121*, 114, 118-120, 123-124, *123*, 126, 134 **3**: 393 **4**: 458, 514 **5**: *702*, 709, 712 **6**: 854 **7**: *904*, *915*, 975, *975*, 987, 997 **9**: *1163*, *1174*, 1187, *1189*, 1206, 1209-1211, 1213, 1221, 1225, 1236, 1268, 1270, *1273*, 1273-1274, 1276-1278, 1285, 1287 **10**: 1305, 1307, *1311*, 1316-1317, 1321, 1323, 1326-1327, *1328*, 1329-1330, 1332, 1337, *1342*, 1343, *1347*, 1348, 1350, 1352-1354, 1356, *1356-1357*, 1358-1359, 1363-1364, *1364*, 1366, 1369-1372, 1374-1375, *1375-1376*, 1377-1381, *1378-1381*, 1383-1384, *1383*, *1386-1387*, 1386-1387, 1392, 1398, 1406-1407, 1411-1412, *1416*, 1418, 1420 **11**: 1560-1561

Francesco Sforza, condottiere who played a crucial role in fifteenth-century Italian politics and duke of Milan **10**: *1397*, 1398

Francis I, last Holy Roman emperor (1768-1835) **11**: 1561, 1563

Francis of Assisi, original name Francesco di Pietro di Bernardone (1181/82-1226); canonized July 15, 1228; founder of the Franciscan orders **10**: 1314, *1315*

Franconia **10**: 1321. *See also* Franks

Franconian dynasty **9**: 1214, 1221

Frankfurt **10**: 1318

Frankish; - Empire **8**: 1108 **9**: 1159-1160, 1163, 1171, 1182, 1193-1194, 1196, 1199, 1202, *1202*, *1206*, 1231, 1286-1287; - kingdom **7**: 990 **8**: 1032, 1143; - law **8**: 1040, 1042 **9**: 1159; - rule **9**: 1178

Franks **6**: 820 **7**: 950, 985, 990 **8**: 1024, 1026, *1029*, 1031-1034, 1107-1108, 1124, 1141-1142 **9**: 1161, 1163, 1165-1166, 1168, 1171, 1175-1176, 1178, 1182, *1182*, 1186, 1191, 1193, 1202-1203, 1227, 1239, 1272, 1286-1288

Fraunhofer, Joseph von (1787-1826) **1**: *8*, 12, 133,

Frederick Barbarossa. *See* Frederick I

Frederick I Barbarossa (c.1123-1190), Holy Roman emperor (1155-1190) **9**: 1276 **10**: 1317, *1333*, *1334*, *1335-1338*, *1340*, 1337-1338, 1388

Frederick II (1194-1250), king of Sicily (1197-1250),

duke of Swabia (as Frederick VI, 1228-1235), German king (1212-1250), and Holy Roman emperor (1220-1250) **9**: 1277 **10**: 1340, *1346*, *1348*, 1354, 1388, 1394, 1404, 1420

Frederick III (1415-1493), Holy Roman emperor from 1452 and German king from 1440 **10**: 1390, 1393

Frederick of Hohenstaufen. *See* Frederick I

Freemen **4**: 453-454, 469, 471-472, 515, 567 **8**: 1016, 1038, 1040, 1042 **10**: 1391

Freiherren **10**: 1391

French Revolution **10**: 1320

Fresco **5**: 1018, 1031 **10**: 1313, 1341, 1344, 1368

Frescoes **2**: *197*, 201-203 **4**: 497 **6**: 772, *773*, 805; house of the - **2**: 201

Freya, in Norse mythology, god **8**: 1032

Friars **10**: 1314

Friars Preachers, Order of **11**: 1561

Fribourg **10**: 1390

Friesland **9**: 1187

Frigidarium **6**: *810*

Frisian language **8**: 1043

Frisians **8**: *1029*, 1039 **9**: 1161-1162, 1167, 1176, *1180*, 1286

Frontinus, Sextus Julius (c.35-c.103), Roman soldier, governor of Britain, author of *De aquis urbis Romae* **6**: 783

Frumentius, Saint (fourth century AD) **11**: 1544

Fuji, volcano **11**: 1527

Fujiwara period (858-1160) **11**: 1526-1528, 1574

Funerary temple **2**: 174, 177

Funnel-beakers **1**: 83-84; - culture **1**: 80, 87, 92, 98, 133; - people **1**: 81

Fustat **8**: *1113*, *1119*, 1121, 1126, 1132, 1134

Fustian **8**: 1126

Gabriel, archangel **7**: 972 **8**: *1081*, 1085-1087, *1094*, *1096*

Gad **3**: 319

Gainas **8**: 1142

Gaiseric **8**: 1026, 1029-1031, 1142

Gaius (Flaminius) (217 BC), Roman political leader **5**: 687-688, 690, 695-696, 700, *700*, 710-712

Gaius Aurelius Valerius **8**: 1016, 1142

Gaius Gracchus (160/153 BC?-121 BC), Roman tribune (123-122 BC) **5**: 696

Gaius Julius Caesar. *See* Caesar

Gaius Terentius Varro **5**: 688. *See also* Varro

Galaxy **1**: 11, 14, 16-17, 19, *20*, 21, 133-135

Galba, Servius Sulpicius (3 BC-AD 69), Roman emperor for seven months (68-69) **6**: 774-775, *775*

Galeazzo, Gian, Visconti, byname Count of Valour (1351-1402), Milanese leader who brought the Visconti dynasty to the height of its power and almost succeeded in becoming the ruler of all northern Italy **10**: 1397

Galerius, Gaius Galerius Valerius Maximianus (?-AD 311), Roman emperor (305-311) **6**: 828, 830-831, *831* **7**: 942, 997 **8**: 1016

Galicia **9**: 1226, 1230, 1234 **11**: 1516

Galilee **3**: 313 **7**: 926

Galileo Galilei, astronomer, mathematician and physicist (1564-1642) **1**: 10-11

Galla Placidia **8**: 1024, *1025*, 1142

Galley **4**: 471 **6**: *742-743*

Gallia (Gaul) **5**: 669, 690, 710 **7**: 933; - Cisalpina **5**: 690, 710; - Transalpina **5**: 669. *See also* Gaul

Gallia Lugdunensis **6**: 774

Gallia Narbonensis **6**: 854

Gallic **5**: 668-669, 686-687, *702* **10**: 1412

Gallic Wars (58-50 BC) **6**: 736, 738

Gallienus, Publius Licinius Egnatius (c.218-268), Roman emperor jointly with Valerian (253-260), sole emperor to 268 **6**: 819-820, *822*

Gallienus, son of emperor Valerian **7**: 941

Gallus, Gaius Vibius Trebonianus (?-253), Roman emperor (251-253) **6**: 832, *834*

Gamiko **4**: 566

Gamma-ray **1**: 12, 19

Gamow, George, nuclear physicist and cosmologist (1904-1968) **1**: 19-20

Ganaka, Hindu king **3**: 390

Ganda **3**: 411

Gandhi, Mohandas Karamchand, preeminent leader of Indian nationalism and the prophet of nonviolence in the twentieth century **3**: 384 **7**: 893, 997

Ganges **3**: 362 **7**: 871, 875, 891, 892

Ganges River **6**: 845

Gao **11**: 1547-1548, 1574

Gath **3**: 328

Gathas **3**: 367, 371

Gau **9**: 1175-1176, 1187, 1286

Gaugamela, city in northern Mesopotamia **5**: *620*, 621, *622*, 709-710

Gaul **6**: 736-738, 740, 744, 792, 813, 820, 822, 827-828, 830, 832-834, 837, 853-854 **7**: 950, 954, 959, 975, 985, 997 **8**: 1019-1021, 1023-1028, 1032, 1037, 1066, 1124, 1141-1142, 1144 **9**: 1174, 1187, 1194, 1287 **10**: 1412

Gauls **1**: 123, 126 **5**: *628*, 669, 700 **6**: 738, 774, 836, 854

Gautama, Siddhartha (c.480-400 BC), a prince of the Shakya clan; called the Buddha, founder of Buddhism **7**: 871-873, *872-874*, 877, 882, 884-885, 997

Gautier Sans-Avoir. *See* Walter the Penniless

Gaza **2**: 186 **3**: 328, 330-331 **5**: 620, *620*

Gaza Empire **11**: 1554

Gdansk **10**: 1408

Gelasius II (?-1119), pope (1118-1119) **9**: 1220

Gelon **5**: 680

Gemma augustea cameo **6**: *750*

Gemmyo, Japanese empress **11**: 1526

Genealogy **11**: 1459, 1462

General Stilicho. *See* Flavius Stilicho

Genesis **2**: 168 **3**: 298, 316, 317, 319-320

Genetic changes **1**: 38

Genghis Khan. *See* Chingiz Khan

Genoa **9**: 1242, 1274 **10**: 1312, *1395*, 1396, 1398 **11**: 1559

Gens (people), Roman clan led by chieftains called patres (fathers) **5**: 655, 710

Gentes **6**: 728

Genua **11**: 1574

Genus **1**: 38, 45, 134

Geocentrism **1**: 8

Geoffrey (of Monmouth), author of *Historia regum Britanniae* (c.1136), acquaintance of Thomas Becket **10**: *1322*, 1326, 1330

Geography **2**: 151 **5**: 607, 642, 712 **11**: 1573

Geologic; - Periods **1**: 33, 133; - time **1**: 38, 41-42; - timescale **1**: 30, 33, 133

Geologists **1**: 33, 43

Geometry (*Geometria*) **4**: 503, 549 **5**: 641-643, 712 **9**: 1179

Georgia **11**: 1539, 1542

Georgica **6**: 856

Gepides, Germanic people **8**: 1026

Gerbert. *See* Sylvester II

German **1**: 9, 30, 46, 108, 134

German Empire **10**: 1316, 1318, 1332, 1335, *1346*, 1388, 1390, 1411, 1418-1419

German tribes **8**: 1021

Germania **8**: 1021, 1038, 1142

Germania Inferior **6**: 775-776, 778

Germanic **5**: 700

Germanic kings **8**: 1044, 1060, 1142

Germanic tribes **1**: 126 **7**: 946 **9**: 1167

Germanic migration **7**: 980

Germanics **1**: 120, 126, 133

Germanicus, Caesar (15 BC-AD 19), nephew and adopted son of emperor Tiberius **6**: 760-762, 765, 853, 855

Germans **6**: 738, *750*, 755, 772, 817-818, 820, 824, 827, 842-843, 854

Germany **1**: *44*, 45-46, 52, 62, 76, 80-81, 86, 90, 110, 113-114, *114*, 126 **5**: 626 **6**: *749*, 755, 761, 775-776, *777*, 778, 783-784, *825*, 830, *843*, 856 **7**: 990 **8**: 1016, 1021-1022, *1038*, 1141-1142, 1144 **9**: 1162, *1170*, 1171, 1187, 1191, 1204, 1206, *1211*, 1213-1214, *1216*, 1219, *1222*, 1224, 1231, 1272, 1276, 1285-1287 **10**: *1330*, 1333-1335, *1336-1337*, 1338, 1340, 1346-1347, 1349, 1363, 1373-1374, *1387*, 1388, 1392, 1394, 1402, 1409, 1412, *1415*, 1416, 1418 **11**: 1459, 1545

Gerontium **5**: 688

Gerousia, Council of Elders in Sparta **4**: 473, 566

Gerzean (Naqada II and III), Egyptian predynastic cultural phase **2**: 152

Geta, Publius Septimus (189-212), Roman emperor 209-212 **6**: *812*, 815

Gethsemane **7**: *930*, 931

Gézo, king of India (reigned 1818-1858) **11**: 1551

Ghana, empire of (400-1240) **11**: 1544-1545, 1574

Ghazan Khan (reigned 1295-1304) **11**: 1539

Ghazni **8:** 1080 **11:** 1492, 1494, 1496

Ghengis Khan, Mongol ruler. *See* Chingiz Khan

Ghent **10:** 1317-1318, 1377

Ghettos **9:** 1270 **10:** 1373

Ghibellines **10:** 1333, 1349, 1363, *1394*, 1396

Gibraltar **1:** 46, *46* **3:** 295, 302-303 **8:** 1029, 1107, 1144 **11:** 1498

Gideon **3:** 328, 330

Gigilda (guilds) **10:** 1320

Gilgal **3:** 327

Gilgamesh, Mesopotamian hero **2:** 222, 235, *238*, *240*, 242, 244-246, 277; epic of -, literary composition in Akkadian language **2:** *238*, *240*, 242, 246, 277

Giovanni Maria, son of Gian Galeazzo **10:** 1398

Girsu **2:** 227-228

Giza **2:** 154, 156

GL229 (star) **1:** 24

Gla **2:** 215-216, 277

Gladiator **6:** *729*, 730, *778*, *800*, 801-802, *802*, 811-812, *815*, 854, 856

Gladiatorial combat **6:** 801-803, 812

Gladiators **8:** 1056

Glarus **10:** 1390

Glassware **1:** 118

Gleb **11:** 1515

Go-Daigo, emperor (1333-1338) **11:** 1529, 1573

Gobi Desert **8:** 1128 **11:** 1504, 1531, 1574

Gobir **3:** 414 **11:** 1550

God of aggression and chaos **2:** 170

God of death **2:** 165

God of science and writing **2:** 165

Goddess of dawn. *See* Eos

Godfrey of Bouillon (1060-1100), duke of Lower Lotharingia and a leader of the First Crusade **9:** *1267*, 1270, 1274, 1285-1286 **10:** 1338

Godigiselus, king of the Vandals **8:** 1028-1029

Gog, monster in Shah-nama. *See* Magog

Golconda **11:** 1497

Gold **1:** 88, 102, *102*, 104, *105*, 112, *112*, 117, *119*, 120, 122, *123* **4:** *484*, *486*, 487, 492, 512, *532*, 565

Gold River **3:** 303

Gold solidus **6:** 832

Golden Age **4:** 527, 532 **6:** *783* **7:** 951

Golden Book or Gospels **9:** *1220*, *1224*

Golden Gate **8:** 1052

Golden Horde **11:** 1516, 1518, 1536, 1538, 1542, 1574; Empire of the - **11:** 1574

Golden Horn **8:** 1046, 1110

Golden House. *See Domus Aurea*

Golden One. *See* El Dorado

Golgotha **7:** 931

Gondwanaland **1:** 30

Gonja **11:** 1548

Gordian III, Marcus Antonius Gordianus (225-244), Roman emperor 238-244 **6:** 818

Gordian knot, Greek legend **5:** 619

Gordius **5:** 619, *620*, 710

Gorgias **5:** 596, 712

Gorgon **5:** 629

Gospel of Jesus **8:** 1090

Goth Gainas. *See* Gainas

Gothic **6:** 1021, 1023-1024, 1032-1035, 1043, 1059-1060, 1064-1065, 1142, 1144

Gothic Kingdom **8:** 1060

Goths **6:** 817, 819-820, 841, 853-854 **7:** 940 **8:** 1019-1021, 1024-1025, 1027-1028, 1035, 1037, 1043-1044, 1057-1058, 1060, 1064, 1066, 1144 **9:** *1168* **10:** 1339

Gotland **9:** 1188 **10:** *1402*, 1408

Gournia **2:** 200, 278

Government Reforms **8:** 1018

Gracchus, Gaius Sempronius (153-121 BC) **6:** 728, 799

Graces, the three Roman goddesses of beauty, joy, and charm **5:** 638, 710

Graeci **9:** 1244

Graffiti **6:** 805 **8:** 1134

Grain distribution **6:** 749, 799

Grain silos **2:** 175

Grammar **9:** 1179

Grammatica **9:** 1179

Granada **8:** *1119*, 1122 **9:** 1230, 1238, 1286

Grand Canal **11:** 1508

Grand Canyon **1:** 26, 32

Grand National Assembly of Turkey **8:** 1122

Granicus (River), site of a battle in northwestern Asia

Minor **5:** *616*, 617, 619, 710

Gratian, Flavius Gratianus Augustus (359-383), Roman emperor (367-383) **6:** 834 **7:** 951, 953, 997 **8:** 1020, 1142

Grave circle **2:** 208-209, *210-211*, 211, 213; - plundering **2:** 173

Gravettian **1:** *51*, 53-55, 62, *64*, 136

Great Attack **8:** 1100

Great Britain **3:** 300 **9:** 1193, *1194*

Great Enlightenment **7:** 874

Great Gate (Mongolian) in Delhi **11:** 1500

Great Goddess **7:** *894*, *897*, 900

Great Interregnum, the period of twenty years between 1254-1273 **10:** 1388

Great Migration **8:** 1022, 1033

Great Moguls, Mogul dynasty in northern India (sixteenth-eighteenth century) **11:** 1574

Great Palace **11:** 1500

Great Renunciation **7:** 873

Great Schism (1054) **9:** 1222, 1224, 1263, 1287

Great Wall **3:** 360 **11:** 1508, 1511, 1531, 1534—1535

Great War, (Peloponnesian War) (431-404 BC) **5:** 587

Great Yasa **11:** 1534

Greater Greece **4:** 458

Greco-Roman **3:** 387 **6:** 845-846 **7:** *883*, 892, 948-951

Greece **1:** *29*, 72-73, 75, 106, 108, 114, 118-120 **2:** 151, 193-194, 207, 212, 215-216 **3:** 307, 347, 378, 387 **4:** 439, 445-448, 454, 457-458, 461, 475-476, 482-483, *484*, 490, 492, 497-498, 503, 513, 515, 517-524, 526, 534, *550*, 565-566, 568 **5:** 583, 587, 590-591, 598, 601, 609-612, 617, 624, 626, 628, 630, 636, 639, 642-643, 672, 674, 680, 691, 693, 698, 709-712 **6:** 727, 740, 744, 767, 771, *788*, 817, *835*, 838-839, 853 **7:** 917, *925*, *928*, 934, 937, 954, 956, 972, 978 **8:** 1023, 1030, 1077 **9:** *1251*, *1257*, *1263*, 1264, 1268, 1277, 1286 **11:** 1497, 1543—1544, 1559, 1574

Greek **3:** 298-299, 302, 305, 307, 310, *312-313*, 333, 347, 361-363, 365, 372, 378, 387-388, 392 **7:** 886, 917-918, 920, 925, 932-934, *934*, 937-938, *939*, 943, 945, 948, 956, 962, 968, 974, 976, 980, 984, 988, 990, *990*, 997 **9:** 1178, 1180, *1197*, 1227, *1238*, 1240, *1240*, 1243-1244, 1248, 1252, 1254, 1263, 1265-1266, 1269, 1272, 1286 **10:** 1339, 1345, 1410

Greek; - art **5:** 587; - cities **4:** 458, 492, 511, 517, 565; - civilization **4:** 440, 445, 498; - colonies **5:** 595, 597, 654, 672 **6:** 767; - colony **1:** 8 **8:** 1017, 1045; - culture **5:** 624, 633; - expansion **4:** 457; - fire **8:** *1108*, 1110, 1142; - gods **5:** 629; - history **4:** 452, 565; - language **5:** 604, 633; - mainland **4:** 448, 458, 504, 525, 547; - mythology **4:** 445, 546, 565 **5:** 619, 638, 711; - philosophers **4:** 475, *549*, *556*, 565-568 **9:** 1227; - philosophy **4:** 503, 565, 567; - poetry **4:** 457; - polis **4:** 450; - society **5:** 584, 634; - temple **4:** 497; - theater(s) **4:** 535 **6:** 807; - tragedy **4:** 534, 543, 545; - vases **1:** 117; - vocabulary **4:** 450; - world **4:** 448-450, 452, 454, 461-462, 468, 474, 482, 489-490, 498, 503, 509, 548, 567 **5:** 584, 602, 609, 613, 616, 620, 646, 697

Greek-Aegean area **1:** 116

Greeks **1:** 7-8, 107, 120, 122-124 **2:** 158, 165, 192, 195, 199, 206, 208, 217 **3:** 300, 305-308, 310, 312, 315, 338, 347, 365, 367, 372, 387 **4:** 439, 441, 445, 448-450, 452-454, 456-457, 459, 461-462, 474, 476, 482, 487, 490, 493-494, 508, 514-515, 517-518, 520-522, 524, 529, *530*, 531, 540, 543, *545*, 552, 565-568 **5:** 587, *587*, 596, 609, 611, 615, 617, 620-621, 623, *625*, 628, *629*, 630, 633, 636, 641-642, 649, 667, 673-675, 680-681, 685, 688, 711 **6:** 752, 767, 798, 836, 845 **8:** 1132

Greenland **1:** 33, 41 **3:** 392 **9:** 1206, 1287 **10:** 1401

Greens, party in Constantinople **8:** 1050, 1052-1053, 1056, 1141-1143. *See also* Blues

Gregorian **7:** 925, 978, 982-984, 997

Gregorian calendar **6:** 854. *See also* Calendars

Gregorian Reform (1073) **9:** 1215, 1286

Gregory I, the Great, Saint; pope (590-604) **7:** 944, *968*, 974, 976, *979-980*, 981-984, *983*, *986-987*, 986-988, 997 **9:** 1193, 1213, 1219, 1221-1222, *1221-1222*, 1268, 1273, 1276, 1278, 1286

Gregory VI (?-1048), pope (1045-1046) **9:** 1215, 1286

Gregory VII, original name Hildebrand (c.1020-1085), one of the great reform popes of the Middle Ages (reigned 1073-1085) **9:** 1215, 1219, 1221, *1222*, 1232, 1268, 1286 **10:** 1333-1334, 1348

Gregory VIII (?-c.1137), antipope (1118-1121) **9:** 1220-1221, 1273, 1276

Gregory IX, original name Ugo, or Ugolino, di Segni

(c.1170-1241), one of the most vigorous of the thirteenth-century popes (reigned 1227-1241), a canon lawyer, theologian, defender of papal prerogatives, and founder of the papal Inquisition **9:** 1278 **10:** 1347

Gregory XI, original name Pierre-Roger de Beaufort (c.1329-1378), the last French pope and the last of the Avignonese popes, when Avignon was the papal seat (1309-1377) (reigned 1370-1378) **10:** 1365

Gregory XIII (1502-1585), pope (1572-1585) **6:** 854

Grenada **9:** 1239

Griffin, mythological creature, part eagle, part lion **2:** 199

Guangzhou **11:** 1508

Guatemala **11:** 1447, 1453—1454, *1454—1455*, *1464*, 1574

Gudea, ruler of Lagash (c.2144-c.2124 BC) **2:** *226*, 227-229, *228-229*, 232, 233

Guelphs **10:** 1333, *1335*, 1340, 1342, 1363, *1394*, 1396

Guerrero **11:** 1450

Guerrilla tactics **5:** 590 **10:** 1380

Guerrillas **8:** 1121

Guibert of Ravenna. *See* Clement III

Guienne **10:** 1377, 1386

Guilds **10:** 1313, 1319-1320, 1360, 1369

Guillaume de Nogaret (1260/70-1313), magistrate under King Philip IV the Fair of France **10:** 1356

Guinea, Gulf of **11:** 1551

Guizhou **3:** 360

Gula, a name written with the prefix for deity **2:** 258

Gulf of; - Aegina **5:** 585; - Corinth **5:** 709; - Guinea **3:** 404, 409; - Mexico **11:** 1449, 1451; - Neapolis **5:** 667; - Oman **3:** 361; - Tunis **5:** 679

Gulf Stream **1:** 41, 134

Gumma **11:** 1520

Gunderic, king of the Vandals **8:** 1028

Gundobad **8:** 1034

Günz-Mindel interglacial **1:** 45

Gupta Empire, northeastern India (fourth-sixth century) **11:** *1490-1491*, 1491, 1574

Guru, teacher **3:** 390

Guthian interregnum (twenty-second century BC) **2:** 278; - period **2:** 227

Gutians **2:** 226-227, 232, 235, 277

Haakon VI, byname Haakon Magnusson the Younger, king of Norway (1355-1380) whose marriage to Margaret, daughter of the Danish king Valdemar IV in 1363, paved the way for the eventual union (1397) of the three major Scandinavian nations: Denmark, Norway, and Sweden **10:** 1409

Hadad, Semitic god of storms **2:** 250

Hadejia River **11:** 1548

Hades, Greek god of the underworld **4:** 444, 500, 566-567

Hadith, companion book to the Koran **8:** 1089-1090, 1142

Hadramaut **8:** 1083

Hadrian, Publius Aelius Hadrianus (76-138) Roman emperor (117-138) **5:** 614 **6:** 754, 787-789, *787-789*, *791*, 810, 813, 833, 844, 853-855 **8:** 1067

Hadrianople **6:** 831, 834

Hadrianus. *See* Hadrian

Hadrian's Wall **6:** 787, *789*, 813, 843, 853-854

Hadrosaurus **1:** 36

Hagar, Abraham's concubine and the mother of his son Ishmael **3:** 319 **8:** 1091, 1142

Haggai, prophet (fl. sixth century BC) **7:** 916

Hagia Sophia (St. Sophia, Church of the Holy Wisdom) **8:** 1050, 1052, *1054-1055*, 1056, *1057*, *1063*, 1142-1143 **9:** *1243*, 1247, 1251, *1260*, 1263, 1266, 1274 **11:** 1559, *1563*

Hagia Triada, palace of **2:** 200

Hagib **9:** 1228-1230, 1238, 1286

Hagiography **7:** 968, 970, 975, 986, 997

Hainan **11:** 1504

Hainault **10:** 1330, 1343, 1390, 1413

Hajib **8:** 1134

Hajj, journey to Mecca **8:** 1090, 1142

Halab **9:** 1272, 1286

Halicarnassus **4:** 448, 515, 566

Halley's comet **1:** 11, 23

Hallstatt **1:** *111-113*, 114, 116-120, *119*, 123, *125*, 133-134; - culture (c.1475-1200 BC) **1:** *111-113*, 114, 116-120, *119*, *125*, 133-134

Hamburg **1:** 62 **10:** 1388

Hamilcar Barca (c.270-228 BC) Carthaginian general; father of Hannibal **5:** 680, 682, 684, 710

Hamites, African peoples who speak related Hamito-Semitic languages **3:** 413

Hamito-Semitic **2:** 152 **3:** 412-414

Hammam **9:** 1239

Hammock **11:** 1448

Hammurabi, ruler of the first dynasty of Babylon (c.1792-1750 BC) **2:** 226, 231-232, 234-237, *235-236*, 241-242, *241*, 247-248, 252-254, 260, 277-278; code of - **2:** 235, 241, 248, 252 **3:** 315

Han; - Confucianism **11:** 1502; - emperors **11:** 1502, 1504, *1504*, 1520; - Feizi, (d. 233 BC) councilors to the first emperor Shih Huang Ti **7:** 910

Han dynasty (206 BC-AD 220), second great Chinese Imperial dynasty **3:** 357, 360 **6:** 845 **7:** *906-907*, 909, 910-911, *911-912*, 997 **11:** 1501, *1502*, 1504-1506, *1506*, 1508, *1508*, *1512*, 1574

Han-fei-tzu (d. 233 BC), greatest of China's Legalist philosophers **3:** 357-358

Han-li Academy **11:** 1508

Hand-axe **1:** 50-51, *50*, 134

Hanging gardens (Babylon) **2:** 258

Hangzhou **11:** 1510

Haniwa **11:** 1522

Hannibal (247-183 BC) legendary Carthaginian general; son of Hamilcar **5:** *679*, 682, 684-685, *686-688*, 687-691, 709-710, 712 **6:** 799, 838-839 **7:** 952-953

Hanno (fl. second half of the third century BC), leader of the aristocratic pro-Roman faction at Carthage during the Second Punic War **3:** 303-304

Hansa. *See* Hanseatic League

Hanseatic League, also called Hansa, organization founded in the thirteenth century by North German towns and German merchant communities abroad to protect their mutual trading interests **10:** *1388*, 1391, 1401, *1402*, 1406, *1406*, 1408-1409 **11:** 1516

Hanukkah **5:** 630, 710

Happy Arabia. *See* Arabia felix

Hapsburg **10:** 1391-1393, 1398, 1422

Harald Hardraada, byname Harald the Ruthless, king of Norway (1045-1066) **10:** 1324-1325

Harappa **3:** 380, *382* **7:** 889

Harem **8:** 1078, 1118

Harley Gospels **9:** *1180*

Harmodius, Greek legendary hero (fifth century BC) **4:** 487-488, *490*. *See also* Aristogeiton

Harokag **3:** 363

Harpalus **5:** 615

Harpists **2:** 165

Harran **2:** 270 **3:** 316

Harris papyrus **2:** 189

Harsha, Buddist king (reigned 606-647) **11:** 1491-1492, 1574

Harun al Rashid (c.766-809), fifth caliph of the Abbasid dynasty **9:** *1174*

Harun ar-Rashid, caliph **8:** 1142

Hasdrubal (221 BC), Carthaginian general, the son-in-law of Hamilcar Barca **5:** 684, 689-690

Hasid (pious) **10:** 1372-1373

Hasidism **10:** 1372-1373

Hasmonaeans **5:** 629, 630, 710 **7:** 918

Hassan **8:** 1094, 1104, 1111, 1143

Hastings **10:** *1323*, 1324-1325

Hathor, Egyptian goddess of the sky **2:** 177, 186

Hatshepsut, queen of Egypt (1473-1458 BC) **2:** *158*, 171, 173-175, *179*, 277, 280

Hatti **3:** 338, 345, 347

Hattusas, Hittite city **2:** 244 **3:** 339-341, *342*, 344-345, 347

Hattusilis I (reigned c.1650-1620 BC), Hittite king in the Old Hittite Kingdom **3:** 344

Hattusilis III (reigned c.1285-1265 BC), Hittite king in the Hittite Empire **1:** 116 **2:** 186 **3:** 339, 345, 347

Hausa city-states (900-1591) **11:** 1549

Heaven **7:** 902, 905, 912, 956

Hebei **11:** 1510

Hebrew **2:** 152, 155, 183 **3:** 308, 310, *312*, 319, 321, 323 **7:** 913, 917-918, *919*, 925, 934, 976, 997 **10:** *1370*, 1370-1373

Hebrews **3:** 319, 321-322

Hebrides **3:** 393, *399* **9:** 1206 **10:** 1400

Hebron **3:** 316, 327, 330, 337

Hector, Greek legendary Trojan hero **4:** *440*, 441-444, 566

Heftakites **11:** 1574

Hegira, journey of Muhammad from Mecca to Medina **8:** 1092, *1095*, 1143

Heian-Kyo. *See* Kyoto **11:**

Heian period (794-1185) **11:** *1526*, *1524-1530*

Heidelberg **1:** *44*, 45

Heiji War (1159-1160) **11:** 1528

Hejaz **8:** 1114, 1122

Hekabe, in Greek mythology, wife of King Priam **4:** 444

Hekanakhte, letters of **2:** 162

Hekau-Chasut, desert kings (thirteenth dynasty) **2:** 168

Helen, in Greek mythology, wife of Menelaus **4:** 441, 568

Helena, Roman empress **8:** 1017, 1052

Helena, Saint (c. 248-328), wife of the Roman emperor Constantius I and mother of Constantine the Great, emperor of Rome **7:** 943, 997

Heliocentric solar system **1:** 9, 133-134

Heliogabalus. *See* Elagabalus

Heliopause **1:** 22

Heliopolis **2:** 155, 177, 189, 279

Helios (sun) **1:** 9 **5:** 648

Helios, Greek god of the sun **4:** 497 **6:** *816*

Helium **1:** 13, 17, 20, 23, 25, 27-28, 135

Hell **7:** 879, 956, 960, 966, 997

Helladic; - civilization **2:** 205, 279; - culture **2:** 195, 277

Hellas, Greece **5:** 636

Hellen, legendary ancestor of the Hellenes **4:** 445, 565-566

Hellenes, Greeks **4:** 445, 565-566

Hellenic world **6:** 837

Hellenism, Greek civilization **5:** 625, 630, 634, 709-710 **7:** 917-918, 920, 925

Hellenistic **5:** 624, *631*, 632-633, *637*, 638-639, *639*, 641, *641-642*, *679*, 710-711

Hellenistic buildings **6:** 752

Hellenistic mythology **6:** 752, 767

Hellenization, the process of making a culture Greek **5:** 629, 633, 710 **7:** 918

Hellespont **4:** 458, 520, 548; - Strait **4:** 520 **5:** 596, 613, 616-617, 627

Helot rebellion **4:** 472

Helots, people enslaved by the Spartans **4:** 469, 471-473, 522, 524-525, 566 **5:** 608

Hemisphere **1:** 14, 24, 42, 63, 135

Henan **3:** 349

Henotheism **4:** 502

Henry I (the Fowler) of Saxony (876?-939), German king (925-939) **9:** 1202, 1221, 1286-1287

Henry I, byname Henry Beauclerc (Good Scholar), king of England (1100-1135) **10:** 1322

Henry II (1133-1189), byname Henry of Anjou, duke of Normandy (from 1150), count of Anjou (from 1151), duke of Aquitaine (from 1152), and king of England (from 1154) **10:** *1321-1322*, 1325-1326, 1352, 1379

Henry II (the Saint) of Bavaria (973-1024), king of Germany (1002-1024), king of the Lombards (1004-1024) and Holy Roman emperor (1014-1024) **9:** *1211*, 1213, 1286

Henry III (1207-1272), king of England (1216-1272) **10:** 1344, 1352-1353

Henry III the Black (1017-1056), king of Germany (1028-1056) and Holy Roman emperor (1039-1056) **9:** 1214-1215, *1220*, 1286

Henry IV (1050-1106), king of Germany (1056-1106) and Holy Roman emperor (1084-1106) **9:** 1215-1216, 1218-1219, *1221-1222*, 1286-1287

Henry IV, also called Earl of Derby (1377-1397); or Duke of Hereford (1397-1399); byname Henry Bolingbroke, or Henry of Lancaster (1366?-1413), king of England (1399-1413) **10:** 1338, 1363, *1380*, 1381

Henry V (1086-1125), German king (from 1099) and Holy Roman emperor (1111-1125), last of the Salian dynasty **9:** 1219-1221, 1285 **10:** 1333, 1381, 1383, *1385-1386*, 1412

Henry VI (1165-1197), German king and Holy Roman emperor of the Hohenstaufen dynasty **10:** 1330, 1335, 1338, 1340, 1342, 1383, 1386

Henry of Bavaria. *See* Henry II

Henry of Burgundy, Count of Portugal (twelfth century) **9:** 1237, 1288

Henry the Fowler. *See* Henry I

Henry the Lion, duke of Saxony (1142-1180) and of Bavaria (as Henry XII, 1156-1180), a strong supporter of the emperor Frederick I Barbarossa **10:** 1334, *1337*, 1338, 1340

Henry the Saint. *See* Henry II

Hera, Greek goddess of birth and marriage **4:** *450*, 496-497, *496*, 499, *501*, *547*, 558, 566

Hera, in Greek religion, a daughter of the Titans Cronus and Rhea, sister-wife of Zeus, and queen of the Olympian gods **5:** 690

Heraclitus, Ionian natural philosopher (c.500 BC) **4:** 504, 553, 555, 566

Heraclius, Byzantine emperor (610-641) **8:** 1078, *1078*, 1099-1100, 1142-1143 **9:** 1244, 1246, 1248

Herakleopolis **2:** 158, 277

Herat **8:** 1078

Herbivores **1:** 35

Herculaneum **5:** 616 **6:** 779, *804*, 804-805

Hercules, famous Greco-Roman legendary hero **3:** 299, 303, 387 **5:** 659 **6:** *729*, 812, 830

Herculius, byname of Maximian. *See* Maximian

Hereafter **2:** 154, 165, 278-279

Herero people **11:** 1554

Heretic **10:** 1316, *1383*, 1386

Herihor, Egyptian army officer and high priest of Amon (eleventh century BC) **2:** 191, 277

Hermes, Greek god of commerce, invention, travel **4:** 496, 566 **6:** 855

Hermus and Cayster Rivers, Valleys of the **4:** 511

Hernici **6:** 836

Hero **5:** 641, 711

Herod Antipas (21 BC-AD 39), son of Herod I the Great **7:** 921, 925, 997

Herod the Great, Roman-appointed king of Judaea (37-4 BC) **1:** 68-69 **7:** 920, 997

Herodotus (c.484-c.430/420 BC), Greek author of the *History of the Greco-Persian Wars* **1:** 121 **2:** 152, 258 **3:** 302, 306, 310, 365, 372-373, 375-376 **5:** 587-588, 675

Herodotus of Halicarnassus, historian (c.484-424 BC) **4:** 484-486, 506, *512-513*, 515, 517-518, 522, 534, 566-567

Heroes **4:** 446, *450*, 488, 494, 544

Heroic poems **4:** 440

Herophilus (c.335-280 BC), Alexandrian physician **5:** 643, 710

Herschel, Caroline, astronomer (1750-1848) **1:** 11

Herschel, William, astronomer (1738-1822) **1:** 11

Heruli, a Germanic people originally from Scandinavia **6:** 817 **8:** 1028

Hesiod (Hesiodus), epic poet (c.700 BC) **4:** 462, 493, *502*, 566

Hestia, Greek goddess of the hearth **4:** 496

Hetairoi, personal retinue of the Macedonian king **5:** 616, 624

Hexameter **6:** 854

Heyerdahl, Thor (b. 1914), ethnologist and adventurer **3:** 394, 399-400

Heys **11:** 1574

Hezekiah (reigned c.727-698 BC), king of Judah and friend of Isaiah **3:** 335

Hicma **8:** 1142

Hiera **9:** 1180

Hieratic **2:** 165, 168, 277

Hieria **9:** 1254

Hiero **5:** 681, 689

Hieroglyph(ic)s **2:** 152-153, 164-165, 180, 186, 187, 199, 209, 277-279 **3:** 308, 312, 339-341, *344*, 398, 413 **4:** 450 **11:** 1459

High and Low German **8:** 1043

High priest **2:** 191, 277 **7:** 916-918, 920, 930, 932

Hilary of Poitiers, Saint (c.315-367) pagan convert to Christianity, doctor of the Church, bishop of Poitiers **7:** 997

Hildebrand **10:** 1333, 1363. *See also* Gregory VII

Hildebrand, hero of *Song of Hildebrand* (*Hildebrandslied*) **9:** 1215, 1218, 1224, 1286

Hildesheim **3:** 334 **9:** *1219*

Himalayas **3:** 379 **7:** 889, 897 **8:** 1071, 1144 **11:** 1489-1490

Himera **4:** 458

Hinayana **7:** 882, 997

Hincks, Edward **2:** 218

Hindu **3:** 363, 380, 384, 388, 390 **7:** 879, *889-893*, 890-891, 893-894, *896*, 897, 898, 900, 997 **11:** 1496-1497

Hindu Kush **5:** 622

Hindu Pallava dynasty (fourth-ninth century) **11:** 1493; - princes **11:** 1492; - Tamils **11:** 1574; - temple **11:** 1496

Hinduism **3:** 380, 383, 384, *386*, 388, 390 **7:** 871, 878,

513 **5:** *621*, 622-623, *623*, *639*, 709-710 **6:** 845
Indus Delta **11:** 1494
Indus River **1:** 74 **3:** 362, 380, 384 **7:** 871, 889 **8:** 1069, 1076, 1108 **11:** 1489-1491, 1494
Indus Valley **3:** 361, 379-380, *381*, 390 **5:** *621*, 622, 710 **7:** 889 **11:** 1490
Infamia **6:** 728, 854
Infantrymen **2:** 176, 264
Infrared rays **1:** 12, 21
Ingeborg, second wife of King Philip Augustus **10:** 1343-1344
Initiates **4:** 499
Inland kingdoms (1200-1400) **11:** 1551
Innocent II, original name Gregorio Papareschi (?-1143), pope (reigned 1130-1143) **10:** 1333
Innocent III, original name Lothair of Segni (1160/61-1216), pope (reigned 1198-1216) **9:** 1277 **10:** 1317, 1339-1340, *1340-1341*, 1342, 1344, 1347, 1354
Innocent IV, original name Sinibaldo Fieschi (c.1200-1254), one of the great pontiffs of the Middle Ages (reigned 1243-1254) **10:** *1347*, 1348, 1404
Inquisition **9:** 1236 **11:** 1561
Insignia **6:** 774-775 **8:** 1028
Insubres **5:** 687
Insula (pl. *insulae*) **6:** 793, 854 **8:** 1034, 1048, 1142
Interdict **10:** 1317, 1343-1344
Interglacial episodes **1:** 134
Intermarriage **8:** 1043
Internal administration **2:** 161
Interpluvials (drier periods) **1:** 41, 134-135
Inti (sun god) **11:** 1483, *1487*, 1573-1574
Intiwatana **11:** 1488
Invasion of Gaul **8:** 1026
Invention of the wheel **1:** 94
Investiture **10:** 1334-1335, 1340, *1340*
Investiture controversy, power struggle between papacy and Holy Roman Empire (eleventh-twelfth centuries) **9:** 1215-1216, 1218-1221, 1224, 1285-1286 **10:** 1340
Invincible Sun **6:** 822
Iolkos **2:** 213
Ionia **3:** 378 **4:** 452, *463*, 468, 503, 517, 522, 534, 548, 565 **5:** 584, 711
Ionian **5:** 587, 609, 710, 711; - temple **5:** 587
Ionian Greeks, Greek tribe **4:** 487
Ionian natural philosophy **4:** 503-504, 567
Ionian rebellion, rebellion of Ionian cities in Asia Minor against Persia (499-495 BC) **4:** 515, 517, 519, 566-567; - school **4:** 503, 552
Ionians **4:** 448, 462, *465*, 517, 566
Ionic, Greek dialect **4:** 448, 566
Ipuwer, ancient Egyptian sage **2:** 158
Ira **6:** 856
Iran **1:** 67, 73 **2:** 221, 230, 235, *248*, 256, 262, 268 **3:** 361-362, 366, 373, 375-376, 407 **6:** 843, 845 **8:** 1069, 1072, 1074, *1123*, 1143 **9:** *1174* **11:** 1496, 1536, 1539, 1542, 1555, 1563-1564
Irani **3:** 361
Irania. *See* Iran
Iranian plateau **2:** 252
Iraq **1:** 70, 73 **2:** 151, 218, 258, 268 **3:** 361 **8:** 1104, *1107*, 1113, 1116, *1117*, 1120-1121 **11:** 1494, 1536, 1539, 1555, 1562, 1564
Iraqi **2:** 234
Ireland **1:** 90 **3:** 392 **5:** 668 **7:** 988, *988*, 990 **9:** 1192, 1206, *1218* **10:** 1353, 1400
Irene (752-803), Byzantine empress (797-802), married to Emperor Leo IV in 769 and regent for her son Constantine VI (780-790 and 792-797) **9:** 1170-1171, 1180, 1255-1256, 1285-1287
Irish Christianity **7:** 997
Iron **1:** 18, 23, 25, 102, 106-107, 111, 115-120, *116-123*, 123, *125*, 126, 134 **4:** 447, 449, 453, 461, 567
Iron Age (begin: c.1200 BC) **1:** 107, 115-116, *116-123*, *125*, 126, 134
Iron Age cultures **4:** 461
Irsu, Egyptian official **2:** 189
Isaac **8:** 1090-1091, 1144
Isaac I Comnenus (c.1005-1061), Byzantine emperor (1057-1059) **9:** 1269
Isaac II Angelus (c.1135-1204), Byzantine emperor (1185-1204) **9:** 1276
Isaac, second of the patriarchs of Israel, only son of Abraham and Sarah, and father of Esau and Jacob **3:** 315-316, *317-318*, 319, 322

Isabel of Castile (1451-1504), queen of Castile and Aragon **9:** 1236
Isabella (of Hainault), first wife of King Philip Augustus **10:** 1343, *1348*, 1356, *1381*, 1383
Isaiah, Israelite prophet (eighth century BC) **3:** 334-335, *334* **7:** 930
Isaius, famous litigator **5:** 604
Isaurian **8:** 1058, 1110, 1143
Isaurian dynasty, founded by Leo III the Isaurian (Byzantine Empire, 717-802) **8:** 1110 **9:** 1255-1256, 1286
Isaurians **8:** 1056, 1142
Ishbi-Erra, king of Isin (c.2017-c.1985 BC) **2:** 233
Ishmael, Abraham's son by his concubine Hagar **3:** 315, 319 **8:** 1090, 1142-1143
Ishme-Dagan I, king of Assyria (fl. second millennium BC) **2:** 247, 260
Ishtar, Canaanite deity of war **3:** 327, 347 **4:** 498. *See also* Astarte, Shauska
Ishtar Gate (built c.575 BC) **2:** 247, *257-258*, 258
Ishtar, goddess of the Sumero-Akkadian pantheon **2:** 223, 225-226, 230-231, *234*, 245-246, *247*, 250, *257-258*, 258, *263*, 278
Ishvara (Sanskrit: Lord) in Hinduism, the personal, or immanent, god, as distinct from the absolute, or transcendent, supreme being (Brahman) **7:** 900
Isidorus of Miletus **8:** 1068 **9:** 1251
Isin, Second dynasty of **2:2:** 218, 233-234, 247, 256, 278, 280
Isis, Egyptian goddess **2:** *188*, 280 **5:** 633 **6:** 752, *764*, 767, 801, 854
Iskenderich (Alexandria) **8:** 1080
Islam **3:** 362-363, 378 **7:** 888 **8:** 1078, 1082, *1082-1083*, 1087-1088, 1090, 1092, 1095-1096, *1098*, 1103, 1105, *1105*, 1107, 1113-1114, 1118, 1120-1121, 1123, 1126, 1129-1130, 1132, 1141-1144 **9:** 1226-1227, *1229*, *1238*, 1288 **10:** 1345, 1348 **11:** 1494, 1496, 1539, 1544, *1544*, 1549, 1555, 1557, 1562, 1566, 1573-1574
Islamic kingdoms **11:** 1497, 1536
Islamic; - civilization **9:** 1226; - community **8:** 1104; - culture **9:** 1227, 1241-1242, 1259, 1288; - Empire, expanded out of Arabia in the seventh and eighth centuries to Syria, Egypt, North Africa, Spain, and Asia to the Chinese border **8:** 1142; - expansion **8:** *1105*, 1110, *1113*, 1143; - history **8:** 1096; - holy men **8:** 1106; - law **8:** 1106, 1143; - raids **8:** 1108; - rule **8:** 1106; - state **8:** 1114, 1141; - world **8:** 1110, 1112, *1119*, 1126, 1131-1132, *1132* **9:** *1174*, 1230, *1242*
Ismael **8:** 1091, 1142
Ismail I, Persian ruler who founded Safavid dynasty in 1501 **11:** 1564
Isocrates (436-338 BC) Athenian orator, logographer, and teacher of eloquence **5:** 604, *609*, 609-611, 710
Isotope **1:** 33-34, 43, 133
Isphahan **8:** 1078
Israel **1:** 46, *67*, 73 **2:** 170, 187, 267 **3:** 310, 313, 318, 319-320, 322, *327*, 328, 332-335, *332* **6:** *801* **7:** 913-914, *915*, 923, 927
Israelites **1:** 68-69 **3:** 313, 320, 322, *322-324*, 325, 327-331, *328*, 333, *334*, 336, 337 **7:** 913-914
Issachar, son of Jacob **3:** 319
Issus, coastal city **5:** 619-620, 709-710
Istanbul **6:** 831, 853-854 **7:** 952, 954 **8:** 1046, *1057*, *1064*, 1068, *1091*, 1141 **9:** *1243* **11:** *1557*, 1559, 1564, 1573
Isthmus **4:** 476, 483-484, 521-522, 525
Italian campaign **10:** 1338
Italian cultures **1:** 116
Italian Peninsula **1:** 74 **4:** 459 **5:** 667, *669*, 669-670, 672, 674-676, 678-679, 684-685, 687-692, 701, 711 **6:** 732, 737, 743, 748, 754, 759, 765, 801, 814, 824, 827-828, 832, 834-837, 854
Italian region **4:** 461
Italy **1:** 46, 78, *79*, 80, *83*, 90, 108, 114, 116-117, 120, 123, 126 **2:** 214 **4:** *457*, 458, 461-462, 483, *502*, 504, 514-515, 534, *547*, 548, 566, 568 **5:** *595*, 595-597, 604, 612, *649*, 650, *653*, 654, *655-656*, 658, *659*, *664*, 666, *674*, 675, 685, 690, 709-710, 712 **6:** 727, 729-730, 732, *732*, 740, 748, 755, 767, 775, 784, 789, 831, 836-837, 853-856 **7:** 920, 949, 951, 953-954, 975-976, 980, 982, 987, 997 **8:** 1016, 1019-1020, 1023-1025, 1027-1029, 1032, 1034, 1038, 1059-1060, *1060*, 1064-1066, 1068, 1141, 1143-1144 **9:** 1162, 1164, 1166, 1168, 1170-1171, 1179, 1183, 1187-1188, 1191, 1193-1194, 1205-1207, 1212-1214, 1218, *1218*, 1221, 1231, 1233, 1239-1244,

1242, 1251, 1254, 1263, 1269-1270, 1272, 1277-1278, 1286-1288 **10:** 1304, *1307*, 1313, *1314-1315*, 1317-1318, 1323, 1333, *1334*, 1335, 1337-1338, 1346-1350, 1356, *1359*, 1363-1366, 1370, 1373-1374, 1387-1388, 1393-1394, *1393-1396*, 1398, 1422 **11:** 1545, 1561
Ithaca, in Greek mythology homeland of Odysseus **2:** 207 **3:** 306 **4:** 442, 446, 566
Itzá, tribe of Mayans **11:** 1457
Itzamna, Mayan deity **11:** 1462
Ivan I (1304-1340) **11:** 1518
Ivan III the Great, grand duke of Muscovy (1462-1505) **11:** 1518, *1518*, 1538, 1574
Ivan IV Vasilyevich (Ivan the Terrible, reigned 1533-1584) **11:** 1518

Jacob van Artevelde (c.1295-1345), Flemish leader who played a leading role in the preliminary phase of the Hundred Years' War (1337-1453) **10:** *1370*, 1377
Jacob **8:** 1090
Jacob, grandson of Abraham, son of Isaac and Rebekah **2:** 168 **3:** *318*, 319-320, 322, *323*, *333*, 399
Jacoba (of Bavaria), daughter of William of Bavaria **10:** 1413
Jadwiga (of Anjou), originally Hungarian Hedvig (1373/74-1399), queen of Poland (1384-1399) **10:** 1410
Jaén **9:** 1230, 1234
Jagati **11:** 1538
Jagiello, Vladislav, grand duke of Lithuania (as Jogaila, 1377-1401) and king of Poland (1386-1434), who joined two states that became the leading power of eastern Europe **10:** 1410
Jaguar god **11:** 1462
Jainism **7:** 893, 900
Jalisco **11:** 1450
James Cook (1728-1779), British naval captain, navigator, and explorer **3:** 399, *399*, 402
Janiculum Hill **5:** 651
Janissaries **11:** 1557, 1559, 1564, 1566, 1574
Janissary revolt **11:** 1558
Janizaries. *See* Janissaries
János Hundayi, Hungarian general (c.1407-1456) **11:** 1559
Japan **11:** 1508, 1519-1520, 1522-1524, 1526, 1528-1530, 1542, 1573-1574; - emergence of **11:** 1519
Japan **7:** 876, 885-886, 888, 902, 997
Japanese; - archipelago **11:** 1519-1520, 1529; - art **11:** 1530; - culture **11:** 1527; - poetry **11:** 1527
Japan's Inland Sea **11:** 1520
Jarmo (also called Qalat Jarmo) **1:** 70
Jarrow **7:** 984, 990
Jason, high priest in Jerusalem in 168 **7:** 918
Java **1:** *39*, *41-42*, 44, 47-48, 134-135 **3:** 396 **7:** 900 **11:** 1500, 1542
Jaxartes River **11:** 1504
Jehovah, Judeo-Christian name for God **3:** 322
Jehovah. *See* Jahweh
Jemdet Nasr **2:** 218
Jephtah **3:** 330
Jeremiah, Israelite prophet (seventh century BC) **3:** 335-336, *335* **7:** 914
Jericho **1:** 67-70, 72, 95-96; - culture (from ninth century BC) **1:** 70
Jeroboam, the first king of the new state of Israel **3:** 332
Jerome, Saint (c.345-c.420) father and doctor of the Church; translated Bible into Latin version called the Vulgate **7:** 975-976, 987, 997 **9:** *1178*
Jerusalem **2:** 167, 229, 253 **3:** 298, 316, 321, 329-330, *329*, 332-333, 335-337, *335* **5:** 620, *620*, 629-630, 710 **6:** 731, 764, 774, 776, 778-779, *781*, 785, *785*, 787 **7:** 914, 916-918, *917*, 920, *921*, 922-923, *924*, 926, 928, 929, 931-932, 937, 955, 965, 997 **8:** 1068, 1077, *1078*, *1095*, 1098, 1101, *1102-1103*, *1105*, *1119*, *1132*, 1143-1144 **9:** 1263, 1267, *1267*, 1269, 1272-1274, *1274*, 1276, 1278, 1285-1288 **10:** *1338*, 1339, 1344, *1346*, 1348, 1370, *1387*, 1406 **11:** 1539, 1562
Jester God **11:** 1462
Jesus **6:** 748, 758, 771-772, 790 **7:** 920, 925-934, *927-928*, *930-932*, 931, 933, *934-936*, 938, *938*, 943-944, 945, 948, 955-956, 959-960, 962-964, 969, 972, 974, 975, 980, 990, 997 **8:** 1017, 1035, 1053-1054, *1057*, 1060, 1072, 1076, 1088, 1090, 1100, 1113, 1141, 1143 **10:** 1340, *1352*, *1365*, 1369, 1374, 1407
Jesus Christ (Jesus of Nazareth or Jesus of Galilee) (c.6 BC-AD 30) **6:** 730, 758, 771-772, 817, 855 **7:** *931*, 960,

Charlemagne **9:** 1180

Libya **2:** 156 **3:** 303, 361 **4:** 458, 544 **5:** 620, 626, 679, 684 **6:** *839* **7:** 997

Libyan desert **2:** 151, 184; - domination **2:** 192

Libyans **2:** 167, 186, 189, 192, 278, 280

Licinian-Sextian Laws **5:** 664

Licinius (c.270-325) Roman emperor **6:** 831-832 **7:** 942, 944, 949, 997 **8:** 1017-1018, 1045, 1142

Licinius, Roman tribune (c.367 BC) **5:** 664

Lictors **5:** 654, 656

Liegnitz (Legnica) **11:** 1536. *See also* Battle of Liegnitz

Life of Charlemagne **9:** 1182

Light-year **1:** 14

Lighthouse **6:** *820*

Ligurian **5:** 687

Lilybaeum **5:** *595*, 682

Limburg **10:** 1413

Limerick **9:** 1206

Limitanei **6:** 831

Limpopo River **11:** 1553

Lindisfarne **7:** 988, *988* **9:** 1206

Linear A **2:** 199, 201, 206, 209, 278-279

Linear B **2:** 206, 209, *209*, 278-279 **4:** 446, 448, 456, 496-497; - scripts **4:** 446; - tablets **4:** 446, 456, 496-497

Lingam **11:** 1496

Lingua franca **5:** 632

Linguistic groups **4:** 448

Linnaean classification **1:** 38

Linnaeus, Carolus (1707-1778) **1:** 37-38, 133-134

Lion gate **2:** *205*, 208, 211

Lisbon **8:** 1124 **9:** 1230, 1237-1238

Literacy **1:** 90

Literary arts **4:** 534

Literature **5:** 604, 615, 637-638, 641

Lithosphere **1:** 30

Lithospheric plates **1:** 29

Lithuania **10:** 1391, 1410

Lithuanians **11:** 1574

Liturgy **4:** 566 **7:** 938, 959, 988, 997

Liu Chi (256-195 BC) **11:** 1501

Liu Pang, first Han emperor (256-195 BC) **11:** 1501

Livia Drusilla (58 BC-29 AD), also called Julia Augusta, wife of Augustus **6:** *745*, *747-748*, 751, 756, *760*

Livia's palace **6:** *749*

Livilla, wife of Drusus **6:** *758*

Livy, Titus Livius (59/64 BC-AD 17), Roman historian **6:** 733, 750, 855 **9:** 1179

Lixos **3:** 303

Llama **11:** 1448-1449, 1487; - wool **11:** 1448

Locris **5:** *595*, 597

Lodi, Ibrahim (d.1526) **11:** 1497

Loge River **11:** 1553

Logic **5:** 607, 641, 648, 710

Logographers **5:** 602, 604, 710-711

Logos **5:** 648, 712 **6:** 808

Loire **8:** 1025 **9:** 1161, 1186, *1189* **10:** 1383

Lombard kingdom **9:** 1166

Lombard law **8:** 1040

Lombard League **10:** 1338

Lombards **7:** 980, 982, 997 **8:** 1028, 1033-1034, 1037, 1042, 1068, 1143-1144 **9:** 1164-1166, 1168, 1170, 1175-1176, 1179, 1213-1214, 1239, 1244, 1285-1288 **10:** 1308, 1369

Lombardy **9:** 1178, 1206, 1213, 1285, 1287 **10:** 1305, 1307, 1317, 1337, 1340, 1349, 1392, 1397-1398

Londinium **6:** 773

London **1:** 11 **6:** 773 **9:** 1193 **10:** 1318, 1323-1324, *1377*, 1378, 1381, 1391, 1406, 1416

Long Count **11:** 1461

Long Walls, stone walls connecting Athens with the port city of Piraeus **5:** 588, 711

Lope de Vega (1562-1635), Spanish dramatist **9:** 1238

Lord of the four quarters **2:** 226

Lorraine **9:** 1187, 1199, 1202-1203, 1213-1214, 1270, 1286-1288 **10:** 1384-1385, 1422

Losis **11:** 1496

Lost-wax method **11:** 1449

Lot, nephew of Abraham **3:** 316

Lothar I (795-855), Frankish emperor **9:** 1182, 1184, *1184*, *1186*, 1187, 1190, 1199, 1213, 1287-1288

Lothar III (1075-1137), German king (1125-1137) and Holy Roman emperor (1133-1137) **10:** 1333

Lotharingia. *See* Lorraine

Lotus Sutra **7:** 885

Louis I the Pious (778-840), Holy Roman emperor (814-840), king of France (814-840), king of Germany (814-840) and king of Aquitaine (781-840) **9:** 1285, 1287

Louis II, king (1845-1886) **11:** 1563

Louis II the German (c.806-876), king of Germany (840-876) **9:** 1184, 1187, 1190-1191, 1199, 1240, 1286-1288

Louis IV, byname Louis d'outremer (Louis from Overseas) (921-954), king of France (reigned 936-954) **10:** 1349, 1391

Louis VI, byname Louis the Fat, (1081-1137), king of France (reigned 1108-1137) **9:** 1221 **10:** 1328

Louis VII, byname Louis the Younger (c.1120-1180), Capetian king of France who pursued a long rivalry, marked by recurrent warfare and continuous intrigue, with Henry II of England **9:** 1273, *1273*, 1276 **10:** 1328

Louis IX, also called Saint Louis (1214-1270), king of France (reigned 1226-1270), most popular of the Capetian monarchs; he led the Seventh Crusade to the Holy Land 1248-1250 and died on another crusade to Tunisia **9:** 1278 **10:** *1350*, *1352-1354*, 1354

Louis XI, king of France (reigned 1461-1483) **10:** 1420, 1422

Louis the Child (893-911), king of Germany (899-911) **9:** 1202

Louvre Museum (Paris) **2:** 235

Low Countries **1:** 76 **9:** 1287-1288. *See also* Netherlands

Lowell, Percival, astronomer (1855-1916) **1:** 28

Lower Egypt **2:** 153-154, 158, 278-280

Lower Germany **6:** 775-776, 778, 783

Lower Mesopotamia **2:** 218

Lower Moesia **9:** 1264

Lower Paleolithic Age (c.2,500,000-200,000 years ago) **1:** 53

Lowlands **9:** 1187 **10:** 1418

Lu **3:** 357

Luba Empire (peak: AD 1500) **11:** 1553

Lubeck **10:** 1402

Lublin **11:** 1536

Luca **6:** 737

Lucan, Marcus Annaeus Lucanus (39-65), poet and Roman republican patriot **6:** 798

Luceres, tribe mentioned in the legend of Romulus **5:** 653

Lucerne **10:** 1390

Lucifer, "bearer of light," fallen angel **7:** 956

Lucius Cornelius Sulla **5:** 700-701. *See also* Sulla

Lucius Septimius, Roman emperor **8:** 1046, 1069

Lucius Tarquinius Priscus, traditionally the fifth king of Rome **5:** 651. *See also* Tarquin the Elder

Lucius Verus **8:** 1069

Lucretia **5:** 653

Lucretius **5:** 647

Lucumo **5:** 651

Ludi **6:** 799, 801, 855

Ludi magni **6:** 799, 855

Ludwig. *See* Louis

Lugal, ruler of a city-state in Babylonia **2:** 219, 278, 280

Lugalbanda, Sumerian epic **2:** 222

Lugalzaggesi, king of the Mesopotamian city of Umma (c.2375-2350 BC) **2:** 278, 280

Lugdunensis **10:** 1412

Lugdunum **6:** 813

Luke (fl. first century AD), in Christian tradition, the author of the third Gospel and the Acts of the Apostles **7:** 926-927, 930, 933, *933*, 997

Lullubians **2:** 225

Lumbini Grove **7:** 871

Lun yu **3:** 356

Lunda Empire **11:** 1553-1554

Lung-shan culture, Neolithic culture of central China **3:** 350

Luo people **11:** 1553

Lupercalia (wolves' feasts), Roman festival **5:** 650, 711 **6:** 742

Lurs **3:** 361

Lusitani **6:** 838

Lusitania **8:** 1025

Luxembourg **10:** *1390*, 1391, 1413

Luxor **2:** 159-160, *166*, 170, 176-177, 186; - Museum **2:** 170

Lybia **8:** 1105

Lyceum, the academy in Athens founded by Aristotle **5:** 607, 648

Lycia **6:** 766

Lycurgus, Spartan lawgiver (ninth century BC) **4:** *471*,

472-473, 478, 485, 566; biography of - **4:** 473

Lydia **3:** 373, 375 **4:** 492, 511-513, *512* **5:** 584, 675, 709

Lydian; - kings **4:** 492; - language **4:** 481

Lylibaeum **8:** 1029

Lyon **8:** 1020 **9:** 1270

Lyric poetry **4:** 466, 566

Lysandrus Spartan general **5:** 601

Lysias (459-380) orator and metoikos (foreigner) logographer in Athens **5:** *602*, 604-607, 711

Maat, Egyptian goddess of truth and justice **2:** 278-279

Maccabees, Jewish movement that fought for political autonomy **7:** 918-919, 997

Macedonia **2:** 194 **4:** 517, 522, 526, 534, 565 **5:** *609-611*, 610-612, *613*, 614-615, *617*, 620, 624, 628, 630, 636, *695*, 697-698, 709-711 **6:** 838-839, 853 **7:** 917 **9:** 1260, 1264 **11:** 1556, 1558

Macedonian **5:** *608*, 611-613, 615-616, *616*, 619, 621, 624, 628, 630, 632, 633, 691, 695, 697, 709-711; - armies **5:** 612; - dynasty **9:** 1259-1260, 1265, 1285; - power **5:** 612; - Renaissance **9:** 1265; - rule **5:** 615

Macedonian Wars **5:** 691, *695*, 697, 711 **6:** *838*, 837-838

Macedonians **4:** 512 **5:** 598, 601, 612, 616-617, 619, 624, 630 **8:** 1069 **9:** 1287

Macehualtin **11:** 1468, 1470, 1474, 1574

Macina **11:** 1548

Macrina **7:** 974

Macrinus, Marcus Opellius (c.164-218), Roman emperor (217-218) **6:** 815-816

Madagascar **3:** 405, 414 **11:** 1553

Madain **8:** 1105

Madhva (1199-1278) **7:** 898

Madras **11:** 1493

Madrid **11:** 1459, 1561, 1563

Maecenas, Gaius Cilnius (c.70-8 BC), Roman diplomat **6:** 750, *751*, 855

Maeonia (Lydia) **4:** 511

Magadha **7:** 886

Magatama **11:** 1522, 1574

Magdalena River **11:** 1452

Magdalenian **1:** *50*, 53, *54-56*, 55-57, 134, 136; - culture (11,000-17,000 years ago) **1:** 55-56, 134

Magellan, Ferdinand (1480-1521), Portuguese navigator **3:** 392

Magellanic Clouds **1:** 16, 133-134

Magi **3:** 370, 372, 376 **7:** 925

Magistracy **5:** 636, 662

Magistrates **4:** 453, 472-473, 477, 480, 507, 527, 539, 565-566 **5:** *601*, 661, 664, 709-710 **6:** 728, 741, 747, 790, 853-856

Magma **1:** 30-31

Magna Carta **10:** 1330, *1342*, 1344, 1353

Magna Grecia (region in Southern Italy) **4:** 458, 461, 566

Magnentius, in full Flavius Magnus Magnentius (d. 353), usurping Roman emperor **7:** 948

Magnesia **5:** 690-691

Magnetic field **1:** 12, 18, 27, 43, 135

Magnetosphere **1:** 27

Magnus Clemens Maximus, usurping Roman emperor who ruled Britain, Gaul, and Spain (reigned 383-388) **7:** 951 **8:** 1020, 1066

Magnus the Lawmender, Haakon's son and successor, Magnus VI (reigned 1263-1280) **10:** 1400

Magog. *See* Gog

Magyars **9:** *1190*, 1193, 1202-1204, 1206, 1231, 1264, 1287

Mahabharata, epic poem of Hinduism **7:** 891, 894, 997

Mahasanghikas **7:** 882

Mahatma Gandhi **3:** 384 **7:** 893, 997. *See also* Gandhi

Mahayana **7:** 882, 884, 886, 888, 912, 997

Mahayanins **7:** 884

Mahdi **9:** 1230

Mahendra, Buddhist monastery founded in the late third century BC in Anuradhapura, the ancient capital of Sri Lanka **7:** 888

Mahmud II, Ottoman sultan (1785-1839) **11:** 1574

Mahmud of Ghazni, sultan (reigned 998-1030) **8:** 1080 **11:** 1492, 1494, 1496

Mai Idris Alooma (reigned 1580-1617) **11:** 1549

Maidiomana, cousin of Zarathushtra **3:** 369

Main River **8:** 1032

Mainz **6:** 787, 817 **10:** 1371-1372, 1391

Maior domus (Mayor of the palace). *See* Majordomo

Maize god **11:** 1462

Majjhima **7:** 881

Majordomo **8:** 1039, 1141, 1143 **9:** 1160-1161, 1287

Makamat, by al-Hariri **8:** 1101, 1104, 1109, 1126-1127

Makua **3:** 412

Málaga **8:** 1132

Malagasy **3:** 414

Malaysia **1:** 52, 74 **11:** 1493

Mali **11:** *1544*, 1547-1548, *1547-1548*, *1550*, 1573-1574 ;

Malik Shah (1055-1092), third Seljuq sultan **9:** 1288

Malindi **11:** 1551

Mallia **2:** 197, 199, 279

Mallorca **1:** 73, *91*

Malta **5:** 679

Malventum, renamed by the Romans in Beneventum **5:** 674

Mameluke dynasty, ruled Egypt and Syria (1250-1517) **9:** 1278

Mamelukes **8:** 1143

Mamertines, Italian mercenaries and pirates on Sicily **5:** 681, 711

Mamluk Empire (1250-1517) **11:** 1562

Mamluks **11:** 1562, 1574

Mammals **1:** 35-36, 39, 50, 134-135; dawn of - **1:** 36

Mammoth **1:** *41*, 42, 50, 56, 63, *71*, 134

Manchuria **11:** 1504, 1508, 1510, 1522

Manchus **11:** 1535

Manco Capac **11:** 1478, 1480-1481, 1573

Mandalas **7:** 886

Mandarins **11:** 1508, 1574

Mandinka **11:** 1545, 1574

Manes **6:** 752, 767

Manetho, Egyptian priest who wrote a history of Egypt (c.300 BC) **2:** 154, 157, 160, 168, 180, 192, 278

Manfred, half-brother of Conrad IV **10:** 1349-1350

Mangu (1251-1260) **11:** 1512, 1537-1540, 1574

Mani (216-274?), Iranian founder of the Manichaean religion, a church advocating a dualistic doctrine that viewed the world as a fusion of spirit and matter **7:** 963-964, 997 **8:** 1072, 1074, 1143

Manichaeanism **7:** 962-963, 997 **8:** 1072, 1134

Maniples, military formation **5:** 678, 711

Manisa **5:** 690

Manna **3:** 327

Mansa Süleyman **11:** 1547

Mansu, emperor Congo Musa (1307-1332) **11:** 1547

Mans-ra **8:** 1113

Mantras **7:** 885-886

Mantua **10:** 1395

Manu, in Indian mythology the first man, and the legendary author of an important Sanskrit code of law, the Manu-smrti **7:** 894

Manus, Roman concept of possession **3:** 392 **6:** 796-798 **8:** 1042

Manuscripts **8:** 1119, 1129, 1141-1142 **9:** *1159*, *1162*, *1173*, *1177*, 1179, *1180*, *1197*, *1199*, *1223*, *1233*, *1238*, *1244-1245*, *1247*, 1261, *1269*

Manzikert, Battle at (1072), marking the end of Byzantine imperial power in Asia Minor **9:** 1266, 1268, 1285, 1288

Maori, Polynesian people **3:** 394, 396, *400*, *402*

Mara, evil god who tempted Buddha **7:** 873

Marathon **4:** 487, *515-519*, 517-519, 565-566 **5:** 585; Battle of - (490 BC) **4:** 565; Bay of - **4:** 517

Marcel, Etienne **10:** 1379

Marcian **7:** 980 **8:** 1058-1059

Marco Polo, Venetian merchant (1254-1324) **11:** 1536-1537, *1537*, 1540, 1574 ;

Marcus Aurelius Antonius (121-180), Roman emperor (161-180) **6:** 730-731, 789, *790*, *792*, 802, 808, 812, 814, 816, 819, 824, *836*, 853-855 **8:** 1016, 1069

Marcus Aurelius Numerianus **8:** 1016

Marcus Aurelius Valerius Maximianus **8:** 1016

Marcus Livius Drusus (c.124-91 BC), son of the tribune of 122 by the same name **5:** 701

Marcus Pomponius, Roman praetor **5:** 687

Marcus Porcius Cato (234-149BC), Roman statesman **5:** 693. *See also* Cato

Marcus Tullius Cicero **7:** 962. *See also* Cicero

Marcy, Geoffrey **1:** 24

Mardonius, Achaemenian Persian general, nephew of King Darius I (?-479 BC) **4:** 517, 522 **5:** 584

Marduk (Bel), chief god of Babylon, national god of Babylonia **2:** 236, 251, 254, 258, 270, 278

Mare nostrum **5:** 684 **6:** 855 **8:** 1029

Margaret (of Denmark) (1353-1412), regent of Denmark

(from 1375), of Norway (from 1380), and of Sweden (from 1389), who, by diplomacy and war, pursued dynastic policies that led to the Kalmar Union (1397) **10:** 1401

Margrave (marquise) **9:** 1287

Mari **2:** 196, 224, 230-231, *230-232*, 233-234, *234*, 247-248, *250*, 253-254, 277-278 **3:** 315; Golden age of - **2:** 230; - letters **2:** 234

Marienburg **10:** 1407

Mariner 4 **1:** 27

Mariner 9 **1:** 27

Marius, Gaius (c.156-86 BC), Roman general and politician **1:** 126 **5:** 699-702, *700*, 709, 711-712 **6:** 855 **7:** 950

Marjorian Roman emperor **8:** 1030

Mark (fl. first century AD), traditional author of the second Synoptic Gospel **7:** 926, 928, 930-931, 933, *933*, 956, 997

Mark Antony. *See* Anthony

Market economy **10:** 1304

Marketplaces **5:** 588 **10:** 1313

Markets of Trajan **6:** 794

Marmoutier **7:** 975

Marquesas Islands **3:** 394

Marrakesh **9:** *1237*

Marriage; - contracts **2:** 241; - document **2:** 241

Mars (planet) **1:** 9, *9*, 23, 26-27, 133, 135

Mars, Roman god **5:** *622*, 642, 650, *691* **6:** *746*, 853, 855

Mars Ultor **6:** *746*

Marseilles **3:** 300 **7:** 975 **8:** 1132 **10:** 1366

Marsupials (animals) **1:** 36

Martigny **6:** *769*

Martin of Tours, Saint (316-397), bishop of Tours; one of the founders of Monasticism in the West **7:** 954, 975, 978, 997

Martin V, original name Oddo, or Oddone, Colonna (1368-1431), pope (reigned 1417-1431) **10:** *1366*, 1368, *1368*

Martius **5:** 651, 658, 710. *See also* Ancus Marcius

Martyrs **7:** 938, *942*, 955, 982, 997 **10:** 1372

Mary, heiress to Burgundy **10:** *1322*, 1393, 1421-1422

Mary, mother of Jesus **7:** 926, *936*, 955-956, 997

Masai **1:** 72

Masinissa (c.240-148 BC), ruler of the North African kingdom of Numidia **5:** 690 **6:** 839

Masons **10:** 1310, 1320

Masqat **8:** 1095, 1105

Masses **5:** 634, 655, 676, 695, 711

Massilia (Marseille) **4:** 458 **6:** 740

Mastaba chapels **2:** 156, 280

Masterpiece **10:** 1320

Masvingo **11:** 1553

Matabeleland **11:** 1554

Mathematics **5:** 607, 641-642 **9:** 1178, 1227, 1261 **11:** 1500

Matsya, the "Noah" of the Hindus **7:** 894

Mattathias, patriarch of the Hasmonaeans **5:** 629 **7:** 918

Matthew, first in order of the four canonical Gospels and often called the "ecclesiastical" Gospel **7:** 926, 930-931, 933, *933*, 970, 997

Matthew, Saint, the Evangelist, one of the twelve apostles **9:** 1222, 1263

Maui, hero in Polynesian creation legend **3:** 396

Mauretania **5:** 700 **6:** 766, 839

Maurice Bourdin, archbishop of Braga, later antipope Gregory VIII **9:** 1220

Mauricius, Flavius Tiberius (c.539-602), general and Byzantine emperor (582-602) **8:** 1077 **9:** 1244

Mauritania **8:** 1031 **11:** 1545

Maurya, major kingdom in India (c.320-185 BC) **3:** 387 **11:** 1491-1492

Mauryan dynasty **7:** 886

Mausoleum **5:** 604 **6:** *832*, 855

Mawali **8:** 1114, 1143

Maxentius, Marcus Aurelius Valerius (?-312), Roman emperor 306-312 **6:** 831 **7:** 943, *946* **8:** 1017, *1017*, 1141

Maximian, Marcus Aurelius Valerius Maximianus (?-310), Roman emperor with Diocletian (286-305) **6:** 827-828, *827*, 830-831, *831*

Maximian. *See* Marcus Aurelius Valerius Maximianus

Maximianus **8:** 1016, *1063*, *1067*

Maximianus, bishop of Ravenna **8:** 1063

Maximianus, Roman emperor (286-305) **7:** *946*

Maximilian, son of Frederick III **10:** 1393, 1421-1422

Maximinus Daia, Galerius Valerius (?-313), Roman emperor (310-113) **6:** 830-831

Maya **7:** 872, 898 **11:** 1447-1449, 1451, 1453-1456, *1454-1455*, *1458*, 1458-1462, 1464, 1574

Mayan **3:** 308; - calendar **11:** 1460; - dress **11:** 1464; - religion **11:** 1461-1462; - ritual **11:** 1458; - tribes **11:** 1453

Mayan civilization (third-seventeenth century) **1:** 75, 102

Mayapán **11:** 1454, 1456, 1458

Mayor of the palace. *See* Majordomo

Mayoral dynasty. *See* Carolingians

Mazdak **8:** 1076

Meander River **5:** 609

Mecca **6:** 844 **8:** 1081-1087, *1083*, *1086-1087*, *1090*, 1090-1093, 1095, *1095*, *1099*, 1103, 1111, *1113*, 1114, *1119*, *1132*, 1142-1144 **9:** 1226-1227, 1288 **11:** 1547-1548

Meccan rebellion **8:** 1113

Meccans **8:** 1092-1093, 1113

Mechanism of genetics **1:** 38

Medea, in Greek mythology, an enchantress **3:** 347 **5:** *585-586*, 600, 710

Medes **2:** 252, 258, 268, 270, 277, 279 **3:** 375, 377 **8:** 1069

Media **5:** *620*, 624 **8:** 1078

Median tribe **3:** 370

Medians **8:** 1078

Mediator **4:** 479

Medimnoi. *See* Council of 500

Medina **8:** 1081, *1083-1085*, 1084, 1086, *1090-1091*, 1092, *1095*, 1096, 1099, 1101-1104, 1111, *1113*, 1119, 1142-1144

Medinet Habu **2:** 189

Mediolanum **6:** 820 **8:** 1016

Meditation **7:** 873, 875, 878, 885-886, 894, 997

Meditations **6:** 789

Mediterranean **2:** 152-153, 186, 193, 197, 214, 216, 222, 247, 258, 260, 263, 267, 279 **3:** 295-298, 300, *301*, 302, *303*, 305-306, 308, 312-313, 315, 328, 330, 340, 345, 387, 403-404, 407, 409, 413 **4:** 445, 448, 450, 457-459, *460*, 461, *464*, 484, 487, 514, 524, 532, 565 **5:** 596-597, 613, 619-621, 626, 628, 667-668, 675, 679, 684-686, 710, 712 **6:** *728*, 730-731, *740*, 790, 835, 837-838, 855-856 **7:** 934, 937 **8:** 1026, 1029, 1038, 1045, 1064, 1066, 1081, 1084, 1108, 1122, 1130, 1141 **9:** 1193, 1227, 1232-1233, 1236, 1242-1244, 1264, 1273, 1276, 1278, 1288 **10:** 1350, 1395 **11:** 1532, 1542-1543, 1547, 1562-1563, 1574

Mediterranean; - peoples **4:** 450; - region **4:** 445; - world **4:** 448

Mediterranean Sea **1:** 64, 95, 97, 119-120 **2:** 193, 279 **3:** 295, 298, 305, 313 **4:** 514 **6:** *728*, *740*, 835, 856

Meerssen, Treaty of (870), divided the northern part of Lothar I's empire between Charles the Bald and Louis the German **9:** 1199, 1288

Megacles, member of the family of the Alcmaeonids, who helped the tyrant Peisistratus (sixth century BC) **4:** 485-486

Megalithism **1:** 87

Megaliths **1:** 83, 87, *87*, 133-134 **11:** 1450

Megalopolis **5:** 628

Megara **5:** 587

Megaron **2:** 212-214, 278-279 **4:** 497, 566

Megasthenes (c.350-290 BC), ancient Greek historian and diplomat **6:** 845

Mehmed I (Muhammad, reigned 1413-1421) **11:** *1558*, 1559, *1561*, 1561-1562, *1563*, 1564, 1566

Mehmed II, Sultan of Ottoman Turkey (reigned 1444-1446 and 1451-1481) **11:** 1559, *1561*, 1561-1562, *1563*, 1564, 1566, *1566*

Melanesia, region in Oceania **3:** 391-392, *393-394*

Melanesians **3:** 392-394, *394*

Melchizedek, king of Salem (Jerusalem) **3:** 316

Melitene **8:** 1076

Melkart-Baal-Tsor, Phoenician god of trade and shipping. *Also known as Moloch* **3:** 299

Melpomene **5:** 638, 711

Memnon, mythological hero **2:** 177 **5:** 619; Colossi of - **2:** 177

Memphis **2:** 153-154, 157-158, 161, 167, 170, 184, *184*, 189, 270, 277-278, 280 **3:** 296 **5:** *620*, 627

Memphite astronomers **2:** 156; - kingdom **2:** 154

Menander (?-293 BC) Greek playwright of comedy **5:** 639, 711

Menander (c.160 BC-c.135 BC), Indo-Greek king **6:** 798

Mencius. *See* Mengzi

Mendicant **10:** 1314

320-323, *322, 324*, 325 **7:** 917, 964 **8:** 1088, 1090 **10:** 1345, 1374

Mosesh, Sotho leader (1786-1870) **11:** 1554

Mosque **8:** *1055*, 1068, 1092, 1101, *1102, 1105-1107, 1109-1110, 1112*, 1113, *1115-1117, 1120*, 1143

Mosque of Ibn Tulum **8:** 1120

Mossi-Dagomba group **11:** 1574

Mosul **8:** *1105, 1119*, 1126, 1131, *1132*, 1141

Motecuhzuma I (c.1468) **11:** 1469, 1573

Motecuhzuma II **11:** 1469, 1476

Mount Athos **5:** 584

Mount Elgon **3:** 403

Mount Kenya **3:** 403

Mount Kilimanjaro **3:** 403

Mount Olympus **5:** 583

Mount Vesuvius **6:** 779, 804

Mouseion (museum) **5:** 628, 637-638, 711

Mousterian culture (c.40,000 BC) **1:** 50, 52, 135; - customs **1:** 54

Mozambique **3:** 412 **11:** 1553

Msir (Egypt) **8:** 1080

Mstislav **11:** 1517

Mu`āwiyah **8:** 1103-1105, 1111-1112, 1124, 1132

Mucius Scaevola, legendary Roman hero **5:** 668

Mudras **7:** 886

Muezzin **8:** 1091, 1143 **9:** 1225

Mughal dynasty **11:** 1497, 1542

Muhammad (c.570-632), prophet of Islam **8:** 1081, *1081, 1083-1085*, 1084-1088, *1088, 1090-1092*, 1090-1096, *1094-1098*, 1099-1101, 1103, *1105*, 1105-1106, 1111-1114, 1119, 1121-1122, 1128, 1132, 1141-1144 **9:** 1194, 1225, 1227, 1230 **11:** 1566

Muhammad Ibn Tughluq (reigned 1325-1351) **11:** 1496-1497

Muhammad of Ghor (d.1216) **11:** 1496, 1574

Muhammad, or Abu al-Qasim Muhammad ibn 'Abd Allah ibn' Abd al-Muttalib ibn Hashim, prophet of Islam **3:** 368, 375

Muhammadans **9:** *1162, 1167*

Muisca. *See* Chibcha

Mukurra **11:** 1544

Multan **8:** 1113

Mummies **2:** 173 **3:** 350

Munda, Battle of (45 BC) **6:** 742

Mundium **8:** 1042, 1143

Municipium (pl. *municipia*) **6:** 748, 766, 790, 836, 855

Murad I, sultan (reigned 1359-1389) **11:** 1557, *1557*

Murad II, sultan of the Ottoman Empire (1421-1444 and 1446-1451) **11:** *1558-1559*, 1559

Murals **2:** 176, 201, 212, 231, 278 **11:** 1449-1450, 1491

Murcia **9:** 1230, 1239

Murex **3:** 298

Muromachi **11:** 1530

Mursilis I, Hittite king during the Old Kingdom (c.1620-c.1590 BC) **2:** 256 **3:** 345

Mursilis II, Hittite king in the Hittite Empire (reigned c.1350-1320 BC) **3:** 339, 345

Muscovite power **11:** 1518

Muscovy. *See* Moscow

Muses, in Greek mythology, nine goddesses who inspired philosophers, poets, musicians, and artists **5:** 628, 637-638, 642, 711

Mushkenu **2:** 237; class of the - **2:** 237

Muslim **3:** 363 **8:** *1055*, 1072, 1080, *1086*, 1088-1089, *1090*, 1092, 1092-1093, 1095, 1095-1096, 1098, 1101-1102, *1104-1105*, 1104-1108, *1108*, 1111-1114, *1112-1114*, 1116, 1118-1119, 1122-1123, 1125-1126, 1129-1130, 1132-1133, 1141-1144 **10:** 1308, *1311, 1338*, 1346, 1357

Muslim dynasty **9:** 1288

Muslim orthodoxy **8:** 1113

Muslims **7:** 985 **9:** 1162, 1164, 1172, 1194, 1213, 1225, 1227, 1230, 1233-1234, 1237-1242, *1239*, 1262, 1264, 1270, 1272, 1274, 1276, 1278, 1285-1288 **11:** 1491-1492, 1494, 1497, *1498*, 1536, 1538, 1540, 1544-1545, 1555, 1559, 1562, 1566, 1574

Muslin **11:** 1498

Mustasib **9:** 1228, 1287

Mutina **6:** 743

Muwatallis, son of Mursilis II, Hittite king during the New Kingdom (c.1360-1282 BC) **2:** 184 **3:** 339, 345

Muwatallis II **3:** 345

Mwene Mutapa Empire (c.800-c.1800) **11:** 1553

Myanmar **7:** 888

Mycale **4:** 522-524, 566

Mycenae **2:** 197, 205-216, *205, 207-208, 210-211, 213*, 279 **3:** 347 **4:** 441, 445-446, 543, *545*

Mycenaean **2:** 151, 170, 195, 197, 204-210, *206-207, 210*, 212-216, 214-216, 277-280

Mycenaean; - civilization **1:** 114 **2:** 195, 204, 216, 278 **4:** 445; - communities **4:** 446; - culture **2:** 205-207, 212, 279 **4:** 447; - Greece **1:** 106 **4:** 445; - kings **4:** 446; tombs - **4:** 446; - settlement(s) **2:** 151 **4:** 476; - world **4:** 446

Mycenaeans **2:** 151, 204, 206, 212, 214, 216, 280 **3:** 312 **4:** 445, 461, 497

Mycerinus. *See* Menkaure

Mylae **5:** 681, *684*

Mysore **11:** 1573

Mysteries **4:** 498-500, *502*, 566

Mystery cults **4:** 498, 500

Mythology **1:** 7 **2:** 177, 195, *208* **4:** 445, 449, 464, 497, 503, 546-547, 565-566 **6:** 752, 767, 806, 823, 855 **11:** 1455

Mzilikazi **11:** 1554

Nabatean Kingdom **8:** 1081

Nabis **5:** 636

Nabonidus, king of Babylonia (556-539 BC) **2:** 253

Nabopolassar, king of the Chaldean dynasty of Babylonia (625-605 BC) **2:** 252, 258, 277

Nabu, Assyro-Babylonian god of writing and vegetation **2:** 268

Nahuatl **11:** 1468, 1476

Naksh-i-Rustam **8:** 1069, 1071-1072, 1076-1077

Nala **7:** 891

Nalanda **11:** 1500

Namibia **11:** 1554

Namur **10:** 1413

Nanking **11:** 1506, 1512

Nanna (Sin), Sumero-Akkadian god of the moon **2:** 221, 225, 250 **3:** 315

Nanshe, Sumerian city goddess of Nina **2:** 228

Napata **2:** 175

Naphtali, younger of two sons born to Jacob and Bilhah, a maidservant of Jacob's second wife, Rachel **3:** 319

Naples **4:** 458, 461, *466*, 550, 566 **5:** 688 **6:** 762, 779, 796, 804-805 **8:** 1113 **9:** 1213, 1236, 1244, 1288 **10:** 1350, 1366, 1394, 1398. *See also* Neapolis

Naqia, Assyrian queen mother (fl. seventh century BC) **2:** 270

Nara **11:** *1519, 1523-1524*, 1526, 1530, 1574

Naram-Sin, king of the Mesopotamian dynasty of Akkad **2:** 225-227, *227*, 248, 279

Narasimha, appearance of Vishnu as the demon-defeating man-lion **7:** 894

Narbonne **8:** 1132 **9:** *1162* **10:** 1372

Narcissus (?-54), freedman who became minister of state **6:** 765, 768

Narmer. *See* Menes

Narses **8:** 1065-1066, 1143-1144

Nasser Lake. *See* Lake Nasser

Nataraja, four-handed dancing Hindu god **7:** 896

Natatio **6:** 810

Natural; - philosophers **4:** 503, 566; - science **4:** 503

Naucratis **4:** 457

Naumachiae **6:** 803

Nauru **3:** 393

Navarre **9:** 1227, 1233-1234, 1287 **10:** *1356*, 1379

Navas de Tolosa, Battle of (1212), major battle of the Christian reconquest of Spain **9:** *1232*, 1237

Navigation **2:** 152, 156 **3:** 297, 299-300, 305, 394, 404

Naxos **3:** 378 **4:** 477, 525

Nayarit **11:** 1450

Nayran **8:** 1095

Ndebele **11:** 1554

Ndwandwe **11:** 1554

Neander Valley **1:** 46

Neandertal (*Homo sapiens neanderthalensis*) **1:** *39*, 45-46, *46-47*, 49-50, 52-53, 134-135 **2:** 259

Neapolis (Naples) **4:** 458-459, *462* **5:** *595*, 667, *674*, 688

Near East **1:** 64, 67-68, 70, 100, 106, 108, 121, 133, 135 **2:** 168, 175, 183, 186, 196-197, 278

Neareastern history **2:** 247

Nearer Spain **6:** 838

Nebuchadnezzar, king of Babylonia (588 BC) **3:** 315, 336 **7:** 914, 997 **8:** 1072

Nebuchadnezzar I, king of Babylonia and Mesopotamia

(c.1124-1103 BC) **2:** 256

Nebuchadnezzar II, king of the Chaldean Empire (c.630-562 BC) **2:** 252, *254*, 257-258, *258*, 279

Nebulae (clouds) **1:** 11, *15-16*, 16, *18*, 20, 22-23, 133

Necho, Egyptian pharaoh (fl. c.672-664 BC) **3:** 302

Nefertari, queen of Egypt and wife of Ramses II **2:** 186

Neferti, Prophecy of **2:** 160, 164, *183*

Nefertiti, queen of Egypt and wife of Akhenaton (1379-1362 BC) **2:** 178, 180

Negev Desert **3:** 314

Negritos **3:** 392

Nehemiah, Jewish governor who arranged for Jewish self-rule **7:** 916-917, 997

Nejd **8:** 1083

Nekawend **8:** 1078

Nekho, king of Egypt (thirteenth dynasty) **2:** 192, 279

Neo-Assyrian Empire **2:** 263-264, 266

Neo-Babylonian dynasty **2:** 270

Neo-Babylonian Empire **2:** 252, 258

Neo-Hittite (Empire), period in Hittite history (c.1400-1200 BC) **3:** 340, 346, 348

Neo-Sumerian period **2:** 227

Neolithic **1:** 50, 61, *61-62*, 64-68, *64, 66-70*, 70, 72-76, *74-80*, 78, 80, *83*, 86-88, 90-98, *90*, 100, 103, 105, 116, 133, 135; -Age **2:** 194; - culture(s) **1:** *64*, 73-76, 78, 94, 133, 135 **11:** 1520; - farmers **1:** 76 **2:** 194; - Greek culture **1:** 73; - horses **1:** 93; - people **1:** 67, 80, 94, 100, 103; - Period (c.8000-2000 BC) **1:** 61, *61-62*, 65, *66-67*, 67, *69-70*, 72-73, *74*, 76, 78, *78-80*, 88, 91, 97-98, 100, 105, 135; - revolution **1:** 66, 135; - settlements **1:** 67, 96

Neolithical Japanese civilizations **11:** 1574

Neon **1:** 26

Nepal **7:** 876, 878 **11:** 1491

Neptune (planet) **1:** 23, 27-28, 135

Nero, Claudius Caesar Drusus Germanicus (37-68), originally named Lucius Domitius Ahenobarbus, Roman emperor (reigned 54-68) **6:** 768-775, *771-773, 775*, 778, 783, 785, 793, 809, 812, 815, 853-856 **7:** 923, 936, 955, 997 **11:** 1500, 1543

Nerva, Marcus Cocceius (c.30-98), Roman emperor (96-98) **6:** *782-783*, 784

Nestor of Pylos, in Greek legend, king of Pylos **2:** 206, 213

Nestorian Church. *See* Nestorius

Nestorian monasteries **8:** 1133

Nestorianism **7:** 997 **8:** 1076, 1143

Nestorius (d. c.451) Syrian monk who disputed the Greek title Theotokos (Mother of God) for Mary **7:** 956, 997

Nestorius, archbishop of Constantinople (428-431) **8:** 1076, 1133, 1143

Nestor's palace **2:** 214

Netherlandic **8:** 1043

Netherlands **1:** 63, 75-77, 80, 84, 89, 90, 97, *108, 110*, 113, 119-120 **6:** 856 **7:** 990 **8:** 1022 **9:** *1180* **10:** 1393, 1402, 1412, 1418, 1420, 1422. *See also* Low Countries

Neumagen **6:** *843*

Neustadt, siege of (1275) **11:** 1536

Neustria **9:** 1161, 1287

Neutron star **1:** 18, 135

Neva **10:** 1403

Nevsky, Alexander. *See* Alexander Nevsky

New Academy **5:** 644

New Assyrian Empire **2:** 277, 279

New Babylonian Empire **2:** 277, 279

New Caledonia **3:** 392-393

New Carthage **5:** 685, *688*, 690

New Comedy, genre of comedy from the Hellenistic era **5:** 600, 639

New Guinea **3:** 391-393, *395*

New Kingdom (1550-1070 BC) **2:** *168*, 171, *172*, 173, *174*, 175-176, *179*, 181, 189, 191, *192*, 277-280 **3:** 345

New Monastic Orders **10:** 1306, 1314, 1406

New Persian Empire **8:** 1069-1071, *1078*, 1083, 1095

New Persian kingdom **8:** 1143-1144

New Rome **11:** 1559. *See also Nova Roma*

New Stone Age. *See* Neolithic Period

New Testament **1:** 68 **7:** 926, 933-934, 937, 946, 964, 974, 997

New World **1:** 75, 102

New Zealand **3:** 391-392, 394, 396-397, *401*, 402

Newton, Isaac (1642-1727) **1:** 9-10, 12, 135

Ngazargamu **11:** 1549

Ngoni **11:** 1553-1554

Niani **11:** 1547-1548

Roland. *See* Cardinal Roland; *Song of Roland*
Roma **5:** 649, 654, *674*
Roma Nova **8:** 1017-1018
Romaioi **9:** 1244
Roman alphabet **4:** 450
Roman army **5:** 658, 687-688, 691, 695, 700, 709 **6:** 729-730, *749*, 817-818, 824, 826, 853-854 **7:** 920, 950, 975 **8:** 1019, 1023, 1028, 1032, 1142
Roman art **8:** 1034
Roman Catholic Church **1:** 9 **6:** *826* **7:** 948, 968, 983, 997
Roman census **6:** 745
Roman Church **9:** 1224, 1263 **11:** 1559
Roman citizenship **5:** 642, 678 **6:** 728, 731, 748, 755, 765, 772, 776, *776*, 790, 815, 824, 836 **8:** 1015
Roman civilization **8:** 1034, 1060
Roman class **5:** 660
Roman clergymen **9:** 1215
Roman colony **6:** 787, 854
Roman Egypt **11:** 1543
Roman emperors **8:** 1017, 1028, 1074, 1143
Roman Empire **3:** 308 **5:** 657, *664*, *674*, 685, *695*, 698, 712 **6:** 745, *754*, 758, *783*, 808, 811, 817, 823, 827-828, *827*, 831, *834*, 835, 838, *840*, 841, 843-845, 853-854, 856 **7:** 925, 932, 937, 939, 940, 941-942, 944, 947, 948, 966, 968, 979-980, 982, 988, 997 **8:** 1015-1016, 1018-1021, *1020*, *1022*, 1023, 1025, 1027-1028, *1029*, 1032, 1039, 1043-1044, 1057-1059, *1060*, 1066, 1068-1069, 1074, 1095, 1108, 1141-1144 **9:** *1165*, 1168, 1171-1172, 1177, 1192, 1213, *1215*, 1216, *1218*, 1239, *1242*, 1243, 1246, 1256, 1285-1287 **10:** 1303, 1317, 1335, 1343, 1345, 1352, 1363, *1364*, 1370, 1384, 1388, 1391-1393, *1392*
Roman encampments **6:** 755
Roman languages **8:** 1043, 1144
Roman law (753 BC-fifth century AD) **6:** 741, 772, 796 **7:** 936, 988 **8:** 1035, 1042, 1067 **9:** 1183
Roman legions **8:** 1026
Roman literature **6:** 733, 750
Roman mercatores **6:** 795
Roman orator **6:** *730*, 808
Roman prefect **8:** 1023
Roman religion **8:** 1020
Roman Republic (c.509-31 BC) **5:** 657, 660, *685*, 690, 709, 711 **6:** 727, *730*, 732, 734-736, 738, 741-742, 750-751, 754, 764, 774, 799, 801, 854-855 **10:** 1315
Roman Senate **5:** 668, 685 **6:** 730, *745* **7:** 997. *See also* Senate
Roman soldier **6:** *730*, *777*, *818*, *840*
Roman students **9:** 1179
Roman Synod of 1075 **9:** 1216
Roman territory **6:** 755
Roman theaters **6:** 807
Roman tragedy **6:** 808
Romania **6:** *782* **8:** 1030
Romanization **6:** 765, *776*, 781, 792, 841
Romanova, Anastasia. *See* Anastasia
Romans **1:** 107, 114, 120, 123-124, 126 **3:** 300, 305, 307-308, 312, 367, 387-388 **4:** 450, *466*, 512 **5:** 627-628, 636, 650-651, *651*, 654-655, 657, 664, 666, 668-670, *669-670*, 672-676, 678, *679-680*, 680-682, *682-684*, 684-686, 688-692, *693*, 696, 698-701, 709-712 **6:** *727*, 733, 742, *751*, 752, 755, 761, 764, 767, *770*, 771, 773, 776, 778, *782*, 785, *786*, 792, *792*, 794-795, *794*, 797, 801, *806*, 808, 815-816, *816-817*, *819*, 824, *830*, 835-836, *836*, 839, 841-845, 853-856 **7:** 892, *917-918*, 922, 924, 927, 930, 936, *938*, 954-955, 962, 988, 997 **8:** 1021-1022, 1024-1025, *1028*, 1028-1029, 1034-1035, 1039, 1042, 1045, 1060, 1063, 1065, 1071, 1076, 1098, 1141-1142, 1144 **11:** 1498, 1500
Romanus I, Byzantine co-emperor **9:** 1261
Romanus II (939-963), Byzantine emperor (959-963) **9:** 1208, 1261, 1264, *1265*
Romanus III, prefect of Constantinople (eleventh century) **9:** 1265
Romanus IV Diogenes, Byzantine emperor (1068-1071) **9:** 1266, 1288
Rome **3:** 299 **5:** 612, *628*, 630, 648-651, *650*, 653-658, 660-662, 666-676, *670*, *674*, 678-679, *681*, 681-682, 684-693, *686*, *691*, *693*, 695-702, *697*, *700*, *702*, 709-712 **6:** 727-734, *729*, *731-732*, *735*, 736-746, *741*, *746*, 748-752, *749*, *753-754*, 754, 759-762, *764*, 766-768, *766*, 770-776, *770*, *773*, 778, *778-779*, 780, 782, *782*, 784, *785-787*, 787-790, *790-791*, 792-796, *794*, *796*, 799-801, *802*, 806-810, *810*, 812-813, *814*, 815-816, 819-820, 822, 824, 828,

830-831, *833-834*, 833-840, *842*, 843-844, 846, 853-856 **7:** 921-922, 933-934, 936-938, *937*, *939-940*, 940-942, *942*, 944, *946*, 948, *950-951*, 951-953, 955, 959, 962-963, 965-966, 975-976, *976*, 978-982, *981*, 983, 984, 986-988, *988*, 997 **8:** *1015-1016*, 1015-1019, *1021*, *1023*, 1024-1025, 1027-1029, *1029*, 1031, *1031*, 1033-1035, 1039, 1044-1046, 1048, 1052-1053, *1053*, 1060, 1064-1066, 1068, 1072, 1074, 1076, 1099, *1105*, *1113*, *1119*, 1130, 1141-1142, 1144 **9:** 1164, 1166, 1168, *1168*, 1170-1171, 1178, 1180, 1184, 1187, 1191, 1193-1194, 1206, *1208*, 1212-1215, *1216*, 1219-1223, 1226, 1240, 1244, 1249-1250, 1254, 1263, 1285, 1287 **10:** 1310, 1312, 1314-1317, 1335, 1337, 1342, 1356, *1360*, *1362*, 1363-1368, *1364*, 1394, *1414*, 1416 **11:** 1497-1498, 1500, 1518, 1543-1544, 1559, 1561, 1574
Romulus, one of the legendary founders of Rome **2:** 223 **5:** 650-651, 653-654, *691*, 709-710, 712 **6:** 733, 855. *See also* Remus
Romulus Augustulus **8:** 1028, 1033, 1144
Roncaglia **10:** 1337
Roncesvalles, Battle at (788), massacre by the Basques of the rear guard of Charlemagne's army in the Pyrenees **9:** 1172, *1173*
Ronda **9:** *1239*
Rössen culture **1:** 80
Rostrum **5:** 681
Rouen **9:** 1186 **10:** 1381, 1386, *1386*
Roxana (?-c.311 BC), daughter of Oxyartes of Sogdiana; Persian wife of Alexander the Great **5:** 627, 712
Roxelana **11:** 1564
Royal dynasty **8:** 1038
Royal palace **3:** 340, *370* **8:** 1050, 1052, *1070*
Royal Society **1:** 11
Rta, truth **3:** 378
Rub` Al Khali **8:** 1083
Rubber **11:** 1448, 1457, 1462
Rubicon **6:** 740
Rubidium (elements) **1:** 12
Rudna Glavna **1:** 104
Rudolf, duke of Swabia (?-1080) **9:** 1219
Rudolf I (1218-1291), first German king of the Habsburg dynasty **10:** *1388*, 1391-1392
Rudolf III, king of Burgundy (eleventh century) **9:** 1213-1214
Rule of the Four emperors. *See* Tetrachy
Ruler of the Believers **8:** 1134
Rum **8:** 1080
Rum, sultanate of **11:** 1556
Rumania **6:** 854 **9:** *1252*
Rumiras **8:** 1080
Rundi **3:** 412
Runic characters **9:** *1188*
Rurik, House of (until 1598) **11:** 1514-1515
Rus in urbe **6:** 772
Rus Khagan (prince of princes) **11:** 1513
Rus river **11:** 1513
Russia **1:** 42, 63-64, 73-74, 76, 86, 97, 102 **3:** 362 **4:** 461 **6:** 856 **8:** 1068 **9:** 1261 **10:** 1387, *1399*, 1410 **11:** 1513-1518, 1536, 1538, 1574
Russian steppes **1:** 86, 114
Rwanda **3:** 412 **11:** 1553
Ryazan **11:** 1513
Ryu-jyu Islands **11:** 1520

Sabbath, seventh day of the week and day of rest according to the Ten Commandments of the Israelites **3:** 322-323 **7:** 917, 928, 931, 997 **8:** 1092
Sabina, Poppaea (?-65), second wife of Nero **6:** 771, 775
Sabines **5:** 650-651, 653, 654 **6:** 836
Sack of Rome **8:** 1024
Sacramentum **8:** 1042
Sacrifices **4:** 496
Saddharmapundarika Sutra **7:** 885
Sadducees, from the name Zadok, Old Testament priest under Kings David and Solomon (2 Samuel 15:24-29) **6:** 785 **7:** 918-920, 930, 997
Safavid dynasty (1502-1736) **11:** 1564
Sagunto **5:** 684
Saguntum, Spanish city south of the Ebro River **5:** 684, *686*, 712
Sahara **2:** 151 **3:** 403-405, *404*, 408-412, 414 **8:** 1126 **9:** 1285
Sahara Desert **1:** 52 **6:** 839 **11:** *1544*, 1548, 1574
Saharan salt **11:** 1545

Said **8:** 1091, *1130*
Saifawa dynasty (eighth-nineteenth century) **11:** 1549
Saint Benedict. *See* Benedict XIII
Saint Catharine. *See* Catherine of Siena
Saint Denis **9:** *1161*, *1163*
Saint-Hilaire, Geoffrey **1:** 38
Saint Irene **8:** 1064
Saint John Lateran **9:** *1168*
Saint Louis IV. *See* Louis IV
Saint Margaret (1556-1586), one of the forty British martyrs who were executed for harbouring priests during the reign of Queen Elizabeth I of England **10:** 1384
Saint Paul **9:** *1214*. *See also* Paul
Saint Peter **9:** 1170, *1214*. *See also* Peter
Saint Peter's Basilica **9:** 1166, 1170
Saint Sophia **9:** *1243*. *See also* Hagia Sophia
Sakya clan **7:** 871
Sakyamuni **7:** 871. *See also* Buddha
Saladin, Arabic: Salah Ad-Din Yusuf Ibn Ayyub (Righteousness of the Faith, Joseph, Son of Job): (1137/38-1193), Muslim sultan of Egypt, Syria, Yemen, and Palestine, founder of the Ayyubid dynasty, and the most famous of Muslim heroes **8:** 1122 **9:** 1273, 1276 **10:** *1333*, *1338*, 1339
Salah, ritual prayer **8:** 1090
Salamis **4:** 521, 523-524, 534, 544, 567
Salamis, Battle of (480 BC) **4:** 534, 544, 567 **5:** 585. *See also* Themistocles
Salerno **9:** 1213-1214, 1219, 1232, *1242*
Salian dynasty. *See* Franconian dynasty
Salian Franks **8:** 1032, 1034, 1142
Salic law (*Lex Salica*), code of the Salian Franks, issued c. 507/511 **9:** 1184
Salt **1:** 64, 90, 116-117, 120
Sama-Veda **3:** 384-385 **7:** 891
Samadhi **7:** 875
Samaria **2:** 267 **3:** 313, 332, 335 **7:** 913-914, 916, 920, 997
Samaritans **7:** 915, 921, 997
Samarkand **7:** 363 **8:** 1078, 1108, 1109-1110, 1113, 1119, 1132 **11:** 1497, 1504, 1536, *1541*
Samarra **8:** *1117*, *1120*, 1128, 1134
Samhitas **7:** 891
Samnite Wars (343-341 BC, 316-304 BC, 298-290 BC) **6:** 836
Samnites, mountain people of the southern Apennines **5:** *669*, *670-672*, 671-672, 674, *678*, 688, *702*, *711-712* **6:** 836, 856
Samoa **3:** 392, 394, 396, 402
Samos **3:** 378 **4:** 448, 452, 513, 517, 548, 566
Samothrace **5:** *614*, 641
Samsara **7:** 879, 893, 997
Samson, one of the judges of the Bible **3:** *320*, 328, 330-331, *331*
Samsu-Iluna, king of Babylon (1749-1712 BC) **2:** 254
Samudra Gupta, Indian Emperor (c.330-380) **11:** 1491, 1574
Samuel (fl. c. eleventh century BC), religious hero in the history of Israel **3:** *327*, 329 **7:** 919, 997
Samurai **11:** 1528, *1530*
Samyutta **7:** 881
San (Bushman) **3:** *325*, 405, 410-411 **11:** 1551, 1554
San Andreas Fault **1:** 30
San Vitale **8:** 1061, 1063, 1065 **9:** *1170*, 1251
San`a **8:** *1083*, *1095*, *1119*
Sancho I (?-925), king of Navarre from 905 **9:** 1227
Sancho II of Castile (c.1038-1072), king of Castile from 1065 **9:** 1237
Sancho III (c.992-1035), king of Navarre (1000-1035) **9:** 1234
Sanctum **2:** 176
Sangha **7:** 879, 881-882, 997
Sanhaja Berbers **11:** 1545
Sanhedrin **7:** 918, 920, 922, 930-932, 955, 997
Sankhya **7:** 891
Sanskrit **7:** 871, 881, 885-886, 889-891, 997 **11:** 1491, 1497
Santa Maria Maggiore **9:** 1215
Santa Maria Rotunda **6:** *833*
Santiago de Compostela **9:** *1236*
Sant' Apolinare Nuovo **8:** 1060
Sapa Inca, king of Incas **11:** 1480, 1574
Sappho, poet (c.600 BC) **4:** 466, 468, *468*, 567
Saqqara **2:** 154

Zoroaster **3:** 367
Spoleto **9:** 1178
Spyglass **1:** 10
Sremska Mitrovica. *See* Sirmium
Sri Lanka **6:** 845 **7:** *871*, 874, 884, 888 **11:** 1493, 1498, 1573
Ssu-ma Chien, astronomer and historian (145-97 BC) **11:** 1506, 1508, 1573
Ssu-ma Yen, emperor of Chin dynasty (236-290) **11:** 1508
St. Augustine **7:** *959, 960, 961, 963*, 987. *See also* Augustine
St. Benedict **7:** 976, 986 **8:** 1059. *See also* Benedict of Nursia
St. Helena. *See* Helena
St. John, Knights of, Christian Hospitalers **11:** 1561-1562, 1574
St. John's Basilica **8:** 1113
St. Pachomius (c.290-346), founder of Christian cenobitic (communal) monasticism **7:** 969
St. Peter's Church (Rome) **6:** 772
St. Roman **11:** 1559
St. Seurin **8:** 1035
St. Zeno **8:** 1037
Stabiae **6:** 805
Stadium **6:** 764, *802*
Stamford Bridge **10:** 1325
Star clusters. *See* Galaxy
Starcero **1:** 75
Starry Messenger **1:** 10
Stars **1:** 7-14, 16-22, 133-135
State prefect **8:** 1048
State religion **6:** 734, 855 **7:** 881, 888, 937, 979, 997 **8:** 1035, 1054, 1078
Stateira, second wife of Alexander the Great **5:** 624, 709
States-General **10:** 1379, 1418, *1419*, 1420, 1422
Stauracius **9:** 1256
Steady state theory **1:** 19
Steinheim **1:** 45
Stele **11:** 1459, *1496*
Steles (tombstones) **2:** 166, 179, 225
Step pyramid **2:** 154, 279
Stephen II (?-757), pope (752-757) **9:** 1164, 1288
Steppe horses **8:** 1025
Sthaviras **7:** 882
Stilicho. *See* Flavius Stilicho
Stoa **4:** 474, *526*, 567
Stoa poikile **5:** 648 **6:** 808
Stockholm **10:** 1402, *1404*
Stoic **5:** 648, 710; - School **5:** 648
Stoic fatalism **6:** 808
Stoic philosopher **5:** 710 **6:** 768-769, 808, 856
Stoicism, Greek school of philosophy **5:** 648, 712 **6:** 808, 856
Stone Age. *See* Paleolithic -, Mesolithic - and Neolithic Period
Stone monuments **2:** 165
Stone tools **1:** 49
Stone tower **6:** 846
Stonecutters **10:** 1320
Stonehenge **1:** 87, *87-88*, 134
Strabo, Greek geographer and historian (64/65 BC-AD 23) **3:** 299 **11:** 1543
Straits of Bosporus **1:** 73 **8:** 1045
Straits of Gibraltar **3:** 295, 302 **6:** 835 **8:** 1029 **9:** 1225
Straits of Messana **5:** 681
Strategist, one of ten commanders in chief in Athens **4:** 567 **5:** 595, 682, 711
Stratēgos, strategist **5:** 595 **8:** 1110 **9:** 1248
Strike **2:** 189
Stupas **7:** 876
Styx, mythical river **6:** 752, 767, 802
Sub-Mycenaean period **4:** 445
Sub-Sahara **11:** 1544
Subduction **1:** 30
Suche Bator (1893-1923) **11:** 1574
Sudan **1:** 74 **2:** 152, 156, 192 **3:** 404, 411-412, 414 **6:** 840 **11:** 1548, 1553, 1574
Suetonius, Gaius Suetonius Tranquillus (69-c.122), Roman biographer **6:** 752, 758, 768 **9:** 1179, 1182
Suevi (tribe) **1:** 126 **8:** 1024, 1028, 1029
Suez, Gulf of **2:** 151
Sui dynasty (581-618) **11:** 1508
Suiko, empress of Japan (554-628) **11:** 1524

Sukuma **3:** 411
Süleyman I the Magnificent, sultan of Turkey (reigned 1520-1566) **11:** 1547, 1556-1557, 1562-1564, 1566
Sulfur dioxide **1:** 26
Sulla, Lucius Cornelius (Felix) (138-78 BC), Roman general and statesman **5:** 700-702, *702*, 710-712 **6:** 727-732, 743, 854-856
Sultan **8:** *1104*, 1121-1122, *1133*, 1141, 1144
Sultan of Egypt **8:** 1122 **10:** 1348
Sumatra **1:** 44 **11:** 1500
Sumer **2:** 217-218, *219*, 220, *221*, 222-225, 227, 233-234, 247, 259, 277-278, 280 **3:** 342
Sumerian **2:** 218-228, *219, 223-225*, 230, 232-235, 237, 241, *243-244*, 244-245, 247-248, 250, 270, 277-280; - law **2:** 241; - period **2:** 225; - religion **2:** 220; - renaissance **2:** 223, 227, 278, 280
Sumerian culture (c.4000-c.1900 BC) **1:** 106 **2:** 218, 221, 225
Sumerians **2:** 217-218, *219*, 220-221, 222, 223, 227, 232, 235, 252, 277, 279-280
Sumero-Akkadian civilization **2:** 259
Sumu-Abum, Amorite king (fl. nineteenth century BC) **2:** 234, 247
Sun **1:** 7-9, *8-9*, 11-14, *13*, 17, 22-24, 26-29, 34, *102*, 133-135
Sun god **2:** 155, 159, 176-177, *187*, 221, 236, 246, 277-279 **7:** 943 **11:** 1462
Sun Line **11:** 1523-1524
Sunda Islands **1:** 42
Sundiata Keita, West African king (d.1255) **11:** 1545, 1547
Sung dynasty, Chinese dynasty (960-1271) **11:** 1510, *1510-1511*, 1541, 1574
Sung emperors **11:** 1510, 1512
Sung empire of the north (960-1125) **11:** 1574
Sung empire of the south (1125-1271) **11:** 1574
Sunna (conduct of the Prophet Muhammad) **11:** 1566
Sunnah (Islamic custom) **8:** 1112
Sunni Ali (1465-1492) **11:** 1548
Sunni caliph of Baghdad **11:** 1555, 1564; - Ottomans **11:** 1564
Sunnites Muslims **8:** 1112, 1119, 1142, 1144
Supernova **1:** 18, *18*, 133
Superposition, Law of **1:** 32
Suppiluliuma I, Hittite king (c.1375-c.1335 BC) **2:** 182 **3:** 345
SUQ (*sine una querella*) **6:** 798
Surgery **2:** 156, 252
Susa **2:** 226, 235, 270 **3:** 365, 376-378, *378* **5:** 618, *620*, 621, *623*, 624 **8:** 1078
Susu **11:** 1547
Sutra Pitaka **7:** 881
Suzdal **9:** 1253 **11:** 1516
Svadharma **7:** 893
Svyatoslav, Grand Prince of Kiev (d.972) **11:** 1514, *1514*
Swabia **9:** 1202, 1219, 1285-1286, 1288 **10:** 1340, 1342, 1390
Swabian League **10:** 1390
Swahili **11:** 1551
Swanscombe skull **1:** 45
Swazi kingdom **11:** 1554
Sweden **1:** 80 **9:** 1186 **10:** 1399, 1401-1402, *1404*, 1408-1409, *1408*
Swedes **9:** 1206, 1287
Swedish **10:** 1043 **10:** 1402, *1402*, 1409
Swiss **10:** 1368, 1390, 1421-1422
Swiss Confederation **10:** 1390
Swiss League **10:** 1390
Switzerland **1:** 24, 76, 78, 95 **6:** 769 **8:** 1022 **10:** 1390, 1412
Syagrius **8:** 1025, 1032, 1142
Sybaris **4:** 458, 462
Syene **5:** 643
Syllabary **4:** 450
Syllable **4:** 441, 450, 466, 566
Sylvester II (c.945-1003), head of the Roman Catholic Church (999-1003) **9:** 1213
Sylvester III (?-c.1046), pope (1045) **9:** 1215
Symbolism **2:** 268
Symmachus, Quintus Aurelius (c.345-c.402), Roman statesman, a brilliant orator and writer who was a leading opponent of Christianity **7:** *950*, 951-953, 962
Syncretism **5:** *631*, 633
Synod **7:** 964, 990 **9:** 1218, 1263 **10:** 1356

Syracuse **4:** 458, *459*, 526 **5:** *595-596*, 596-597, 604, 607, 641, 680-681, *681*, 689, 711-712
Syraz **8:** 1132
Syria **1:** 64, 68, 73, 105, 116 **2:** 167, 169-170, 177, 182, 184, 196, 214, 218, 226, 230-231, 234, 252-253, 258, 262, 266, 268, 270, 278-279 **3:** 296, 298, 301, 314-316, *316*, 320-321, 334, 337-340, 345, 347, 404, 407 **4:** 448, 450, 567 **5:** 619, 628, *639, 689*, 691, 709-710, 712 **6:** 731, 737, 755, 787, 808, 813, 815-816, 820, 838, 843-846 **7:** 918, 920-921, 969-970, 976, 997 **8:** 1054, 1071, 1074, 1077, 1081-1082, 1084, 1100-1101, 1103-1104, *1106*, 1107, 1110-1111, 1122, 1141-1144 **9:** 1244, 1250, 1261, 1263-1264, 1268-1269, 1272, 1278, *1278*, 1285-1286, 1288 **11:** 1542, 1562, 1574
Syrian **5:** 630, 633, 690, 710
Syrian Christians **8:** 1072
Syrian Coast **4:** 457
Syrian Desert **1:** 67
Syrian Empire **2:** 192
Syrian regions **4:** 498
Syrians **2:** 192 **8:** 1106, 1132
Syro-Palestinian region **2:** 175, 180, 183
Systema naturae **1:** 37
Szeletian culture **1:** 54
Szigetvár **11:** 1563
Szombathely **7:** 975

Ta-tsi Tsin (Chinese for Imperium Romanum) **11:** 1506
Tabasco **11:** 1453
Tablets **2:** 177, 183, 206, 209, *209*, 214, 216, 218, 222, *222*, 234, 237, 241, 244, *248*, 252, 253, 270, 277-279
Tabula Peutigeriana **6:** *736*
Tabularium **6:** *754*
Tacitus, Gaius Cornelius (56-120), Roman historian, orator, and public official **1:** 126 **6:** 758, 768, 770-772, 824, 827, 842 **7:** 936 **9:** 1171
Tagaste **7:** 962
Tagmata **8:** 1110 **9:** 1248
Tagus River **1:** 119 **5:** 684 **8:** 1124 **9:** 1237
Tahuantinsuyu (Empire of the Four Winds) **11:** 1480, 1573-1574
Taif **8:** 1083, 1095
Taika, the Great Change (645) **11:** *1519*, 1524, 1574 ; - reforms, period in Japan (645-702) **11:** 1524, 1574
Taira, Japanse clan (twelfth century) **11:** 1528, 1574
Takauji **11:** 1529
Taklimakan Desert **3:** 350
Takrur **11:** 1545
Talas **11:** 1510
Tale of Genji **11:** *1524*, 1527
Talents, ancient units of weight and money **5:** 591, 634, 682, 690, 702
Talha **8:** 1091
Talmud **10:** 1370-1373
Tamarshak **3:** 414
Tamerlane (Timurlenk), Mongolian ruler (1370-1405) **4:** 512 **11:** 1497, 1538, *1541-1542*, 1542, 1558, 1573-1574
Tamil **11:** 1492-1493
Tammuz (the Greek Adonis), son of Baal (the god of rain and fertility) and Astarte **2:** 221 **3:** 307-308
Tampumachay, ruins of **11:** 1478
Tamralipti **11:** 1500
Tanaquil, legendary Etruscan prophet, wife of Tarquinius Priscus, traditionally the fifth king of Rome **5:** 651
Tancred de Hauteville (?-1112), one of the leaders of the First Crusade **9:** 1242
Tane **3:** 402
Tang dynasty, Chinese dynasty (618-907) **7:** 912 **11:** *1505*, 1508, 1510, 1526, 1574
Tanganyika Lake **11:** 1553
Tangaroa, hero of Polynesian myth, great god of the ocean **3:** 396, *396*
Tangut tribe **11:** 1510
Tanis **2:** 191
Tantalus, mythical figure **6:** 767
Tantras **7:** 886, 900, 997
Tantrism **7:** 886, 900, 997
Tanzania **1:** 48 **11:** 1553
Tao **3:** 357 **7:** 910, 997 **11:** 1510
Tao-te-Ching. See Daode Jing
Taoism **7:** 909-911, *912*, 997 **11:** 1508, 1510
Taoist societies **11:** 1506
Tapestry **3:** 320 **8:** 1073, 1111 **10:** 1323-1324, 1404
Tapioca **11:** 1455

tem **3**: 384 **7**: 871, 893
Upanishads **3**: 387 **7**: 871, 891, 893-894, 897, 997
Upper and Lower Germany **6**: 783-784 **10**: 1412
Upper Egypt **2**: 153, 154, 158, 169, 280
Upper Paleolithic **1**: 53-54, *53*, 56-57, *56, 62, 71*, 72, 99, 103; - Period (c.34,000-10,000 BC) **1**: 53, 72, 135
Ur **1**: 77 **2**: 218, 222, *225*, 227, 230, 232-233, *232*, 235, *242-244*, 247-248, 278, 280 **3**: *314*, 315-316; - dynasty **2**: 227, 233
Ur III period **2**: 227, 232-233, 248, 280
Ur-Nammu, king of the third dynasty of Ur (2112-2095 BC) **2**: 232, 235 **3**: 315
Ural Mountains **1**: 54
Ural River **8**: 1026 **11**: 1536
Urania, in Greek religion, one of the nine Muses, patron of astronomy **5**: 638, 711
Uranus (planet) **1**: 11, 23, 27, 29, 135
Uranus, in Greek mythology, the personification of heaven **3**: 388
Urartu **2**: 262, 267, 278-279
Urban II (1040-1099), pope (1088-1099) **9**: 1267-1269, *1269*, 1285-1286, 1288
Urbs **6**: 856
Uri **10**: 1390
Urnfield culture (1600-800 BC) **1**: 112-114, 117, 119, 133, 136
Uru-Salem **3**: 329
Urubamba River **11**: 1488
Uruinimgina (Urukagina), ruler of Lagasch (fl. twenty-fourth century BC) **2**: 222-223, 278
Uruk **2**: 218-220, 226-227, 232, 235, 244-246, 251, 277-278; - period **2**: 218-219
Urukagina. *See* Uruinimgina
Usamacinta River Basin **11**: 1456
Usas. *See* Dawn
Ushebtis (Shawabtis) **2**: 165, 280
Usurper **5**: 621
Usus **6**: 797-798
Uta-Napishtim, figure in epic of Gilgamesh **2**: 246
Utica **3**: 300
Utrecht **9**: 1161, 1221 **10**: 1413
Utu, Sumero-Akkadian god of the sun **2**: 221
Utuhegal, king of Uruk (c.2116-c.2110 BC) **2**: 232, 235
Uxmal **11**: 1456
uyi **11**: 1526
Uzbekistan **5**: 632 **6**: 845

Vaballath **6**: 820
Vae victis **5**: 669
Vai **3**: 411
Vaipulya Sutras **7**: 997
Vaishali **7**: 881
Vaishesika **7**: 900, 997
Vaishnavas **7**: 894
Vaisyas, third inherited social status in the caste system of India **3**: 381 **7**: 871
Vajjian Confederacy **7**: 881
Vajrayana **7**: 886
Valdayskaya Hills **11**: 1513
Valdemar (d. 1275), Swedish king of the Foljungar dynasty **10**: 1402
Valencia **9**: 1230, 1236, 1238-1239
Valens, Eastern Roman emperor (reigned 364-378) **6**: 833 **7**: 946 **8**: *1018*, 1019-1022, 1034, 1037, 1048, 1050, 1054, 1141, 1144
Valentinian, Flavius Valentianus (321-375), Roman emperor (346-375) **6**: 833-834
Valentinian I, in full Flavius Valentinianus, Roman emperor (reigned 364-375) **7**: 951, 997 **8**: *1018*, 1019-1020, 1144
Valentinian II, Flavius Valentianus (371-392), Roman emperor (375-392) **6**: 834 **7**: 951, 953, 997 **8**: 1020, 1144
Valentinian III, Western Roman Emperor (425-455)
Valerian, Publius Licinius Valerianus, Roman emperor (reigned 253-260) **6**: 819 **7**: 941, 997 **8**: 1071, *1071*
Valhalla **9**: *1188*
Vallabha, supreme being in Hindu religion **7**: 898
Valley of Mexico **11**: 1450, 1456, *1464*, 1465
Valley of the Kings (Luxor) **2**: 173, *176*, 180, 182, 184, 189, 277, 280
Valois **10**: 1376, 1398, 1412, *1419*
Vamana, fifth appearance of Vishnu as a dwarf, who tricks the demon Bali into thinking he is a giant **7**: 894
Van Artevelde, Jacob. *See* Jacob (van Artevelde)

Vandal; - population **8**: 1028; - kingdom **8**: 1029, 1063-1064; - plundering **8**: 1029
Vandals **7**: 966 **8**: *1021*, 1024-1026, 1028-1031, *1029*, 1035, 1038, 1063, 1142, 1144
Vanuatu **3**: 392-393
Varaha, third appearance of Vishnu as a boar, who slays a demon who had dragged the world to the depths of the cosmic ocean **7**: 894
Varanasi **7**: 874
Varangians **11**: 1514
Varna, Battle of (1444) **11**: 1559
Varro, Gaius Terentius (?-c.200 BC) consul **5**: 688, 712
Varuna, Aryan god **3**: 371, 388
Varus, Publius Quintilius (?-9 AD), Roman general and consul (13 BC), governor of Syria (6-4 BC) **6**: 755
Vasco de Balboa (1475-1519) **11**: 1477
Vassals (Vassi) **3**: 352 **9**: 1174-1175, 1190, 1201, 1209-1210, 1214, 1232, 1286, 1288 **10**: 1319, 1321, 1323, 1326-1327, 1329, 1332-1333, 1335, 1339, 1344, 1353, 1387-1388, 1391, 1418
Vatican **8**: 1031, 1059 **10**: 1314, 1364
Vatican palace **6**: 772
Veche **11**: 1517
Veda **3**: 384-385 **7**: 890-891
Vedanta **7**: 897-898, 997
Vedas, earliest Indian literature in the original language of the Aryans **3**: 381, 384, 387, 390 **7**: 871, 889-894, 897, 997
Veii **5**: 668, 678 **6**: 836
Vendida **3**: 372
Veneti people **8**: 1027
Venetian **10**: 1306, 1339, *1418*
Venezuela **11**: 1447
Venice **3**: 300 **8**: *1027, 1045*, 1054, 1132 **9**: 1171, 1232, 1278 **10**: 1312, 1339, *1373*, 1395-1396, *1396*, 1398, 1414
Ventris, Michael (1922-1956), architect and cryptographer **2**: 206, 209
Venus (planet) **1**: 9-10, *9*, 17, 23, 26, *51, 53, 64, 71*, 134
Venus 1 and 2 **1**: 26
Venus of Brassempouy **1**: *64*
Venus of Laussel **1**: *51*
Venus of Willendorf **1**: *53*
Venus, Roman goddess **5**: 606, 642 **6**: *753*, 807, 856. *See also* Aphrodite
Venus Victrix **6**: 807
Vera Cruz **11**: 1451, 1453
Vercellae **5**: 701
Verdun **8**: 1132
Verdun, Treaty of (843), divided up the Carolingian Empire between Charles the Bald, Louis the German and Lothar I **9**: 1187, 1287-1288
Verona **8**: 1037 **10**: 1395
Verres, Gaius (c.115-43 BC), Roman magistrate of Sicily **6**: 731-732
Vertebrate animals **1**: 35, 135
Vertesszollos **1**: 45
Verulamium **6**: 772
Verus, Lucius Aurelius (130-169), Roman emperor (161-169) with Marcus Aurelius **6**: 789
Vespasian, Titus Flavius Sabinus Vespasianus (9-79), Roman emperor (69-79) **6**: 773, 776, *776*, 778, *778, 780*, 781, 783, 785, 787, 798, 856 **7**: 923
Vespasianus. *See* Vespasian
Vesta **5**: 650, *693* **6**: 816, 856
Vestal Virgins **5**: 650 **6**: 856
Vesuvius **6**: 730, 779, 804, *805*, 855
Veto **5**: 660, 695, 709
Via Appia **6**: *732*, 737, 784, 856
Via Biberatica **6**: *794*
Via Traiana **6**: 784
Victoria Lake **11**: 1553. *See also* Lake Victoria
Vicuna **11**: 1449
Vienna **6**: 789 **10**: 1409 **11**: 1563, 1566
Vietnam **3**: 360 **7**: 888 **11**: 1504, 1508
Vigintivirate **6**: 747
Vijayanagar, Hindu kingdom founded in 1336 **11**: 1497
Viking ship **8**: 1037 **9**: 1206, *1207*
Vikings **9**: 1175, 1184, 1186-1187, 1191-1192, 1206, 1246, 1285-1287 **10**: 1303, 1323, 1325
Villa **2**: 200-201, 279 **6**: *747*, 772, 788, 795-796
Villanova **5**: *653, 668*, 675
Villas **8**: 1050
Vinaya Pitaka **7**: 881
Vindex, Gaius Julius (?-68), governor of Lugdunensis

(Gaul) **6**: 774
Vindobona **6**: 789
Viracocha (the Creator), Inca emperor (fifteenth century AD) **11**: 1478-1479, *1479*, 1483, 1574
Virgil (Publius Vergilius Maro) (70-21 BC), Roman poet **5**: 638, 650 **6**: 733, 750, 752, *752*, 767, 798, 853-856 **9**: 1179
Viriathus (?-c.139 BC), leader Lusitanian rebels (147-139 BC) **6**: 838
Viscontis **10**: 1396-1398
Vishnu, Hindu god called the Preserver; forms a trinity with Brahma and Shiva; takes human form as Krishna **3**: 383, 388 **7**: *889*, 891, 894, 897, *898*, 997 **11**: 1496
Vishtaspa, king of Chorasmia **3**: 362
Visigoth kingdom **9**: 1225
Visigothic; - dynasty **8**: 1025; - Empire **8**: 1108; -kingdom **8**: 1066; - warriors, *See* Goths
Visigoths **9**: 1226-1227, 1285
Vistula River **1**: 122 **8**: *1021* **10**: 1409
Visudhim **7**: 884
Vita apostolica **10**: 1314
Vitellius, Aulus (15-69), Roman emperor (69) **6**: 774-776
Vix **4**: 461
Vix, Grave of **1**: 118
Vizier **2**: 156-157, 160, 167, 175, 189, 280 **3**: 348, 369 **9**: 1228, 1230
Vladimir-Suzdal region **11**: 1516, 1536
Vladimir the Great (Vladimir I), king of Kyyivan (980-1015) **11**: *1513*, 1514-1517, 1574
Vlèardingen; - culture **1**: 84, 86; - settlements **1**: 86
Volcanoes **1**: *25*, 30
Volga **8**: 1025 **10**: 1404 **11**: 1513, 1516, 1542, 1574
Volhynia **11**: 1516
Volkhov **11**: 1513
Volsci **6**: 836
Volta **11**: 1551
Voronet **9**: *1252*
Votive offerings **4**: 496
Vowels **4**: 450
Voyager 1 and 2 **1**: 27
Vulgate **7**: 976, 990, 997

Wadai **11**: 1549
Waddenzee **9**: 1286
Wadi Hammammat **2**: 160
Wadis (oasis) **8**: 1082
Wahlstatt **11**: 1536
Wai Wang **11**: 1535
Waiblingen **10**: 1333
Wailing Wall **6**: 779, 785 **7**: 924
Waldemar IV (Atterdag), king of Denmark (elected 1340) **10**: 1408
Wales **5**: 668 **6**: 783 **10**: 1353
Wallio, Visigoth king **8**: 1025, 1144
Walls of Athens **5**: 598, 601
Walter the Penniless (?-1097), French knight, a leader of the Peasants' Crusade **9**: 1269, 1287
Wanax, Minoan word for king **2**: 214, 277-278, 280 **4**: 456, 568
Wang Binghua **3**: 350
Wang Mang **11**: 1504-1505
Wangara Region **11**: 1545
War **5**: 587, 589, *590*, 634, *674, 681*, 691, *695*, 698, 701, 709-712
War booty **4**: 472, 490
Wardu, Minoan word for slaves **2**: 237
Warring States period (1467-1568) **11**: 1520, 1530, 1573-1574
Warring States period (480-221 BC), Chinese era when Zhou dynasty disintegrated into vying politically independent principalities **7**: 997
Warriors **4**: *454, 458-459, 463*, 469, *469*, 471, 473-474, *492* **5**: 608, *651*, 657, 671
Warriors, Temple of the **11**: 1457
Warships **9**: *1249*
Wat Tyler, byname of Walter Tyler (d. 1381), leader of the Peasants' Revolt of 1381, the first great popular rebellion in English history **10**: 1381
Waterford **9**: 1206
Way of the Prophet **8**: 1112
Weavers **10**: 1304
Wegener, Alfred, meteorologist (1880-1930) **1**: 30
Wei **11**: 1506, 1508, 1574; - kingdom (453-225 BC) **11**: 1506